ALBEMARLE PARISH VESTRY BOOK,
1742-1786

SURRY AND SUSSEX COUNTIES,
VIRGINIA

ALBEMARLE PARISH VESTRY BOOK,
1742-1786

SURRY AND SUSSEX COUNTIES, VIRGINIA

Virginia Lee Hutcheson Davis
Andrew Wilburn Hogwood

Reprinted for
Clearfield Company by
Genealogical Publishing Co.
Baltimore, Maryland
2008

ISBN-13: 978-0-8063-1756-4
ISBN-10: 0-8063-1756--6

Copyright © 2005 by Virginia Lee Hutcheson Davis
All rights reserved, including the right of
Reproduction in whole or in part in any form.

Published for Clearfield Company, Inc., by
Genealogical Publishing Co., Inc.
Baltimore, Maryland

Made in the United States of America

[Original Vestry Book Introductory Note]

Restored

In honor of

Mrs James Hopkins Davis

State President — 1967-1970

by the

Jamestown Virginia Chapter

National Society

Colonial Daughters

of the

Seventeenth Century

1969

To J. Thomas Wadkins, III

For his untiring efforts in making our early records available
in a manner that will preserve our heritage
and make it accessible to all.

It is said that the written word is the only means of communication
that has survived through the centuries.

Tom has spanned the time from the early eighteenth century
into the twenty-first century in giving unstintingly of his technical expertise
to convert these early records to a form that will contribute
to their endurance for posterity beyond the next century.

THE ALBEMARLE PARISH VESTRY BOOK, 1742-1786

Introduction

The Vestry Book of Albemarle Parish[1] is one of the priceless original Public Records of the Old Dominion which has survived the vicissitudes of time, wars, invasions, fire and neglect. Albemarle Parish is a lineal descendant of James City Parish, the first established in the new world and included both the north and south sides of the James River.[2]

Surry County was formed in 1652 from that part of James City County south of the James River; the new county included the two parishes that had been created earlier out of James City County: Lawne's Creek Parish (1640) and Southwark Parish (1647). In 1738 these two parishes were divided with parts of both parishes north of the Blackwater River united into one parish and retaining the name Southwark. The parts on the south side of the Blackwater River became another distinct parish named Albemarle. With the changes in boundaries, Lawne's Creek Parish then became extinct. Sussex County was created from Surry County in 1754 with Surry County remaining in Southwark Parish, and Albemarle Parish encompassing the new county.

Beginning in 1738 and until his death in 1776, the Reverend William Willie was the rector of the parish. The Reverend William Andrews was his successor, having been received by the vestry in July 1776. He apparently remained as minister through the birth of a son, William Conner Andrews, entered in the parish register in May 1777. No further entry remains in the records indicating that he remained longer in the parish.[3] Bishop William Meade mistakenly wrote that the parish ended with the death of the Reverend Willie as its minister;[4] however, it is known that there were minutes of a meeting on April 28, 1787 of the "Overseers of the Poor", which had as an act of the Legislature succeeded to the functions of the vestries with respect to the care of the poor of the counties.[5] It was also mistakenly believed that Bishop Meade had access to the parish vestry book, but his writings show he had seen the parish register, but lamented the fact that he did not have available the old vestry books from either Surry or Sussex County.[6]

While Bishop Meade wrote of the four churches in Albemarle Parish as he identified them, it is now known it appears the more recent names were preceeded by earlier named, or identified chapels in three instances. Nottoway Church, identified as on the north side of Nottoway River, appears to have been the first and always been so named. The predecessor of St. Andrew's Church appears in the records, by inference to have been known as Spring Swamp Chapel. St. Paul's Church, by court order no longer extant, was preceeded by Secaurees Chapel. The name St. Mark's first appeared in the vestry minutes as a chapel at Stoney Creek.[7]

Pages at the beginning of the vestry book are missing; and that part of the extant record of the first meeting which would show its date is lost. However, the record of the succeeding meeting held on November 16th, 1742, shows that the preceding meeting was on October 12, 1742. The Reverend William Willie kept and signed the minutes of the proceedings of the vestry. In Colonial Virginia the practice in this regard was not uniform, in some parishes the clerk of the vestry kept and signed the record. There appear to be no vestry records preceding 1742; the first extant record of a vestry meeting being an incomplete one (October 12, 1742), thus the earlier history of the parish for the first two or three years can only be surmised.[8]

In working with a complete set of photostats, and also by examination of the original, Landon C. Bell goes into detail describing the assembling, and ultimate binding of the vestry book. He writes that the pages were not originally numbered; after the sheets, some of them, had become separated, and disorganized, they were reassembled, for better preservation, and were then numbered. It was then found that there were 327 pages, some of them blank, subsequently a few sheets have been found and added to the volume. Two of these are numbered 12a and 12b and another assigned the number 329. Upon careful examination it appears that the numbering of the pages of the volume is meaningless, except to indicate the total number of pages, of the now bound volumes, which have survived.[9]

There are many missing sheets and the extant pages have not been assembled in proper sequence in several instances. After copying the pages Mr. Bell felt that careful examination allowed one to arrange them in proper chronological order. It is now felt that as these pages have now been numbered and bound, that even allowing for those missing, the extant pages were not bound in proper date order.[10] No attempt has been made by the present transcribers to alter the sequence of the pages, beyond the order in which the pages have been numbered, bound by volume, and now made available by photostatic copy. It is left to the researcher, for his use, to verify the dates and proper sequence of entries in the vestry book.

Posterity can be grateful for the execution of this directive found on page 300 of the Albemarle Parish Vestry Book, and the return of the early parish vestry minutes. It is a brief notation but an interesting part of the history of the vestry Book of Albemarle Parish. It is believed that the vestry book was deposited with the Sussex County Court Clerk's office and subsequently confiscated by Federal troops and left at a local tavern:

> To be returned to
> Genl' W. B. Shands[11]
> Jerusalem, Va
> Southampton Co
> When directed
> Vestry Book of Albemarle Parish Sussex Co — left by
> Federal Soldiers under
> Tauerrant at Sussex Ct house
> when they occupied P.S.[12]

The Albemarle Parish Vestry Book, 1742-1786. 2 Volumes (15 by 9½ inches, 319 leaves), negative photostats can be found at the Library of Virginia, Richmond, Virginia 23219.[13] This record is in two parts. Part I covers the period 16 November 1742-8 through April 1760. Part II covers the period 12 May 1760 through 20 September 1786. Also included are many records of the processioners' returns. While it is the original volume, found in poor condition, the photostats are necessarily incomplete; however, given the passage of time, they are surprisingly clear. The pagination is not indicated in the entries of the vestry book, but in some instances it appears to have been noted on some pages in the lower left hand corner at a later time, thus the pagination indicated in brackets in upper left hand corner is that of the sequence of the pages as photocopied. Recordation of the minutes by different persons makes it even more difficult to decipher the writing. Capitalization and spelling of words in the text is inconsistent, as is the punctuation, by today's standards. Transcription has been as the text appears and is evidence of accurate transcription rather than typographical errors made by the transcribers. Spellings of proper names, both given and surnames vary widely, some spelled phonetically, some as abbreviations, and some virtually indecipherable. Names have been indexed according to the variant spellings, so as to draw no inferences that may be erroneous as to the identity of that person. It is advised that the researcher refer to the photostatic or microfilm copy for verification. Spelling of geographic locations vary widely also, as does the handwriting. To verify place names, one should check a modern topographic map for the closest approximation.[14]

This transcription is made from a photocopy of the restored volumes from the microfilm copies made by the Library of Virginia staff. This copy has only been made available through a generous contribution by Gary Murdock Williams, Clerk of the Circuit Court, Sussex County and has been transcribed by Virginia Lee Hutcheson Davis, 2004. Editor/Publisher of the former publication, *TIDEWATER VIRGINIA FAMILIES: A Magazine of History and Genealogy* and Andrew Wilburn Hogwood, President, The Genealogical Research Institute of Virginia. Publishing and Technical assistance has been graciously provided by J. Thomas Wadkins, III, Information Specialist.

V.L.H. Davis

Notes

1. *The Albemarle Parish Vestry Book*: Restored in honor of Mrs. James Hopkins Davis (Priscilla Shepherd) State President 1967-1970 by the Jamestown Virginia Chapter National Society Colonial Daughters of the Seventeenth Century. 1969
2. Landon C. Bell, *"Albemarle Parish: Surry and Sussex Counties, Virginia"*, *Tyler's Quarterly Magazine*, 1950 147-180. LVA F232.A35 B5. This is a well researched history of the parish.
3. The last record of attendance of William Willie at a vestry meeting was dated 20 December 1775. The next vestry meeting of record was 18 July 1776 at which time William Andrews was in attendance.
4. Bishop William Meade. *Old Churches, Ministers, and Families of Virginia, 1* 309. Bell 152.
5. Bell 179. It was these records that had been deposited with the Sussex County Clerk's office probably along with the parish vestry minutes.
6. The Albemarle Parish Vestry Book was given to the Virginia State Library from the Protestant Episcopal Seminary, Alexandria, VA. in 1931. Bell 178.
7. Bell 154-156, 159-163.
8. Bell 177.
9. Bell 177.
10. Bell 176.
11. *Brigadier-General William B. Shands appointed by Governor John Letcher. April 10, 1861.* Bell 179.
12. It is probable that the initials P. S. signed in the notations are those of the Reverend Philip Slaughter, and may have been though his offices that the volume was placed in custody of the Theological Seminary, Alexandria, Va. Bell 180.
13. Accession No. 19734.
14. Accession 30085 is the manuscript copy of this volume. It is also available on Miscellaneous Reel 382 and Miscellaneous Reel 648. Library of Virginia, Richmond, VA.

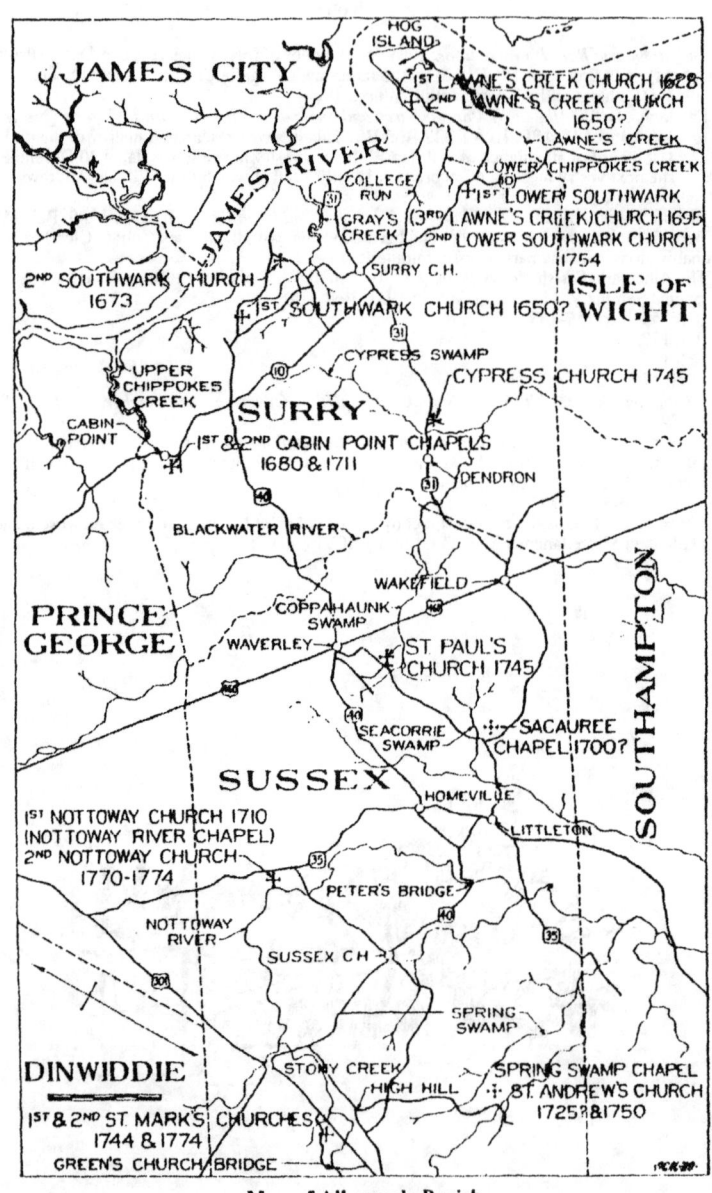

Map of Albemarle Parish

Taken from *The Colonial Churches of Surry and Sussex Counties, Virginia*, George Carrington Mason. *William & Mary Quarterly Historical Magazine*, 2nd Ser., Vol.20, No.2 (Apr.1940) 287.

THE VESTRY BOOK OF ALBEMARLE PARISH

1742-1786

SURRY AND SUSSEX COUNTIES, VIRGINIA

[2]

Albemarle Parish
By 1449 Tythables at 30^w Tob^o ℔ poll...... ....W Tob^o Cd 43,470

Orderd
    That Richard Blunt and Thomas Avent Gent^m. on their entering into Bond with sufficient suretie, to the Vestry of this Parish (to be taken by any of e'm) appointed Collectors of this Parish and that they do demand and recieve of evry Tythable person in the sd Parish the sum of thirty pounds of Tob^o, being the Parish levy of this Parish from the 15th Day of October 1741 to the 15th Day of Octob^r 42. And that they do make payment to the several Parish Creditors (to whom the same is paible the several sums of Tob^o, so recv'd and Levied; and upon refusal of payment of any part of the s^d sum of thirty pounds of Tobacco, any person chargeable therewith, that then they do levy the same by distress.

An acco^t offer'd against this Parish by the Rev^d Wm Willie for 12 months and 27 Days board Viz^t from the 11th Day of 7ber 1741 Till ye 8th Day of Octob^r 1742. And the question being put whether the sd acco^t be allowd, it pass'd in the negative.

Order'd that the s^d acco^t be rejected.

Upon the motion of Robert Wynne Gent^m. Tis order'd that an entry be made that the s^d Wynne agreed to allow Mr Willie's acco^t.

A Petition from the Inhabitants above Stoney Creek in this Parish Direct to the Rev^d. Wm Willie and the Vestry of this Parish praying that a Church or Chapel may be built for the convenience of the s^d Inhabitants.

Order'd that the s^d Petition be rec^d and that Major Wynne appoint the s^d Inhabitants to meet at some certain place in order to Vote for a place that shall be most to the convenience of the s^d Inhabitants and good Water; and the Major Wynne make a report of his proceedings therein to the next Vestry to be held for this Parish.

Order'd that Richard Griffin be exempted from pay his Parish Levy for the fut[ure] and that the Collectors pay his Levy of the Year last past; and recount with the Vestry for the same at the laying of the next Parish Levy.

Order'd that the Church Wardens take Edwd Morrice[sic], a Pensioner of this Parish and agree with Suit[able] person as they shall think proper for his Support.

Order'd that the Church Wardens pay for Richd Carter the sum of Twelve pounds Curr^t Money, for a Ballance of all acco^t against this Parish by ye s^d Carter.

The Vestry having this Day covenanted and agree'd to and with the Revd William Willie, for his finding and providing Elements sufficient for the Celebration of the Holy Communion four several times a Year at each Church and Chapel of this Parish: In consideration whereof the s^d Re^d Wm Willie to recieve of this Parish the sum of seven pounds Curr' Money of Viz'.: for his performing the same, for the Year next ensuing.

Ord^d that the Church Wardens pay to Lewis Delong the sum of thirty pounds Curr' Money for and in p' of work to be completed in the Glebe Land of this Parish.

Order'd that notice be given by the Church Wardens of this Parish, that on 16th Day of Octb' next, a Vestry will be held at the Church in order to treat with workmen for building a Church or Chapel, above Stoney Creek for the use of the upper Inhabitants of this parish.
Wm Willie Mins'

[3]

PCom' Tobacco sold by Major Rob' Wynne for the use of this Parish Augst 1748 Viz'

	Tob^o			£ S d
To Lewis Deloney junr	9,635	a'	12/9 P C'	61: 8: 5
To Colo^l Thomas Cocke	5,216	a'	12/8 P C'	33: - 8
To D^o	4,000	a'	12/9 P C'	25: 10:
To Mr Jno Hood	6,742	a'	12/9 P C'	42: 19: 7
To M' Booge	1,064	a'	12/. P C'	6: 7: 8
a'	26.657			£169: 16: 7

[4]

At a vestry for the Parish of Albemarle in the County of Surry at the Church on the North side of Nottoway River in the County of Surry on the 16th Day of November anno Domini 1742.

Present
To the Revd Wm Willie

Thomas Avent	Richard Blunt
Howel Briggs	James Gee Gent^n
Chris' Tatum	Robert Wynne
James Chapel	Moses Johnson
John Mason j'	Ephaim Parham

Consideration being had to the inconveniency attending an order of this Vestry made the 12th Day of Octo' last past, in relations to the placing a Chapel to be built in the upper end of this Parish, above the mouth of Stoney Creek; its resolv'd that the s^d order be revers'd.

The Question being put whether the s^d Chapel be built, on the upper end of this Parish above the mouth of Stoney Creek as aforesd. it past in the affirmative.

Ordered That the s^d Chapel be placed upon the Land of Peter Green on the North side of Nottaway River, convenient to the best Water:

Order'd that George Pasmore, be exempted from paying his Parish Levy for the future.

A Bond given this Vestry by the Church Wardens (Avent & Blunt) with surities for their Collection of the Parish Tob^o, Levied the 12th Day of Octo' 1742.

The Vestry having this Day covenanted and agree'd to and with Collo^l Jno Wall of Brunswick County for the building a Church or Chapel, on the Land of Peter Green on the North side of Nottaway River, in this Parish according to the Dimensions and Manner following. Viz' 48 foot Long and 24 foot wide in the clear: 11 foot pitch to the spring of the Arch: To be underpined with good well burnt Bricks 18 Inches above the surface of the ground; a good substantial girt floor the Corner posts 14 Inches by 6, in assize the other posts 6 by 6 Inches, to be weather boarded with good prime poplar quarter'd plank plain'd and beaded to Show 6 Inches the roof to be Arc'd without beams a cross /at least such as will appear/ and to be cover'd with good burr[?] Cypress or Pine Shingles, 18 Inches long at lest and in breadth proportionable on good saw'd lathe: the Walls within and cielling to be lath'd plaister'd and whitewash'd or lin'd with poplar or pine plank plain'd and beaded or Cypher'd, only tie to be observ'd that if tie plaistered, it is to be plank'd as before 4 foot high; To have two folding Doors. quarter round and raise'd pannel 4 foot wide 7 or 8 foot high, one made fast with a good Lock and Key; the other with a Barr and Iron Hooks, 3 windows with foreside and 4 in the back side, 3 by 32 foot, one in the East end 32 by 7 foot, to be glaiz'd with good fast glass in proper sashes, and supported at the windows of that Chapel to be built in the Lower end of this Parish and in order to save the Windows from being broke to have plain wainscot window shutters; made fast as the Chapel before mont^d: the Doors and Windows to be plac'd according to the plan: The floor to be laid with good quarter'd and well season'd pine plank the whole framed to be a good sound poplar, pine or white oak saw'd the Pughs to be plain Wainscot front & Seats. the Door (to wit) the Pugh Doors to be hung with good H hinges, the Pughs to be in size and situation according to the plan. The Pulpit Reading & Clerks Pughs and Communion according to the Direction of the Minister. of plain neat work. All the outside (to wit Walls, Roof and Doors and Windows, Shutters to be well Tarr'd the whole to be compleated and finished after a good workmanlike manner at the sole charge of the s^d John Wall and that by the 1st Day of June 1744. In consideration whereof the s^d Wall is to receive

[5]

of this Parish the sum of one hundred and Eighteen pounds seventeen shil^g & no pence Curr^t Money of Virginia fifty nine pounds eight Shillings and nine pence, where of to be p'd when said Chapel is ris'd and the residue of the said Sum when the s^d work shall be fully compleated.

Ord^d That an agreen^t made with Jacob Warrick on the 12th Day of Octo^r last past for the keeping and providing for Owin Jones sufficient Washing Lodging Diet and apparel for w^c he is to recieve of this Parish five hundred pounds of Tob^o P annum. for his Trouble therein being omitted, being entered in the orders of the Day Tis order'd that it be here invested.

Wm Willie Minst^r

[6]

At a Vestry held at the Church on the Northside of Nott'y River for the Parish of Albemarle in the County Surry on the fifth Day of April Anno Domini 1743.

               Present
       The Revd William Willie
  Thomas Avent   Richard Blunt
  John Mason   James Gee } Gent^m
  James Chappell   Moses Johnson
  Chris' Tatum   Ephraim Parham
       John Mason Junr

Capt John Mason & Capt James Gee are Elected Church Wardens, for the Year next ensuing; and sworn according to Law.

Ord^d That Willet Roberts be allow'd his account against this Parish for looking after & burying Elizabeth King, two pounds five Shillings and that the Church Wardens do pay the same out of the Money in their hands belonging to this Parish.

The Vestry having Covenanted & agreed to and with M'r James Mason for the keeping and providing for Joshua Obly sufficient Cloathing Meat Washing and Lodging, Drink and Diet for the year next ensuing and that he be allow'd for the trouble therein after the Rate of two hundred pounds of Tobacco P annum during such Time as he shall keep & provide for the said Obly as aforesaid.

William Willie Min'r

[7]

At a Vestry held at Nottoway Church on the north Side of the Nottoway River for the Parish of Albemarle in the County of Surry on the 14th of June Anno Domini 1743

Present
The Revd William Willie

John Mason	Thomas Avent
James Gee	Richd Blunt } Gent.
James Chappel	Christopher Tatum
John Mason j^r	

Peter Green appear'd and with him the Vestry agreed for two acres of Land on the River part of that Tract of Land whereon he the said Green lives to be laid off by the Revd Wm Willie, Capt James Gee & Capt Thos Avent in such a manner and Form as they shall think proper & at a time they shall think convenient.

Mem: The price of the above Land agreed on between the Vestry & the said Green, is 1 pistole or twenty one shillings & six pence p[r] acre.
By Order of Vestry bearing Date 20th July 1741, a Church being orderd or appointed to be built on the North Side of Coppahanock on the Beaver dams, on the public Road leading from the Court-house to Peters Bridge on the road belonging to Wm Rose.

Ord^d That Capt Mason and Capt Gee Church Wardens do agree with said Rose for so much of the said Land adjoining to that appointed by the Re^d Wm^m Willie as they shall think proper on which to erect the said Church, and include the most convenient spring: And that after such Land is agreed for Robt Jones j^r Clerk of the Vestry do prepare Deeds for that and the Land agreed for with Peter Green aforesaid.

Ord^d That the Church Wardens do pay D^o Hays bill 16/.&.

Ord^d That the Church Wardens do repay to Robt Jones j^r a pistole being a Consultation fee to Mr Barradall on the Dispute betwixt Messenes[sic] Eldridge & Briggs late Church Wardens vs the Vestry, about allowing Commission for receiving and paying away the parish money.

Mem: That Mr Barradalls opinion was ag^t Messines[sic] Eldridge & Briggs.

Ord^d That the Church Wardens pay 1/S[sic] to John Underhill for keeping Wm Holmes a Pensioner 14 days.

[8]

Ord^d That William Mitchell & Thomas Beddingfield be dischard^d for the future from paying their parish Levy.

Mem: That the Church Wardens have agreed with John Ellis for keeping Wm Holmes a Pensioner to the 15th of Octr next and find the said Holmes meat, drink, washing & Lodging, during the Space aforesaid, in Consideration where of the said Ellis is to receive from the Church Wardens 250 pounds Tob^o to be assess'd at the next Levy laying.

Mem: That Capt James Gee agree to keep Mary Delahay a Pensioner from that time to the next Levy laying, at his own proper charge, without any consideration.

Wm Willie Mins^r

St. Mark's Chapel, c.1744)

Conjectural drawing by Andrew Hogwood from specifications as written in the Albemarle Parish Vestry Minutes (page 4 of original minutes).

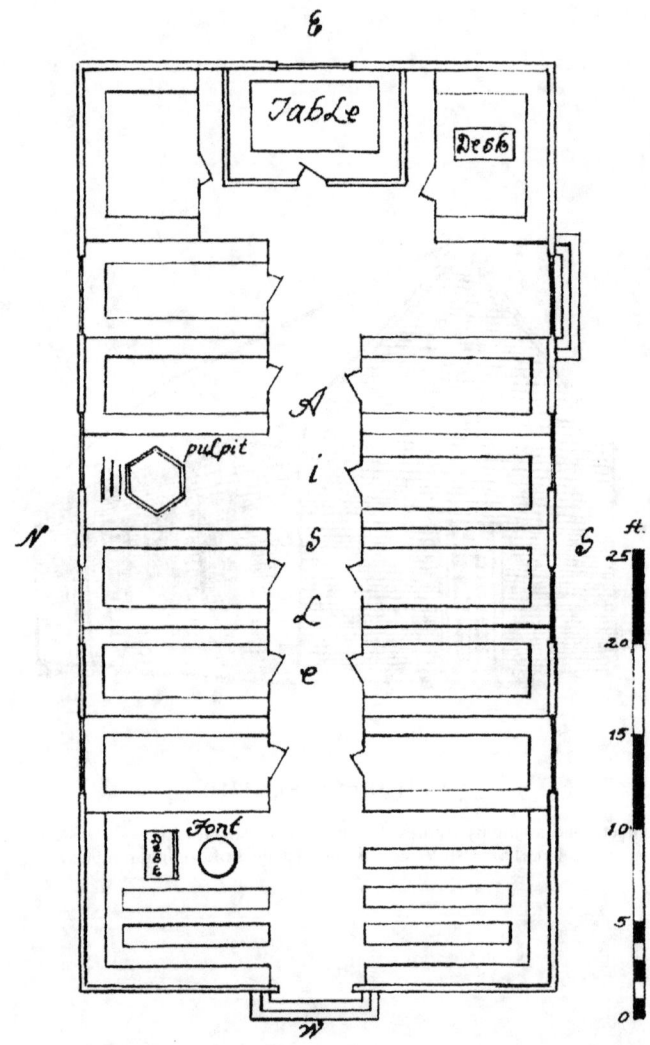

St. Mark's Chapel, c.1744)
Interior Arrangement

Conjectural drawing by Andrew Hogwood from specifications as written in the
Albemarle Parish Vestry Minutes (page 4 of original minutes).

[9]

At a Vestry held for the Parish of Albemarle in the County of Surry, at the Church on the Northside of the Nottaway River, on the thirteen Day of October Anno Domini 1743

Present
The Revd William Willie

John Mason	James Gee
Thomas Avent	Moses Johnson
Richard Blunt	Richard Blow } Gent^n
James Chappell	Chris' Tatum
Howell Briggs	Ephraim Parham
Chris^r Tatum Jun	John Mason Junr

  In pursuant to an order of Surry County Court dated the 20th day of July 1743 directing the Vestry of This Parish to divide the same into precincts for the processioning every persons Land with in the s^d Parish: We do appoint Joseph Petway and William Evans to see every persons Land processioned and the Land Marks renewed, beginning from the Isle of Wight Line, thence up Black Water; all the Land between Tarrapin Swamp and Birchan Island: And that they do assemble all the Freeholders with in that precinct to attend the performance thereof, and that the said Joseph Petway & William Evans do return to the Vestry an account of every particular persons Land that they shall procession and of the persons present at the same and of whose Land they shall fail to procession & of the particular reasons of such failure and that the same be done and perform'd between the first Day of Novem^r and last day of March next ensuing.

William Handcocke & Robert Nicolson are appointed to procession the Land between Seacock and Tarrapin Swamps to Birchan Island Road.

Richard Blow and John Smith are appointed to procession from from[sic] the South side of Seacocke Swamp to the head of Lightwood Swamp and Seacorree Swamp and then to Birchan Island Road.

George Briggs & Walter Baley are appointed to procession from Isle of Wight County Line up Assamussock Swamp to Seacorree Swamp & then to the head of Seacorrees.

Batholomew Figgures and Howell Briggs all upon Black Watter & between Birchan Island Road and the Old Parish line up to the head of Seacorrees and to Seacorree Road.

William Briggs and Richard Blunt from the old Parish Line up Black Water to Cooks Road along the New Road to Black Swamp and from thence to the head of Copohonk.

Nicholas Patridge and David Peebles are appointed to procession from Seacorree up Assamussock to William Johnsons and from Johnsons down Copohonk to Seacorree road then to the beginning.

Richard Carter & David Jones from Cooks Bridge along the Road to Joseph Swamp then thence up the Swamp to Prince George Line and along that line to the beginning.

[10]

Josephs[sic] Masons and Ivey from Cooks Road out the new Road to the Governours Road all between the said Cooks Road and Governours Road to Joseph Swamp.

John Mason Junr and Edwd Weaver from the new Road at Black swamp to the Governours Road all between Assamussock and Joseph Swamp to the Old Parish line.

William Parker and Robert Jones from the Old Parish line down to the Mouth of Robins Branch, thence down Aulstines Branch to Nottaway River thence up the River to the Old Parish Line.

William Edmunds and David Edmunds all between Nottaway River & Assamussock below the Mouth of Robin branch and Austins branch to the Isle of Wight County Line.

Henry Lee and Edward Eppes from the Governours Road down Joseph swamp to Nottaway River and up Nottaway River to the Church at Jones Hole.

Christopher Tatum and Henry Mitchell are appointed to procession all between Joseph Swamp & Jones hole and Governours Road & Prince George County Line.

William Parham & William Moore all between Joseph Swamp and Monkannock Creek, from the line that divides Prince George & this County & Nottaway River.

Thomas Wynne and Major Robt Wynne are appointed to procession all between Monkannock Creek and Stoney Creek and up Saponey Creek to the Line that divides Prince George and this County.

William Gilliam and Peter Green are appointed to procession from Stoney Creek to Saponey Mill and from thence to Peter Greens then down Nott:y to the beginning.

James Cain & Robert Farrington from Peter Greens to Saponey Mill all between the Lines that divide P. George and this County and Nott:y River and Harry's Swamp.

[bottom third of page torn off]

[11]

Wm Knight and John Battle are appointed to procession on the East side of Stoakes's Pond between the line that divides Isle of Wight and this County and to the Rackoon Swamp.

John Avent and John Shands are appointed to procession from the South side of the Poplar Swamp to the three Creeks between Brunswick & Isle of Wight County line.

James Wyche and Jos. Thorp are appointed to procession from the Southside of the three Creeks between Isle of Wight & Brunswick County Lines.

Edward Petway & Wm Petway are appointed to procession frm Stoakes's Road up Nott:y River to the flat Swamp and from the head of the same a strait Course to the head of the Hunting Qua^r Swamp

Sloman Wynne and Henry Sturdivant are appointed to procession from flat swamp to Island Swamp & thence to the Hunting Quar^r

Albemarle Parish Debitor	W Tob^o
To the Revd William Willie as minister of this Parish 12M^o	16,000
To Cash for the same a^t 4 P Ct	640
To Chris^r Tatum as Clk & Sexton for one Year	1,603
To Robt Jones Junr as Clk to Secauree Chapel	1,200
To Ditto as Clk of the Vestry	400
To Gregory Rawlings as Clk to Sp:[ring] Swamp Chapel	1,200
To Josiah Hix as Sexton to Secauree Chapel	1,400
To Edwd Shelton as Sexton to Sp.[ring] Sw. Chapel	400
To Wm Jones in Ball: of his keep: of Tos^a Obly	275

Surry and Sussex Counties, Virginia, 1742-1786

To allowance to Thos Peebles for 4 Months at 800 P annum	266
To Chris Tatum for keeping Mary Delahay a^t 790 P an 100 deducted	427
To Mary Delahay as above deducted from C^r.T.	100
To Wm Ezell for 4 Months board &c of Wm Holman a^t 300 P annum	100
To Ditto for Making Cloaths for Ditto	24
To Lewis Solomon for Making Jacket & Breeches for s^d	24
To Ditto for keeping Ditto Holman 3½ M^o a 350w Tob^o	102

[beginning here the page is torn]

To Josh Hix for mend. of Secauree window shutters	12
To the Revd Wm Willie for building a St[torn]	245
To Wm Rose for keeping Alex^s Con[?][torn]	700
To Ditto for Sundries as p[er] [torn]	
To John Ellis for keeping W^m [torn]	
To Capt Blunt as per [torn]	
To John Ellis for 1 pr of [torn]	
To Jacob Warrick [torn]	
To Thos Peters for [torn]	
To Mr Davis [torn]	

[bottom part of a third of the page torn]

[12]

[the minutes beginning on the next page of the record book are in the handwriting of yet a third person, the first two lines illegible and the first paragraph exceedingly dim].

Robert Jones Junr clerk of the Vestry [illegible] this Parish and that they be ordered and assessed of every [illeg.] person in the s^d Parish the sum of twenty five pounds of Tobacco being the Parish Levy of the Parish from the 15 of October 1742 to the 15th of Oct 1743. and that they do make payment to the several Parish Creditors to whom the same is paiable, the several sums of Tobacco Raised[?] Levied, and that upon refusal of payment shall and any paid of the sum of twenty five pounds of Tobacco by any person charged that then they do Levey the same by distress.

Robert Jones Junr Gent^d Cont^d Clk of Secauree Chapel the Year ensuing.
Chris^r Tatum cont^d Clk of Notaway Chapel the Year ensuing.
Gregory Rawlins cont^d Clk of Sp[ring] Swamp Chapel the Year ensuing.
Joseph Hix continued Sexton of Secauree Chapel the Year ensuing.
Edward Shelton cont^d Sexton of Sp[ring] Swamp Chapel.
Chris^r Tatum cont^d Sexton of Nottoway Church the Year ensuing.
Robert Jones Junr Cont^d Clk of the Vestry for the Year ensuing.

Matthew Gibb covenanted and agreed with this Vestry [rest of this entry is indistinct or illeg.: it seems that Gibb was judged to be a drunk and insolvent. without lodging and the Vestry would assume responsibility].

Capt Mason agrees to [illeg.] Mary Dillahay formerly a pensioner [rest of entry illeg.]
Wm Jones Covenanted and agreed with this Vestry to keep Owen Jones Pensioner to find for and allow the s^d Jones Meat Drink [rest of entry illeg.]
[The next two are indistinct and illegible to the extent that they cannot be transcribed accurately]

Order^d that 10/6 be paid by the Church Warden to the Rev^d [-?-] Ball of his acco^t this Day given

Ord^d that the Church Wardens do agree with [illeg.] made and set up a window in [-?-] Church [rest of entry illeg.]

[13]
At a Vestry held at the Church on the Northside of Nottoway River the Parish of Albemarle in the County of Surry on the 27th Day of March 1744.

Present
The Revd Wm Willie

John Mason	James Gee	
Howell Briggs	Richd Blunt	
Chris' Tatum	Thomas Avent	}Gent^m
Moses Johnson &	John Mason Junr	}

Moses Johnson and James Chappell Gent^m are elected Church wardens for this ~~Year~~ Parish for the Year next ensuing.

On the Motion of Jethro Barker an Antient[sic] infirm Man T'is ordered that he be exempted from pay his Parish levy for the future.

Order'd That the Church Wardens lay out twenty Shillings/4 the Fines recov'd by this parish towards the relief of Mary Woodhard a poor Indigant Woman.

Order'd That twenty Shillings arising by fines recover'd by this Parish be laid out by the Church Wardens of this Parish for Sarah Wallace in proper Medicins for recovering her of a Dropsie.

Order'd That the Church Wardens lay out Thirty Shillings arising as afores^d towards the relief of Richard Griffin a poor infirm Man.

Order'd That the Church Wardens lay out thirty Shillings of the arising as above ment^d toward the relief of Wm Barlow an old infirm man.

William Willie Minst^r
Recorded P — R. Jones Junr Clk Vest.

[14]

(N° 1)   Pursuant to Order of Vestry bearing the Date the 13th Day of October in the Year of our Lord Christ 1743. We the prosessioners appointed by the above orderd have been and prosession'd the above Lands in the above Order. Proprietors Names Peter Green's, Nathl Green's, Wm Green's, Willm Richardson's, Henry Freeman's, Charles Dillihay's [Delahay], Wm Malone's, John Malone's, Joshua Ellis's, Robert Webb's, Mical [Michael] Hill's, Collonel Robt Bollings. The persons present, Mr Geo. Booth, Wm Richardson, Wm Green, Nathan^l Malone, Wm Malone, Isaac Robertson, Charles Dillihay, Joshua Ellis, Henry Freeman & Mical Hill.

Wm Gillam's, Wm Thrower's, Wm Winfield's, James Windfield's & Mr Geo. Booth, Persons present George Booth, Nathan^l Molone, Henry Freeman, Wm Winfield, James Robertson & Thomas Wynne.

Nathl Malone's, James Gillian's, Mr Wm Harper's, Isaac Robertson & ~~Robt Farrington~~ Persons present. Geo. Booth James Gilliam.

Robert Farrington's, Person present Henry Freeman & Mical Hill
Procession'd & return'd by
                                                                              Will: Gilliam
                                                                              & Peter Green

(N° 2)   Pursuant to an Order of Vestry to us directed, to procession all the therein marks, Accordingly we with the assistance of the Freeholders have done it as the Law directs us &c.[etcetera]
                                                                              Wm Evans
                                                                              & Jos: Petway

N° 3   In pursuance of an Ord^r of Vestry, held for the Parish of Albemarle in the County of Surry Octo^r 13th 1743. Have precession'd according Exd Vizt. 23^d March 1743.

Nam^d[sic] Land prosession'd part of a Line at Thomas Briggs's, People present, Jno Stevens, Richd King, John King, Thos Peddington & Saml Stevens, Richard Kings, John Stevens wth John Kings, Thos Peddington & Saml Stokes.

part of a line belonging to [illeg.] Present Nich^s Collihams, John Weaver's, Thos Grantham———————present John Weaver, Thos Pennington, James Stevans, Ric^d King, Saml Stokes, Sil:^{s} [Sylvanus] Stokes, Thos Davis, John Knight, Caliham[?] first days work.

Thos Pennington's Land, Silvanus Stokes Senr Saml Stokes, Abra: Brown, present, Ja^s Stevens, Thos Grantham, Thos Davis, John Stokes, Arthur Freeman, Silv:^{s} Stokes Junr Thos Grantham.

Thos Penningtons Lands present James Stevens, John Stokes, Thos Grantham, part of a line belong' to Sarah Brown's present Ja^s Stevens, Thos Grantham, Thos Pennington, John Stokes, Arthur Freeman, Sil^s Stokes, Tho: Davis, [torn] line Sarah Brown's All people present last Day. John Stevens

[15]
In compliance to an Order of Vestry Dated 13thof Oct. We the Subscribers have procession'd the several Tracts of Land in our precinct belong to these hereafter Names, Charles Maberry, Dury Parker, James Cooper, Morris Trippet, Robert Webb, James Carter, James Stokes, Edward Shelton, Gregory Rawlings, George Long, John Richardson, John Battle, Benj^m Richardson, Hen^y Mannery, Wm Brown, Thos Newsom, George Cornet, Joseph Harwood, Robert Bullock, Hen^y Tyler, Wm Knight, Philip Harwood, Fran^s Felps. The persons present are those hereafter named, Chas Mabry, Druy Parker James Cooper, Amos Newsom, Gregory Rawlaings, Thos Battle, John Richardson, Benjn Richardson, Henry Mannery, Thos Newsom George Cornet, Joseph Harwood, Robt Bullock, George Butler, Philip Harwood, Fran^s Felps. [Procession Masters]
Wm Knight
John Buttler

(N° 5) In obedience to an Order of Vestry dated October 13th 1743 We the Subscribers have processio'd the several Tracks of Land in our precinct belonging to those hereafter nam'd

Thos. Avent	John Golightly,	John Morgan	John Rowlings
John Morgan	Thos. Avent	Matt^w. Hubbard	Thos. Underwood
Lewis Solomon	Thos. Avent	John Rowlings	Rich^d. Hay
Rich^d. Hay	Thos. Avent	W^m. Martin	Richard Barlow
Thos.Underwood	Thos. Avent	W^m. Martin	Rich^d. Hay
Thos. Avent	Gilbert Prince	Saml. Carlile	W^m. Solomon
James Sammons	Thos. Avent	Rich^d. Hay	W^m. Solomon
Ja^s Sammons J^r.	Thos. Avent	Rich^d. Hay	W^m. Solomon
Marm. Hamilton	Thos.Underwood	Rich^d. Hay	W^m. Solomon
W^m. Solomon	Samuel Carlile	Gilbert Prince	Thos. Underwood
John Shands	Thos. Avent	W^m. Solomon	Samuel Carlile
John Avent	Thos. Avent	W^m. Solomon	Samuel Carlile
Gilbert Hay	Saml. Carlile	W^m. Solomon	Gilbert Prince
Samuel Carlile	W^m. Solomon	W^m. Barlow	Gilbert Prince
Gilbert Prince	Samuel Carlile	W^m. Barlow	W^m. Solomon
John Bass	W^m. Barlow	W^m. Solomon	W^m. Barlow Junr.
Peter Marten	W^m. Marten	W^m. Barlow	W^m. Barlow Junr.
Maj^{er} Tiller	W^m. Barlow,	W^m. Solomon,	W^m. Barlow Junr.

Colⁱ. Bland	Thoˢ. Avent	Thoˢ. Underwood	Jnᵒ. Morgan
Thoˢ. Pate	Wᵐ. Tomson	Wᵐ. Tomson Junʳ.	Jaˢ. Evans
James Snensick [Sansenick]	Thoˢ. Pate	Wᵐ. Tomson	Wᵐ. Tomson Junʳ.
John Mᶜlemore	Wᵐ. Jones	Wᵐ. Tomson	John Mᶜlemore Junʳ.
Burrel Mᶜlemore	John Mᶜlemore	Wᵐ. Jones	Wᵐ. Tomson
Benjᵐ. Adams	Edmond Pate	Thoˢ. Pate	Wᵐ. Tomson
Adam Ivey	John Mᶜlemore,	Wᵐ. Tomson,	Wᵐ. Jones
Mattʷ.[?] Wilkason	John Hill	Jer [eremiah] Bullock	Benjᵐ. Adams[?]

[NB: the bottom of the page is partly torn, making the last line of names somewhat difficult to distinguish]

[16]

Daniel Roberts	John Hill	Jer. Bullock	Matthew Wilkason
Grace Williamson	Matthew Wilksason	Jer. Bullock	John Hill,
Jer. Bullock	Mattʷ. Wilkason,	Benjᵃ. Adams	John Hill
Richᵈ. Wiggins	Mattʷ. Wilkason	Benjᵃ. Adams	John Hill
Edʷ. Ellis	Richard Wiggins	Matthew Wilkason	John Hill,
John Hill	Richᵈ. Wiggins	Edʷ. Ellis	Matthew Wilkason

John Avent &
John Shands
[Procession Masters]

Nᵒ. 6) In Obedience to an order of the Vestry of the Parish of Albemarle bearing date the 13ᵗʰ day of October 1743, We the Subscribers hereof have procession'd every persons Lands within the precinct herein ment'd as followeth, to wit, 1743 March 8ᵗʰ procession'd the Lands of Moses Johnson, the Land lately belongᵍ. to Colloᵉ. John Allen, John Sands, Alex. Dickings, John Pennington, Clement Handcocke. In presence of John Pennington, John Hatly, Thoˢ. Brewer, Wᵐ. Johnson & Thomas Ren.
March 9ᵗʰ The Lands of Philip Lightfoot Esqʳ. Majʳ. Benjᵃ. Harrison, Thoˢ. Ren, Wᵐ. Bishop, Lambert Zell.
17ᵗʰ. Wᵐ Pear, Richᵈ. Jones, Thomas Harrison, John Hatley, Philip Baley & John Zell. In presence of John Pennington, Thoˢ. Brewer, John Zell, Maurice Zell & Wᵐ. Pear.
26ᵗʰ. The Land of the Revᵈ. Wᵐ Willie.

In presence of John Pennington, Philip Baley, John Hatley & Robert Jones Junʳ.

Witness our hand 26ᵗʰ Day of Mar. 1744
Moses Johnson} pᵉʳ
Clement Handcocke }
[Procession Masters]

Nᵒ. 7) Pursuant to an Order of Vestry Dated Octoʳ 10ᵗʰ 1743 We the Subscribers have procession'd the Land between Joseph Swamp and Jones Hole, the Governours Road & Prince George County Line as followeth.

Proprietors names, March 12th Richard Tomlinson, Thos. Adkins, pt. of Jno Youngs Ld. part of the Glebe Land, John Hawthon, Petr. Hawthon, Frac. Maberry, Persons present, Thos. Adkins, Petr. Hawthon, ~~Thos. Adkins~~, John Moss, Mr. Wm Willie, ~~Peter Hawthon~~ & George Rieves.
March 13th. George Rieves's, Lewis Green's, Burrel Greens, Frac. Eppess', Henry Mitchell, John Howell, Matt. Gibbs, Wm. Maberry & Wm. Dobey, present, George Rieves, Frances Maberry, Matt. Gibbs & Wm. Dobey.
March 14th. Chrisr. Tatums, Stephen Housmans, John Edwards's, James Williams', Robert Dobey. Josa. Hawthon's (present) John Housman, John Edwards, James Williams, Robert Dobey, Joshua Hawthon.

Chrisr. Tatum }
Henry Mitchell }
[Procession Masters]

[17]

No. 8) In obedience to an order of Vestry ~~held for Albemarle~~ dated last Octor. 13th day 1743 directing us to Assemble the freeholders together and to renew their Land Marks and procession all the Lands from the Mouth of the Raccoon Swamp, so to the Mouth of ye Little Swamp, thence up the Little Swamp to Stoakes's Road thence by Stoaks's Road to the Hunting Quarter thence down the Hunting Quarter to Nottaway River to the beginning. Accordingly the 8th of March we met and procession'd the following Land viz.
Mar. 8 Coll. Benja. Harrison, Charles Gillam, Thos. Gillam, Nathl. Clanton, Charles Maberry, Burrell Gillam, John Gillam, Ralph Maggee, Thos. Dunn, Hinchia Gillam, Richard Clanton, Wm. Land, Richd. Phelps, John Clanton, Wm. Loften, Cornelius Loften, John Rochell, John Knight, Thos. Moor, Richd. King Junr., Richd. Avary, Wm. Andrews, John Pennington Minor, John Pennington & Benja. Swonsby. In presence of us, Maurice Pritchard, Charles Gillam, Thomas Gillam, Nathl. Clanton, Charles Maberry, Burrel Gillam, John Gillam, Ralph Maggee, Thos. Dunn, Hinchia Gillam, Richard Clanton, Richd. Phelps, John Clanton, Wm. Loften, Cornelius Loften, John Rochel, John Knight, Richd. King Junr., Richard Avary, Wm. Andrews, John Pennington Minor, John Pennington Junr. Benja. [Swonsby?] & Wm. Rogers.

Richd. Avary}
John Gillam}
[Procession Masters]

No. 9 In obedience to an order of Vestry held for Albemarle. Octor. 13 day 1743, We have assembled the Free holders from the Old Parish Line up Black Water to Cooks Road and along the new Road to Black Swamp, and from thence to the land of Copohonk and have renewed the Land Marks within the same as followeth. Tracts of Land, part of James Rookings's, Andrew Lester, Richard Blunt, Edmund Ruffin, Col. Willis, John Irby, Wm. Briggs, Thos. Beddingfield, Walter Lashly, Henry Barker, John Barker, part of Reuben Cook's, David Jones, Peter Bayly, John Scot, Edwd. Ellis, Hannah Gilbert, John Tomlinson, Wm. Johnson, Willit Roberts, Samuel Tatum. Persons present Robt. Tucker, Andrew Lester, Edmund Ruffin, Edwd. Alman, John Irby, Willit Roberts, Walter Lashly, Samuel Tatum, Nathl. Johnson, John Tomlinson, Reuben Cook, David Jones, John Barker, Henry Barker, Thomas Beddingfield

Retd. by R. Blunt}
W. Briggs}
[Procession Masters]

[18]

N°. 10 In Obedient pursuance to an order of Vestry made the 13th day of October 1743, We the Subscriber being appointed to procession every persons Land between Assamusauk & Joseph Swamp, from the Old Parish line, to the Governours Road In pursuance to the s^d. Order on the 27th Day of Feby we did procession the Land of John Mason Junr. John Collier, John Sledge, John Peebles, Alexr. Finnia, Theo^c. Bland, and there was present, John Sledge, John Peebles, John Underhill.

Witness our hands this 27th Day of
March 1744 John Mason Junr.}
Edwd. Weaver}
[Procession Masters]

N°. 11 March 9th 1743 In obedience to an Order of Vestry held for the Parish of Albemarle in the County of Surry Octo^r. 13th 1743. We Subscribers have met and procession'd all the lines, as in the s^d. Order exprest, Viz^t. the lines between Coll. Benj^a. Harrison & Rich^d. Pepper & Lawrence Gibbons, and Mary Randall & W^m. Smith Senr. & Thos. Jones Senr., Thos. Vines, James Banks. Present W^m. Smith Senr. John Ogbourn, James Cain, James Banks, Lawrence Gibbons, W^m. Mitchell, Thos. Jones, John Jones, Haugh [Hugh] Davis, Allen Addison, Peter Mitchell, John Mitchell. The lines between Rich^d. Pepper, Mary Randall, Lawrence Gibbons. Thomas Jones, Thos. Butler, Hugh Davis, John Jones & John Moss. present Ditto. ' 19th. The lines between Law^{ce}. Gibbons, W^m. Smith & between the s^d. Smith & James Cain & James Banks present Ditto. The lines between Thos. Butler and Henry Mitchell, James Porch, Rich^d. Pepper & John Moss. Present W^m. Mitchell, Peter Mitchell, John Mitchell, Henry Mitchell, Thos. Butler. The lines between Henry Mitchell, James Porch, John Mitchell, W^m. Mitchell & Edwd. Wyat, present Ditto, 21st. The lines between W^m. Mitchell, John Mitchell, Robert Rivers and Thomas Addison, present Ditto. The lines between John Mitchell, Peter Mitchell, Thomas Vines and Thomas Addison, present Thos. Jones, Senr., John Jones, W^m. Mitchell, John Mitchell, Peter Mitchell, Stephen Jones, Edwd. Jones. The Lines between Thomas Vines, John Mitchell, Peter Mitchell. Thos. Jones & Thos. Addison present Ditto, The lines between Thos. Jones, Richard Pepper & Peter Mitchell, present Ditto,.

28th The lines between Thos. Addison & Pat. Dempsey, present W^m. Mitchell, Thos. Hurst, Thos. Addison, The lines between the Colledge and Patrick Dempsey, present Ditto,. The s^d. Dempsey's Land is not procession'd, being removed out of this Governour.

Thos. Vines}
Rich^d. Pepper}
[Procession Masters]

[19]

N°. 12 In Compliance to an order of Vestry Dated October the 13th 1743 We Subscribers have procession'd the Several Tracts of Land in our precinct belonging to the s^d hereafter named. James Carter's, Henry Browns, Charles Judkin's, Joseph Moody's Silv^s. Stokes's Junr., Robert Owins', John Bells's, Jonas Stokes', Thos. Adkins, Thos. Weathers's, Richard Roses's, W^m. Roland's, Joshua Roland's Matthew Wilkason's, Thomas Felps's, Robert Scot's, W^m. Craggs, W^m. Atkins's. W^m. Woodlands's, Rich^d. Norcross's, the persons present are those hereafter named, Charles Judkins, Thos. Felps, Robert Scot. Thos. Dunn Junr., Jos^a. Roland, W^m. Roland.

John Bell}
Jonas Stoakes}
[Procession Masters]

Surry and Sussex Counties, Virginia, 1742-1786

N°. 13 Pursuant to an order of Albemarle Vestry bearing Date the 13th day of Oct[r]. 1743. Robert Wynne & Thomas Wynne were appointed, to call together all the Free holders from Monkannock [Monks Neck] Creek to Stoney Creek & up the s[d]. Creek to Sapponey Creek to the County line that Divides Surry and Prince George County and go and renew all the Land marks within that precinct, and that it be done by the last Day of March in the same Year, and it is done accordingly by Robert Wynne & Thomas Wynne Procession Masters.

Proprietors Names		persons present			
				Rich[d]. Huson	Jn°. Curtis
Jn°. Williamson	W[m]. Harper	Tho[s]. Malone	~~Jn[r]. Curtis~~	~~Rich[d]. Huson~~
Jos. Jn°. Clinch	W[m]. Harper	Tho[s]. Malone		Rich[d]. Huson	John Curtis
John Curtis	W[m]. Harper	Tho[s]. Malone		Rich[d]. Huson	Tho[s]. Burnet
Tho[s]. Malone	W[m]. Harper	Tho[s]. Burnet		Rich[d]. Huson	Jn°. Curtis
W[m]. Harper	Tho[s]. Burnet	Tho[s]. Malone		Richd. Huson	John Curtis
Rich[d]. Huson	W[m]. Harper	Tho[s]. Malone		Tho[s]. Burnet	Jn°. Curtis
Robert Wynne	W[m]. Harper	Tho[s]. Malone		John Jackson	Jn°. Freeman
Tho[s]. Wynne	W[m]. Harper	Tho[s]. Malone		Jn°. Jackson	Jn°. Freeman
Alex[r]. Bolling	W[m]. Harper	Tho[s]. Malone		Jn°. Jackson	Jn°. Freeman
John Freeman	W[m]. Harper	Tho[s]. Malone		Jn°. Jackson	Edw[d]. Eacols
John Freeman J[r]	W[m]. Harper	Tho[s]. Malone		Jn°. Jackson	Edw[d]. Eacols
Mr. Munford	W[m]. Harper	Tho[s]. Malone		John Jackson	Edw[d]. Eacols
Edw[d]. Eacols	W[m]. Harper	Tho[s]. Malone		Jn°. Jackson	Jn°. Freeman
John Jackson	W[m]. Harper	Tho[s]. Malone		Edw[d]. Eacols	Jn°. Freeman
Mr. Poythress	W[m]. Harper	Tho[s]. Malone		Edw[d]. Eacols	Jn°. Freeman
Col.Rob[t]. Bolling	W[m]. Harper	Tho[s]. Malone		Edw[d]. Eacols	Jn°. Freeman
Edw[d]. Broadnax	W[m]. Harper	Tho[s]. Malone		Edw[d]. Eacols	Jn°. Freeman
Rob[t]. Wynne	W[m]. Harper	Tho[s]. Malone		Edw[d]. Eacols	Jn°. Freeman
Joseph Tucker	W[m]. Harper	Tho[s]. Malone		Jn°. Freeman ~~Edw[d]. Eacols~~	John ~~Freeman~~ Jackson

[20]

N°. 14 In obedience to an order of y[e] Vestry of the Parish of Albemarle dated the 13th of Octo[r]. 1743 We have assembled all the Freeholders within our precinct according to the directions of the s[d]. order & have renewed the Land Marks of every persons Land in the s[d]. Precinct in the presence of Henry Hartwell Marvell, William Freeman, W[m]. Bridges, W[m]. Stewart, W[m]. Partin, Richard Wooddrooff, being all the Freeholders residing in the s[d]. precinct perform'd the 17th day of March 1743 by us.

W[m]. Petway }
& Edw[d]. Petway }
[Procession Masters]

N°. 15 In compliance with an order of Vestry held for Albemarle Parish Octo[r]. 13th 1743. All the Land on the south side of Nottaway River from the Island Swamp to Brunswick Line and to the old Parish line, was quietly procession'd by

Persons present
Tho[s]. Oliver
John Passmore
John Wilbourn

Matt. Parham }
Ephra[:]: Parham }
[Procession Masters]

Nº. 16 In pursuance to an Order of Vestry dated the 13th. of Octor. 1743. We the Subscribers have procession'd the Land of the Several persons hereafter ment.d that is to say the Land of Majr. Benja. Harrison, Capt. John Mason, Mrs. Judith Eldridge, Wm. Shands, Wm. Shands Junr. Wm. Saunder[s?] John Heath. John Peebles. Sarah Peebles, Edwd. Prince. Jos. Prince, Francs. Redding, John Ivey, Joseph Barker, Hugh Ivey, Jos. Mason. John Mason Junr. John Wilkason, John Underhill, John Rosser, Mary Dean, David Jones, Wm. Cook, In presence of the persons above ment.d Witness our hands ye 26th March 1744.

Jos. Mason}
Hugh Ivey}
[Procession Masters]

Nº. 17 Pursuant to an Order of Vestry Dated the 13th Octor. 1743 We the Subscribers have assembled all the freeholders within our precinct to attend the performance thereof. Whose lands procession'd, part of Wm. Roses, Joel Barkers, John Warbitons, Benja. Ellis's, Bathow. Figgures, James Nicholsons, Samuel Magots, Benja. Jordans, Robert Judkin's. Benja. Rogers, Rob. ~~Judkins~~ Proctors, Josa. Proctors, Richard Fitzpatrick, John Jeffries. John Richardson, John Groves, Howell Briggs, Richd. Blunt, pt. James Rooking, Thos. Alsobrooks. Persons present, Wm. Rose, Joel Barker, Jos. Warbiton Benja. Ellis, James Nicholson, Samuel Maget, Benja. Jordan, Robt. Judkins, Benja. ~~Jordan~~ Rogers, Robt. Proctor, Richd. Fitzpatrick. John Jeffries, John Richardson, John Groves, Thos. Alsobrook. The above Land, was procession'd in the presence of us.

Howl. Briggs}
Batho. Figgures}
[Procession Masters]

[21]
Nº. 18 We whose Names are underwritten being by order of Vestry bearing Date Octor. 13th 1743, appointed Procession Masters of all the Land lying within these bounds vizt. Joseph Swamp, Jones Hole Swamp, the Governour's Road, and Nottoway River, have procession'd the sd. Lands at time, & in manner following. Frebrary [sic] 6th 1743/4 procession'd the Land of Henry Lee, of Peter & Robert Doby, Orphans of Clemt. Handcocke, of Thos. Thrower, Persons present, Clement Handcocke Robert Handcocke, Wm. Moss, Peter Smith and ~~Robert Doby~~ Thos. Thrower. Freby. 7th 1743/4 the Land of Hartwell Marvel, of Gilbert Weaver, of Wm. Moss, of Edwd. Eppes, part of James Masons, and part of John Youngs, of Henry Meacham, of Timothy Ezell, of Mountfort Elbeck, Persons present Thoss. Thrower. Wm. Moss, Gilbert Weaver, Timothy Ezzel, Junr., Hartwell Marvel and Heny. Meacham. Freby. 8th 1743/4. The Land of Henry Porch & part of the Glebe Land, Persons present Henry Porch, Wm. Moss, & Peter Hawthorn. March 17th 1743/4. The Land of Frans. Mabry. Persons present. Frans. Mabry & Gilbert Weaver.
Given undr. our hands this 26th March 1744.

Henry Lee, }
Edward Eppes}
[Procession Masters]

Nº. 19 In Obedience to an order of the Vestry of the Parish of Albemarle bearing Date the 13th Day of Octor. 1743. We the Subscribers hereof have procession'd all the Lands within the precinct therein ∞ mentd. . to wit, On the 6th & 7th Days of Feby. 1743/4. The Lands of Reuben Cook, Wm. Cook, David Jones, John Goodwin, Wm Shands, James Gee. Wike[?] Hunnicut, Thos. Taylor, Charles Gee, Richard Carter, Thos. Tomlinson, Judith Eldridge, Wm. Heath, Adam Heath, Wm. Heath Junr., John Tatum, Peter Tatum, Peter Tatum Junr. Thos. Young, Benja. Harrison. In presence of Reuben Cook, Wm. Cook, Wm. Heath, Adam Heath, Peter Tatum, James Gee, Willm. Shands, John Goodwin.

Davd. Jones}
Richd. Carter}
[Procession Masters]

N°. 20 Pursuant to Order of Vestry bearing Date 13th Octr. In the year of our Lord N°. 20 Christ.1743 We the processioners Ja^s. Cain, & Robert Farrington, appointed by the above order have been and ~~procession'd~~ procession'd the above Lands in the above order. Proprietors names, W^m. Rainey Junr., Edwd. Farrington, Hinchia Mabry, Mary Randall, James Cain. Persons present W^m. Rainey Junr., Ja^s. Cain Junr., Duke Kainborough, James Banks, John Woodard, Jno. Davis, Ja^s. Moss, Richard Pepper, Rich^d. Huson, John Jones. Persons present James Banks, John Woodard, John Davis, W^m. Rainey Junr., Rich^d. Huson, John Jones, Thos. Wade.

Procession'd & ret^d. by

James Cain &}
Robt. Farrington}

[22]

N°. 21 We the Subscribers being appointed by order of Vestry to procession and renew the Land Marks of all the Land in our Precinct, we have according meet the Freeholders of the several parcels of Land, and in the presence of Jones Stokes, Thomas Moore, Curtis Land, W^m. Loften, Cornelius Loften, Sarah Gillam, Fran^s. Hutchings, Thomas Caponell[?]. And have peaceably and quietly procession'd all the Several Lines, in the s^d. precinct (Abram Evans was absent, but have procession'd his Land) without whatsoever [illegible] any disturbance or disturbances of any person or persons whasoever.
Given Under our hands this 15th Day of Mar 1743

Robert Webb Junr. }
Charles "His *CB* Mark" Battle. }
[Procession Masters]

N°. 22 In obedience to the Order of ye every [Vestry] of Albemarle Parish Dated Octo^r. 13th 1743, We the procession Masters appointed by the Order of the Vestry, have procession'd all the Land within our Precinct. And the proprietors Names as followeth. Tim^y. Ezell, James Mason, John Coats, Henry Mitchell Junr., Peter Poythress, Thos Heath, John Smith, Charles Leath, John Parham, James Parham, Abra . Parham, Matt : Parham. Given under our hands this 15th of Mar. 1743/4.

W^m. Parham}
W^m. Moor }
[Procession Masters]

N°. 23 Pursuant to an Order of Vestry for the Parish of Albemarle in the County of Surry the 13th day of Octo^r. 1743 for processioning of Lands, we the Subscribers have procession'd the Several Tract here in mentiond. Viz^t. Wm. Barlows Land present James Pully in his behalf. James Wyche s Land present Jos. Thorp, John Reads Land present John Read, John Nanny's D^o. present John Nanny, Samuel Alsobrooks D^o. present Samuel Alsobrook, Joseph Thorps D^o. present James Wyche, Timothy Thorps Do. present Adam Ivey in his behalf. Isaac Williams's Ditto present Nathl. Edwards in his behalf. Maj^r. Tillers Land not procession'd for want of his appearing or some person in his behalf. Richard Ransom's Ditto present. Robt. Bird.

James Wyche}
Jos. Thorpe}
[Procession Masters]

[23]

N°. 24 In Obedience to an Order of ye Vestry of the Parish of Albemarle bearing Date the 13th of Octr. 1743. We the Subscribers hereof have procession'd the Lands within the precincts therein ment'^{d}, to wit, On the 20th Day of January & the 5th & 6th Days of March 1743. The Lands of Capt. John Mason, James Chappell, Samuel Chappell, John Peebles, Sarah Jones, Mr. John Cargill, George Wyche, Rich^d. Griffin, Col. John Allen, W^m. Hall, Rich^d. Parker, Robt. Jones J^r., Robt. Jones Senr., W^m. Parker. In presence of James Chappell, John Peebles, Howell Jones, Benj^a. Wyche, Richard Griffin, John Harrison, Thos. Mores, Peter Railey.

Robt. Jones Senr.}
W^m. Parker}
[Procession Masters]

N°. 25 March 20th 1743/4 Procession'd by George Briggs & Walter Bailey all the Land in their precinct in presence of Thomas Deloch, Robert Long, Simon Murphey, Nathaniel Briggs, Stephen Hamlin, Thomas Gresswit, Nicholas Jones, Henry Sorrow, Ja^s. Turner.

26 We procession'd the Lands of Henry Johnson, Joel Barker, Richard Parker, Samuel Lanier, Benj^a. Clements, Nich^s. Bush, Col^o. Benj^a. Harrison. 2nd Day of March 1743/4 And March the 16th We procession'd Thos. Peters's, John Hunt, William Hines Senr., W^m. Hines Junr., Thomas Hines, W^m. Edmunds, James Chappell, John Wasdon, Thomas Renn, John Cargill, W^m. Hines, John Edmunds, David Edmunds.
And in presence of Henry Johnson, Joel Barker, Richard Parker, John Hunt, W^m. Hines, W^m. Hines Junr., Samuel Lanier, John Wasdon, Thos. Renn, John Edmunds, Thos. Peters.

W^m. Edmunds}
David Edmunds}
[Procession Masters]

[24]

(27) October the 6th 1744

Pursuant to an Ord^r. of Vestry the 13th of October 1743 Wee the Subscribers have assembled the Freeholders of the precinct between Seacocke Swamp and Tarrapin Swamp to Birchan Island Road and have procession'd the Lands following Viz^t. the Lands of Thos. Clary, the Land of Mr. Howell Briggs, the Land of John Jeffries, the Land of William Carrill, the Land of Charles White, the Lands of John Handcocke, the L^d. of Robert Nicolson, the Land of William Handcocke, the Land of William Bradly, the Land of David Andrews, the Land of Robert Atkins, the Land of Thos. Wrenn, the L^d. of Augustine Hargrave, the Land of Jos. Hargrave, the Lands of John Holliman, the Land of Elizabeth Atkins.
Present Howell Briggs, Thos. Clary, John Handcocke, Robert Atkins, Augt. Hargrave, W^m. Carrill, Jno. Jeffries, W^m. Bradly, Dav^d. Andrews, Joseph Hargrave, Jno. Holliman, Thos. Wrenn.

The Lands of Harry Vaughan, the Land of W^m. Cripps, the Land of Jno. Judkins, the Land of Anselm Bailey, the Land of Samuel Cornwell not procession'd, the reason was because they did not attend [the processioning] the Lines the Land of Jos. Petway not procession'd the reason was he had made a new Entry round three sides and expected ~~and expected~~ the Surveyor in a Short time and would not have the old lines renewed.

Robert Nicolson } Procession Masters of the
W^m. Handcocke } Precinct above ment^d.

The aforegoing returns of the persons whose Names are thereto written were duly comprated [compared?] & examined [illegible] with the Origals [sic] and are found to be truly Recorded; in attestation whereof we the Church Wardens of the Parish of Albemarle for the time being have hereunto set our hands the Day & Year afores^d.

[25]

At a Vestry held at Saint Mark's Chapel on the North side of Nottoway River for the Parish of Albemarle in the County of Surry on the XXVIth. Day of July 1744.

Present
The Rev^d. William Willie

James Chappell	Thomas Avent }	
James Gee	Ephraim Parham }	Gent.
Christ^r. Tatum	John Mason }	

Upon a View of the Chapel Built by Colo^l. John Wall pursuant to an agreemt. entred into with this Vestry by the s^d. Wall on the xvith Day of Novem^r. anno Dom. MDCCXLii: 'Tis Ordered & agreed upon the s^d. Wall's placing & putting in two strong & substantial Crosbeams in the s^d. Chapel for the better supporting & strengthening the Roof of the same and also upon making a platform & steps for ascending to the Reading Pughs according to the directings of the Minister: That that [sic] the s^d. Chapel be from thenceforth recd to the use of this Parish.

Ordered That the Churchwardens of this Parish pay to Colo. John Wall the sum of one hundred & eighteen pounds seventeen shillings & six pence, Currant Money as the consideration Money to be paid the s^d. Wall for the Building the Chapel aforementioned. And also the further sum of Ten Shill^s. for Erecting a small window in the backside of the s^d. Chapel more than is contained in the abovement^d. agreement.

Robert Farrington being recommended by the Worshipful Vestry to the Minister as a proper person to be Clk of the aforement^d. Chapel; Tis thereupon ordered that the s^d. Farrington be received as Clerk of the same til the laying the next Parish Levy of this Parish and that he receive, for the due performance of his office therein, after the rate of twelve hundred pounds of Tobacco pe^r annum during such Time as he shall so perform his Duty.

Peter Green is appointed Sexton to the s^d. Chapel till the laying of the next Parish Levy; And ordered that he receive of this Parish after the rate of three hundred pounds of Tobacco pe^r annum during such Time as he shall so continue & duly perform the Duty of his s^d. office.

In regard John Mason & James Gee Gent. have not made an agreement with William Rose for Land sufficient whereon to seat the Church, Churchyards, &c. which is to be built at Beverdam Bridge pursuant to an Order of this Vestry bearing Date 14th Day of June 1743. Tis therefore now ordered that the Rev. William Willie & James Chappell do agree with the s^d. Rose for so much Land as they shall think necessary for the purposes afores^d.

W^m. Willie Min.

Copy
Test   Robert Jones jun^r. Clk Vest^y.

[26]

At a Vestry held for the Parish of Albemarle at the Church on the North side of Nottoway River, on the 11th Day of October 1744 for laying the Parish Levy of the s^d. Parish.

Present
The Rev^d. M^r. William Willie Min^r.

Moses Johnson	John Mason	
Chris^r. Tatum	Rich^d. Blunt	} Gent
James Gee	Richard Blow	
John Mason j^r.		

Albemarle Parish[-?-]	Dr. Lbs. Tob°.
To the Rev^d. Mr. Willie as Min^r	16,000
To Cask for the same, ^{at} 4 p C^t.	640
To Xtopher Tatum as Clk & sexton to the Church 12 M°.	1,600
To Gregory Rawlings as Clk to Spring Swamp Chapel 12 M°	1,200
To Edward Shelton as Sexton to Ditto.	400
To Robert Jones j^r. as Clk to Secaurees Chapel & Vestry one Year	1,600
To Joseph Hicks Sexton to D°.	400
To Pet^r. Green as Sexton to S^t. Mark's Chapel six weeks	50
To Robert Farrington as Clerk to the same, 1 M°	100
To Matt^w. Gibbs for keeping William Homes 9 M°. & 14 Daies	508
To William Jones j^r. for keeping Owin Jones one year	500
To William Rose for keeping Alex^r. Pendix 1 year	700
To James Mason for keeping Jos. Obly 1 year	200
To Charles Gillam for keeping his Son Hinchia Gillam one Year	400
To an allowance to William Rogers &[sic] Impotent Man to be laid out at the Discretion of the Churchwardens	600
To William Rose for his Acco^t. against this Parish	221
To John Jeffries j^r. for his Acco^t. the Parish	144
To Samuel Lancaster for his Acco^t.	372
To an allowance to William Malone to be laid out at the Churchwardens Discretion}	400
To Levied for the Use of the Parish	3,796
To the Collector for collecting & paying 29,831 ^{lb}. of Tob°. in Inspectors Notes at Six p^{er} Cent	1,789
Lbs	31,620
pe r Contra	C^r.
By 1581 Tythables at 20 ^{lb}. Tob°. p^r poll	31,620

Ordered That Capt. Howell Briggs & his Deputies on their entering into Bond with sufficient Sureties to the Church Wardens & Vestry of this Parish, to be taken by the Clerk of the Vestry, be appointed Collectors of this Parish, And that they do demand & receive of every Tythable person in the s^d. Parish the sum of twenty pounds of Tobacco, being the Parish Levy of the Parish from the 15th Day of Octob^r. 1743 to the 15th Day of October 1744. And that they so make paiment to the several Parish Creditors, to whom the same is paiable, the several sums of Tob°. so raised & levied. And that upon refusal of paiment of all or any part of the afores^d. Twenty pounds of Tob°., by any person chargeable therewith, that then they do Levy the same by Distress.

[N.B. The bottom right side of the page bears the handwritten letters "An", which correspond to the first word of the following page. It appears that the clerk used this technique to keep track of the sequence of the ledger pages.]

[27]

An Acco^t. was exhibited by Capt. John Mason & Capt. James Gee of disbursements &c. by them made whilst Church Wardens in the Year 1743, which by the Vestry is approved.
Ordered That William Rose have an allowance of one hundred pounds of Tob^o. p Annum for the future more than he formerly had, for keeping of Alex^r. Pendix a Pensioner.
Ordered That Maj^r. Robert Wynne pay the Sum of Two pounds seven shillings & one penny, the Balance from him due to this Parish, to the new ChurchWardens, of this Parish, for the Use of the Same.
Ordered That the Churchwardens of This Parish pay to Matthew Gibbs the Sum of thirty two Shillings & six pence, for disbursement [illegible] by him made in Burying &c. of William Holmes as p his Acco^t.
Ordered That John Andrews, who is recommended to the Minister by the Vestry be appointed Clerk of Secaurees Chapel in Stead of Robert Jones j^r. who hath resigned it. And that he be allowed the sum of twelve hundred pounds of Tobacco p annum during such Time as he continues therein.

W^m. Willie Min^r.

Test   Robert Jones j^r. Cler^k. Vest

[28]

At a Vestry held for the Parish of Albemarle in the County of Surry, at the Church on the North Side of Nottoway River on Barlethorp Creek April 16th 1745

Present
The Rev^d. William Willie

Moses Johnson	James Gee
James Chappell	Thomas Avent
John Mason	Richard Blunt
John Mason j^r.	Christopher Tatum

Ephraim Parham.

M^r. John Mason j^r. & M^r. Christopher Tatum are appointed Churchwardens for the Parish of Albemarle for the Year ensuing.
The late Churchwardens not being ready to settle their Accts. with the Vestry this Day; Order'd therefore that they settle their Accts. with the New Churchwardens as soon as conveniently they can: and that the Churchwardens Messrs. Tatum & Mason do take up Money at Interest on the Parish Acct. in order to discharge the Ballance that shall appear to be due to the late Churchwardens.
The Vestry having agreed with John Smith to keep, one year from the Date hereof two Orphan Children. vizt. Sarah & Selah Children of William Walace deceas'd, and to find for the s^d. Children Victuals, Drink, Apparel & Lodging in a decent & Christian like Manner. 'Tis ordered that twelve hundred pounds of Tobacco be paid to the said Smith, at the Expiration of the Time afores^d. for his trouble & Charges.
Ordered that M^r. Parham does employ some Workman to secure the West Door of St. Mark's Chapel, to prevent the Water driving in, and that M^r. Parham or the s^d. Workman bring in his Charges to the Vestry.

W. Willie Min^r..
Copy Teste
Robert Jones j^r. Clk. Vest.

[29]

At a Vestry held at St. Paul's Chapel on Copohonk for the Parish of Albemarle in the County of Surry, for laying the Levy of the s^d. Parish for the Year 1744 on the 9th Day of October 1745.

Present
The Rev^d. William Willie

Christopher Tatum	John Mason j'.
John Mason	Thomas Avent
James Gee	Richard Blunt
Moses Johnson	James Chappell

Ephraim Parham.

Albemarle Parish	D^r.
To the Rev^d. William Willie as Min^r.	16,000
To Cask for s^d. Tobacco at 4 p C^t.	640
To Chris^r. Tatum as Clk & Sexton to the Church	1,600
To Gregory Rawlings as Clk. to Spring Swamp Chappell	1,200
To Edward Shelton as Sexton to the same	400
To Robert Nicolson as Clk to the Secaurees Chappel 9 M^o.	900
To John Andrews as Clk to the same 3 M^o.	300
To Joseph Hix as Sexton to the same	400
To Robert Jones jun^r. as Clk to the Vestry	400
To William Ross for keeping Alex^r. Pendix One Year	800
To William Jones for keeping Owin Jones one Year	500
To Charles Gillam for keeping Hinchia Gillam One Year	400
To William Rogers an Allowance..Lame Man	600
To Robert Farrington as Clk to S^t. Marks Chappel	1,200
To Peter Green as Sexton to the same	400
To M^r. Aug$^{..}$. Claiborne for his Acct. against the Parish	738
To John Jones for his acc^t. against the Parish	100
To Thomas Butler for 4 parish Levies p^d. Capt. Briggs twice	
To Ephraim Parham for his Acco^t. against the Parish a^t 11/3	224
To Robert Jones junior for his acc^t. against the Parish	666
To William Rogers for keeping Celia Rogers 11 M^o.	900
To John Smith for keeping 2 Orphan Children 6 M^o.	600
To Will. Ross for his Ac^t. against the Parish	259
To an Allowance to W^m. Barlow an Infirm Man	300
To an Allowance to John Tomkins In[illeg.]	300
To Levied for the use of the Parish	39,989
To the Collector for Colltg. & pay g. 69896 in Insp^{rs} Notes at 6 pC^t	4,193
	74,089
P^r.	C^r.
By 1723 Tythables at 43 p poll	74,089

[30]
Ord^r. That Christopher Tatum & John Mason j^r. on their Entering into Bond with sufficient Sureties to the Vestry of this Parish to be taken by the Clk of the Vestry, be & are appointed Collectors of this Parish, and that they do collect & receive of every Tythable person in the s^d. Parish the Sum of 43^{lb}. Nett Tob^o. being the Parish Levy of this Parish from the 15th. of October 1744 to the 15th of October 1745. And that they do make paiment to the several Parish Creditors, to whom the same is paible, the several Sums of Tobacco so raised & Levied, And that upon refusal of paiment of all or any part of the afores^d. Fourty Three pounds of Tob^o. by any person Chargeable therewith that then they do levy the same by Distress.

Ord. That the Church – Wardens pay to M^r. Thomas Eldridge £ 11.16.9½ for Ballance of his Acc^t. agst. this Parish to this Day & that the s^d. ChurchWardens take up Money at Int. to discharge the same.

Ord^d. That the Church Wardens pay £ 6.3.0 to M^r. Moses Johnson in full of his Acc^t. against the Parish, & that the same be paid as soon as Money can be raised by a Sale of Tob^o. this Day Levied.

Mem: The Vestry this Day agreed to & with Will. Rogers for the keeping of Celia Rogers an Infant & finding the s^d. Celia, Washing, Lodging & Apparel in a Christian like Manner, for which the s^d. William is to receive of this Parish after the Rate of 900^{lb}. of Tob^o. p annum during such Time as He shall so keep & provide for the s^d. Child.

Ord^d. That the Churchwardens put W^m. Barlow a poor Man, who labours under some Indispositions under Care with some Doct^r. & that they bring in an Acc^t. of their disbursements for the same to this Vestry.

Mem: The Vestry this Day enter'd into an agreem^t. with W^m. Jones for the keeping of Owin Jones a Lunitick person, and finding & providing for the s^d. Owin Sufficient Washing & Lodging, for which the s^d. William is to receive of this parish after the Rate of 700^{lb}. Tob^o. p annum during the time he shall keep him.

Mem. The Vestry this Day agreed with M^r. Moses Johnson for keeping Jno. King McGary [McGarraty?] an Impotent Infant & finding the s^d. John sufficient Meat, Apparel, Drink & Washing, for which he is to receive of this Parish after the Rate of 800^{lb}. Tob^o. p annum during such Time he shall find &c. for the s^d. John.

Robert Nicolson is appointed Clk to S^t. Pauls Chapel for the year next ensuing, And 'tis Ordered that he give his attendance & perform the Duty of Clk on all Sundays & Holy Dais throughout the year.

Joel Barker is appointed Sexton to S^t. Pauls Chapel & tis Ordered that he give his attendance & perform his Duty as Sexton on all Sundays & Holy Dais throughout the year.

An Ac^t. exhibited by M^r. Chappell & M^r. Johnson late Churchwardens [which?] by the Vestry is approved.

Ord. That the Churchwardens pay the Rev^d. Will. Willie £. 3/10. for an Oven built by M^r. Delony on the Glebe, pursuant to M^r. Delony's Ord^r. and Ordered that the Church Wardens take up Money on Acc^t. of the parish to pay the same.

W^m. Willie
Copy Test. Robt. Jones j^r. Clk. Vest.

[31]
At a Vestry held for the Parish of Albemarle in the County of Surry, at Nottaway Church on Barlthorp Creek; on the 1st Day of April, 1746

Present
The Reverend Will: Willie

Christopher Tatum	John Mason j^r.	
John Mason	James Chappell	} Gent.^{mn}
James Gee	Richard Blunt	
	Ephraim Parham	

Mr. Christopher Tatum & John Mason j^r. are Elected & Appointed Churchwardens for the Year next ensuring.

Ord. That Chris^r. Tatum & John Mason j^t. Churchwardens do apply themselves to Howel Briggs Gent. Sher^f. of Surry County for an acc^t. of & paiment for some Supernumerary Levies recd of Several Tythable persons of this Parish in the year 1745 & not accounted for to the Parish.

Ord. That the Churchwardens pay unto M^r. Moses Johnson the Bal that shall appear to be due from this Parish to him upon his Acc^t.

Ord. That the Churchwardens pay Joshua Mecham seventeen shillings Cash for his Acc^t. exhibited against this Parish.

Ord. That the Churchwardens lay out twenty shillings at their discretion / out of the fines recovered by this Parish against several delinquents / in relieving the necessities & wants of Geo. Malone & his Wife poor Indigent & impotent persons.

Ord. That the Churchwardens lay out 20^s/ at their discrietion / out of the Monies in their Hands recover'd by this Parish against several delinquents / in relieving the necessities & wants of Frances Crosland a poor & impotent Widow.

W^m. Willie Min^r.

Copy Test

Robt. Jones j^r. Clk Vest^ry

[32]

At a Vestry held for Albemarle Parish in the County of Surry on the 14th Day of October 1746, at the Church on the Northside of Nottaway River in the s^d. Parish.

Present
The Rev^d. William Willie Min^r.

Thomas Avent	Moses Johnson	
James Gee	Chris^r. Tatum	
James Chappell	John Mason j^r.	} Gent.
Richard Blow	John Mason	

Ephraim Parham

Albemarle Parish	D^r.
To the Rev^d. Mr. Willie's Salary	16,000
To Cask for the same	640
To Chris^t. Tatum Clk at Nottaway Church	1,200
To Ditto............Sexton at Ditto	400
To Robert Nicolson Clk at St. Pauls Church	1,200
To Joel Barker Sexton at Ditto	400
To Gregory Rawlings Clk at Spring Swamp Chapel	1,200
To Edward Shelton Sexton at Ditto	400
To Robert Farrington Clk at S^t. Marks Chapel	1,200
To Mary Green Sexton at the Same	400
To M^r. Johnson for keeping & cloathing a Child, John King McGary for one Year	800
To Samuel Lancaster for keeping & cloathing a certain Bastard Child one Year	650

To Charles Gillam for keeping & cloathing his Son Hinchea a disabled person one year	400
To W^m. Barlow for keeping his son Thomas a sick person 5 months & burying him	500
To John Smith for keeping & cloathing two Orphan Children of W^m. Wallace Dec^d.	1,200
To W^m. Rogers for keeping & cloathing a bastard Child for one year	800
To W^m. Rose for keeping Alex. Pandex an infirm Person	800
To Ditto for setting up Horse Blocks &c. at S^t. Pauls Church	200
To Peter Hawthorn for setting up Horse Blocks at Nottaway Church	100
To Thos. Mitchell for a set of Stops to the West Door at Ditto	160
To Ephraim Parham for raising the Pulpit &c. at S^t. Mark's Chapel	100
To W^m. Rogers an infirm Person for one year a Pension	600
To W^m. Jones for keeping & cloathing his bro^r. Owen Jones a disabled Person one Year	700
To the ChurchWardens for one Levy over-charged 1745	43
To Tobacco levied for the Use of the Parish	20,027
To 6 pC^t. for Collecting & paying away 49860 lib. Tob^o.	2,991
C^t.	52,851
By 1768 Tythables a^t 30 p poll	53,040

[33]

The Vestry having agreed to & with Christ^r. Tatum & John Mason j^r. Gent. for the collecting of 53111 lib. Tob^o. for the Use & Behalf of the s^d. Parish of Albemarle, tis hereby Ordered that the s^d. Christ^r. Tatum & John Mason have authority to receive from the several Persons chargeable therewith 30 lib. p poll according to the list of Tythables for the s^d. Parish, and that out of the s^d. 30 p poll they pay & discharge the several Parish Debts to the respective Creditors; and that if the persons Chargeable with the s^d. 30^{lb} p poll shall refuse or delay paying the same within the Time limitted by Law -- the s^d. Chris^t. Tatum & John Mason have authority to levy the same by Distress.

Ordrd. That the s^d. Christopher Tatum & John Mason j^r. give Bond & Security for the due performance of their Office, to the Clerk of the Vestry.

Ordrd. That the ChurchWardens pay M^r. Robert Jones j^r. 400^{lb}. of Tob^o. as Clk. of the Vestry the same having been omitted in the Parish Debit.

Ordrd. That the Churchwardens agree with some Person to send for a set of Church Plate for the Use of Albemarle Parish the Price not to exceed 40 £ Ster. and that the s^d. Plate be sent for according to the directions of the Rev^d. Mr. Willie.

Ordrd. That the Church Wardens do agree with some Person to send for four folio Common Prayer Books & one folio Church Bible for the Use of the s^d. Parish.

Ordrd. That the Churchwardens take Care of a Certain Child now kept by Samuel Lancaster.

Ordrd. That the Churchwardens pay Jno. Carril his ac^t. agst. the parish out of the Money in their Hands.

Ordrd. That the Churchwardens pay M^r. Hunter his ac^t. agst. the parish out of the Money in their Hands.

       W^m. Willie Min.
     Copy Test
       Robt. Jones j^r. Clk. Vest^y.

[34]

At a Vestry held for the Parish of Albemarle in the County of Surry on the 20th Day of August 1747. at the Church on Barlthorp Creek.

Present
The Rev[d]. William Willie Min[r].

Thomas Avent	Howell Briggs	
John Mason	James Gee	} Gentlemen
James Chappell	Chris[r]. Tatum	
John Mason j[r].	Moses Johnson	

In pursuance to an Order of Surry County Court bearing Date the 21st Day of July 1747 directing the Vestry of this Parish to divide the same into precincts for the processioning of every person's Land within the s[d]. Parish: We do appoint Thomas Bell & William Evans to see every person's Land Procession'd and the Land Marks thereof renew'd beginning from the Isle of wight County Line at Black Water thence up Black Water all the Land between Tarrapin Swamp & Blow Road. And that they Assemble all the Freeholders within that Precinct to attend the performance thereof; and that the s[d]. Thomas Bell & William Evans do return to this Vestry an Account of every particular persons Land that they shall Procession and of every person present at the processioning thereof, and also of whose Land they shall fail to procession & the particular Reasons of such failure, and that the same be done & perform'd between the first Day of November & last Day of March Next ensuing.
William Hancock & Robert Nicolson are appointed to procession all the Land between Seacock & Tarrapin Swamp to Birchan Island Road.
Richard Blow & John Smith are appointed to Procession from the S[o]. side of Seacock Swamp to the Head of Lightwood Swamp & Seacaurees Swamp thence to Birchan Island Road.
George Briggs & Walter Baley are appointed to procession from Isle of wight County Line up Arsamosauk Swamp to Secaurees Swamp thence up Secaurees to the Head.
James Chappell j[r]. & John Jarrard are appointed to procession from the Mouth of Secaurees Swamp up Arsamosauk to Allens Road & along that Road to Copohonk thence to Secaurees Road & thence to the beginning.
Nicholas Partridge & Howell Jones are appointed to procession from Allens Road up Assamoosock and including William Johnson's Land thence to the Head of Copohonk Swamp.
David Jones & William Cook are appointed to procession from Cook's Bridge along Cook's Road to Joseph Swamp thence up the s[d]. swamp to Prince George County Line thence by the s[d]. Line to Black Water thence to the beginning.
John Mason & Hugh Ivey are appointed to procession from Cook's Road or the New Road to the Black Swamp thence to the Governors Road all between the s[d]. Roads out to Joseph Swamp.
John Mason j[r]. & Edward Weaver from the Governors Road the Old Parish Line and between Arsamoosock all between Joseph Swamp & Arsamoosock to the Old Parish Line.
William Parker & George Wyche are appointed to Procession from the Old Parish Line down to the Mouth of Robins Branch thence down Austins Branch to Nottaway River thence up Nottaway to the beginning.
William Edmunds & David Edmunds are appointed to procession all between Nottaway River & Asamoosock below the Mouth of Robin's Branch & Austin's Branch to Isle of wight County Line.
[written at edge of page] Edward

[35]

Edward Lee & Peter Hay are appointed to procession from Greens Old Mill along John Hawthorn's Line to the Colledge. Line thence by that Line to Joseph Swamp & down that Swamp to Nottaway River & up the same to the Mouth of Barlthorp Creek & up that Creek

to the beginning.
William Parham & James Mason are appointed to procession all between Barlthorp Creek & Monkasneck from Prince George County Line to Nottaway River.
Maj^r. Robert Wynne & Thomas Wynne are appointed to procession all between Monkasneck Creek & Stony Creek & up Sappony Creek to the line that Divides Prince George & this County.
William Gillam & Henry Freeman are appointed to procession from Stony Creek to Sappony Mill from thence to the Plantation of Peter Green Dec^d. so down Nottaway River to the beginning.
James Cain & Robert Farrington are appointed to procession from the Plantation of Peter Green Dec^d. to Sappony Mill all between the line that divides Prince George & this County and up Nottaway River to Harry's Swamp.
Thomas Vines & Richard Pepper are appointed to procession from Harry's Swamp up Nottaway to the extent of this County.
Hinchia Gillam & Richard Avery are appointed to procession from the Mouth of Rackoon up to the mouth of Little Swamp thence up Little Swamp to Stokes's Road thence by Stokes's Road to Hunting Quarter, and down the same to Nottaway River thence down Nottaway River to the beginning.
Robert Webb & Charles Battle are appointed to procession all between Rackoon Swamp, Little Swamp and Stokes's Road.
Moses Johnson & Clem^t. Hancock between Hunting Quarter, Nottaway River & Stokes Road.
Matthew Parham & Ephraim Parham are appointed to procession from the Island Swamp to the Old Parish Line & along that line to the line that divides Brunswick County & this County all between Nottaway River &c.
John Stevens & Will. Ezzel between the Rackoon & Hunting Quarter out to the Head of Hunting Quarter.
Charles Judkins & John Bell are appointed to procession from the West Side of Stokes's Road between the Poplar and Rackoon to the Old Parish Line.
William Knight & John Battle are appointed to procession all the Land on the East Side of Stoke's Road between the Line that divides Isle of wight County from this to the Rackoon Swamp.
John Avent & Peter Avent are appointed to procession from the S^o. side of the Poplar Swamp to the three Creeks all between Brunswick County Line & the s^d. Creek & Swamp.
James Wyche & Joseph Thorp between the S^o. side of three Creeks & Isle of wight & Brunswick County Lines.
Edward Petway & William Petway are appointed to procession from Stokes's Road up Nottaway River the flat Swamp and from the Head of that a Strait Course to the Hunting Quarter Swamp.
Sloman Wynne & Henry Sturdivant are appointed to procession all from flat Swamp up Nottaway River to Island Swamp and from thence to the Hunting Quarter Swamp.
Howel Briggs & Samuel Magget from the mouth of Copohonk Swamp to Birchan Island & by that Road till it intersects with Secaurees Road & by that to Copohonk & down the same to the beginning.
David Hunter & Robert Judkins all between Black Water the Mouth of Copohonk and the Old Parish Line.
Peter Bagley & John Barker are appointed to procession from the Mouth of Town Swamp & up that to Head of the Tar Kiln Branch & down the s^d. Branch to the Mill Swamp & including Samuel Tatum's Land & thence to the new Road thence to Cooks Road & by that to Black Water thence to the beginning.
William Briggs & Edmund Ruffin are appointed to procession from Black Water at the Old Parish Line by that Line to Copohonk Swamp thence up that to the Head thence to the Head of the Mill Swamp and down that to Black Water Swamp and thence to the beginning.

[36]

Whereas Robert Wynne Gent'. has neglected to serve this Parish in the Capacity of a Vestry Man and to attend the vestries held for the same ever since the 16 Day of November 1742. Tis Ordered that the Church Wardens of this parish wait on the s^d. Wynne & require his reasons for neglecting his Duty as afores^d. and whether the s^d. Wynne does resign his Office of Vestryman for the parish. And that the s^d. Churchwardens do make a report of their proceedings therein to this Vestry.
Order'd and Agreed that Robert Jones Junr. be & is elected a Vestry Man for this Parish in the place & stead of Capt. Richard Blunt deceas'd and that he qualify as soon as conveniently he can for serving this Parish in that Capacity.
On the petition of Daniel Weldon Ordered that he be and is appointed Clk of this Vestry instead of Robert Jones Junr. who has this Day resigned his Clerkship.
Ordered that Chris^r. Tatum & John Mason j^r. Churchwardens do give publick notice by advertisements at such places in this County & the Counties Adjacent as they shall think proper, that on Thursday the 15th of October Next a Vestry will be held at the Church on Barlthorp Creek in Order to treat with workmen for building & erecting a Church 70 by 26 at or near where the Chapel at Spring Swamp now stands for the Use of the s^d. Parish.
Ordered that the Rev^d. M^r. Willie agree with a person to repair the Steps of the Glebe House of this Parish which are out of repair. And an account of the Charge to be return'd to this Vestry.
Ordered that the Sum of four pounds be paid to Thomas Cooper by the Chrchwardens of this Parish out of the Money in their Hands raised by Fines, the wife of the s^d. Thomas being much Afflicted.
Ordered that the Churchwardens of this Parish at their discretion lay out thirty Shillings of the Money in their Hands which has arisen by fines for the use of Cannon Roe & an infirm Person.

W^m. Willie Min^r.
Copy
Test   D. Weldon Clk Vest^y

[37]

At Vestry held for Albemarle Parish at Nottaway Church the 25th Day of October 1747.

Present
The Rev^d. William Willie

James Gee	Christopher Tatum	
James Chappel	John Mason j^r.	
Moses Johnson	Richard Blow	} Gent^n.
John Mason	Ephraim Parham	
Robert Wynne	Howel Briggs	

Albemarle Parish	D^r.	lbs Tob^o.
To the Reverend William Willie's Sallery		16,000
To Cask for the same		640
To Christopher Tatum Clerk of Nottaway Church		1,200
To Ditto............Sexton at Ditto		400
To Robert Nicholson Clk at S^t. Pauls Church		1,200
To Joel Barker Sexton at Ditto		400
To Gregory Rawlings Clk at Spring Swamp Chapel		1,200
To Edward Shelton Sexton at Ditto		400

To Robert Farrington Clk at S[t]. Mark's Chapel	1,200
To Mary Green Sexton at the Same	400
To Edward Shelton for keeping the Church Ornaments	33
To Christopher Tatum for Ditto	25
To Joel Barker for Ditto	25
To M[r]. Willie on Ac[t]. of John King McGary now at M[r]. Johnson's	700
To Samuel Lancaster for keeping & cloathing a certain Bastard Child	650
To Charles Gillam for keeping & cloathing his son Hinchia one year	400
To W[m]. Rogers for keeping & cloathing a certain Bastard Child one year	900
To W[m]. Jones for keeping his Bro[r]. Owin Jones an infirm person one Year	700
To Maj[r]. Robert Wynne for summoning Several Evidences	456
To Robert Jones j[r]. Clk of this Vestry	400
To John Warrick for keeping & cloathing Barnet Johnson	300
To William Ross for finding Sundry Things & burying Alex. Pandix	200
To M[r]. John Mason j[r]. for keeping John Myers a sick Person 6 Weeks	100
To William Parker for keeping Tho[s]. Beddingfield a sick Person 6 Weeks	200
To Tobaco levied for the Use of the Parish	28,129
	30,000
To 6 p C[t]. for Collecting the above Tob[o]. & paying away the same	58,129
	3,487
	61,616
Albemarle Parish	C[r].
By 1873 Tythables at 33[lb]. Tob[o]. p poll	61,809

M[r]. Chris[r]. Tatum & John Mason j[r]. are appointed Church wardens until Easter Tuesday next.

The

[38]

The Vestry having agreed to & with Christopher Tatum & John Mason j[r]. Gent[n]. for the collecting of 61616[lbs] of Tob[o]. for the Use & behoof of the s[d]. Parish of Albemarle tis hereby ordered that the s[d]. Christopher Tatum & John Mason j[r]. have authority to Receive from the several Persons chargeable therewith 33[lb] Tob[o]. p poll according to the list of Tythables for the s[d]. Parish & that out of the s[d]. 33[lb]. p poll they pay & discarge the several parish Debts to the respective Creditors; and that if the persons Chargeable therewith shall refuse or delay paying the same within the Time limited by Law the s[d]. Christopher Tatum & John Mason have authority to levy the same by Distress.
Order'd that the s[d]. Christopher Tatum & John Mason j[r]. give Bond & Security for the Collecting of the same Tob[o]. to be taken by the Clk of the Vestry.
Order'd that the Churchwardens pay to Christopher Mason his Ac[t]. against the Parish which is £15. for work done at Nottaway Church.
Order'd that the Churchwardens pay to William Carlisle thirty Shillings for diging a Well &c. at S[t]. Pauls Chapel.
Order'd that the Churchwardens do find for & allow Joshua Fitch Patrick such Cloaths as they shall think proper.
The Vestry having covenanted & agreed with James Anderson of Amelia County for the building of a Church or Chapel at or near where the Chapel at Spring Swamp now stands, for which he is to have £290. Curr[.] Money of Virginia, according the Demensions & Manner following Viz[t]. 69 feet in Length & 26 feet in Bredth in the Clear: 16 feet Pitch underpin'd 2 feet high viz[t]. w a foot below & 12 foot above the surface of the Ground with good well burnt Bricks & air Holes at proper Distance, a strong substantial Girt Floor laid with sound well season'd quarter'd pine plank in bredth not above 10 Inches, all the Pews to be 6 feet wide & 10 feet long, except two Viz[t]. one on each side of the Communion Table, which are

to be 9 by 7 the Ally to be 6 feet wide. The Church to have two Doors in the South Side & one in the West and 4 feet wide and 9 feet high all to be folding, and the work quarter Round & Rais'd pannel; the two Doors in the South Side to be made fast with Bars & Iron Hooks, that in the West End with two spring Bolts & a neat & strong Lock: all to be hung with suitable HL Hinges; the pews to be 4 feet high & close the Front to be quarter Round & raised pannel, the Partitions plain Wainscot; all the pews to be neatly cap'd plank seats on three sides, the Doors to be of size according to the plan & hung with substantial H Hinges, the Communion Table to be rais'd two steps above the Floor of the Church, and inclos'd with Rails & neatly turn'd Ballusters, the Door thereof to [be] hung with neat substantial Hinges, a Pulpit with a neat & suitable Canopy & Door hung with H Hinges & both that & the two Reading pews Viz^t. for the Minister & Clerk to be the sort of work with the Front of the pews & of Demension according to the plan, Rails & Ballusters from the Minister's reading pew to the pulpit: The length & width of the space for the Communion Table & number of steps to ascend to the reading pews & pulpit to be deter-mind

[39]

mind & directed by the Minister. The span of two pews on the North Side at the West end of the Church to be set apart for a Baptistry with Seats all round: A neat turn'd Post erected in the area with handsom Mouldings round the Top, whereon to place the Font or Bason, & a Desk adjoining to ~~lay it~~ lay the Book on: two plank seats to be put up in the Westmost front Door way & one in that of the Eastermost. The Church to have 6 Windows in the South Side 7 in the North side of [sic] on & size in the clear according to the plan, a large window in the East End 6 feet wide in the Clear & of a proportional highth divided by a post in the Middle a window in the West End above the plate of Demension suitable to the place: all the Windows to be glaz'd with good Crown Glass, the runing sashes to be supported when up with Iron pins made fast to the Frame with a Leather thong the Church to be done up the highth of the pins with Feather Edge plank plain'd & beaded, to have a common Substantial Roof with a Compass Cieling the Wall's & Roof to be strengthen'd with great Beams across in Number & size suitable, the Walls above the pews & cieling to be well plaister'd & whitewash'd: The Window Frames on the inside & Door Cases on both sides to be architrav'd: a small Window in the back of the pulpit of size suitable to the plan, Shutters for all the Windows of Plain Wainscot, to be hung with substantial H. Hinges & made fast when open with Iron Hooks & Staples & when shut with an Iron Spring Bolt, the Walls & Gable Ends to be done with Feather Edg plank plain'd & beaded to show not above 6 Inches, with Cornish Eaves, the Roof to be cover'd on saw'd Laths with good Cypress Heart Shingles in length 20 Inches in thickness 1 Inch & in Bredth not above 4 Inches & nail'd with 6^d. nails the Roof to be hip'd from the Coller Beams, the Side & Gabel End Walls to be well tar'd: the Window Shutters on both sides the out side of the Doors & Door Cases, the out side of the window Frames & Sashes the Cornish the Corner & Barge Boards all to be well painted with White Lead & oil: a Fronton or Pediment over each Door Shingled &c. as the Roof: White Oak or Light Wood Steps at each Door mitred at the Corners. A gallery in the West End of the Church of Pitch, Demention & Form according to the plan with a proper stair case & close Breast or Front of Wainscot quarter'd round & rais'd pannel with architrave frese & Cornish & proper Bars, one pew in the fore part on the Northside 6 feet by 11½ with seats round 3 sides the Back Door & Eads: on the South side plane wainscot 3 feet by 11½ a passage from the stairs of 3 feet wide, a passage to the back side of 3 feet wide, 8 seats on each side, four 2 by 11½ feet to rise above one another 9 Inches, a Partition betwixt each Seat 2 feet high above each respective Floor of plain Wainscot, The Gallery plastered underneath the whole to be completed & finished at the proper Cost, & Charges of the s^d. James Anderson and that in a neat & workmanlike Manner; by the 15th of June which shall Happen in the Year 1750. For the Performance whereof the s^d. James Anderson is to give Bond with Sufficient Security as soon as may be to the Church wardens of the s^d. Parish for the Time being.

W^m. Willie Min^r.
Copy Test   Daniel Weldon Clk Vest

Spring Swamp Chapel, c.1748

Conjectural drawing by Andrew Hogwood from specifications as written in the Albemarle Parish Vestry Minutes (pages [38]-[39] of original minutes).

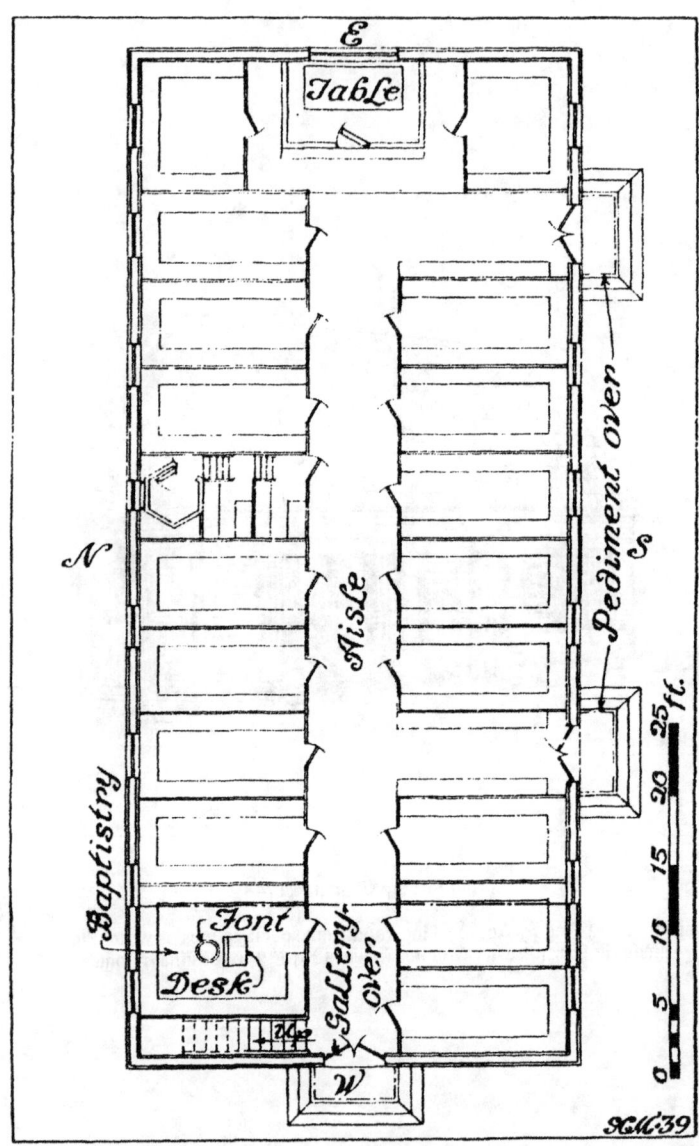

St. Andrew's Church, c.1754 (Spring Swamp Chapel)
Interior Arrangement

George Carrinton Mason, Colonial Churches of Tidewater Virginia. (1945)
(Richmond, VA: Whittet and Shepperson). Plate 10.

[40]

At a Vestry held at Nottaway Church in the Parish of Albermarle on on [sic] the 12th Day of April (being Easter Tuesday) 1748.

Present
The Reverend William Willie

Thomas Avent	Christopher Tatum	
John Mason	John Mason jr.	
Robert Wynne	Moses Johnson	} Gent
James Gee	Ephraim Parham	
	James Chappell	

Christopher Tatum & John Mason jr Appointed Church Wardens for the year ensuing.
A Letter from Mr. Robert Jones junior setting forth the Misfortunes of a Certain Jordan Knight son of John Knight, being read, it is ordered that the said Jordan be Exempt from paying his Parish Levies, during his Continuance Under his Calamity.

Ordered that the Church Wardens do pay, out of the Fines in their hands, Ten Shillings Currency to Mary Coles, an Indigent woman,

Ordered that the Church Wardens do pay out of the Fines in their Hands thirty Shillings Curr^{cy}. to Major Robert Wynne for Jane Matthews an Indigent woman.

Orderd that the Church Wardens do pay out of the Fines in their Hands, ten Shillings Currency to Eliz. Arnold an Indigent Woman.

Orderd that the Church Wardens do pay, out of the Fines in Their Hands for one year's Schooling of a Child of a Certain Frances Crossland Widow, a Woman under Low Circumstances.

Order'd that the Church Wardens do lay out, out of the Fines in their Hands Thirty Shillings Currency, in such Things, as they Shall Think most Proper and Convenient for Supplying the necessities of a certain Thomas Davis junior an Infirm Man.

Order'd that the Church Wardens do pay, out of the Fines in their Hands twenty Shillings Currency to Major Robert Wynne, for a Certain Mary Woodham an Infirm & Indigent Woman.

Order'd that the Church Wardens do agree with some Person or Persons to set up Seats in Certain Places Convenient for the People to sit on before Divine Service begins, at Nottaway Church, St. Pauls Church, & St. Mark's Chappel in this Parish.

Upon the Motion of Major Robt. Wynne tis Order'd that for the more decent Performance of preaching in three Churches of this Parish, where there is not a gown the Minister for want, thereof is Oblig'd to Preach in the Surplice, that Three gowns be purchas'd] by the Reverend William Willie, or the Minister for the Time being, at the Charge and Cost of Albermarle Parish, which Gowns to be kept at the Several Churches viz: St. Pauls Church, St. Mark's Chappel & the Church at Spring Swamp, under the Care of the several sextons and to be [??m'd] as Vestments of the said Parish.

[41]

Daniel Weldon Clerk of the Vestry, having resign'd, Joseph Mason is appointed to succeed him & tis Ordred [sic] that he the s^d. Mason do enter upon his Office & receive Under his Care the Vestry Books and all the Parish Papers now in the hand of the said Weldon, after the s^d. Weldon hat enter'd all the returns of Processioning in the Vestry Book.
Order'd that ten Pounds Curr^t. Money, be paid by the Church Wardens out of the Parish Money now in their Hands to James Anderson Undertaker of the Church to be built at Spring Swamp in This Parish; and likewise that the Church Wardens do pay to the said Anderson Seventy Pounds Current Money, when the Tob^o. levied for the Use of the Parish shall be Sold and the Money arising from such Sale in the hands of the Church Wardens.

W^m. Willie Minist^r

(1) Pursuant to an Order of Vestry Dated Agust 26:1747 we Henry Mitchell & Christopher Tatum have seen all the Lands procession'd between the College [land] and John Hawthorn's lines, and the line that divides Surry and Prince George County and between Joseph Swamp & Jones Hole as followeth

Proprietor ~~Lands~~	Land	Persons Present
John Reeves's	Land	Matthew Gibbs & Thomas Mitchel
Matthew Gibbs's	Land	John Reeves, Thomas Mitchel
Henry Mitchel's	Land	Jno. Reeves, Matthew Gibbs, Thos. Mitchel
Francis Mabry's	Land	Jno. Reeves, M. Gibbs, T. Mitchel
Thomas Mitchel's	Land	J. Reeves, M: Gibbs.
Francis Eppes's	Land	Thomas Mitchell, M: Gibbs
George Reeves's	Land	T. Mitchel, M: Gibbs
Wm Dobey's	Land	John Reeves, Thomas Mitchel
Robt. Dobey	Land	Jno. Reeves, Wm. Dobey
Joshua Hawthorn	Land	R: Dobey, Chris^{to}. Tatum j^r.
Chris^{to}. Tatum	Land	R: Dobey
Capt. Aug. Claiborne	Land	R: Dobey

p^r Chris. Tatum
[Procession Masters] Henry Mitchel

(2) In Obedience to an Order of Vestry of Albermarle Parish bearing date Ag^t 26 1747 & directed to us whose names are hereunto set we have, after due notice given quietly procession'd all the Lines & renew'd the Land Marks within the Precinct in the s^d. Order Mention'd, the several Persons whose Names are hereunto subjoyn'd being present. viz:

Proprietors names.	Persons present
Peter Dobey	R: Hancock, H: Meachum, Tim Ezell j^r
Clem: Hancock	Dit^o & Clem: Hancock
Henry Lee	H: Moss, H. Porch, J: Porch
Munford Ellbeck	R. Hancock. H. Meachum, T. Ezell j^r

[42]

Brought Over

Proprietors Names}	Persons present
Wm Moss	Dit^o. & Wm Moss
Timothy Ezell j^r.	Clem: Hancock, R: Hancock, Tim Ezell j^r.

Surry and Sussex Counties, Virginia, 1742-1786   35

Henry Moss	H. Porch, Ja^s. Porch, R: Hancock, H. Moss
Henry Porch	Ditto
Edwd Lee	Ditto
Ja^s Porch	Ditto & Henry Meachum
Henry Meachum	Wm Moss, Jno Atkins, H: Meachum
Edwd Eppes	H: Meachum, R: Hancock, T Ezell, W Moss
Richd Tomlinson	Jno Atkins, Nathaniel Tomlinson
Thos Adkins	Ditto & H. Meachum
———— Young	H: Meachum. Jno Adkins
Wm Moss	R: Hancock, Wm Moss
Glebe	Ditto
Peter Hawthorn	Robert Hancock
Rebecca Hawthorn	D^o
Thos Eldridge	Robt Hancock, Clem Hancock, Tim Ezel j^r.
Francis Mabry	Robt Hancock

Given under our Hands   p Peter Hawthorn
this 20th of April 1747   Edward Lee [Procession Masters]

(3) In pursuance to an Order of Vestry held for the parish of Albermarle Augt 26 in the year of our Lord 1747 we the said James Cain & Robt Farrington have seen every person's Land procession'd within our precinct & the land marks renew'd except a line between James Cain & George Robinson which the said George Robinson refused to have procession'd the reason was the former lines are Cut down And the s^d Robinson says the s^d. James Cain hath removed his Land mark.

Proprietors ~~Land~~	Land	Persons present
Edwd. Farrington	Land	[illegible]
Hinchy Mabry	Land	Wm Raney & Jno Farrington
Wm Raney	Land	Wm Young & Geo. Robinson
Geo: Randolph	Land	Ja^s Oliver & Thos Wilkinson
Ja^s Banks	Land	Matthew Hill & Jno Davis
Ben. Harrison's	Land	Thos Hunt & Jno Jones
Jo^s. Sewell	Land	Jo. Sewell & Thos Butler
Matthew Hill	Land	Thos Huson & John Kelly
Thos Burrough	Land	Henry Mitchel & Thos Ward
Jno Davis	Land	
James Moss	Land	
Arch^d Pepper	Land	
Thos Wilkenson	Land	
Thos Hunt	Land	Witness our Hands the 27th
Thos Butler	Land	of February 1747.
Richd Carter	Land	p James Cain [Procession Masters}
John Jones Senr	Land	Robert Farrington
Jno Jones j^r		
Wm Harper	Land	
Jno Kelly	Land	
Richd Huson 's	Land	
Henry Mitchel	Land	
Jno Farrington	Land	

[43]

(4) Pursuant to an Order of Vestry of the Parish of Albermarle made 26 of Aug[t] 1747 we have procession'd the Lands within our precinct belonging to the persons hereafter mention'd. Viz. Samuel Alsobrook, John Nanny, Maj[r] Tillar, Joseph Thorp, James Wyche, Agnes Williams, William Barlow, Timothy Thorp, Richard Ransom, persons Present at the Processioning, Major Tillar, Sam. Alsobrook j[r], Jn[o] Nanny, James Wyche Jun[r], Nathaniel Wyche, Tho[s] Bridges, William Barlow.

Jo' Thorp
[Procession Masters] James Wych

(5) In Obedience to an Order of Vestry of the Parish of Albermarle Dated 26 of August 1747 directing us to Assemble the Freeholder together within the Precinct Viz: on the Southside of Nottaway River and below Stokes's Road to the Hunting Quarter Swamp, thence down the said Swamp to the Mouth. to Conclude. Accordingly we Assembled the Freeholders together the seventeenth of March and went in Quiet procession of the Lands of the following Persons Viz.

Mar. 17		Moses Johnson	Persons present	Clement Hancock
		John Land		Jn[o] Pennington
		Alexander Dickins		Moses Johnson
		John Pennington		John Zeels
		Major Baker		Morris Zeels
	Col[o]	———		Wm Johnson
		Lightfoot		
		Clem: Hancock		———
Mar. 18		Lambert Zeels		———
		John Zeels	Mar. 18 Persons Pres[nt].	Clement Hancock
		Morris Zeels		John Pennington
		Wm Zeels		Moses Jonson
		Tho[s] Renn		John Zeels
	Col[o]	Ben Harrison		Morris Zeels
		Wm Bishop		Wm Zeels
		Wm Pare's		Lambert Zeels
		Tho[s] Harrison		Philip Bailey
Mar 26		Philip Bailey		Wm Pare
		R. Jones j[r]		Charles Abbington
		Jn[o] Hunt		Wm Johnson
				Thomas Renn
		————	Persons present M[ah] 26 day	Clem. Hacocke
		————		John Pennington
		————		Moses Johnson
				Philip Bailey
				Wm Pare

Clem: Handcock
& Moses Johnson
[Procession Masters]

(6) By Virtue & pursuant to an Order of Vestry bearing Date 26 of August 1747 We the Subscribers have procession'd and saw the Land Marks of Several Persons Renew'd, to wit, Capt John Masons, Wm Johnsons & the Land between R: Jones & James Jones and out [-?-]. Present Robert Jones, Daniel Guthry, Nicholas Partridge j^{ior}, & Wm Johnsons, given under our hands this the 15 day of March 1747.

                                              Howell Jones
[Procession Masters] Nichol^s. Partridge

(7) Pursuant to An Order of Vestry dated the 26 of August 1747, it is order'd that Robert Wynne & Thomas Wynne procession every mans Land & the Land Marks Renew'd between Monksneck Creek & Stony Creek, & Sappony Creek And the Line between Prince George County & Surry County and it is done Accordingly.

[44]

Proprietors Names	The persons names when Procession'd
M^{rs}. Eliz: Poythress	John Jackson, Edwd Eacols, Jno Freeman j^r,
Col^o Robert Bolling	Solomon Graves & James Gearton
Edward Broadnax	
John Jackson	
Edward Munford	
Edward Eacols	
John Freeman jun^r	
Capt Alexander Bolling	
Andrew King	
William Raines	
William Malone	
Robert Wynne	
Thomas Wynne	
George Booth	John Williamson, John Curtis, Thomas Huson,
Thomas Malone	Thomas Malone, Wyat Harper, John Williamson,
John Williamson	John Curtis, George Booth, Tho. Huson, Wyat Harper,
John Curtis	
William Harper	
Thomas Hunt	done p Robt Wynne
Richard Huson	[Procession Masters] Thos Wynne

(8) Pursuant to an Order of Vestry bearing date August 26 day 1747 we the Subscribers have Procession'd the following Lands, to wit, Thomas Clapps[?], John Handcock, John Bradley, William Bradleys, William Carrills, John Jeffreys, Robert Carrels, John Groves, William Capp[?], Samuel Cornwell, David Andrus, Robert Adkins, Thomas Renn, Joseph Handcock, Augustine Hargrave, Joseph Hargrave, Anselm Bailey, John Holloman, Eliz: Adkins and our own, Present all the Proprietors of the aforesaid Lands Excepting Eliz: Adkins, Capt Howell Brigg's Land and Michael Petway's Land not Procession'd the reason, because they was no Body attended to do the same in their behalf. Given Under our hands this 26 day of March, 1748.

                                              William Hancock
[Procession Masters] Robert Nicolson

38   The Vestry Book of Albemarle Parish

(9) In Obedience to an Order of Vestry held for Albermarle Parish Augt 26 day 1747. We the Subscribers have Quietly & peacibly procession'd all the Land mention'd in the said Order, from the Old Parish line to the Mouth of Robins Branch, thence down Austin's Branch to Nottaway River thence up the s^d River to the Parish line Aforesaid.

Proprietors Names	~~Proprie~~ present
Robt Jones	M^r. Robt Jones
Sam: Chappel	M^r. Sam: Chappel
Sarah Jones	James Chappell
Mr James Chappel	John Harrison
Hall 's Land	
Maj^r James Baker	Edwd Allmond
Richd Parker	Geo: Davis
Rich^d. Griffin	
Wm Hines	
M^r Wm Barker	
Cargill 's Land	
Capt Jno Mason	
Geo: Wych	

                                              Geo Wych
                                              Wm Parker
                                        [Procession Masters]

[45]

(10) In Obedience to an Order of Vestry of Albermarle Parish Dated the 26 day of August 1747 we the Subscribers being Appointed by the said Vestry to see the Land of Several Persons procession'd did on the 26 day of February procession the land of John Sledge, Reuben Cooke, Alexander Finney, Joseph Mason, John Underhill and our own Land and there was present the above mention'd Persons and William Tomlinson and Daniel Sledge witness [our?] Hands this 20th Day of March 1748

                                              John Mason Junr
                                              Edward Wever
                                        [Procession Masters]

(11) In pursuance to an Order of Vestry held for the parish of Albermarle of 26 of August in the Year of our Lord ~~God~~ 1747 We the s^d. Wm Gilliam & Henry Freeman have seen every persons Land Procession'd and the Land marks renew'd in our precinct.

Proprieters ~~Names~~	Persons present
Nathaniel Green j^r.	
Nathaniel Green Senr	Robt Farrington, Arthur Freeman
William Green	Charles Dillelay, Wm Malone
John Hale	Joshua Ellis, Rich^d. Hill
Martha Richardson	Nathaniel Green, Jo^s King
William Wynns	William Green
Robert Farrington	
Wm Richardson	
Charles Dillelay	
Drury Roberson	
Joshua Ellis	
Henry Freemans	Land
Arthur Freemans	

Rob: Webbs
Miles Hills
Rob: Bolling
William Gillum
Rich⁴ Hills
John Hills
William Wilburn's   John Tyus, Wm Winkfield
John Tyus   Jarvis Winkfield, George Booth
William Winkfield   Nat: Malone, Isaac Roberson
Jarvis Winkfield   James Gillum
Geo: Booths
Nat: Malone
James Gillum
Wm Harper
Isaac Roberson
Tho⁵ Waide
John Bonner   witness our Hands
                                              William Gillum
                                              Henry Freeman
                                              [Procession Masters]
[46]

(12) In Obedience to an Order of Vestry of Albermarle Parish bearing Date August 26, day 1747 we the Subscribers have assembled the Freeholders together and procession'd the Land of Henry Jarrad, John Barker & the Land of Sarah Jones, and the Land of Howell Briggs and the Land of James Chappell, and the Land of John Harrison, & the Land of Thomas Wallis jun', & the Land of William Hines jun' & the Land of William Lowry[?], and the Land of Robert Jones, & the Land of Esther Winkles & the Land of John Jarrad and the Land of James Chappell, Junior.
present when the afores⁴. Lands were procession'd

                 Howell Briggs   John Barker
                 James Chappell   Henry Jarrad
                 John Harrison   Thomas Wallis j'
                 Robert Jones   Wm Lowry
Mar. 16 1747 p Certified Given under our hands   James Chappell j'
                                              [Procession Masters] John Jarrad

(13) Pursuant to an Order of Albemarle Vestry of Albemarle Parish dated Aug' 26 day 1747. We Wm Parham & James Mason, have seen all the Land procession'd between the mouth of Barlethorpe Creek & Prince George County Line & Nottaway River to the mouth of Monksneck Creek as followeth processiond the 7ᵗʰ & 8ᵗʰ days of March 1747/8'

Proprietors Names	Land	
Timothy Ezell	Land	The Persons all present
James Mason	Land	&
Edw⁴. Petway	Land	all the lines quietly
Wᵐ. Moore	Land	procession'd
Eppes Moore	Land	
John Coats	Land	
Henry Mitchel j'.	Land	
James Heath	Land	
Peter Poythress	Land	
Tho⁵. Heath	Land	
John Smith	Land	

40   The Vestry Book of Albemarle Parish

    Charles Leeth   Land
    James Parham   Land
    John Parham   Land
    Matthew Parham   Land
    John Leeth   Land
    James Brown   Land
    Abraham Parham   Land
    Joshua Poythress   Land
    William Parham   Land   William Parham
                           James Mason
                          [Procession Masters]

(14) In Obedience to an Order of Vestry of Albermarle Parish dated Augt 26 day 1747 we the Subscribers after Due notice given have quietly procession'd the Several Persons Lands hereafter mentiond and have [illegible] assign'd reasons wy the Lands of Wm Clifton, Richard Knight, & Christopher Golithely were not procession'd.

Proprietors names   Persons present

William Eldridge   Nathaniel Hood, Holman Sturdivant,
             Land Jno Wynne, Richd Reeves, Edw'd
                    Petway, Wm Petway, Jo Wheless, Wm
                    Weathers, Jno Threwitt, Jno
                    Rottenberry, Stith Parham
Richd Reeves   Ditto
                               continued

[47]

Edward Petway   Ditto
Wm Petway   Ditto
William Weathers   Ditto
Joseph Wheeless   Ditto
Robert Petway   Ditto
Maj^r Robert Wynne   Ditto
Stith Parham   Ditto
Sloman Wynne   Ditto
Hollman Sturdivant   Ditto
Henry Sturdivant   Ditto
John Wynne   Ditto
Matthew Wynne   Ditto
Edward Eckles   Ditto
John Rottenberry   Ditto
Robert Green   John Threwitt, John Rottenberry,
                    Richard Rives, Matthew Whitehead,
                    John Shands
John Threwit   Ditto
Col^o. Robert Bolling   Ditto
Matthew Whitehead   Ditto
John Sturdivant   Ditto
Nat. Hood   Ditto
John Shands   Ditto
Capt Howell Briggs   By his Order to us
William Bridges

William Clifton's Land not Procession'd because he wou'd not attend unless he was fetch'd from his House.

Richard Knight's land not procession'd because he wou'd not attend & he alledg'd he never had done it.

Christopher Golikely's land not procession'd he not attending not withstanding due notice given him.

Sloman Wynne
Henry Studivant
[Procession Masters]

(15) In Obedience to an Order of the Worshipful Vestry of Albemarle Parish bearing Date the 26 Day of August 1747 we have procession'd & renew'd & all the Land & Land Marks in our Precint Viz^t.

The Land of	Thos. Newson	John Richardson	Persons Present
Fran^s. Felps	Henry Manery	John Battle	Fran^s. Felps Phil.
Philip Harwood	Benj. Richardson	Charles Mabry	Harwood
W^m. Knight	Mary Brown	Gregory Rawlings	Robt. Bullock Jos
Henry Tyler	Sil. Stokes	Gregory Rawlings j^r.	Harwood
Robt. Bullock	James Carter	Robert Long	George Cornet,
Jos. Harwood	Fran^s. Hutchens		Thos. Newsom
Geo. Corney	James Cooper		Henry Mannery
	John Moss		Ben. Richardson
			Sil. Stokes Ja^s.
			Carter, Fran^s.
			Hutchens
			Ja^s. Cooper John
			Moss John
			Richardson
			Charles Mabry
			Gregory
			Rawlings
			Gregory
			Rawlings j^r.

John Battle
& W^m. Knight
[Procession Masters]

(16) This is to Certify that we the Subscibers have procession'd all the Lands within our Precinct according to order of Vestry. Which are as follows. Viz^t.

	The Names of People Present	
The Land of Thos. Capel		
The Land of Chas. Battle	Thos. Capel	Jones Stokes j^r. for
The Land of Levi Gilliam	Chas. Battle	Sil. Stokes j^r.
The Land of W^m. Loftin	Levi Gillam	Thos. Moore for W^m.
The Land of Curtis Land	W^m. Loftin	Moore
The Land of Thos. Moore	Curtis Land	Robt. Webb
The Land of Sil. Stokes Senr.	Thos. Moore	Fran^s. Hutchens
The Land of W^m. Moore		
The Land of Robt. Webb		
The Land of Fran^s. Hutchens		

Robert Webb
Charles Battle
[Procession Masters]

[48]
March 14. 1747/8

(17) Pursuant to an Order of Albemarle Parish & the County of Surry we the Subscribers in company of Capt. Howel Briggs, Benj^a. Jordan, W^m. Rogers, Benj^a. Ellis, James Nicolls, W^m. Judkins, Nich^s. Judkins, Simon Stacy & Emanuel James Possession the Lands after ment^d. Viz^t. Joel Barkers, ~~Line~~ Part of W^m. Ross Line, part of Capt. Briggs's, David Hunter's, John Warbirton's, Benjamin Ellis's, Nicholas Judkins's and James Nicolson.

March 17. 1747/8

Then we the above mention'd possession'd the Lines of Capt. Rich^d. Blunt dec^d., W^m. Blunts, Benj^a. Jordan's, W^m. Rogers, Robert Judkins's, W^m. Judkins, Simon Stacy's, Nathl. James & Joshua Procters dec^d.

[Procession Masters]
David Hunter
Robert Judkins

(18) In Obedience to an Order of the Worshipful Vestry, held for Albemarle Parish in the County of Surry, dated August 26. 1747. We the Subscribers have met and procession'd all the Lines as in the s^d. order Expressed; Except the Line between the Colledg & Patrick Dempsey; the Reason is the Overseer of the Colledge came in order to procession when we were from home & he & two or three Neighbours went & procession the s^d. Line and left Word that he cou'd not spare the Time to come again.

May 7th The Lines between Col^o. Benj^a. Harrison & W^m. Smith & Jno. Wilkerson and Col^o. Harrison & Ja^s. Banks & Colo^o. Harrison & Banks & John Wilkerson and Thos. Wilkerson and Joseph Scouls & W^m. Smith & Scouls & Smith and Lawrence Gibbons

pres. W^m. Smith, Law. Gibbons, Jno. Wilkerson, Jos. Scouls, Thomas Wilkerson, James Banks.

The Lines between Col^o. Harrison & Law. Gibbons & Gibbons & W^m. Yarbrough & Gibbons & Pepper & Chris^r. Jean & Pepper & Yarbrough

pres. W^m. Smith, Law. Gibbons, W^m. Mitchell, Thos. Vaughan, Thos. Jones

8th The Lines between Col^o. Harrison & Thos. Vines & Col^o. Harrison and Thos. Vaughan & Vaughan & Vines & Vaughan & Dempsey

pres. Thos. Jones, Thos. Vaughan, W^m. Mitchel

The Lines between W^m. Mitchell & Henry Mitchel & Willm. Mitchel & John Mitchel & Vines & Jno. Mitchel & Vines & Pepper, Mitchel & Vines & Thos. Jones & Jones and Peter Mitchel, Peter Mitchel & Thos. Mitchel

pres. W^m. Mitchel, Hen^{ry}. Mitchel, Peter Mitchel, Jno. Mitchel, Thos. Jones, Thos. Butler, Edward Jones

21st. The lines between Henry Mitchel & Thos. Mitchel & Henry Mitchel & Thomas Butler & Pepper & T. Butler & R. Pepper & John Woodard & Woodard & Thos. Butler

pres. Henry Mitchel, Peter Mitchel, Thos. Butler

The Lines between Rich^d. Pepper & Thos. Jones & T. Jones & Benjamin Ball

pres. Thos. Jones, W^m. Mitchell, John Mitchel, Edwd. Jones

The Lines between Thos. Butler & Ja^s. Porch & Henry Mitchel & Ja^s. Porch & Porch to the County Line & Edward Buckner to the s^d. Line & James Porch & Edwd. Buckner and Buckner & Rich^d. Pepper}

Present. Henry Mitchel, Thos. Butler, Ja^s. Porch & Robert Mitchell

Thos. Vines
Rich^d. Pepper
[Procession Masters]

[49]

(19) In Obedience to an Order of the Vestry of the Parish of Albermarle to us directed and bearing Date the 26 Day of August 1747 we have on the twenty Eighth and twenty ninth day of January, procession'd all the Lands within our precincts as in the afores^d. Order Mention'd and renew'd all the s^d. Land Marks Viz: from the Isle of Whight Line to Stoke's Road; and from the little swamp to Nottaway River up to the Mouth of the Hunting Quarter Swamp thence up the south Side of the s^d. Swamp to the s^d. Road, Present at the s^d. processioning.

The first day Viz. Jan: 28
Charles Gillam
Burwell Gillam
Anselm Gilliam in the room of Sarah Gillam
Thos. Dunn
Richard Felts
Ralph Magee
Charles Mannry
John Hargrave
& Nat. Clanton
whose Lands were then procession'd as also the land of W^m. Land who was not present living in another County: and part of Col^o. Harrison's Dec'd. Land now in the Care of Col^o. Randolph: for whom John Hargrave

The second day Viz. Jan: 29
Richard Clanton
Cornelius Loftin
Henry Andrews in the Room of his Father.

William Andrews
John Pennington Senr.
John Pennington Junr.
Ben: Sowersberry
Henry Pritchard for Col^o. Randolph
Thomas Briggs
Wm Rogers
Richard King J^r.
and John Knight
whose Lands were then procession'd together with part of a line of W^m. Loftain who attended another procession in another precinct as also the Land of John Rachel whose wife being sick cou'd not attend

Richard Avery
Hinchia Gillum
[Procession Masters]

(20) Pursuant to an Order of Vestry bearing Date August 26 1747 we the Subscribers have renew'd the land Marks in our appointed precinct belonging to the person's hereafter mention'd and the reason of the failure of those that were not procession'd and the persons pres^t. & at the performance of the s^d. Land's procession'.

Thomas Pennington
John Stokes
Samuel Stokes
Abraham Brown
Arthur Freeman
John Owen
Wm Ezell
Sil^r. Stokes Sr.
Thos. ~~Oliver~~ Moore
Jesse Gillum
Jno. Stevens
Jno. Shanns
Jno. King
Rich^d. King
Thos. Briggs

persons pres^t.
John King, Rich^d. King, Abrm. Brown, Thos. Pennington, John Owen, John Stokes, Sam: Stokes & [-?-] Subscriber's
Jno. King, Rich^d. King, Ab: Brown, Thos. Pennington, Jno. Owen, J. Stokes
Rich^d. King, Jno. King, Jesse Gillum, Thos. Pennington, Jno. Owen

W^m. Ezell, Jno. Stevens, Spittle Pulley, Shann's overseer

Jno. Owen, Jno. King, Rich^d. King, Thos. Pennington
D.R.

Silvanus Stokes j'. no attendance therefore not procession'd
James Williams
John Knight

March 31 1748
p Jn°. Stevens
W^m. Ezell
[Procession Masters]

[50]

(21) Surry County Albermarle Parish.} In pursuance to an Order of the Worshipful Vestry of Albermarle Parish bearing Date 26 Day of August 1747. We the Subscribers together with the several Freeholders and inhabitants, did quietly and peacibly on the 18th, 19th and 20th of February 1747/8 Renew the several lines and Land Marks of the Lands in the precinct mention'd in the said Order.

present at the time viz:

Robert Seat	Joseph Roland	W^m. Roland
Nath: Felts	Thos. Felts	Edwd. Powell
Thos. Weathers	Jn°. Ezell	Jn°. Atkins
W^m. Woodland	W^m. Cragg	Thos. Atkins

Drury Stokes son of Sil: Stokes, Ja^s. Hern, Overseer for Mr. Mr. [sic] Henry Brown, W^m. Rose, son of W^m. Rose, Jn°. Battle J^r., D°. for M^{rs}. Mary Brown. Given under our Hands this 20th day of Feby. 1747/8.

Chas. Judkins
John Bell
[Procession Masters]

(22) In Obedience to an Order of Vestry of the parish of Albermarle dated the 26th of August 1747, and directed to use whose Names are hereunto subscribed, we have, according to the s^d. Order after due notice given to the persons concern'd, quietly procession'd the several Lands within the precinct, in the s^d. Order mention'd, and the several Land marks have renew'd.

Proprietors Names	Persons present
Col°. Benj^a. Harrison	Robt. Sandefour, W^m. Stuart, Edwd. Freeman
Hartwell Marble	D°.
Benj^a. Weathers	D°.
Edwd. Petway	D°.
Capt. Aug: Claiborne	D°.
Robert Sandefour	D°.
William Freeman	D°.
William Stewart	D°. and W^m. Bridges
William Bridges	D°. D°.
Christopher Golikely	D°.
W^m. Dansey	W^m. Dansey, W^m. Partin, Rich^d. Woodroof
Christopher Golikely	D°.
Richard Jones	D°. and Rich^d. Jones
Capt. Howell Briggs	D°.
Robt. Jones J^r.	D°.
W^m. Partin	D°.
Richard Woodroof	D°.

This service was completed the 14th day of March 1747 by us.
Edward Petway
and
W^m. Petway
[Procession Masters]

[51]

23^d In Obedience to an Order of Vestry held in Albemarle Parish the 26th day of August 1747. We the Susbscribers have procession'd every Tract & Parcel of Land in our Precinct.

Proprietors Names	Persons present
Thomas Avent	Edward Griffis, James Stuart, Lewis Solomon
John Shands	Wm Solomon, Richard Hay, Ditto
John Morgan	Ditto, Ditto, John Bass
Col^o. Bland	Ditto, John Ezell, Lewis Solomon
William Solomon	John Shands, Richard Hay, Ditto
Thos Underwood	Bedels Underwood, James Sammons j^r, Ja^s Sammons Senr.
John Sammons j^r	Ditto, Thomas Underwood
James Sammons Senr	Thos Underwood, James Bass
John Bass	Ditto, Ditto, James Sammons
Peter Martin	Ditto, Ditto, Ditto
Samuel Bass	John Dortch, Ditto, Ditto
Thomas Pate	Ditto, Ditto, Wm Thompson
Wm Thompson j^r	Thomas Pate, Henry Lee, Samuel Bass
John Maclemore	Burrel Maclemore, Adam Ivy, Wm Thompson
Adam Ivy	Ditto, Henry Lee, Ditto
Burrel Maclemore	Adam Ivy, Thomas Pate, Samuel Bass
Henry Lee	Ditto, Burrel Maclemore, Wm Thompson
Benjamin Adams	Henry Lee, Ditto, Adam Ivy
Matthew Wilkason	Ditto, Daniel Roberts, John Ezell
Daniel Roberts	Ditto, Thos Ezell, Matthew Wilkason
Vol Williamson	John Ezell, Jeremiah Bullock, Ditto
Jeremiah Bullock	Ditto, Daniel Roberts, John Ellis
John Ellis	Ditto, Ditto, Henry Lee
John Hill	John Ellis, Ditto, Ditto
Richard Wiggens	Ditto, John Hill, John Ezell
Edward Ellis	Ditto, Ditto, Ditto
Richard Hay	Lewis Solomon, Ditto, Wm Solomon
Gilbert Prince	Ditto, Samuel Carlile, Richard Hay
Lewis Solomon	Wm Solomon, Ditto, Ditto
Gilbert Hay	Lewis Solomon, Edward Griffis, Ditto
Samuel Carlile	Ditto, Ditto, John Hill

John Avent
Peter Avent
[Procession Masters]

[52]

At a Vestry held for Albemarle Parrish in Surry County at the Church on the North Side of Nottway River on the 26th Day of October 1748 for laying the levy of the s[d]. Parrish.

Present
The Rev[d]. W[m]. Willie

Chris[r]: Tatum	John Mason j[r].
Howell Briggs	Moses Johnson
James Gee	James Chappell
Ephraim Parham Gent.	Rob[t]. Jones j[r]. Gent.

Albemarle Parish   D[r] lb Tob[o].

To the Rev[d]: W[m] Willie as Minis[tr]. for a years Sallery	16,000
To cask for the same a[t] 4 p C[t].	640
To Chris[tr]: Tatum as Clk & Sexton to Nott[y]. Church	1,600
To Rob[t]. Nicholson as Clk to S[t]. Pauls Church	1,200
To Joel Barker as Sexton to D[o].	400
To Gregory Rawlings as Clk to Sp Swamp Chappell	1,200
To Edw[d]. Shelton as Sexto to D[o].	400
To Rob[t]. Farrington as Clk to S[t]. Marks Chappell	1,200
To Nat[l]. Green as Sexton to D[o].	400
To Dan[l] Weldon as Clk of the Vestry from Oct[hr]. 1747 till june 1748	260
To Joseph Mason as D[o]. from thence hitherto	140
To Sam[l] Lancaster for keeping Edmund Deford a year	650
To Rich[d]. Fitzpatrick for keeping & Cloathg Jos[s]: Fitzpatrick a year	400
To Charles Gillam for keeping and providg for his son Hincha a year	400
To W[m]. Jones for keeping Owen Jones	100
To W[m]. Rogers for keeping and providg for a Bastard Child p. agreement with the Church wardens	900
To M[r]: Moses Johnson for keeping John M[c]Gary	800
To Jones Bird for attending on Anne Green a M[o]. in her last Sickness and finding her necessary Sustenance	200
To John Weaver for Digging a Grave for Anne Green Dec'd upon the Parrish Acc[t].}	20
To John Whittington for keeping Eliz[a]. Arnold one Mo. Infirm Impotent Woman from aprill last	300
To Benj[a]. Barker for making seats at S[t]. Pauls Chapple	250
To John Mason j[r]. for D[o]. at Nottaway Church	250
To Ephraim Parham for his Acc[t]. against the Parrish	330
To Rob[t]. Farrington for his Acc[t]. against D[o].	100
To Chris[to]. Tatum for keeping Church ornaments	100
To Joel Barker D[o].	100
To Edw[d]. Shelton D[o].	100

[illeg.]

[53]

Brou'over	28,440
lb.	
To Levied for the use of the Parrish to be sold by the Churchwardens	16,513
To the Collectors for Collecting and pay^g: in Inspectors notes 44,953 lbs. Tobbco at 6 p C^t.}	2.697
	47,650
By 1906 Tythables ^{at} 25 lbs. Tob^{co}. p. pole	47,650

Order'd that Chris^r. Tatum and John Mason jun^r. be and are appointed on their entering into Bond with Sufficient Securities to the Vestry of this Parrish, Collectors of this Parish to Collect, the Levy this Day Levied upon the sd Inhabitats of the Parrish and that they do Collect and receive of every Tithable Person within the sd Parish the sum of 25 ^{lb}. Pounds of Net Tob^o. being the Levy of this Parish from the 15th day of Oct^{br}. 1747 to the 15th Oct^r: 1748 and that they do make payment of the Several sums of Tob^o. so by them to be raised from and levid, to the several Parish Creditors to whom the same are due and payable, and that upon refusal of payment of any part of the sum of 25 ^{lb}. Tob^o. by any person chargeable therewith. that the sd Collectors, do levy the same by Distress.

Orderd the Churchwardens pay Edwd. Pettway Sen'r, Shill^s and C^s out of the Mony in hands belong^g. to this Parish in discharge of his Acc^t. against this Parish of disbursments in searching out the Title of Nottway Church Land.

Orderd that the Churchwardens do pay Doc^r. John Hay £2..18S..0 in Ball^{cc}. his acct: for Levies done and Medicins Administered to Thos. Davis Deceas^d:

Orderd that the Churchwardens pay W^m. Jones 32S out of the Mony in their, belong'g' to this Parish in Ballance of sd Jones's Acct: for Burying Owen Jones Deceas'd: a Parish Pensioner.

Order'd that the Churchwardens pay out of the Mony in their hands belon'g to the Parrish 30S/ to the Rev'd M^r. Willie for repairs to the Glebe House.

Wm Willie Min^r:
Copy Test
Jo^s. Mason Clk Ves^t.

[54]

At a Vestry held for Albemarle Parish at Nottoway Church in the said Parish on the 28 day of March Anno Dom: 1749. being Easter Tuesday

Present
The Rever^d William Willie

Robt Wynn	James Chappell	
Thos Avent	Christopher Tatum	} Gent^n;
James Gee	John Mason Junr	

48   The Vestry Book of Albemarle Parish

Christopher Tatum and John Mason Jun' appointed Church Wardens for the Year ensuing;
    Order'd that the Church Wardens do pay to Thos Cooper for the Support of his Wife, a bed ridden Woman, Twenty Shillings out of the money in their hands, arising from Fines.
    Order'd That the Church Wardens do pay to the Widow Cox for the Support of her small Children Twenty Shilling out of the money in their hands arising from Fines.
    Order'd That the Church Wardens do pay to Sarah Evans an Indigent Woman Fifteen Shillings out of the money in their hands arising from Fines.
    Order'd That the Church Wardens do pay to Elisabeth Duncan an Indigent Woman Fifteen Shillings out of the money in their hands arising from Fines.
    Order'd That the Church Wardens do pay to Mary Cotes an Indigent Woman five Shillings & Six pence out of the money in their hands arising from Fines.
    The Church Wardens having this Day brought in their accompts for the Years 1745, 1746, 1747 & 1748, as may appear Recourse being had to the said acc^{ts} in the hands of the Clerk of the Vestry, The said accts. were examined and allow'd.
    Order'd That John Ivy an infirm and Lame man be Clear'd of his parish Levy for the future.
    Agreed with Edward Shelton for the keeping and maintaining Elisabeth Arnold an Antient & infirm Woman from this Time to the 15 of October next & including nine weeks preceeding this Day, for all which he is to have 300 lbs Tob^o.
                                                              William Willie Min^r

[55]

At a Vestry held for laying the Levy for Albemarle Parish at Nottoway the 16 Day of October 1749.

Present
The Rever^d, William Willie

Howell Briggs	James Chappell	
Robt Wynn	Ephraim Parham	} Gent^n
Moses Johnson	John Mason Junr	
Christopher Tatum	James Gee	

Albemarle Parish	Dr.
To the Reverend William Willie as Min^r	16000
To Cask for the same	640
To Christopher Tatum as Clerk of Nottoway Church	1200
To Robt Nicholson Clerk of S^t. Paul's Church	1200
To Gregory Rawlings as Clerk for Spring Swamp Church	1200
To Robt Harrington as Clerk St Marck Chapel	1200
To Joseph Mason as Clerk of Y^e Vestry	400
To Christop^r Tatum as Sexton of Nottoway Church	400
To Edward Shelton as Sexton for Spring Swamp Chapel	400
To Joel Barker as Sexton for St Paul's	400
To Mary Green as Sexton for St Mark's Chapel	400
To Christop^r Tatum for taking Care of Church Ornaments	100
To Edward Shelton for taking Care of Church Ornaments	100
To Joel Barker for taking Care of Church Ornaments	100
To Samuel Lancaster for keeping an Orphan One Year	650
To Moses Johnson for keeping a base born Child	800
To Charles Gillam for keeping his Son Hincha	450
To John Knight for keeping Sarah Davis	300
To Edward Shelton for keeping Elisabeth Arnold	300

To Levied for the use of the Parish	20666
To 6 p Cent on 49900 lbs Tob°	2994
	49900

[56]

Albemarle Parish   Cr.

By 1996 Titheables at 25 lb Tob° per Poll;   49900 lb

Order'd That Peter Martin an infirm Man be exempted from paying his parish Levy for the future.

Order'd That Joel Barker be exempted from paying his parish Levy for the future.

Agreed with John Night for the keeping of Sarah Davis for the Year ensuing and that he be paid 400 lb Tob°

Agreed with James Williams for keeping John King an Old infirm Man and that he find him Necessary Cloathing & Diet for the Year ensuing and that he be paid for Service 600 lb Tob°

The Surplice at St Paul's Church being damag'd by Rats, 'tis order'd that the Church Wardens do have it repair'd.

Order'd that the Church Wardens do employ a workman to move the Pulpit of Nottoway Church to the North side of said Church and to repair the seats in the Gallery.

Christop^r. Tatum and John Mason Junr. Gent.; being appointed Collectors of the parish Levy now Laid, it is Order'd That they do Collect & receive of each Person Therewith Chargeable Twenty five Pounds of Tob° pr Poll, and that They have authority in case the 25 pr Poll or any Part of it be Delay'd or Refus'd, To Levy the same by Distress, and that they pay to each Respective Creditor The Several Sums due to each, and that they expose to publick Sale The Tob°. Levied for the use of the Parish and pay to the Church Wardens for the Time being the money arising from Such Sales.

Order'd That Christopher Tatum & John Mason Junr. do give Bond with Sufficient Security for the due Performance of Their Office as Collectors to the Clerk of the Vestry in Behalf of the Parish of Albemarle.

                                                William Willie Min^r:

[57]

At a Vestry held for the Parish of Albemarle in the Couny of Surry at Notaway Church April ye 19th 1750

Present
The Rever^d. William Willie Min^r.

Chris^t. Tatum	John Mason Junr.	
James Gee	Thomas Avent	} Gent.
Moses Johnson	James Chappell	
Robt. Wynne	Ephraim Parham	
& Robert Jones J^r.		

A Petition from John Jenkins praying to be Admitted Clerk to this Vestry in the Place of Joseph Mason deceas'd which being Considered Ordered that it be Rejected.

A Petition from James Chappell J^r. Praying to be Admitted Clerk to this Vestry in the place of Joseph Mason Deceas'd which being considered Ordered that the said James Chappell

J^r. be Admitted to that Office and that he Attend As often as Occasion may require to perform the Duty of his Office.

Ephraim Parham and Christopher Tatum are elected & Appointed Church wardens for the Year Next ensuing.

Ordered that the late Churchwardens pay Thomas Woodham out of the Money in their hands which have accured [accrued] to this Parish for Fines for Basturdy &c the sum of Thirty Shillings for the Releif of Mary Woodham a Poor Impotent Person.

Ordered that the Church wardens pay Isaac Robertson a Poor Infirm man the sum of Thirty Shillings Out of the Money which has Accurd[sic] to this Parish for Bastard Fines &c for releiving his Necessity.

Ordered that the late Churchwardens pay Sarah Evins a poor Infirm Woman the sum of Fifteen Shillings Out of the Money which has Accurd to this Parish for Bastard Fines &c. towards her releiveing her Necessity.

Ordered that the Churchwardens pay Ann Malone a poor Infirm woman the sum of Fifteen Shillings Out of the Money which has Accurd to this Parish for Bastard fines &c towards her Releif.

Ordered that the late Church wardens pay Moses Johnson Gent. sum of Thirty Shillings Out of the Money which has accurd to this Parish for Bastard fines &c to be by him laid out towards Releiveing the Necessities of an Infirm and Diseased Daughter of Cannon Roes.

[58]

Ordered that late Church wardens pay Jane Matthews a poor Impotent woman the sum of Fifteen shillings Our of the Money which has Accurd to this Parish for bastard fines &c towards her releif.

Ordered that the late Churchwardens pay Mary Coats a Poor Infirm woman the sum of Fifteen Shillings Out of the Money which has Accurd to this [parish] for bastard Fines &c towards her Releif.

Ordered that the late Churchwardens pay Lenda Cox a poor Impotent woman Twenty Five Shillings Out of the Money which has Accurd to this Parish for Bastard fines &c towards her Releif.

Ordered that the late Churchwardens lay out of the Money that has Acurd [accrued] to this Parish for bastard fines &c Thirty Shillings for the Releif of Mary Crosland a poor Impotent Widow.

Ordered that the late Churchwardens pay Izodaniachristian[sic] Higgs a poor Impotent Widow Out of the Money that has Accurd to this parish for bastard fines &c the sum of thirty Shillings towards her Releif.

Ordered that the late Churchwardens pay Thomas Cooper a poor Decriped Man Fifteen shillings Out of the Money that has Accurd to this Parish for bastard fines &c towards his releif.

Ordered that the late Churchwardens pay Ann Greswit a poor Impotent widow fifteen Shillings Out of the Money that has Accurd to this parish for bastard Fines &c towards her Releif.

Ordered that the late Church wardens out of the Money in their hands belonging to this

Parish pay Doc[r]. Samuel Peete Fifty Shillings for Medicines Exhibited to Edward Facecy by Order of the Churchwardens.

The Petition of divers Inhabitants of the lower part of this Parish praying a Chapel may be built & Situated so as to enable the Petitioners to Attend Divine Service with Covenancy tis Ordered that the Consideration thereof be refazed [sic] till Next vestry to be held for this Parish.

Ordered that the Collectors of the Parish Levies pay John Freeman Seven hundred pounds of Tobacco out of the Depositum in their hands belonging to this Parish as a Consideration for keeping Jane Matthews a Pensioner of this Parish from Octo[r]. 1748 till Octo[r]. 1749.

Ordered that the late Churchwardens Out of the Money which has Accured to this Parish for bastards fines &c lay out fifteen shilling in releiveing y[e] necessities of Elizabeth Duncan widow an Aged Infirm woman.

Will[m]. Willie Minister
Copy Test James Chappell J[r]. Clk Vestry

[59]

At a Vestry held for the Parish of Albemarle in the County of Surry at Spring Swamp Chappel on the 10th day of October 1750.

Present

Christopher Tatum	Thomas Avent	
James Chappell	James Gee	
Moses Johnson	Robert Wynne	} Gent.
Ephraim Parham	Howel Briggs	
& Robert Jones Jun[r].		

Albemarle Parish	D[r].
To the Reve[d]. William Willie as Minister	16000
To Cask for the same	640
To Chris[r]. Tatum as Clerk of Nottoway Church	1200
To Rob[t]. Nicolson as Clerk at S[t] Pauls Chappel	1200
To Gregory Rawlins as Clerk at Spring Swamp Chappel	1200
To Rob[t]. Farrinton as Clerk at S[t]. Marks Chappel	1200
To Christ[r]. Tatum as Sexton at Nottoway Church	400
To Edward Shelton as Sexton at Spring Swamp Chappel	400
To Rob[t]. Farrinton as Sexton at S[t]. Marks Chappel	400
To Chris[t]. Tatum for Taking Care of the Church Ornaments	100
To Edward Shelton for D[o].	100
To Moses Johnson for keeping a base born Child one year	800
To Charles Gillam for keeping his Son Hinchea	450
To John Knight for keeping Sarah Davis	400
To James Williams for keeping John King	600
To David Stokes for keeping & Providing for Eliz[a]. Arnold, An Impotent Woman from Novem[r]. 1749 till Now	700
To Christ[r]. Tatum for his Account	224
To the Sexton at S[t]. Pauls Chappel	400
To the Adm[r]. of Jos. Mason as Clerk Vestry 6 Month.	200
To Ja[s]. Chappell J[r]. as D[o]. 6 Months	200
To John Freeman J[r]. for keeping Jane Mathis one Year	700
To Levied for the Parish to be Collected & sold for the use of y[e] Parish	12000

	39514
To the Collectors for Collecting and Paying Inspectors Notes 39514 £ at 6 p^{cr} cent	2370
	41884

[60]

P^r. Contra   C^r.
By 2100 Tidables at 20 £ p Poll   £ 42,000

Ordered that Christ^r. Tatum & Ephraim Parham on their entering into Bond & Security to the Vestry of this Parish to be Taken by the Clerk of the Vestry be Appointed Collectors of this Parish for the Year ensueing and that they do Demand & receive of every Tythable Person in this Parish the Quantity of Twenty pounds of N^t. Tob And Pay the Several Quantities of Tob. by them so to be levied to the Several Parish Creditors to whom the same is due & paiable And that upon refusal of Payment by any Person Chargable with the said Quantity of Twenty pounds of Tob. that then the Said Collectors do levy the same by Distress.

The Petition of Divers Inhabitants of the lower part of this Parish which was prefered to this Vestry at their last Meeting was now again read & Considered whereupon tis resolved by the Vestry that the same be rejected being of Openion [sic] that as there are already four Churches in this Parish they are Sufficient and that they cannot consistant with Justice and duty of their office grant the Prayer of the said Petition.

                                                      Chris^t. Tatum   Church
                                                      Ephraim Parham   Wardens
                       Copy Test.   James Chappell Junr. Ck Vestry

[61]

At a Vestry held for the Parish of Albemarle in the County of Surry on the 12th Day of November 1750.

                              Present

Christ^r. Tatum	Ephraim Parham	
Robert Wynne	Thomas Avent	
James Gee	Moses Johnson	} Gent.
Ja^s. Chappell	John Mason Junr.	

The Vestry Met in Order to take the Spring Swamp Chapel and the said Chapel being not completely finishd the said Vestry Thought not fit to Receive the Said Chapel.

Ordered that the Church wardens Pay James Anderson so Much Money as will Make 232£ = 12£ = 08 ½ up 290 Pounds.

Mr. James Anderson has Given this Parish liberty to make use of the Chapel that he has built from this day till such time as he can finish the said Chapel.

Joseph Rolun [sic] is Appointed Sexton at Spring Swamp Chappel instead of Edward Shelton and that he Perform the Duty of his Office so long as he shall Continue Sexton.

                                                    Christ. Tatum   Church
                                                      & Ephraim Parham   Wardens
                       Copy Test   James Chappell Junr. Clk Vestry

[62]

At a Vestry held for the Parish of Albemarle in the County of Surry at Nottoway Church on the 9th day of April 1751 being Easter Tuesday.

        Present
      The Reverend William Willie
   John Mason   James Gee   Gentlemen
   Ephraim Parham Moses Johnson
   James Chappell & John Mason Junr.

Tis Ordered Agreed Appointed & Elected that Augustine Claiborne be a Vestry Man in this Parish in the Place & Stead of Christopher Tatum Deceas'd and that he Qualify as Soon as Conveniantly he can to Serve this Parish in that Capacity.

Ephraim Parham & Augustine Claiborne are appointed Church wardens for the Year Next ensuing.

Joshua Tatum is Appointed Collector of the Parish Levies in the Room of his Father Christ^r. Tatum Dec^d. & he is herby Invested with the same Authority that his said Father was for Collecting & Paying Away the Several sums of Tobacco Assest upon the Several Tythables of the said Parish.

Ordered that the said Joshua give bond with Security for the Due & faithful Performance of his said Office.

The Reverend William Willie haveing Appointed John Tatum Clerk at Nottoway Church in the Room of his Father Christ^r. Tatum Dec^d. it is agreeable to the Vestry.

John Wever is Appointed Sexton at Nottoway Church insend [sic] of Christ^r. Tatum Dec^d. whose time Commencd the first of March 1750/1.

Ordered that the Collectors do pay unto Bridget Tatum Widow of Christ^r. Tatum Dec^d. Out of the Tobacco Levied for the use of the Parish 636 pounds of Tobacco being the Sallary Due to the said Chris^r. Tatum as clerk & Sexton at Nottoway Church from the 15th of October 1750 till the first of March 1750/1.

Ordered that the Church wardens do pay to Moses Johnson for the use of Susannah Jones an Object of Charity out of the Money in their hands Arisen from fines and forfeitures.

Ordered that the Churchwardens do Pay unto Sarah Owin an Object of Charity Twelve Shilling & Six Pence Out of the Money in their hands Arisen from fines & forfeitures.

Ordered that the Church warden do pay unto Ann Malone An Object of Charity Twelve Shillings & Six Pence out of the Money in their hands Arisen from fines & forfeitures.

            William Willie Minister
       Copy Test Ja^s. Chappell Junr. Clk Vestry

[63]

At a Vestry held for the Parish of Albemarle in the County of Surry at Nottoway Church on the 15th Day September 1751.

Present
The Rev^d. William Willie

Augus^e: Claiborne	Ephraim Parham	
Thos. Avent	Robert Wynne	} Gent.
James Gee	James Chappell	
John Mason J^r.	& Moses Johnson	

In Pursuance to an Order of Surry County Court bearing Date The Sixteenth Day of July One Thousand Seven Hundred & Fifty One Directing the Vestry of this Parish to Divide the Same into Precincts for the Processioning of every Persons Lands within the Said Parish We do Appoint Thomas Bell & William Evins to see Every Persons Land Processioned & the Land Marks thereof Renewed from South hamton County on black Water thence up black water All the Land Between Tarripin Swamp & blows Road and that They Do Assemble all the Free holders within that Precinct to Attend the Performance thereof and that the said Thomas Bell And William Evins do return to this Vestry an Account of Every Particular Persons Land they Shall Procession and of every Person ~~Presen~~ Present at the Processioning thereof and Also of whose Land they Shall Fail to Procession & the Particular Reasons of Such failure & that the Same be done & Performed between the first Day of Novem^{er}: And the last Day of March Next ensuing

John Hancock & Robert Nicolson are Appointed to Procession all the land between Secock & Tarripin Swamp to Birchisland Road.

Richard Blow & John Smith are Appointed to Procession from the South Side of Secock Swamp to the head of lightwood Swamp And Secauries Swamp thence to Birchisland Road.

George Briggs & Stephen Hamlin Are Appointed to Procession from South hamton County Line up Assamoosock to Secauries Swamp thence up Secauries to the head.

[64]

James Chappell J^r. and John Jarrad are Appointed to Procession from the Mouth of Secauries up Assamoosock to the Majors Branch & up the s^d. branch to Secaurie Road & along that Road to Secaurie Swamp thence to the Begining.

Nicholas Partridge & Nicholas Partridge J^r. are Appointed to Procession from the Majors Branch up Assamoosock to and Including William Johnsons Land thence to the head of Coperhawnk Swamp Down the s^d. Swamp to Secaury Road & by that Road to the head of the Majors branch thence to the Begining.

David Jones & William Cook are Appointed to Procession From Cooks Bridge along Cooks Road to Joseph Swamp Thence up the said Swamp to Prince George County Line and by that Line to Black water thence to the begining.

Hugh Ivy & John Baird are Appointed to Procession from Cooks Road on the New Road to black Swamp thence to the Governours Road all between the s^d. Roads Out to Joseph Swamp.

John Mason J^r. & Edward Wever are Appointed to Procession From the Governours Road to the Old Parish Line & all Between Joseph swamp & Assamoosock to the Old Parish Line.

William Parker & George Wyche are Appointed to Procession from the Old Parish Line Down Assamoosock to Robins branch thence Down Austins branch to Nottoway River and up the River to the old Parish line thence to the begining.

William Edmunds & Thomas Peters J^r. are Appointed to Procession all between Assamoosock & Nottoway River below robins Branch & Austins branch to South hamton County line.

Edward Lee & Peter Harthorn are Appointed to Procession from Petaways Mill along John Harthorns line to the Colledge Line by that Line to Joseph Swamp & Down that Swa^p. to Nottoway River & up the River to Barlthorp Creek & up the same to the begining.

James Mason & Edward Pettaway are Appointed to Procession all between Jones hole and Indian Swamp and from Prince George Line & Nottoway River

[65]

Thomas Wynne & John Curtis are Apointed to Procession all between Monks Neck Creek & Stony Creek & up Sappony Creek to the line Divideing this County from Prince George.

Richard Hill & William Gillam J^r. are Appointed to Procession from Stony Creek to Sappony Mill from thence to Natt^l. Greens and so down Nottoway River to the begining.

William Rainey & Robt. Farrinton are Appointed to Procession from the Plantation of Nathl. Greens to Sappony Mill all between the line that Divides this County & Prince George and Up Nottoway River to Harris Swamp.

Thos. Vines & Thomas Butler are Appointed to Procession from Harris Swamp up Nottoway River to the Extent of this County.

Robt. Webb & Charles Battle are Appointed to Procession all between Rackoon Swamp & Little Swamp & Stokes's Road.

Matthew Parham & Ephraim Parham are Appointed to Procession from the Island Swamp to the Old Parish line & along that Line to the line Divideing this County from Brunswick and between the said Line & Nottoway River.

John Stevens & Willm. Ezill are Appointed to Procession between the Rackoon & Hunting Quarter Out to the head of Hunting Quarter.

Charles Judkins & Sil^s. Stokes are Appointed to Procession from the West side of Stokes's Road between the Poplar & Rackoon Swamps to the Old Parish Line.

Willm. Knight & John Battle are Appointed to Procession all the lines on the East side of Stokes's Road between the Line Divideing this County from Southhamton to the Rackoon Swamp.

Ja^s. Wyche & Joseph Thorp are Appointed to Procession between the South side of the three Creek & Southhamton & Brunswick County Lines.

Mathew Wynne & Henry Hartwell Marvel are Appointed to Procession from Stokes's Road up Nottoway River to the flat Swamp from the head of that a Strait Course to Hunting Quarter Swamp.

[66]

Howel Briggs & Samuel Magget are Appointed to Procession from the Mouth of Copohonk swamp to Birchisland & by the Road Leading Over Birchisland bridge to Secorrie & that to Copohonk and Down the Same to the Begining.

David Hunter & Robt. Judkins are Appointed to Procession all between black water & Copohonk and the old Parish Line.

Peter Bagley & John Parker are Appointed to Procession from the Mouth of the Town Swamp & up that to the head of the Tar Kiln branch & Down the same to the Mill Swamp Including Samuel Tatums Land & Thence to the New Road & so to Cooks road And by that to Black Water & Down the Swamp to the begining.

Edmund Ruffin and Willard Roberts are Appointed to Procession from black Water at the Old Parish line by that line to Copohonk Swamp so up that to the head thence to the Tar Kiln branch On the Mill Swamp thence up the said branch to the Town Swamp & Down the said Swamp to black [water]& thence to the begining.

Henry Mitchel & Joshua Tatum are Appointed to Procession all between John Harthorns the Colledge line & the line Divideing this County & Prince George & between Joseph Swamp & Jones hole.

John Avent & Peter Avent are Appointed to Procession from ye South side of Great Swamp to the three Creeks & up the three Creeks & Outerdams [sic] to Brunswick Line.

Henry Lee Junr. & William Tompson Junr. are Appointed to Procession from the great Swamp & down the same to the County line & to the Poplar Swamp & up the Poplar to Brunswick line.

Hinchea Gillam & Nathl. Clanton are Appointed to Procession from Nottoway River between Rackoon & Hunting Quarter Swamp & up to the Mill & thence along Loftins Mill Path to the little swamp & Down the same to the begining.

Cornelius Loftin & Richard Avery are Appointed to Procession all from Loftins Mill Path up Hunting Quarter & little Swamp to Stokes's Road.

Moses Johnson & Clem^t. Hancock all between Hunting Quarter, Nottoway River & Stokes's Road.

Thomas Parham & Matthew Parham are Appointed to Procession from Indian Swamp to Monks Neck & the County line & Nottoway River

Sloman Wynne & Henry Sturdivant are Appointed to Procession from flat swamp up Nottoway River to frying Pan & up frying Pan to the head thereof thence to threewitts & Down the River to the begining.

[67]

William Stuart & Peter Rives are to Procession from the head of the frying Pan to Hunting Quarter & down the same to island Branch & down Island branch to the River.

Albemarle Parish	D^r.
	W^t. Tob^c:
To William Willie as Minister	17305
To John Tatum as Clerk at Nottoway Church	750

To Rob:^t. Nicolson as Clerk at S^t. Pauls Church	1200
To Gregory Rawlins as Clerk at St. Andrews D^o.	1200
To Robt. Farrinton Clerk at S^t. Marks Chapel	1200
To John Wever Sexton at Nottoway Church	307
To Joseph Rolin Sexton at St Andrews D^o.	500
To Robt. Farrinton Sexton at S^t. Marks D^o.	500
To Moses Johnson for keeping a base born Child 1 year	800
To Charles Gillam for keeping his Son Hinchea 1 year	500
To Ja^s. Williams for keeping John King one year	700
To John Bain Sexton at S^t. Pauls Church	500
To Rich^d. Huson for keeping Jane Matthis 1 year	679
To Ja^s. Chappell J^r. Clerk of the Vestry	400
To Jo^s. Roland for Grubing S^t. Andrews Church Yard	150
To Jo^s. Clark for Setting up horse blocks at S^t. Pauls & other Services	100
To Edward Shelton for keeping Eliz. Arnold 3 Mo^s,	250
To Levied for the use of the Parish	22309
To 6 p^r Cent for Collecting 52500 £ Tob:	3150
	52500
Albemarle Parish	C^r.
By 2100 Tithables at 25 £ Tob. p^r Poll	52500

[68]

Ordered that John Irby on his entring into bond & Security to the Vestry of this Parish to be taken by the Clerk of the Vestry he is Appointed Collector of this Parish for the Year ensuing and that he Collect and Receive from every Person Chargeable therewith 25 Pounds of Tobacco p Poll and that have Authority in case the said 25 pounds of Tobacco p Pool or any Part thereof be Delayed or refused to Levy the same by Distress And that he Pay to each respective Creditor the Several Sums of Tobacco due to them and that he expose to Publick Sale the Tobacco Levied for the use of the use of the [sic] Parish and that he Pay to the Churchwardens for the time being the Money Arising from Such Sale.

Ordered that the Collector pay to Augustine Claiborne what Tob^o. is now due to him for Copies of the list of Tythables upon the Quantity being assertained by him the said Claiborne.

Ordered that the Ch wardens pay to Ephraim Parham out of the Money in their hand arising by the sales of Tobacco Levied for the use of the use of the [sic] Parish forty Shillings as a Consideration for his Labour & Trouble in Takeing Down & removing the old Church at Spring Swamp.

Ordered that Daniel Epes, Peter Martin & Isaac Robertson be exempted from paying their Parish Levies for their own Persons.

Ordered that the Churchwardens pay to Nathl. Hood Twenty Shillings for Disbursments by him Already & to be made in Supporting Frances Hood till the 16th of October Next.

Matthew Whitfeild personally Appear'd & Undertakes to Provide at his house for Rebeckah Bird a poor Infirm Woman till the 15th of October 1752 for the Consideration of five hundred pds of Tobacco then to be Levied for him.

The Vestry Proceeded to take under Consideration the Present Situation of the building & Improvments on the Glebe and report being made by James Gee & Augustine Claiborne who was formerly Appointed and the Vestry being of Openion the Present Minister has not been Guilty of any waste on the Said Glebe therefore it is Ordered all repairs & buildings Particularly Mention'd together with some Addition thereto made by the Vestry this day be forthwith made and done and that James Gee & Augustine Claiborne do Advertise the same

[69]

In the Virginia Gazettee in order that workmen come in to undertake the same & that they the said Gee & Claiborne Do let the same & take bond and Security for the performance of such Undertakeing.

Ordered that the Ch wardens pay to the Reverend William Willie out of the Money arising by the Sales of the Tob: £10 in full Satisfaction of a barn & Chaise house by him Built on the Glebe Lands at his own Expence.

Ordered that the Ch wardens out of the Money arising by the Sales of the Tob: pay to John Jenkins 12/6 for the Diall by him made for Nottoway Church.

William Willie Min^r.

Copy Test. Ja^s. Chappell J^r. Clk Vestry

[70]

At a Vestry held for the Parish of Albemarle in the County of Surry at Nottoway Church on the 31 Day of March 1752.

Present
The Rever'd William Willie

Epraim Parham	Robert Wynne	
Ja^s. Gee	Ja^s. Chappell	} Gent.
Howel Briggs	John Mason J^r.	

and Moses Johnson

Major Robert Wynne & Robert Jones Junr. are Appointed Ch wardens for the Year ensuing.

Memorandum of the wrongs returns of Processioning made by the Several Persons as follows to Wit George Briggs and Stephen Hamlin, Richard Blow & John Smith, William Cook & David Jones, Robt. Judkins & David Hunter, William Evins & John White, Robt. Nicolson & John Hancock, William Edmunds & Thos. Peters, Joseph Thorp & Ja^s. Wyche, W^m. Tomson Junr. & Henry Lee J^r., Hinchea Gillam & Nathanel Clanton, Charles Judkins & Silvanus Stokes, Sloman Wynne & Henry Sturdivant, Matthew Wynne & Henry Hartwel Marvel, W^m. Gilliam J^r. & Richard Hill, John Avent & Peter Avent,

Whereas there was a Mistake in the last Order of Vestry Concerning the Citchen that was to be built on the Glebe it is the Opinion of the Vestry that the addition that was to be made to the said Citchen Ought to be Twenty foot in the Clear.

Ordered that John Mason J^r. who was late Ch warden pay to Thomas Burgis the Sum of 30 Shillings out of the Money in his hand that has Accurd to this Parish from fines & forfeitures.

Ordered that the Ch wardens pay to Cannon Roe the Sum of 25 Shillings Out of the Money in their hands which has acurd to this Parish from fines & forfeitures.

Ordered that the Ch wardens pay to Edward Facey the Sum of 12S/6 Out of the Money in their hands which has accur'd to this Parish from fines & forfeitures.

[71]

Ordered that the Ch wardens pay to Mary Coats the Sum of 9S/6 out of the Money in their hands which has Accur'd to this parish from fines & forfeitures.

Ordered that the Ch wardens pay to Izodoniah a Christian Higgs the Sum of 9S/6 out of the Money in their hands which has Accur'd to this Parish from fines & forfeitures.

Order.d that the Ch wardens pay to Sarah Evins the Sum of 9S/6 Out of the Money in their hands which has Accur'd to this parish from fines & forfeitures.

Ordered that the Chwardens Pay to Timothy Ezell the Sum of Twelve Shillings Out of the Money in their hands belonging to this Parish for the Cure of Mary Delehays Arm who is an Impotent Woman.

Richard Reives has agreed with the Vestry to Provide for Mary Delihay One Year & he is to have Fifty Shillings For his Trouble.

W^m. Willie Minister

Copy Test Ja^s. Chappell Clk Vestry

No 1
In obedience to an Order of Vestry held for Albemarle Parish on the 15th of September 1751 Appointed John Barker & Peter Bagley to see a Precinct of Land Marks Renewed in the above Mention'd Order we therefore Comploy with our order on the 10th of March in the Presents of William Cook, Henry Barker, Walter Lashley, Samuel Tatum, David Jones, John Lashley, Reubin Cook & Thomas Lashley all Persons Present in Performing the Work.

Peter Bagley
John Barker
[Procession Masters]

[72]

No.2 Pursuant to an Order of Vestry held for Albemarle Parish the 15th of September 1751 we the Subscribers Saw every Persons Land Processioned & the Land Marks thereof renewed within the Precinct therein Specified Viz^t.

	Clement Hancocks	Land	Robt. Newman, $Clem^t$. Hancock
March 9	Robt. Hancocks John Lees	in the Presence	Robt. Hancock, Henry Moss, John Adkins, John Lee, Henry Porch
1752	Thos. Eldridges	of	Edward Epes, Henry Meachum & Peter Doby
D^o. 10th	William Moss's Edward Eppes's Timothy Ezells D^r. John Hays	in Presence of	Henry Meachum, John Adkins John Lee, Edward Eppes Peter Doby
D^o.	Henry Moss's Henry Porch's Edward Lee's	in Presence of	Henry Porch John Adkins

Nathl. Tomlinson's   John Lee
W^m. Young's   Nathaniel Tomlinson
John Adkin's   Peter Doby
Peter Hawthorns
William Moss's
Part of Rebekah Hawthorns
The Glebe Land

                                                Test Peter Hawthorn
                                                            Edward Lee
                                                       [Procession Masters]

No.3 In Obedience to an Order of the Worshipful Vestry of Albemarle Parish in the County of Surry bearing date 15th Day of September 1751 Wee the Subscribers have assembled the Freeholders together within our Precinct & Procession & the Land Marks thereof Renewed of John Jarrads Land, Thomas Wallis's Land, Ja^s. Chappells Land, Henry Jarrads Land, Howel Briggs's Land, Robt. Jones,s Land. Esther Winkles's Land, Ja^s. Chappell Jun^{rs}. Land, Henry Harrisons Land & W^m. Hines's Land. Present when the abovesaid Land were Processioned Ja^s. Chappell, John Jones, John Long, W^m. Howel, Thomas Wallis, Henry Jarrad, & Gray Briggs. Wee did not Procession John Kennebrews Land the why wee did not Procession the said land was because he did not give his attendance Nor any body in his Behalf.

                       March ye 10th: 1752 Certified Under our hands Ja^s. Chappell J^r.
                                                                 & John Jarrad
                                                                   [Procession Masters]

[73]

N°. 4
At a Vestry held for Albemarle Parish the fifteenth Day of Sepr. in the Year One Thousand Seven Hundred & fifty one it was Ordered that wee the Subscribers do Procession & renew the Land Marks in the Precinct there Prescribed & According to Order wee have Processioned the Lands belonging to the Persons hereafter Named & the Persons there Present To Wit January the Seventeenth Then Renewed Jehu Barkers lines, Henry Jarrads lines, Thomas Cullums lines, William Johnsons lines. Israel Cullum Appeard to Procession Nathl. Johnsons Land & According it was done. Mary Briggs's Land Processioned by her Son W^m. Briggs February 29th. Then Processioned Captn. Howel Briggs's Lines, John Lambs Lines, Ja^s. Jones's Lines, Robt. Jones's Lines & the Land belonging to Edmunds Jones Alfin [sic] of Sarah Jones, Capt. John Masons Lines & Nicholas Partridges,s it being all in Our Precinct Witness Our hands this 31st Day of March in 25th: Year of the Reign of Our Sovereign Lord George.

                                                             Nicholas Partridge
                                                           Nicholas Partridge J^r.
                                                          [Procession Masters]

N°. 5
In obedience to an Order of Vestry Dated to us the 25th of September Directing us to assemble the Freeholders & renew the Several Land Marks within Our Precincts Accordingly on the 14th day of March wee Processioned the Lands belonging to the following Persons & renewed their Land Marks.

Charles Mabry   Thos. Dunn
John Richarson   John Hargrove

John Moss
James Cooper
George Long
Gregory Rawlins
Edward Shelton
James Carter
Robt. Bullock
Frances Felps
W^m. Knight
John Battle

Henry Holt
Thos. Battle
Thos. Newsum
Benjn. Richarson
Henry Manry
Henry Richarson
George Cornit
Joseph Harword
Phillip Harword
Saml. Harword
for Tyler

William Knight
John Battle
[Procession Masters]

[74]

In Obedience to an Order of Vestry of Albemarle Held September 15th 1751 We dit the 21st Day of February 1752 Assemble the persons Within Our Precinct together & did Possession & renew the Land Marks of Travis Griffis, Rebekah Sledge, Reubin Cook, Alexandria Finia, John Mason Junr., John Ogborn, John Underhill, Edward Weaver, Charles Sledge & Capt. John Mason, Present John Finia, John Sledge, Ja^s. Tomlinson.

No. 6

John Mason J^r.
Edward Weaver
[Procession Masters]

N° 7

In Obedience to an Order of Vestry dated to us the 15 September Directing us to Assemble the Freeholders and renew the Several Land Marks within Our Precincts Accordingly on the 15th Febru^y we Procession'd the Lands belonging to the following Persons and Renewed their Land Marks.

Persons Present

		Moses Johnson	John Pinnenton
		Coll. Ja^s. Baker	Morris Zill
		John Land	John Zill
		John Pinnenton	Lewis Johnson
			Thomas Brewer
22		-----	-----
Feb		Thomas Dinkins	John Pennenton
		Clem^t. Hancock	Benjn. Hunt
		Willm. Lightfoots	Robt. Hancock
		Thos. Brewer	Morris Zill
		Benjn. Hunt	John Zill
5th		Thos. Reen	Thos. Renn
March		Joseph Renn	John Pinnenton
		Willm. Bishops	Thos. Renn
	Coll:	Benjn. Harrison	Joseph Renn
		Morris Zill	Willm. Bishop
		John Zill	Bethel Pare
		W^m. Pare	Lewis Johnson
		Widow Jones	John Pinnenton

24th March	Rob¹. Jones	Thos. Balie
	Thos. Harison	John Zill
	Phillip Balies	Moris Zill

Moses Johnson
Cleml. Hancock
[Procession Masters]

[75]

N° 8

In Obedience to the Worshipful Vestry of Albemarle Parish held the 15th of September 1751.

Mar 2d 1752 — Pursuant to an Order of the Vestry aforesaid Wee the Subscribers have Processioned the Line Between John Reives:es heires & Matthew Gibbs also a line between Henry Mitchel & Thos. Mitchel also a Line between Matthew Gibbs & George Reives's also a line between Henry Mitchel & George Reiveses heires. Also a Line between Francess Reives Widow & her Son Also a Line between George Reiveses heires & Robt. Glover also a Line between George Reiveses heires & the Colledge Also a Line between George Reiveses heires & Sarah Biggins.
In Presence of Matthew Gibbs, Thos. Mitchel, John Bradley, John Tatum, Christopher Tatum, & George Reives.

Mar 3d. — We Procession'd a Line between Robt. Doby & the Colledge also a line between Majr Augustine Clayborne & the Colledge also a line between Majr. Claiborne & Robt. Doby also a Line between Majr. Cliborne and Chrisr. Tatum also a Line between Chrisr. Tatum & Robt. Doby also a line between Robt. Doby & Joshua Hawthorn also a Line between Robt. Doby & Joshua Tatum also a Line between Robt. Doby & Robt. Tatum also a Line between Majr. Claiborne & Joshua Tatum.
In Presence of John Tatum, Chrisr. Tatum, John Bradley, Joshua Hawthorn, John Verret, Robt. Doby & Robt. Doby Jr.
also a Line between John Tatum & Robt. Tatum also a Line between Robt. Tatum & Joshua Tatum also a line between Chrisr. Tatum and Joshua Tatum.
In Presence of John Tatum, Chrisr. Tatum, Drury Tatum, Robt. Tatum, Henry Tatum & Thos. Young.
We Processioned a Line between Robt. Doby & Willm. Doby also a line between Robt. Doby & Robt. Glover also a Line between Willm. Doby & George Reiveses heres [sic] Also a Line between Robt. Glover & the Colledge.
In Presence of Robt. Doby, William Doby, Robert Glover, Robt Doby Jr.
Also a Line between Sarah Biggins & Peter Hawthorn also a Line between Thomas Mitchell & Willm. Hamelton.
In Presence of Peter Hawthorn, Jas. Rouse & John Bradley & Thomas Mitchel. And the Several Land Marks thereof have Renewed.
All other Lines are Water Courses.

March ye 4th 1752 Henry Mitchell
Joshua Tatum
[Procession Masters]

[76]

N° 9

Pursuant to an Order of Vestry for Albemarle Parish bearing date the 15th Day of September 1751 We the Subscribers have done the Same According to Order & the failures Declar'd.

Willm. Stuart
Peter Reives
[Procession Masters]

31st March 1752

Whose Land	Processiond & Persons Present
A Line of Howel Briggs	Howel Briggs
Willm. Cook	W^m. Cook
Rich^d. Knight	Rich^d. Knight
Matthew Sturdivant	Matthew Sturdivant
The Widow Rotenberry	Holman Sturdivant
John Anderson Sturdivant	Matthew Whitehead
Matthew Whitehead	Robt. Whitehead
Robt. Whitehead	John Anderson Sturdivant
John Spain	John Spain
Peter Reives	Peter Reives
Rich^d. Reives	Rich^d. Rives
Nathl. Hood	Nathaneel Hood
Henry Sturdivant	Henry Sturdivant
Edward Nickels	Edward Nickels
Robert Boling	Solomon Graves
Edward Threewit	Edward Threewit
Peter Threewit	Peter Threewit
Robt. Newman	Robt. Newman
W^m. Stuart	W^m. Stuart

N°. 10

By Virtue of an Order of the Vestry of Albemarle Parish dated the 15th of September 1751 to us Directed we have Processiond the Land therein Mentioned & the same Land Marks thereof Renewd as follows

	Lands	Persons Present
Feby ye 24th	of William Parham	John Parham
	of John Parham	Abraham Parham
	of Ja^s. Parham	Ja^s. Parham
	of Charles Leath	Charles Leath
	of Joshua Poytress	Thos. Moody
	of Matthew Parham	W^m. Parham
	of John Leath	John Leath
	of Abraham Parham	

Thos. Parham
Matthew Parham
[Procession Masters]

[77]

N°. 11

In obedience to an Order of the Worshipful Vestry of Albemarle Parish Dated the 15th Day of September James Mason & Edward Pettway have Assembled the Freeholders of the Precinct hereafter Named to Wit Timothy Ezill J^r., W^m. Moore, Eppes Moore, John Coats, Ja^s. Heath, Thos. Heath & Edward Smith in behalf of his Father John Smith & Procession'd

& renewed the Land Marks of the Several Line of the Lands of the Several Persons Respectively in Presence of all above Named this was done & Performed the fourteenth Day of December by us.   Edward Pettway

Ja^s. Mason haveing Departed this Life before the remaining Line were Processioned or renewed I have in Presence of Peter Poytress, Henry Mitchell, Ja^s. Heath, John Coats & John Heath for Thos. Heath on the ninth day of this Instant March Processioned & remarked the following Lines in Presence of all above Named to Wit the Line betwixt Edward Pettway, M^r. Peter Poytress & betwixt the Said Poytress & Thos. Heath & the Line betwixt Ja^s. Heath & Henry Mitchel as also the Line betwixt Henry Mitchel & John Coats by
     Edward Pettway

N°. 12

In Obedience to an Order of Vestry Dated September ye 15th 1751 We have bin & Processioned & the Land as followeth & the Land Marks Renewed The Land of Thos. Oliver Processioned the Persons Present: Thos. Oliver, W^m. Oliver, W^m. Gilliam, The Land of Willm. Gilliam Processioned ye Persons Present Thos. Oliver, W^m. Oliver. W^m. Gilliam, The Land of Rich^d. Jones Processioned the Persons Present John Willburn, Ja^s. Jones & Thos. Wynne. The Land of Ephraim Parham Procession'd the Persons Present Ja^s. Jones, W^m. Parham, John Gee, W^m. Gilliam. The Land of Thos. Wynne Procession'd the Persons Present Thos Wynne, John Willburn, Ja^s. Jones, The Land of John Willburn Procession'd ye Persons Present John Willburn, Ja^s. Jones & Thos. Wynne, The Land of Matthew Parham Procession'd the Persons Present W^m. Parham, John Gus, the Land of Burrill Green Procession'd the Persons Present W^m. Parham, John Gus, the Land of Ja^s. Green Procession,d Persons Present W^m. Parham, John Gus.

The above Mentioned   Matthew Parham
Land Procession'd by   Ephraim Parham
                              [Procession Masters]

[78]
N°. 13
In obedience to an Order of ye Vestry of Albemarle Parish bearing Date the 15th Day of September 175[1] Wee the Subscribers have Assembled the Freeholders together within Our Precinct & Processioned & the Land Marks Renewed George Wyches Land, W^m. Allens Land, Benjn. Wyches Land, Willm. Parkers Land, John Masons Land, W^m. Halls Land, Elis^h. Chappells Land, Robt. Jones's Land, Ja^s. Jones's Land, Ja^s. Chappells Land. John Cargills Land, W^m. Hines's Land. Present when the Aforesaid Lands were Procession'd Robt. Jones, Ja^s. Chappell, Ja^s. Jones, W^m. Jeen, Thos. Chappell, W^m. Johnson, Michal Singleton, & Joshua Hines.

Feby ye 25 & 26 Days 1752
Certified Under Our hands   W^m. Parker
                                       George Wyche
                                  [Procession Masters]

N°. 14

Pursuant to & Order of Vestry for Albemarle Parish bearing date the 15th Day of September 1751 Wee the Subscribers have done the same According to Order & the failures Declair'd.

                              John Stevens   W^m. Ezell
                                  [Procession Masters]
                                       March 31st 1752

Surry and Sussex Counties, Virginia, 1742-1786

Whose Land Procession,d	& Persons Present	
		The names of those not Pro: cession'd & The reason why
A line of Thos. Briggs	John Stokes	
Solomon Graves	John King	
John King	Jesse Gillam	----------------
John Stevens	Thos. Moore	Abrahams Browne
a line of John Knights	Willm. Ezell	No Atendance
Thos. Moors	John Stevens	----------------
W^m. Ezells	Isom Sills	Arthur Freemans
Jones Stokes's	Saml. Stokes	No Attendance
a line of the Widow Sills	John Stokes	----------------
Lewis Adkins	Lewis Adkins	Silvanus Stokes
Ja^s. Williams	Ja^s. Williams	No Attendance
Thos. Pedinton	Thos. Pedinton	
John Stokes	John Stokes Prst	
Saml. Stokes	Saml. Stokes	
David Stokes	Isom Zills	
a line of W^m. Stuarts	Lewis Atkins	
a line of Matthew Sturdivant		

[79]

N°. 15

By Virtue of Vestry of Albemarle Parish 15th Day of September 1751 Wee Thos. Wynne & John Curtis being Appointed to Call together all the Freeholders from Monksneck Creek, Stony Creek & to Sappony Creek to the County Line have Processioned & Renewed all ye Land Marks as the Law Directs.

Proprietors Names	Persons Present	Per^s. Present	Persons Pre^t.	Per^s. Pre^t.	Persons Pre^t.
George Booth	W^m. Harper	Joseph Williamson	Edwd. Harper		
Danl. Nance	D^o.	D^o.	D^o.		
John Williamson	D^o.	D^o.	D^o.		
John Curtis	D^o.	D^o.	D^o.		
W^m. Harper	D^o.	D^o.	D^o.		
Thos. Hunt	D^o.	D^o.	D^o.		
Rich^d. Huson	D^o.	D^o.	D^o.		
Alex^l. Boling	Ed^d. Eacols	Pet^r. Winfield	Thos. Wynne	Jesse Freeman	John Jack^n.
W^m. Broadnax	D^o.	D^o.	D^o.	D^o.	D^o.
Peter Poytress	D^o.	D^o.	D^o.	D^o.	D^o.
John Jackson	D^o.	D^o.	D^o.	D^o.	D^o.
Edward Eacols	D^o.	D^o.	D^o.	D^o.	D^o.
Edward Mumford	D^o.	D^o.	D^o.	D^o.	D^o.
John Freeman	D^o.	D^o.	D^o.	D^o.	D^o.
W^m. Rains	D^o.	D^o.	D^o.	D^o.	D^o.
W^m. Malone	D^o.	D^o.	D^o.	D^o.	D^o.
Thos. Wynne	D^o.	D^o.	D^o.	D^o.	D^o.
Robt. Wynne	D^o.	D^o.	D^o.	D^o.	D^o.

The report of Thos. Wynne & John Curtis [Procession Masters]

66   The Vestry Book of Albemarle Parish

_____ N°. 16 _____

In obedience to an Order of Vestry held for the parish of Albemarle the 15th of Sept'. 1751 Wee the Subscribers have Seen Every persons Land Procession,d According to Order. Only a line between Ja'. Cain & George Robertson which the said Robertson refuses to Procession the Reason why he Says the Line is Removed.

Propietors Land	Propietors	Person Present	Per'. Pres'.
Rob'. Farrintons Land	John Wilkerson Land	W^m. Whuett	Rob'. Mitchel
W^m. Raneys Se'. Land	Fred^k. Greens Land	George Randall	William Harper
W^m. Whuetts Land	Thos. Butlers Land	Nathl. Rainey	
Mary Randalls Land	Thos. Hunts Land	Ja^s. Cain	
Benjn Harrisons Land	John Jones Land	George Robertson	
James Cains J^r. Land	John Killie Land	W^m. Ellet	
W^m. Raineys J^r. Land	Rob'. Mitchells Land	Thos. Burrows	
Ja^s. Banks Land	W^m. Harpers Land	John Wilkerson	
Thos. Wilkersons Land	John Farrintons Land	Ja^s. Cain J^r.	
W^m. Ellets Land	George Randalls Land	Thos. Hunt	
Thos. Burrows Land	Thos. Huson Land	Thos. Butler	
Fred^k. Jones Land		John Kellie	
John Davis Land		John Jones	
Ja^s. Moss Land		Thos. Huson	

March ye 15th 1752

Rob'. Farrinton
W^m. Rainey Jun'.
[Process. Masters]

[80]
N°. 17

By Virtue of an Order of the Vestry of Albemarle Parish bearing Date the 15th of September 1751 Wee the Subscribers have Assembled the Freeholders Together within the Precinct Specified by the said Order and have Processioned & Renewed the Land Marks of the Several Persons as follows to Wit.

Febr^y
y^e
28
1752

Reuben Cooks Land, William Cooks Land, David Jones Land, John Goodwins Land, James Gees Land, Wyke Hunicutts Land, Charles Gees Land, Richard Carters Land, Benjamin Tomlinsons Land
Present when the abovesaid Land were Processioned
Reuben Cook, John Goodwin, Josiah Heath, Ja^s. Gee, Wyke Hunicut, Charles Gee, Richard Carter, Benjamin Tomlinson.

Febr,
y
y^e
29
1752

William Shands's Land, William Eldridges Land, Mary Dains Land, Adam Heaths Land, W^m. Heaths Land, Benjamin Harrisons Land, Thomas Youngs Land, Peter Tatums Land, Peter Tatums Land [sic]
Present at the Processioning of the Land.
Ja^s. Gee, William Eldridge, Thos. Shands, Thomas Young, Josiah Heath.

David Jones
W^m. Cook
[Procession Masters]

_____ Nº. 18 _____

In Obedience to an Order of Vestry held for the Parish of Albemarle in the County of Surry On the 15th of Septemr. 1751 Wee the Subscribers have Assembled the Freeholders Together within the Precinct Specified by the said Order and have Processioned & Renewed the Land Marks of the following Persons to Witt, George Briggs, Stephen Hamlin, Nathl. Briggs, Robt. Long, Natha1. Davis, Wm. Hicks, Nathl. Jones, Joseph Ellis, Simon Murfee Senr., Wm. Bell, Jas. Turner, Henry Sawrey, Joseph Lane, John Long, Wm. Felps Lands.

Present when the aforesaid Lands was Processioned
Nathl. Briggs, Robt. Long, Nathl. Davis, Wm. Hicks, Nathl. Jones, Joseph Ellis, Simon Murfee Junr., Wm. Bell, Henry Sawrey, Joseph Lane, John Long, Wm. Felps &c.
Jas. Turner Sick & not Present

N.B. the Land Marks was Renewed & Processioned within the time Limitted by the aforesaid Order.
S.H.
G.B.
              Stephen Hamlin
              George Briggs
              [Procession Masters]

[81]
_____ Nº. 19 _____

In Obedence to an Order of the Vestry of the Parish of Albemarle bearing Date September 15th 1751 Wee the Subscribers have Processioned & Renewed the Land Marks of every Persons Land in the said Order Specified in the Presence of John Birdsong, Wm. Brittle, John Hargrave, Henry Blow, Arthur Smith, Wm. Brown, James Bain, Thos. Marsengill, Wm. Marsengill, Henry Marsengill, Joseph Richarson, Joseph Higgs, Edward Bryan, & Jas. Wallace.

    Given under Our hands   Richard Blow
                       John Smith
                     [Procession Masters]

_____ Nº. 20 _____

In Obedience to an Order of Vestry held for the Parish of Albemarle the 15th of September 1751 Wee the Order'd Rich.d Hill and Wm. Gilliam have seen every Person Lands Procession,d & the Land Marks Renewed According to Order.

Proprietors Land	Persons Present
Robt. Farrintons Land	Robert Farrinton
Nathl. Greens Land	Nathl. Green
Wm. Raney Jr. Land	Wm. Raney Junr.
Jas. Mangun Land	Jas. Mangum
Amos Love Land	Amos Love
Wm. Richarson Land	Wm. Richarson
Charles Delihay Land	Charles Delehay
Wm. Malone Land	Wm. Malone
Joshua Ellis Land	Joshua Ellis
John Hill Land	John Hill
Wm. Wilburn Land	Wm. Wilburn

Rich^d. Hill Land
W^m. Gilliam Land
Robt. Boling Land
Mial Hill Land
Robt. Webb Land
Arthur Freman Land
Henry Freeman Land
John Holt Land
W^m. Wynne Land
Burrel Green Land
Isaac Robt.son Land
W^m. Harper Land
John Bonner Land
Thos. Wade Land
George Booth Land
Nathl. Malone Land
W^m. Winfeild Land
Jarvis Winfeild Land

Rich^d. Hill
W^m. Gilliam
Mial Hill
Arthur Freeman
Henry Freeman
W^m. Wynne
Burrel Green
Isaac Robertson
W^m. Harper
John Bonner
Thos. Wade
George Booth
John Malone
W^m. Winfeild

William Gilliam J^r.
Rich^d. Hill
[Procession Masters]

[82]
N°. 21

In Obedience to an Order of the Vestry of Albemarle Parish Dated MDCCLI Wee the Subscribers have Processioned and Renewed the Land Marks of all & every Piece of Land in the Order aforesaid Specified in Presence of Thos. Hines, David Hines, W^m. Hines, Joshua Hines, Peter Hines, Rich^d. Hines, John Edmund, John Worsdon & Thos. Renn.

March 26th 1752

William Edmunds
Thos. Peters Junr.
[Procession Masters]

N°. 22

March ye 9th 1752

In obedience to an Order of the Worshipful Vestry held for the Parish of Albemarle in the County of Surry Dated Septr. y^e 15th 1751 We the Subscribers have met and Processioned all the lines as the said Order Express,d Viz^t.

the lines between Thos. Vaughan & Thos. Vines & Col^o. Harrison & Vines & Harrison & Vaughan & y^e Colledge & Vaughan & the Colledge & Jacob Jones & Col^o. Theo$^-$. Bland & Jones & Vaughan & Jones & W^m. [&?] John Mitchel & Sarah & Randal Mitchell & John Mitchel & Vines.

The lines between Thos. Jones & Vines & Thos. Mitchel & Vines & John & Thos. Mitchel & Harrison & Jones & Harrison, Rich^d. Pepper & Pepper & Jones & Harrison & W^m. Yarbrough & Yarbrough & Lawrance Gibbens & Gibbens & Pepper and Ann Smith & Pepper & Yarbrough & Pepper.

Present

W^m. Mitchell
John Mitchell
Thos. Bryan
Thos. Vaughan
Jacob Jones
Daniel Tucker
Parsons Bradly
John Gordin &
Richard Pepper

Richard Pepper
Thos. Mitchell
Robt. Mitchell
Edward Jones
Thos. Bryan
Lawrence Gibbens

18th The lines between Tho[s]. & Sarah Mitchel & Tho[s]. Butler & Sarah Mitchel & Butler & Ja[s]. Porch & Sarah Mitchel & Porch & Edw[d]. Buckner & Porch & Buckner & Butler & John Wodard & Butler & Benj[n]. Bell & Tho[s]. Jones & Yarbrough & Wade & Wade & Pepper.

The lines between Pepper & Gibbens & Ann Smith & Ellit & Ann Smith & John Wilkerson & Wilkerson & Ja[s]. Banks & Col[o]. Harrison & Banks & Isham Smith & Harrison & Isham & Ann Smith

Present
Rich[d]. Pepper
Tho[s]. Mitchell
Tho[s]. Bryan
Lawrence Gibbens
Isham Smith

Rich[d]. Pepper
Edward Jones

Rich[d]. Pepper
Ja[s]. Porch
Ed: Buckner
John Woodard
Benj. Bell
John Wilkerson
Josiah Smith

Tho[s]. Vines
Tho[s]. Butler
[Procession Masters]

[83]

N°. 23 Albemarle Parish

In Obedience to an Order of Vestry Granted September the 15: 1751 We have Processioned the within Lands.

Prop[to]. Names	Persions Present	Persons Present
Tho[s]. Avent	Tho[s]. Avent	James Samons
John Shans	James Sammons	Tho[s]. Underwood
William Solomon	John Shands	William Bass
John Morgan	William Bass	Rich[d]. Hay
James Sammons Jun[r].	Rich[d]. Hay	William Solomon
James Sammons Sen[r].	Lewis Solomon	Rich[d]. Barlow
Tho[s]. Underwood	Edward Griffis	Joseph Prince
Rich[d]. Hay	Ja[s]. Samons	James Prince
Gilbert Hay	John Shands	Lewis Solomon
Lewis Solomon	John Dennis	John Shands

John Avent
Peter Avent
[Procession Masters]

N°. 24

Albemarle Parish

In Obedience to an Order of Vestry Granted September the 15: 1751 we have Processioned the within Lands.

Propt[r]. Names	Persons Present	Persons Present
Major Tiller	John Nancy	Samuel Alsobrook
Samuel Allsobrook	John Alsobrook	Nath[l]. Wyche
John Nancy	John Alsobrook	John Nancy
John Allsobrook	Nath[l]. Wyche	John Allsobrook
Nath[l]. Wyche	Tho[s]. Alsobrook	Samuel Allsobrook

Joseph Tharp
Ja[s]. Wyche
[Procession Masters]

N°. 25

In Obedience to an Order of the Vestry of the Parish of Albemarle bearing Date 1751 We the Subscribers have Processioned & renewed the Land Marks of all the Tracts Or Percels of Land Prescrib,d us by the afore Mentioned Order.
In the Presence of Thomas Capell, Curtis Land, William Loftin, Nathl. Clanton, Robt. Land, John Rachell, Cornelius Loftin, Levie Gilliam, Thos. More, Henry Freeman Junr., Marcus Stokes, Jones Stokes, W^m. Longbottom, John Hargrave.

Processioned   Robt. Webb Junr.
Feby 25: 1752   Charles Battle
          [Procession Masters]

[84]

N°. 26

In Obedience to an Order of Vestry September the 15th: 1751 We Charles Judkins & Silvanus Stokes have Processioned every Mans Land in Our Precinct except Thos. Ezells who would not attend.

Proprietors Names	had in Company the first Day
Thos. Feltes	Thos. Felts
William Knights	Nathl. Felts
Nathl. Feltes	Joseph Ezell
Joseph Ezells which	John Wilburn Junr.
was formerly	John Carter
Matthew Wilkersons	Rich^d. Norcress
Frances Feltes	John Adkins
Robt. Seats	Thos. Adkins
Mary Brown	W^m. Woodland
Saml. Northinton	Ja^s. Bell
Joseph Roland	Richard Rose
Richard Rose	Robt. Seat
Thos. Weathers	Joseph Roland
Edward Powel	W^m. Roland
John Adkins	Saml. Northinton
Richrd Norcross	The Second Day
John Genings	the same in Company
W^m. Cragg	Except Joseph Ezell
W^m. Woodland	The Third Day
John Carter	Rich^d. Norcross &
Ja^s. Carter	W^m. Roland Missing
Jones Stokes	Their Two Sons
Arthur Freeman	Jesse Roland &
John Wilburn Junr.	Ja^s. Norcross in their
Abraham Brown	Room.
Hannah Bell	The Third Day was
John Owen	Also Added to the
Thos^s. Adkins	Company
W^m. Rolands	William Cragg
Henry Adkins	Edward Powell and
W^m. Richarsons	Frances Sears Liveing

Phebe Bells on Thos. Weatherses
John Darlings Land
Burrel Bells
Charles Judkins
Silvanus Stokes

              Charles Judkins
              Silvanus Stokes
              [Procession Masters]

[85]

N° 27
In Obedience to an Order of Vestry of Albemarle Parish held September 15th AD 1751. We did on the 25th Day of November Assemble the Persons within Our Precinct and did Procession & renew the Land Marks of
John Tomlinson, William Cook, David Jones, John Goodwin, Nathaneel Peebles, William Sandrus Junr. & Peter Bagley.

Present   Proprietors Present
William Bagley
Thos. Shans
December 2nd Reubin Baird, William Sandrus Senr., James Gee
& Edward Prince   Proprietors Present

Present
John Tomlinson
Nathaneel Peebles
William Shands
John Sandrus
William Sandrus
December 9th Col: Benj: Harrison, William Eldridge and William Shands

Present   Proprietors
John Ivy
W^m. Dunn
W^m. Shands Junr.
December 10th John Mason, John Ivy & John Baird
Present   Proprietors
W^m. Dunn

January 9th John Wilkerson, Senr., John Wilkerson, Junr., Hugh Ivy, David Mason, Thos. Adkins, John Mason Junr., John Adkins & John Ogburn.

Present   Proprietors Present   Procession Masters
         Hugh Ivy
         John Bierd

72   The Vestry Book of Albemarle Parish

[86]

N 28
This is to Certifie the Worshipful Vestry that Wee W^m. Thompson and Henry Lee have Processioned every free holders Land between the Poplar Swamp & the great Swamp & Renewed the Lines of the same According to our Order & Within the time Limited &c. In Presence of Thos. Pate, Samuel Bass, W^m. Hill, Joseph Ezel, Joseph Robards, Jeremiah Bullock, Benjamin Andrus, John Hill, John Ellis, George Kersey, Samuel Harwood, Adam Ivy, Burril Maclamore, Joseph Prince, Gilbert Prince.

                                                    Henry Lee
                                                    W^m. Thompson
                                                    [Procession Masters]
              March ye 14. 1752

[87]
              Albemarle Parish to John Mason & Jos^a. Tatum
                                                                          D^r.

			£	S	D
1749		To Ballance of the former Acc^t.	-	4:	5
		To Cash paid M^r. Anderson p^r Order	221	18:	8
		To Ditto paid George Williams for Glazing	4	4:	3
		To M^r. Hunter Acc^t. Agst. the Parish	1	19:	3 ¼
		To Cash paid D^r. Goldey	7	15:	10
		To Goods for Joshua FitzPatrick	1	7:	10
	x	To Cash paid D^r. Peete	2	10	-
		To Ditto paid M^r. Pettway		7:	6
		To a Bucket at S^t. Pauls		4:	-
		To Clearing the Well There		5:	-
		To Mending the Bucket at Nottoway Church		1:	3
		To Ballance of M^r. Eldridges Acc^t.	22	-	8
		To Cash paid Rich^d. FitzPatrick	1	-	-
		To 16 panes of Glass for the Glebe		16	-
May ye 12		To 6 Bottles of Clarret from M^r. Hoods	1	4	-
Oct^{er} 5		To Elements for the Sacrament	7	4	-
1750		To Mending & Repairing the Surplace at S^t. Pauls	-	15	-
May 12 1750		To Elements for the Sacram^t.	7	4	-
May 12 1751		To Ditto	7	4	-
Oct^r		To Cash paid M^r. Massenburg as p^r Acc^t.	2	1:	6
1752		To Cash paid M^r. Willie as p^r Order	11	11:	2
		£	301	18	4 ¼
		To Cash Due from John Mason	30	16:	11: ½
		To Ditto from Capt. Briggs	10	15:	9
		To Ditto from Christopher Mason	2	2:	10
		To Ditto from David Mason	1	-	8
		To Ditto from Daniel Mason	-	16:	9 ½
		To Ditto from M^r. Hunter	16	11:	9
		To Ditto from M^r. Willie	8	5:	2
		To Ditto paid the Ch wardens Robt. Wynne	10	9:	2 ½

To Ditto Due from John Mason & Jos^a. Tatum		22	1:	10	
	£	103	1:	11 ½	
Carried Over		406	-	4 ¼	

[88]

					C^t		
		Contra			£	S	D
1749	By Balance Due from M^r. Hunters Old Acc^t.				74	18 -	9
	By D^o. from M^r. Hood	D^o.			21	13 -	½
	By D^o. from M^r. Willie	D^o.			13	15 -	10
	By D^o. from Cap^{tn}. Briggs	D^o.			22	1 -	3
				£	132	8 -	10 ½
	By Tob: levied for the use of the Parish			16513			
	By 54 Tithables added a^t 25			1350			
				17863			
				281			
				17582			
	Levies Overcharged or romitted Viz						
	W^m. Hill	25					
	Thos. Vaughan	25					
	John Alsobrook	50					
	Eliz. Hargrave	50					
	Francis Turville	25					
	W^m. Judkins	25					
	Commission on 1350	81					
		281					
	By Tob. sold for the use of the Parish 17582 Viz.						
	To M^r. Rae			6898	51	18:	8
	To M^r. Peter			774	5	16:	1
	To M^r. Pritloe			1584	11	2:	10
	To M^r. Cocke			3086	22	14:	9
	To Mr. Jones			872	6	9:	5
	To Capt. Ruffian			686	4	16	-
	To M^r.Hunter			1038	7	13:	8
	To the Ch wardens			2644	19	12:	4
				17582	£ 130	3:	9
1750	By Tob. levied for the use of the Parish			20666			
	levies Overcharged & other allowances			975			
				19691			
	Thos. Warren	75					
	John Davis	25					
	John Rachel	25					
	W^m. Wilborn	50					
	Jo^h. Clark clearg Ch yard	100					
	John Freeman for Jane Matthis	100					
		975					

	By Tob: sold for the use of the Parish	19691			
	Viz. To M^r. Sermont	4202	30	18-	9
	To Capt. Briggs	2947	22	2 -	½
	To M^r. Clintch	1499	10	10	-
	To M^r. Hunter	1600	11	4-	-
	To M^r. Willie	3333	23	6:	7 ½
	To M^r. Noble	1552	11	8:	10 ½
	To M^r. Tyler	225	1	13:	9
		15358	£11	4:	1
			1		
	Carried Over		£37	16:	8
			3		

[89]

Albemarle Parish D^r.

	£	S	D
Brought Over	405	- 4	½
	405	- 4	½

Albemarle Parish D^r. Fines

	£	S	D
To paid Mary Woodham		1	10 -
To paid Isaac Robertson		1	10 -
To paid Sarah Evans		1	10 -
To paid M^r. Johnson for Roe		1	10 -
To paid the Widow Cox		1	15 -
To paid the Widow Crosland		1	10 -
To paid the Widow Higgs		1	10 -
To paid Anne Malone			15 -
To paid Jane Matthews			15 -
To paid Mary Coats			15 -
To paid Thos. Cooper			15 -
To paid Ann Gresswitt			15 -
To paid Eliz. Duncan			15 -
To Thos. Burgiss		1	10 -
To Ballance Due from John Mason J^r.			4 -6
	£	16	19: 6

[90]

Contra C^r

			£	S	D
1750	Brought Over	15358	373	16-	8
	Sold to Thos. Pritloe	103		15:	5
	To Christopher Mason	307	2	2:	10
	To Daniel Mason	112	-	16:	9½

			£	s	d
To David Mason	138	1	-	8
To Cab. P¹. Warehouse	650	4	19:	2
To Jordans Dº.	266	2	-	9
To Maycox Dº.	175	1	6:	8
To Grays Creek Dº.	422	2	19	-
To the Ch wardens	2160	15	2	4¼
		31	3	8¼

Errors Excepted   £   405   -   4¼
by John Mason Jʳ.

& Forfeitures   Contra   Cʳ

	£	S	D
By Ballance of former fines	1	4:	6
By Martha Gilbert	2	10	-
By John Curtis		5	-
By Thoˢ. Booth		5	-
By Simon Flowers		5	-
By Richᵈ. Peppers Maid	2	10	-
By Hollemn Sturdivants Daughter	2	10	-
By Mʳ. Hunters Servant Jane	2	10	-
By Susannah Johnson	2	10	-
By Wᵐ. Pears Daughter	2	10	-
£	16	19	6

Errors Excepted
by John Mason Jʳ.

[91]

1751   the Parish of Albemarle to E. Parham & Josᵃ. Tatum   Dʳ.

		£			
Sepʳ. 19	To paid Nathˡ. Hood p order of Vestry	£	1	-	-
	To removing the Spring Swamp old Chappel		2		
	To 1 Bason for the use of Sᵗ. Marks Chappel			3	6
	To paid John Whittington for keepg Ruana Judkins			3	9
	To paid Mʳ. Willie for Maj. Wynne p. cenᵗ Ch warden		17	8	1

To Ballance due to the Parish   £ 51 14 0

[92]

1751   P   Cʳ.

				£		
By Sold Mʳ. Hunter 2167 lb Tob at Cab Pᵗ.	ᵃᵗ 16/6	£17	17	6½
By Sold ----- Dº. at Jordans 2245 lb	aᵗ 16/2 -	20	11	5¼
By Capᵗ. Howel 477 Briggs	aᵗ 14/11 -	3	11	1¾

The Vestry Book of Albemarle Parish

By David Hunter	352	a' 13/ -	2	5	9
By Cab P¹. Inspectors	1692	a' 13/ -	10	13	4
3 p cent Discount	50	1641			
By Gray Creek Insp'ˢ.	424				
6 p cent Discount	25 [=] 399	a' 14/11	2	19	6
By Jordans Insp'ˢ.	424				
6 p cent Discount	25 -- [=] 389	a' 16/1	3	2	7
By Maycox Insp'ˢ.	128				
6 p cent Discount	8 -- [-] 120	a' 16/ -	-	19	2¼
By Bolings Point Insp'ˢ.	666				
6 p cent Discount	40 -- [=] 626	a' 17/ -	5	6	5
By W[arricksqueek] Bay Inspectors	244				
6 p cent Discount	14 -- [=] 230	a' 13/ -	1	9	10¼
By Ballance due to the Parish by our Tob. Account 635 lb. a' 13/			4	2	6½
		£	72	19	4

E.E. p Ephraim Parham
&
Joshua Tatum
October 16th 1752

[93]

1751	Albemarle Parish to E. Parham & Joshua Tatum		Dʳ.
	To Sold for the Use of the Parish Viz¹.		lb. Tob.
	To David Hunter at Cab. Pᵗ.	at 16/6	2167
	To Jordans Inspectors	at 16/2	2545
	To Capᵗ. Howel Briggs	a' 14/11	477
	To David Hunter	13/	352
	To Cabin Point Inspectors	a' 13/	1692
	To Grays Creek Inspectors	a' 14/11	424
	To Jordans Inspectors	a' 16/1	414
	To Maycox Inspectors	a' 16/	128
	To Bolings Pᵗ. Inspectors	a' 17/	666
	To Warricksqueck Bay Insp'ˢ.	a' 13/	244
	To paid Bridget Tatum p ord of Vest.y		636
	To Deficiency in the Numbers of Taxables on which the Levy was laid Viz¹. 75 pole a' 20 each		1500
	To Sundry Taxables Insolvent & not to be found Viz¹.		
	Absalom Holloway 2 pole		40
	Samuel Sebrel 1 pole		20
	Joseph Clark 1 pole		20
	Thoˢ. Burgiss 1 pole		20
	Thoˢ. Dunn Jʳ. Twice listed 1 pole		20
	John Wilburn Jʳ. Twice listed 1 pole		20
	John Washington 2 pole		40
	Cuthburt Stafford 1 pole		20
	Thoˢ. Zell Jʳ. Twice listed 1 pole		20

Ja^s. More 1 pole	20
Peter Hill 1 pole	20
Robt. Newman Constable 1 pole	20
John Bellemy 1 pole	20
	11565
To Ballance Due to the Parish	635
	lb^s 12200

E.E.p Ephraim Parham
&
Joshua Tatum

[94]

		C^t
1750	p^r	W^t. Tob.
Oct^r.	By levied p Vestry for the use of the Parish	12000
	By received of Sundry Persons not listed Viz^t.	
	Thos. Wallis 2 pole	40
	W^m. Zell 1 pole	20
	W^m. Rowland 3 pole	60
	John Bass 1 pole	20
	James Moss 1 pole	20
	lb^s.	12200

[95]

At a Vestry held for the Parish of Albemarle in County of Surry at Nottoway Church on ye 13th Day of November 1752

Present
The Rev.d W^m. Willie

Robt. Wynne	Robt. Jones J^r.	
Ja^s. Chappell	Ja^s. Gee	} Gent.
Rich^d. Blow	John Mason J^r.	
Ephraim Parham	Moses Johnson	

	D^r.
Albemarle Parish	n^t. Tob.
To the Rev,d W^m. Willie as Minister	17305
To John Tatum Clerk at Nottoway Church	1200
To Robt. Nicolson Clerk at S^t. Pauls Church	1200
To Gregory Rawlins Clerk at S^t. Andrews Church	1200
To Robt. Farrinton Clerk at S^t. Marks Church	1200
To John Weaver Sexton at Nottoway Church	500
To Joseph Roland Sexton at S^t. Andrews D^o.	500
To John Bain Sexton at S^t. Pauls D^o.	500
To Robt. Farrinton Sexton at S^t. Marks D^o.	500
To Moses Johnson for keeping John King a lame C^{hd}.	800

To Charles Gillam for keeping his Son Hinchea	500
To Ja^s. Williams for keeping John King 1 year	700
To Rich^d. Huson for keeping Jane Matthis 1 Yr.	675
To Ja^s. Chappell J^r. Clerk of the Vestry	400
To Matthew Whitfeild for keeping Rebecca Bird 1 Y^r.	500
To Eliz. Jones an Infirm Woman	300
To Matthew Whitfeild for finding Rebecca Bird Shoes & Stockings	50
To John Hood for keeping his Sister Frances 1 Y^r.	400
To John Knight for keeping Sarah Davis 5 Month	250
To Timothy Ezell for keeping Mary Dillahay 6 Month	178
To M^r. Robt. Webb 1 pole Twice Charg,d last year	25
To Charles Mabry D^o. D^o. D^o.	25
	28908
To Ja^s. Chappell J^r. for extraordinary Services	200
To levied for the use of the Parish	1317
To the Collector for Collecting & Paying in Inspectors Notes According to Law 30429 lb Tob.	1925
	32250

p^r. Contra   C^r.
By. 2150 Taxables as tis Supposd a^t 15 ^{lb} p pole   lb. 32250

[96]

Ordered that Ja^s. Jones on his entering into bond and Security to the Vestry of this Parish to be Taken by the Clerk of the Vestry he is Appointed Collector of this Parish for the Year ensuing & that he Collect & Receive of every Person Chargable therewith 15 Pounds of Tobacco p^r. Poll & the have Authority in case the said 15 pounds of Tob. p^r. Poll or any Part Thereof be Delayed or refused to Levy the same by Distress And that he pay to each Respective Parish Creditor the Several Sums of Tob. Due to them & that he expose to Publick Sale the Tob. levied for the use of the Parish & that he pay to the Church wardens the Money arising from Such Sale.

Moses Johnson proposed to the Vestry to keep Sarah Davis an Aged Infirm Woman for one Year Next ensuing & Provide Necessaries for her for 600 ^{lb} Tobo which is agreed to by the Vestry.

Ordered that the Ch wardens pay to John Bain the Sum of Twenty Shillings in full of his Account Exhibited.

Ordered that the Ch wardens pay to John Bain Ten Shill,gs for Building & keeping in repair Seven Years a Chirb [sic] to ye Well at S^t. Pauls Church.

Matthew Whitfeild has agreed to Provide for Rebecca Bird One Year & find her Necessaries for which he is to have Seven hundred Pounds of Tob. which is agreed to by ye Vestry.

John King J^r. propos,d to the Vestry to keep Frances Hood one Year & he is to have five hundred Pounds of Tob. for his Trouble.

Ordered that David Cotten a Cripple be exempted from Paying his Parish Levy for the futer.

Ordered that Moses Johnson & Ephraim Parham view S^t. Andrew Church & Make report to this Vestry whither M^r. Ja^s. Anderson the Undertaker thereof hath Compleated the same According to Agreement.

[97]

Ordered that the Ch wardens pay to Edmund Ruffian the Sum of eighty Pounds out of the Money belonging to the Parish.

Ordered that the Ch wardens pay to Ja^s. Anderson the Sum of Twenty five Pounds five Shillings & Six Pence out of the Money belonging to this Parish.

W^m. Willie Min^r.

Copy Test. Ja^s. Chappell Clk Vestry

[98]

At a Vestry held for the Parish of Albemarle in the County at Nottoway Church on the 24th Day of April 1753 being Easter Tuesday.

Present
The Rev.d William Willie

Augustine Claiborne	Ja^s. Gee	
Robert Wynne	Ja^s. Chappell	} Gent.
John Mason Junr.	Ephraim Parham	
& Thomas Avent		

Robert Wynne & Robert Jones Junr. are Appointed Ch wardens for the Year Ensuing.

Ordered that the Ch wardens Pay to Benjn. Weldon the Sum of four Pounds Six Shillings Out of the Money in their hands belonging to this Parish for four Copies of the Acts of Assembles Ordered to be read in Churches.

Ordered that the Ch wardens Pay to Thomas Cullum the Sum of Three Pounds Out of the Money in their hands which has Accrued to this Parish from fines & forfeitures.

Ordered that the Ch wardens Pay to Ann Malone the Sum of fifteen Shillings Out of the Money in their hands which has Accrued to this Parish from fines & forfeitures.

Ordered that the Ch wardens Pay to Izodoniah Higgs the Sum of Sixteen Shillings Out of the Money in their hands which has Accrued to this Parish from fines & forfeitures.

Ordered that the Ch wardens Pay to Ann Gresswett the Sum of Twelve Shillings & Six Pence Out of the Money in their hands which has acrued to this Parish from fines & forfeitures.

Ordered that the Ch wardens Pay to Eliz^h. Whitehead the Sum of Seventeen Shillings Out of the Money in their hands which has Accrued to this Parish from fines & forfeitures.

Ordered that the Ch wardens Pay to Eliz^h. Spain the Sum of Sixteen Shillings & Nine Pence Out of the Money in their hands which has Accrued to this Parish from fines & forfeitures.

Ordered that the Ch wardens Pay to Edward Morress the Sum of Sixteen Shillings & Nine Pence Out of the Money in their hands which has Accrued to this Parish from fines & forfeitures.

Ordered that the Ch wardens Pay to Sarah Owen the Sum of Sixteen Shillings & Nine Pence out of the Money in their hands which has Accrued to this Parish from fines & forfeitures.

The Vestry takeing under Consideration the Smallness of Nottoway Church and the large Congregation frequenting the Same are of Opinion that its Necessary some alterations be made either by building a new Church or Adding to the Present & therefore do resolve to take the Same Under their farther Consideration at the laying the next levy.

Ordered that Thos. Davis be Exempted from Paying Parish Levies Dureing his Indisposition.

William Willie Min^r.

Copy Test Ja^s. Chappell Jn^r.
Clk Vestry

[99]

At a Vestry held for the Parish of Albemarle in the County of Surry at the Glebe on the 4th Day of October 1753.

Present
The Rev,d William Willie

Robert Jones Junr.	Rich^d. Blow	
Ja^s. Chappell	Moses Johnson	} Gent.
Howel Briggs	& John Mason Junr.	

Albemarle Parish	D^r. W^t. lbs Tob.
To the Rev^d. William Willie as Minister	17305
To John Tatum as Clerk at Nottoway Church	1200
To Robert Nicolson as Clerk of S^t. Pauls D^o.	1200
To Robert Farrinton as Clerk of S^t. Marks D^o.	1200
To Gregory Rawlins as Clerk of S^t. Andrews D^o.	1200
To John Bain Sexton at S^t. Pauls D^o.	500
To Robert Farrinton Sexton at S^t. Marks D^o.	500
To Moses Johnson for keeping John King a lame Child 1 Y^r.	800
To Charles Gilliam for keeping his Son Hinchea 1 Year	500
To Richard Huson for keeping Jane Matthis 1 Year	675
To Moses Johnson for keeping Sarah Davis 1 Year	600
To Matthew Whitfeild for keeping Rebecca Bird 1 Year	700
To John King J^r. for keeping Frances Hood 1 Year	500
To John King J^r. for keeping John King 1 Year	900
To Edward Shelton Sexton at S^t. Andrew Church	500
To John Dento Sexton at Nottoway D^o.	500
To Ja^s. Chappell J^r. as Clerk of the Vestry	400
To William Cook for three Tithes twice Listed last year	45
To William Wynne for two Tithes twice Listed last year	30
To Thos. Briggs for Six Tithes paid to this Parish that beongs [sic] to the Parish of Suthworth [Southwark]	90
To the Collector for Collecting & Paying away 29445 lbs. of Tobacco	29445 1767
To a Depositum in the hands of the Collector including his Commissions for Collecting	31212 2103
	33315
p^r. Contra C^r.	
By 2221 Tythables at 15/ p^r. Pole	33315

[100]

Ordered that Ja^s Chappell Junr on his entering into bond & Security to the Vestry of this Parish to be taken by the Church wards he is appointed ------ Collector of this Parish for the Year Next ensuing & that he Collect & receive of every Person Chargable therewith 46 pounds of Tobacco pe^r Pole & that he have Authority in case the said 16 pounds of Tobacco p^r pole or any Part thereof be Delayed or refused to levy the same by Distress and that he pay to each respective Parish Creditor the Several Sums of Tobacco Due to them & that he expose to Publick Sale the Tobacco locked for the use of the parish & that he pay to the Church wardens for the time being the Money a rising from Such Sale

Ordered that the Church wardens pay to Captn Howel Briggs his Account against this Parish.

Ordered that the Chwardens pay to Moses Johnson the Sum of one pound five Shillings Out of the Money in their hands belonging to this Parish

Ordered that the Chwardens pay to William Rogers the Sum of Six pounds to Reimburse him the Money he has expended with a Doctor in Attempting the cure of Reubin Rogers an infirm man

James Sammons is exemted from paying his Parish Levy for the Future

Captn Edmund Ruffin the Undertaker [overseer, builder] of the Glebe Buildings & repairs appeard & offered the same to view whereupon tis the openion[sic] of the Vestry that the Same is not Compleated[sic] According to the Articles by which the same were let but upon Ruffins agreeing to refund the parish fifteen pounds for the insuffuciencyes tis agreed that the Said work be received at his hands & be discahrged from any Insufficiencies in Compleating the same

The Revd Willie agreed to receive the Glebe Building at the hands of the Vestry & repaie the insuffieiencies of Capt Ruffins work for the fifteen pounds refunded by him which was paid Down accordingly

William Willie Min^r
Copy Test Ja^s Chappell J^r Clerk of the Vestry

[101]

At a Vestry held for the Parish of Albemarle in the County of Sussex at Nottoway Church on the Seventh Day of November 1754

Present
The Revd Wm Willie

Robt Jones Junr	Augustine Claiborne
Thos Avent	Ja^s Gee
Ja^s Chappell	Howell Briggs
Moses Johnson	John Mason J^r

Ephraim Parham

Albemarle Parish	Wt lbs Tob^o D^r
To the Revd Wm Willie as Minister	17305
To John Tatum as Clerk at Nottoway Church	1200
To Robt Nicolson as Clerk at St Pauls D^o	1200
To Gregory Rawlings as Clerk at St Andrews D^o	1200
To Robt Farrinton as Clerk & Sexton at St Marks D^o	1700
To John Denton as Sexton at Nottoway Church	500
To John Bain as Sexton at St Paul's D^o	500
To Edward Shelton as Sexton at St Andrews D^o	500
To Moses Johnson for keeping John King a lame Child 1 year	800
To Mathew Whitfield for keeping Rebecca Bird 1 year	700

To Charles Gilliam for keeping his son Hinchea 1 year	500
To Ja^s Williams for keeping John King 1 year	900
To John Jarrad for 4 Tythes Twice Listed Last Year	60
To Nicholas Prince for one Tythe Twice listed Last Year	15
To Ja^s Chappell J^r as Clerk of the Vestry	400
To Mary Drew for keeping Eliz^h Kersay 6 months	400
To Edward Lee for keeping Thos Musslewhite Orphan of Thos Musslewhite near 20 months	700
To Mary Drew for keeping Eliz^h Kersey a Pensioner	200
To Ja^s Chappell Sh[eriff] for collecting Paying 30741 ^{lbs} Tob^o	1960
To a Depositum in the Hands of the Collector	1944
By 2179 Tythables at 15 lbs Tob^o Pr Pole	32685

[102]

Ordered that Ja^s Chappell on his Entering into Bond & Security to the Vestry of this parish to be taken By the Clerk be Appointed Collector of this Parish for ye year ensuing therewith fifteen Pounds of Tobacco p^r Pole & that he Have Authority in Case the s^d fifteen Pounds of Tobacco Pr Pole or any part thereof be Delayed or Refused to Levy the Same by Distress & that he Pay to each Respective parish the Several Sum of Tobacco Due to them on the fifteenth Day of Last Month & that he Pay the Tobacco Levied for the Use of the Parish to the Ch:wardens for the time being

Ordered that the Ch:wardens Pay to Thos Cullum the Sum of three Pounds Out of the Money in the Hands which has Accrued to this Parish from fines & forfietures

Ordered that the Ch:wardens Pay to John Mason Junr the Sum of Seven Pounds five Shillings & four Pence half Penny Being his Acct against this parish

Ordered that the Collector pay to John Mason J^r the Sum of Tobacco he has Expended in Defending a Suit brought Against him by Ja^s Anderson in behalf of this parish

Mr Gray Briggs is Elected & Appointed as Vestry Man in this Parish in the Room of Major Robt Wynne Dec^d & that he Quallify as Soon as Possible to Serve this Parish in that capacity

Howel Briggs is Appointed Ch:warden in the room of Maj. Robt Wynne Dec^d with Mr Robt Jones Junr till Next Easter Tuesday

Richd King Junr has agreed with the Vestry to keep John King one Year & find him all Necessaries for 1600 lbs of Tob^o

Matthew Whitfield has agreed with the Vestry to keep Rebecca Bird one year & find her all Necessaries for 800 lbs of Tob^o

Ordered that the Collector pay to Wm Parham fifteen Pounds of Tob^o on Acct of his being charged with fifteen Pounds Last Year Not Due

Wm Willie Min^r

Copy Test   Jas Chappell J^r Clk

[103]

At a Vestry held for the Parish of Albemarle in the County of Sussex the 8th Day of August 1755

Present
The Revd William Willie

Ja^s Gee	Moses Johnson
Ja^s Chappell	Ephraim Parham } Gent
Howel Briggs	John Mason J^r

In Pursuance to an Order of Sussex County Court Bearing Date July 1755 Directing the

Vestry of Albemarle Parish to Divide ye Same into Precincts for the Processioning Every Persons Land Within the s^d Parish Wee Do appoint Robt Nicolson & Wm Hancock to see Every Persons Land Processioned & the Land Marks thereof Renewed from Surey[sic] County Line up between Seacock & Tareipin Swamps to Birchan island Road & up the s^d to the Head of Seacock & that they To assemble all the Freeholders within that Precinct to attend the performance thereof & That the s^d Robert Nicolson & Wm Hancock To make Returnd to this Vestry an account of Every Persons Land they shall Procession & of every person Present at ye Processioning thereof also of whose Land they shall fail to procession & the Perticular Reason of Such failure & that ye same be done and performed between the first Day of November & the last Day of March

Henry Blow & Arthur Smith are appointed to procession from ye South side of Seacock swamp to ye Head of the Lightwood Swamp & Secaurico Swamp thence to Birchan island Road

George Briggs & Stephen Hamlin are appointed to procession from Southampton County Line up Assamoosuck to Secaurico thence up Secaurico to the head

Ja^s Chappell Junr & John Jarend are appointed to procession from the Mouth of Seacurios up Assamoosuck to ye Maj. Branch up ye s^d Branch to Secauric road along ye Road to Secauric Swamp Down ye s^d Swamp to the Beginning

Nicholas Partridge & Nicholas Partridge Junr are appointed to Procession from ye Maj: Branch up Assamoosuck Swamp to & including Pettway Johnsons Land thence to the head of Coppahannock Swamp & Down that to Sccauric Road along ye Maj Branch so to the Begining

[104]

David Jones & Wm Cook are appointed to procession from Cooks Bridge along Cooks Road to Joseph Swamp so to Prince George County Line thence by that Line to Blackwater thence to the Begining

Hugh Toy[sic] & John Baird are appointed to procession from Cooks Road on the new Road to the Black Swamp thence to the Governors Road All Between ye s^d Roads out to Joseph Swamp

Edward Weaver & John Ogburn are appointed to procession from ye Governors Road to the Old parish Line all between Joseph Swamp & Assamoosuck Swamp to the Old Parish Line

Wm Parker & David Jones are Appointed to procession from ye Old Parish Line down to the Mouth of Robins Branch thence Down Austins Branch to Nottoway River thence up Nottoway to the Beginning

Wm Edmund & Thos Peters Junr are Appointed to procession All Between Assamoosuck Swamp & Nottoway River below the Mouth of Robins & Austins Branch as to Southamton Line

Edward Lee & Edward Eppes are Appointed to procession from Pettway Mill a long Rebecah Harthorns Line to ye Colledge Lines & a long that line to Joseph Swamp thence Down ye s^d Swamp to Nottoway River up the said River to the Mouth of Baulthorp Creek & Up ye s^d Creek to the Beginning

Edward Pettway & John Jenkins are appointed to procession all Between Jones Hole Swamp & Indian Swamp & from Prince Geo: county line to Nottoway River

John Curtis & Joel Tucker are Appointed to procession all between Monks Neck Creek & Stony Creek & up Sappony Creek to Prince George County Line

Richard Hill & John Tyas are appointed to procession from Stony Creek to Sappony Mill from thence to Lewis Parhams Land So Down Nottoway River to the Begining

Wm Raney J^r & Robt Farrinton are appointed to procession from the Plantation of Lewis Parhams to Sappony Mill all between the Line that Divides this County from Prince George County up Nottoway River to Harris Swamp

Thos Vines & Thos Butler are appointed to procession from Harriss Swamp up Nottoway River to the Extent of this County

[105]

Robt Webb & Charles Battle are appointed to procession all between Racoon Swamp Little Swamp & Stokes's Road

Matthew Parham & Ephraim Parham are Appointed to procession from ye Island Swamp to the Old Parish Line & a long ye s^d Line to the line Dividing this County from Brunswick Between Nottoway River

John Stevens & Wm Ezell are appointed to procession Between ye Rackoon & Hunting Quarter out to the Head of Hunting Quarter

Wm Knight & John Battle are appointed to procession all the Land on the east side of Stokes's Road between the Line Dividing this County & Southamton to the Rackoon Swamp

Ja^s Wyche & Joseph Thorp are Appointed to procession all on the South side of the 3 Creeks & Southamton & Brunswick County Lines

Henry Hartwell Marrible & Matthew Wynne are Appointed to procession from Stokes's road up Nottoway River to the flat Swamp from ye head of ye s^d Swamp a Strait course to Hunting Quarter Swamp

Saml Maggett & John Alsobrook are Appointed to procession from ye Mouth of Copperhannk a long the line Dividing this County & Surey to Birchan island Road & by ye s^d Road to Secuaric Road & by that Road to CopperHannk Swamp & Down ye s^d Swamp to the begining

David Hunter & Robt Judkins are Appointed to procession all between Blackwater Copperhannk & the Old parish Line

Peter Bagley & John Barker are Appointed to procession from all to between Blackwater Copperhannk & the Old parish Line

Willet Roberts & John Irby are Appointed to procession from Black Water at the Old Parish Line by that Line to Copper hank swamp up ye s^d Swamp to the head Thence to the Tarkiln Branch on the Mill swamp Thence up the s^d Branch to the Town Swamp & Down ye s^d Swamp to Blackwater & so to the begining

Thos Mitchell & John Tatum are Appointed to procession all between Rebekah Harthorne Line the Colledge Line & the Line that Divides this County & Prince George & between Joseph Swamp & Jones Hole

Moses Johnson & Joseph Pedington are Appointed to procession all Between Allens Line John Pedingtons Line & Rob' Jones's Line & Stokes Road & the Hunting Quarter Swamp

Clem' Hancock & Rob' Hancock are Appointed to procession all Between Allens Line John Pedingtos Line Rob' Jones Line & Stokes Road & Nottoway River

Peter Vent & Ja' Stuart are Appointed to procession from ye Mouth of the Great Swamp to the 3 creek & up the 3 creeks & Outerdam Swamp to Brunswick Line

Henry Tyler & Sam' Bass are Appointed to procession from ye Great Swamp & Down ye same to the County Line & to the Poplar Swamp & up the Poplar to Brunswick Line

[106]

Hinchea Gilliam & Natha' Clanton are Appointed to procession all Between Nottoway River the Rackoon & Hunting Quarter up to ye Mill Path a Long Loftins Mill Path to the Little Swamp Down the Same to the Begining

Cornelius Loftin & Richd Avery are Appointed to procession up Hunting Quarter & Little Swamp from Loftins Mill path to Stokes Road

Thos Parham & Matthew Parham are appointed to procession from Indian Swamp to Menks Neck & the County Line & Nottoway River

Sloman Wynne & Henry Sturdavant are Appointed to procession from Flat Swamp up Nottoway River to the Mouth of Frying Pan Up Frying Pan to the head therof from thence to 3 witts[threewitts] down the the River to the beginning

Wm Stuart & Peter Reives to procession from head of Frying to Hunting Quarter & Down ye same to Island Branch & Town Island Branch to Nottoway River

Charles Judkins & Sil: Stokes are appointed to procession from ye North side of the Spring Swamp up the s^d Swamp to the County Line & so Down ye Rackoon to Stokes Road

Thos Felts & Rob' Seat are appointed to procession from Stokes road between the Poplar & Spring Swamps up ye s^d Swamps to the County Line

Ordered that Nicholas Jones be Exempted from paying his Parish Levy for ye future

Ordered that Sam' Drake be Exempted from paying his Parish Levy for ye future

Ordered that the Churchwardens pay to Thos Cullum the sum of three three[sic] pounds current Money put of the Money in their Hands Which has accrue^d to this Parish from fines & forfeitures

Wm Willie Min'

Copy Test Ja^s Chappell J^r Clk Vest:

[107]

At a Vestry Held for the Parish of Albemarle in the County of Sussex at Nottoway Church in the 25th Day of November 1755

Present
The Revd William Willie

Howel Briggs	James Gee	
Augustin Claiborne	James Chappell	} Gent
Moses Johnson	Ephraim Parham	
& John Mason		

Albemarle Parish	D^r Wt Tob^o
To the Revd William Willie as Min^r	17305
To John Tatum as Clerk at Nottoway Church	1200
To Robt Nicholson as D^o at St Pauls D^o	1200
To Gregory Rawlings as D^o at St Andrews D^o	1200
To Robt Farrinton as D^o & Sexton at St Marks D^o	1700
To John Denton as Sexton at Nottoway D^o	500
To John Bain as D^o at St Pauls D^o	500
To Edward Shelton as D^o at St Andrews D^o	500
To Moses Johnson for keeping John King a lame child one year	800
To Matthew Whitfield for keeping Rebecca Bird one year	800
To Charles Gilliam for keeping his son Hinchea 9 Months	369
To Richard King for keeping John King one Month	134
To Ja^s Chappell Junr as Clerk of the Vestry	400
To Henry Meachum for three Tythes Twice listed last Year	45
To John King for keeping Frances Hood 1 Year	500
To John Land for keeping Saml Doake 6 Months	500
To Richd Huson for keeping Jane Matthis 8 Months	317
To Thos Cooper for Removing Edward Green out of this Parish to Southworth Parish & for other Services Done	85
	28055
To 6 p^r Cent for Collecting 28055 lbs of Tob^o	1683
To levied for ye use of the parish	12
	29,750
Pr Contra	Cr
By 2125 Tythables at 14 lbs of Tob^o p^r pole	29,750

Ordered that John Wilkerson be Exempted from paying his Parish Levy for ye future

[108]

Ordered that John Mason on his entering into Bond & Security to the Vestry of this Parish to be taken by the Clerk of the Vestry be appointed Collector of this Parish for ye Year ensuing & that he collect & Receive of every Person Chargable therewith fourteen Pounds of Tob^o p^r pole & that he have Authority in case the said fourteen pounds of Tobacco p^r Pole or any part thereof be Delayed or refusd to levy ye same by Distress & that he pay to each respective Parish Creditor the Several sums of Tob^o Due to them & that he pay the Tob^o levied for the use of the Parish to the Churchwardens for ye time being

Ordered that the Churchwardens pay to Charles Gilliam the sum of one pound Seven Shillings & Six pence for Burying his Son Hinchea a Pensioner

Ordered that the Churchwardens pay to Richd Huson the sum of one pound Seven Shillings & Six pence for Burying Jane Mathis a pensioner

Ordered that the Churchwardens pay to Rich^d the sum of one pound Seventeen Shillings & Six pence for Burying John King a Pensioner

Ordered that the Churchwardens pay to Saml Barlow the Sum of twelve Shillings & Six pence for Making a Window Shutter to St Marks Church & Setting it in

Ordered that the Churchwardens pay to James Carter the Sum of Seven Shillings & Six pence for Setting up two pair of Horse Blocks at St Andrews Church

Ordered that the Churchwardens pay to Ephraim Parham ye Sum of Twenty Shillings for services Done as Appears by his Account

Ordered that the Churchwardens pay to Richd Reives the Sum of One pound Nine Shillings for keeping Mary Delshay seven Months

Ordered that the Churchwardens find Mary Coates with two hundred Pounds of Meat & two Barrells of Corn for ye year ensuing

Ordered that the Churchwardens pay to John Bain the Sum of Seven Shillings & Six pence for Setting up a Sweep and finding two Buckets for the Well at St Pauls Church

Ordered that the Churchwardens pay to Charles Flood the Sum of five Shillings for Clearing the Well at St Pauls Church

[109]

As there was an Order of Vestry Made for Edward Pettway and John Jenkins to Procession all the Lands lying Between Jones Hole & the Indian Swamp & Prince George line & Nottoway River & John Jenkins is since Dead whereupon it is ordered that William Moore be put in his stead

Mr John Edmunds is Elected to Serve this Parish as a Vestry Man instead of Captain John Mason Dec^d & that he Qualify as Soon as Possible to Serve this Parish in that Capasity

Resolved that no more than Twenty Seven Shillings be Allowed for Burying any Poor on Account of the Parish

Ordered that the Churchwardens Pay to Edmund Barron the Sum of Two Pounds Twelve Shillings & Six pence for Burying Thos Scarbrough a Poor Prisoner who Dyed in Goal

William Willie Min^r
Copy Test Ja^s Chappell Junr Clk Vest,

At a Vestry held for the Parish of Albemarle in the County of Sussex at the Court House on the 15th Day of December 1755

Present
The Revd William Willie

Ja^s Gee		Ja^s Chappell	
Gray Briggs		Ephraim Parham	} Gent
John Mason		Thos Avent	
Howel Briggs	&	Moses Johnson	

Ordered that Henry Jarrad be Appointed to Procession with Nich° Partridge instead of Nicholas Partridge Dec^d

Ordered that Tho' Pate be Appointed to Procession with Henry Tyler instead of Samuel Bass

Ordered that Nicholas Massenburg & William Danzy be Appointed to Procession in the same Precinct that Henry Hartwell Marrible & Mathew Wynne were formly appointed to Procession

William Willie Min[r]

Copy Test Ja[s] Chappell J[r] Clk Vest

[110]

At a Vestry Held for the Parish of Albemarle at Nottoway Church on the 20th Day of April 1756

Present
The Rev[d] William Willie

Howel Briggs		Augustin Claiborne	
Tho[s] Avent		James Gee	
James Chappell		Ephraim Parham	} Gent
Moses Johnson	&	John Mason	

Thomas Avent & Gray Briggs is appointed Churchwardens for the Year Next Ensuing

Ordered that the Churchwardens pay to John Mason three Pounds for the use of Thomas Cullum Out of the Money in their Hands belonging to this Parish

Ordered that the Churchwardens pay out of the Money in Their Hands belonging to this Parish to John Earwood the Sum of five Pounds for keeping a Child of John Munses [Munns] called Ephraim from the 15th of May 1755 to the 15th Day of May 1756 which said Child the said Earwood Undertook to Keep by order of the Late Churchwardens

Ordered that the Churchwardens Pay to John Piddenton [Pennington] Carp[r] the Sum of two Pounds one Shilling & eight Pence out of the Money in their Hands belonging to this Parish for keeping Two Children of William Goffs named David & Sarah Two months & a half which said Children was put there by the Late Churchwardens

Ordered that the Churchwaardens pay to Ann Malone an aged & Infirm Person the Sum of One Pound Out of the Money in their Hand belonging to this Parish

Upon the Resignation of John Tatum Clerk of Nottoway Church Ordered that the Rev[d] William Willie get Some Person Duly Qualified to act in that office

William Willie Min[r]
Copy Test Ja[s] Chappell Jun[r] Clk of y[e] Vestry

[111]

In due Obedience to an Order of the Worshipfull Vestry of Albemarle Parish August y[e] 8th 1755

Wee have Processioned all the Lands within the Order & have Renewed the Land Marks which are as followeth to Wit

N° 1 Joel Tuckers		John Freeman
William Raines	Present	Edward Eckles
John Freemans		Geo: Parham
William Malones		

Alexander Bolings		Robert Jackson
Joel Tuckers		John Eckles
Peter Poytresss	Present	Henry Hatch
Edward Broadnaxes		Nathan Freeman
John Jacksons		Thomas Wynne &
Thoˢ Wynnes		Peter Winfield

George Booths		George Booth
Daniel Nances		Thoˢ Hunt
John Curtiss	Present	William Harper
Wᵐ Malones		Thoˢ Wynne
Wᵐ Harpers		George Parham
Samˡ Barlow		

Thoˢ Hunts	
Richᵈ Husons	John Curtis
Thoˢ Husons	Joel Tucker

N° 2 To the Worshipfull Vestry of Albemarle Parish Pursuant to a Order of Vestry Dated August yᵉ 8ᵗʰ 1755 We the Subscribers have Processioned & renewed every Mans land Marks in Our Precinct & had Every Freeholder in the said Precinct to Attend at the Performance of the same to Wit; Henry Brown, Charles Judkins, John Wilburn Junʳ, Agness Freeman, James Chappell Junʳ, Abraham Brown, James Bell, John Williss, Silvanus Stokes, Thomas Spain, John Bowen, William Roland, Burrell Bell, Micajah Pettway, William Rose, Thomas Atkins, Edward Slate, William Smith, John Roland, John Atkins

          [Procession Masters] Charles Judkins
                         Silvanus Stokes

[112]

N° 3 An account of the Several Lands Processioned & the land Marks thereof renewed together with the Names of the Several Persons Owning Such Lands Respectively & a list of every Person present at yᵉ time of Processioning each Piece of land taken by us the Subscriber in Obedience to an Order of he Vestry of Albemarle Parish Bearing date the 8ᵗʰ Day of August 1755

Names of the Proprietors of the Several Lands	Persons present at Processioning	
Coll. Benjᵃ Harrison	Benjᵃ Harrison overseer	
John Pidington Senʳ	John Pidington Senʳ	
John Pidington	John Pidington	
Wᵐ Andrus	Wᵐ Andrus	
John Knight	John Knight	
Richᵈ King	Richᵈ King	First Day
John Clanton	John Clanton	
Wᵐ Rogers	Wᵐ Rogers	
Ephraim Knight	Richᵈ King	
Cornelius Loftin	Cornelius Loftin	
Richᵈ Avery	Richᵈ Avery	Second Day
John Rachel		
John Bishop	Cornelius Loftin &	
	Richᵈ Avery's	Return

N° 4 By Virtue of an Order of the Vestry of Albemarle Parish Bearing Date Augˢᵗ 8ᵗʰ 1755 Wee the Subscribers have assembled the Freeholders together within the Precinct Specified by yᵉ said Order & have Processioned & renewed the land Marks of the Several as follows to Wit, Benjamin Tomlinson,

March ye 4   Charles Gee, Richd Carter, Wyke Hunicutt, James Gee, Thomas Goodwynn, Wm Shands, William Eldridge, William Heath, Adam Heath, William Heath Junr, Benjamin Harrison, Thos Young & the Land of Peter Tatum Dec^d, Reubin Cook, William Cook, David Jones, William Shands,
Present when the above Land were Processioned Benj^a Tomlinson, Charles Gee, James Gee, Thos Goodwynn, William Shands, William Eldridge, William Heath, Adam Heath, Glaster Hunicut, Reubin Cook

David Jones &
William Cook   Return

[113]

N° 5 In obedience to an Order of Vestry held for ye Parish of Albemarle the Eight Day of August 1755 Wee the Subscribers have seen every Persons Land Processioned & the Land Marks Renewed according to to[sic] Order Appointed us

Proprietors		Persons Present
Robt Farrintons	Land	Robt Farrinton
Lewis Parhams	Land	Lewis Brown
John Holts	Land	John Roland
Burrell Green	Land	Burrell Green
James Mangums	Land	Jones Freeman
Amos Loves	Land	William Raney
William Richardson	Land	James Mangum
Charles Delihays	Land	Joseph Ingram
William Malones	Land	Josiah Freeman
Joshua Ellis	Land	Mical Hill
Joel Freemans	Land	John Hill
Josiah Freemans	Land	William Wilkerson
Robert Webb	Land	William Gilliam Sen
Agness Freemans	Land	William Winfield Senr
John Hills	Land	Nathl Malone
William Wilburns	Land	John Bonner
Mical Hills	Land	Wyat Harper
William Gilliams S^r	Land	William Richardson
Isaac Robertson	Land	William Winfield Junr
William Harpers	Land	Isaac Robertson
John Bonners	Land	
Nathl Malone	Land	
George Booth	Land	
Jarvis Wynfield	Land	
William Wynfield	Land	Test Richard Hill
John Tyas	Land	John Tyas
Richard Hill	Land	

N° 6   Pursuant to an Order of the Worshipful Vestry of Albemarle Parish Bearing Date the 8th Day of August 1755 Wee the Subscribers did on the 6th day of March 1756 Assemble the Freeholders within the Precinct Specified by the said Order & did Procession & the land Marks Renew of the Lands hereafter Mentioned to Wit — John Jarrads Land, Thomas Wallises Land, William Hineses Jun^{rs} Land, Henry Jarrads Land, James Chappell Jun^{rs} Land, Howel Brigges Land, James Chappells Land, John Kennebrens Land, Ja^s Winkleses Land, Benjamin Harrisons Land, John Joneses Land

Present
Howell Briggs, Ja^s Chappell, John Jones, John Kennebren, Thomas Wallis, William Hines
   [Procession Masters]   Ja^s Chappell, Junr & John Jarrad

[114]

N° 11 In obedience to an Order of Vestry Held for ye Parish of Albemarle the eight Day of August 1755 Wee the Subscribers have seen every Person Land Processioned & the Land Marks Renewed in the Precinct appoint us

Proprietors	Land	Persons Present
Robt Farrington	Land	Nathl Raney
Edward Powel	Land	Edward Powel
Wm Raney Senr	Land	George Robertson
George Randolph	Land	Ja^s Cain Senr
George Robertson	Land	Ja^s Banks
William Ellet	Land	
Benjn Harrison	Land	
Ja^s Cain Senr	Land	
Ja^s Cain Junr	Land	
Peter Cain	Land	Thos Wilkerson
Ja^s Banks	Land	David Owen
Thos Wilkerson	Land	Peter Green
Thos Sikes	Land	Fredrick Green
Fredrick Jones	Land	Thos Burrow
Thos Burrow	Land	Ja^s Moss
William Burrow	Land	
Ja^s Moss	Land	
Thos Butlers	Land	John Kelley
Thos Hunts	Land	Thos Hunt
John Carter	Land	John Hunt
John Kelley	Land	Wm Rachell
Thos Husons	Land	Robt Mitchell
John Jones	Land	Wm Mitchell
W^m & Danl Mitchells	Land	Danl Mitchell
Fredrick & Peter Greens	Land	Wyat Harper
John Farrintons	Land	
Wm Raney Junr	Land	Wyat Harpers

Test Robt Farrington
Wm Raney J^r

N° 12 In Obedience to an Order of Vestry Dated August ye 8th 1755 Directing us to procession the Land in the Precincts laid out to us by ye said Order Accordingly on ye Nineteenth day of March wee assembled the Freeholders & went in Quiet Procession & Renewed the Land Marks of the following Persons

	Persons Present
The Land of Moses Johnson	
The Land of Mr Wm Allen	Lewis Johnson
The Land of John Pidington	John Pidington
The Land of Mr Robt Jones	
The Land of Mr Joseph Pidington	Joshua Dickens
The Land of Lydia Dinkins	John Land
The Land of John Land	
The Land of the Revd Mr Willie	

[Procession Masters]
Moses Johnson   Joseph Pidington

[115]

N° 13 By Virtue of an Order of the Worshipfull the Vestry of the Parish of Albemarle Dated the 8th Day of August 1755 and to us Directed Wee have agreeable to ye said Order seen all the Lands in ye Precinct to us alotted Processioned & the Several land marks Renewed Except a line between Henry Tatum & Augustine Claiborne & a line Between Augustine Claiborne and ye Colledge who did not attend to have it Done in Presence of the Persons hereafter Mentioned

  John Bradley
  Matthew Gibbs   John Bradley
  Nathl Mitchell   Matthew Gibbs
  Thos Mitchell   Nathl Mitchell
  Ann Hulmne   George Reives
  George Reives   Christopher Reives
  Christopher Reives   David Mason
  Frances Reives   Joshua Harthorn
  David Mason   Robt Doby Junr
  Joshua Harthorn   Christopher Tatum
  Robert Doby
  Christopher Tatum

As Witness Our Hand this 4th Day of March 1756
Thos Mitchell
John Tatum

N° 14 By Virtue of an Order of the Worshipfull of the Parish of Albemarle Dated ye 8th Day of August 1755 & to us Directed wee have agreable to ye said Order seen all the land in ye Precinct to us alotted Processioned & the Several land Marks thereof Renewed in Presence of the Persons hereafter mention'd Viz:

  Proprietors Names   Persons Present
  Clement Hancock   Clement Hancock
  Robt Hancock   Dr John Hay
  Dr John Hay   Thos Adkins
  Edward Lee   John Adkins
  Henry Porch   Henry Porch
  Timothy Ezell J^r Joshua Meachum
  Hartwell Marrable   Timothy Ezell Junr
  John Adkins Junr Henry Moss
  Henry Moss
  Henry Meachum
  Wm Moss   Henry Moss
  Edward Eppes   Clement Hancock
  Dorrell Young   Peter Harthorn
  Wm Tomlinson   Jesse Moss
  Nathl Tomlinson   Joseph Denton
  The Glebe Land   John Adkins
  Rachel Harthorn
  Rebeckah Harthorn

As Witness our hands this 25th Day of Feby Anno Domini 1756
Edward Lee
Edward Eppes

[116]

N° 15 By Virtue of an Order of the Vestry of Albemarle Parish Dated the 8th of August 1755 & to us Directed we have Processioned the Land therein Mentioned & the same Lands Marks thereof have Renewed as follows

Lands	Persons Present
Wm Eldridge	Richd Reives
Richd Reives	Wm Petway
Wm Petway	Wm Weathers
Edward Petway	Wm Pettway Junr
Robert Pettway	Robt Pettway
Robt Parham	Stith Parham
Stith Parham	Thos Bobbit
Thos Bobbit	Holm Sturdavant
Susanna Rottenberry	John Wynne
John Threewitts	Matthew Wynne
Matthew Wynne	
John Wynne	
Holm Sturdavant Senr	
Holm Sturdavant Junr	[Procession Masters]
Sloman Wynne	Sloman Wynne
Henry Sturdavant	Henry Sturdavant

N° 16 In Obedience to an Order of the Vestry Dated ye eight Day August 1755 Directing that wee Procession all ye Laid out to us in the Precinct Accordingly on ye 13th day of March wee Assembled all the Freeholders & went in Quiet Procession & renewed the Land Marks of the following Persons Viz: Robt Hancock Present
Lewis Johnson Present

Coll Wm Lightfoot	Land	
Mr Wm Allens	Land	Present
Clem^t Hancock	Land	Present
Thos Wrens	Land	Present
Morriss Zills [Zell]	Land	Present
Joseph Wrens	Land	Present
John Zills	Land	Present
Thos Brewers	Land	Present
Benj^a Hunts	Land	Present
Wm Pain	Land	Present
Lambert Zills	Land	Morriss Zills present
Mr Richd Jones's	Land	John Jones present
Wm Bishops	Land	Present
Henry Jones's	Land	Present
John Pains	Land	Present
Thos Baileys	Land	Present
Thos Munfords	Land	Present
Isham Zills	Land	Present
Thos Harrisons	Land	

[Procession Masters]   Clem^t Hancock Senr
Robt Hancock

[117]

N° 17 Pursuant to an Order of the Worshipfull Vestry of Albemarle Parish Bearing Date the 8th Day of August 1755 Wee the Subscribers have assembled the Freeholders within Our Precinct and have Processioned & the land Marks Renewed of the Several Pieces of land hereafter Mentioned to Wit, George Wyches Land, William Parkers Land, William Allens Land, John Cargills Land, James Chappells Land, Robt Jones's Land, Elisabeth Chappells Land, John Chappells Land, David Jones's Land, Ja^s Jones's Land

Present

Wm Johnson, Ja^s Chappell, Benj^a Wyche, Richd Johnson, John Chappell, Robt Jones, Ja^s Jones
Wm Halls not Processioned because he did not give his attendance
March ye 16th 1756

[Procession Masters]   David Jones
Wm Parker

N° 18 Pursuant to an Order of the Vestry of Albemarle Parish Bearing Date the eight Day of August 1755 Wee the Subscribers have assembled the Freeholders of the land Lying Between Nottoway River & Assamusock Swamp below Robins Branch & Austins Branch Down to Southampton County Line & have Processioned & the Land Marks Renewed of the following Lands to Wit Richd Parkers Land, Ja^s Renns Land, Wm Hines's Land, Thos Hines's Land, David Hines's Land, Lazarus Drakes Land, Wm Howel Land, Wm Hines's Junr Land, Thos Renns Land, John Edmunds's Land, John Wowdons[?] Land, Saml Peetes Land, Benj^a Harrisons Land, Ja^s Chappells Land, William Edmunds's land, Thos Peters's Land, John Hunts, Peter Hines's, Richd Hines's, John Cargills

Present

Richard Parker, Ja^s Renn, Wm Hines, Thos Hines, David Hines, Lazarus Drake, William Howel, Joshua Hines Thos Renn, John Edmunds, John Wowdon, Saml Peete, Ja^s Chappell, Peter Hines
March ye 15th 1756

[Porcession Masters] William Edmunds
Thomas Peters Junr

[118]

N° 19 Pursuant to an Order of the Vestry of Albemarle Parish Bearing Date the 8th Day of August 1755 Wee the Subscribers have Processioned all the Line & Renewed all the Land-marks in ye said Order which are as follows to Witt

Thos Oliver		Thos Oliver
Wm Gilliam	Persons	John Wilborn
Richd Jones	Present	Richd Jones
Charles Delihay		Thos Wynne
Thos Wynne		Ja^s Jones
John Wilborn		Richd Jones J^r
Ephraim Parham		Matthew Parham J^r
Matthew Parham	Persons	Wm Parham
Wm Parham	Present	John Hobbs
Burrell Green		Wm Hunt
Wm Green		George Pryer
John Watkins		Wm Huit
Wm Huit	Persons	Francis Eppes
Francis Eppes	Present	Wm Parham
Isham Smith		Isham Smith
		George Robertson

[Procession Masters]   Matthew Parham
Ephraim Parham

N° 20 In Compliance to an Order of Vestry Held for Albemarle Parish August ye 8th 1755 Wee the Subscribers have seen Every Mans land Mark Renewed in Our Presence

Charles Mabry
John Moss
John Richardson
George Long
John Hargrave
Thos Dunn
James Carter
Edward Shelton
Thos Battle
Thos Newsum
Henry Manncey
Benj^a Richardson

Mary Brown
Henry Richardson
Joseph Harwood
George Cornet
Gregory Rawlings
Richard Rawlings
Martha Bullock
Henry Tyler
Phillip Harwood
Nathl Felts
All those Present

[Procession Masters]   William Knight
John Battle

[119]

N° 21 Pursuant to an Order of Vestry of Albemarle Parish Bearing Date the Eight of August one Thousand Seven Hundred & fifty five Wee the Subscribers have assembled the Proprietors of the Lands from Surry County Lines up Between Tarrapin & Seacock Swamps to Birch island Road & up ye said Road to the Head of the said Seacock Swamp & have processioned & Renewed the Land Marks of the following lands Viz,t.
Benj^a Hancocks Land, David Andrews Land, William Bradleys, John Hançocks, Joseph Pettways, John Pressons, Humphreys Balis's, William Rogers Senr Capt Howel Briggs. Thos Clary's, Ann Fields, Wm Carrels, Timothy Santees, Mrs Bellamy's, Frances Sharp's & Cumboe's[sic], Thos Mias's, Charles Judkins's, & Our Own Lands Present Capt Howel Briggs, Humphry Balis, Wm Rogers Senr, John Poesson, Thos Clary, Thomas Mias, Wm Carrel, Timothy Santee, Benj^a Clary, Nicholas Hancock, John Bradley, Wm Bradley, Henry Bradley, & Benj^a Hancock ——————————— The Lands of Saml Magget, Buford Pleasant & Saml Rogers, not Processioned, the Reason of which was they did not give their attendance to see the same Performrd
March ye 12th: 1756

[Procession Masters]   Robert Nicolson
William Hancock

N° 22 In Obedience to an Order of the Worshipfull Vestry of Albemarle Parish Bearing Date ye 8th Day of August 1755 to us Directed Wee have Procession,^{d} the Several lines in ye order mentioned have Renewed ye Land Marks thereof

Lands Processioned
Mr Gray Briggs
Wm Cook
Ephraim Knight
Matthew Sturdavant
Susannah Rottenberry
Matthew Whitehead
Drewry Spain
Nathl Hood
John Anderson Sturdavant
John Spain
Richd Reives Se^r
Coll Robert Bolling
Robert Newman
Wm Stuart
Peter Reives

Persons Present
Lambert Zills
Ja^s Cook
Richd Knight
Matthew Sturdavant
Brian Senal
Matthew Whitehead
Drewry Spain
Nathl Hood
John Anderson Sturdavant
Ja^s Spain
Wm Reives
Lewis Tyas
Robt Newman
Wm Stuart
Peter Reives

William Stuart   Processioners
Peter Reives

[120]

N° 23 Pursuant to an Order of the Worshipful Vestry of Albemarle Parish Bearing Date ye 8th Day of August 1755 Wee the Subscribers have assembled the Freeholders within our Precinct & have Possessioned & the Land Marks Renewed of the Lands here Mentioned) to Wit. Edward Weavers Land, John Masons Land, Wm Halls Land, John Sledges Land, Alexander Finnies Land, John Ogburns Land, Charles Sledges Land, John Underhill Land, Reubin Cooks Land

Present

Joseph Cotes, John Sledge, Reubin Cook, Ja^s Tomlinson, John Underhill, Charles Sledge
March ye 10th 1756   Edward Weaver} Procession Master
           & John Ogburn} Procession Master

N° 24 Pursuant to an Order of the Worshipfull Vestry of Albemarle Parish Bearing Date ye 8th Day of August 1755 Wee ye Subscribers have Assemble the Freeholders within our Precinct and have Processioned & the Land Marks Renewed of the lands hereafter Mentioned to Wit
Henry Jarrads Land, John Barkers Land, Howle Briggs Land, John Lambs Land, Ja^s Jones's Land, Robert Jones Land, Petway Johnsons Land, Thos Cullums Land, Wm Briggs's Land, Wm Johnsons Land

Present

Jehu Barker, Petway Johnson, Wills Partridge, Howell Briggs, John Lamb, Robt Jones Wm Hite, Wm Johnson, Nathl Johnson Land Mark not Renewed By his not attending Jany 13th & 14th 1756

                                          Nicholas Partridge
                    Procession Masters   & Henry Jarrad

N° 25 By Virture of an Order of the Vestry of Albemarle Parish Dated ye 8th of August 1755 & to us Directed Wee have Processioned the Lands therein Mentioned & Same Land Marks therof have Renew as follow

Land	Persons Present
John Parham	John Parham
Ja^s Parham	Ja^s Parham
Charles Leath	John Leath Senr
John Leath	John Leath Junr
Joshua Poytress	Abraham Parham
Wm Parham	
Matthew Parham	
Abraham Parham	

As Witness Our hand this 25th Day of Feby 1756
                         [Procession Masters]   Thos Parham

                                                          Matthew Parham

[121]

N° 26 In obedience to an Order of Vestry Dated the eight day of August 1755 Wee the Subscribers have Processioned every Person Lands & Renewed the Land Marks thereof between the Poplar and the great Swamp in Albemarle Parish Sussex County

Lines Processioned Between	Persons Present	Lines Processioned Between
Henry Tyler & Adam Toy	John Battle Senr John Maclamore Adam Toy	John Barns & John Bishop

Surry and Sussex Counties, Virginia, 1742-1786

Henry Ty &
Burrell Macklemore

Henry Tyler &
Thoˢ Kersey

Henry Tyler &
Jnº Maclamore

Thoˢ Pate &
Edward Pate

Thoˢ Pate &
Edward Harris

Thoˢ Pate &
Edward Prince

Henry Tyler &
Edward Prince

Edward Prince &
Franˢ Aldridge

Henry Tyler &
Franˢ Aldridge

Benjᵃ Adams &
Jeremiah Bullock

Benjᵃ Adams &
Joseph Ezell

Jeremiah Bullock &
Joseph Ezell

Joseph Roberts &
Joseph Ezell

Jeremiah Bullock &
Vol: Wᵐson

Jeremiah Bullock &
Vol: Wᵐson

Joseph Roberts &
Vol: Wᵐson

John Barnes &
Jeremiah Bullock

Wᵐ Hix &
Jeremiah Bullock

John Barnes &
Vol: Wᵐson

John Battle Senʳ
Jnº Maclamore
Thoˢ Pate Junʳ
Burrel Maclamore

Burrel Maclamore
Edward Prince

Joseph Ezell
Burrell Maclamore
Edward Prince
Jeremiah Bullock

John Hill &
John Bishop

John Battle Senʳ &
John Hill

John Bradley &
John Battle Senʳ

John Battle Junʳ &
Peter Avent

Thoˢ Avent &
Peter Avent

Thoˢ Avent &
John Battle Junʳ

Peter Avent &
John Bradley

John Bradley &
Jaˢ Stuart

Peter Avent &
Jaˢ Stuart

John Battle Senʳ &
John Hill

Wᵐ Hix &
John Bishop

Jeremiah Bullock &
John Bishop

Thoˢ Avent &
Peter Brooks

Thoˢ Avent &
Joseph Prince

Wᵐ Battle &
Joseph Prince

Dread Jelks &
Joseph Prince

98   The Vestry Book of Albemarle Parish

[122]

Persons Present	Lines Processioned Between	Persons Present
John Barns		
Joseph Ezell	Dread Jelks &	Persons Present
Wm Tyler	Wm Battle	
John Bullock		
Wm Hix	Thos Avent &	
John Sandafer	Wm Battle	
Jeremiah Bullock		
	Wm Battle &	
	Robt Linn	
	Thos Avent &	
	Wm Hix	
	Wm Battle &	
	Matthew Hubbud	
	John Sandaford &	
	Wm Hix	
Wm Tyler	Thos Briggs &	
John Barns	Wm Hix	John Battle
John Bullock		John Barns
Wm Hix	Edward Linsey &	Jeremiah Bullock
Edward Prince	Thos Adams	Nathl Johnson
Jeremiah Bullock		Phillip Harwood
John Sandafer	Edward Linsey &	Edward Freeman
Wm Tyler	Thos Adams	
John Battle Junr		John Battle
John Barns	Edward Linsey &	John Barns
John Sandafer	John Morgan	Phillip Harwood
Wm Knight		Edward Freeman
John Barns	Ja^s Bass &	Ja^s Bass
John Sandafer	Matth: Hubbud	
John Battle		
John Hill	Wm Sammons &	Burrell Maclamore
Richd Barlow	Matth: Hubbud	Edward Prince
	Wm Sammons &	
	Robt Lin	
	Wm Sammons &	
	Cornelius Mabry	
		[Procession Masters]
	Matthew Hubbud &	Henry Tyler
	Wm Sammons	Thomas Pate
	Edward Prince &	
	Francis Aldridge	
	Benj^a Adams &	
	Francis Aldridges	

[123]

Nº 27 In obedience to an Order of the Worshipfull Vestry of Albemarle Parish Dated August yᵉ 8ᵗʰ 1755 and to us Directed Wee have on thie 14ᵗʰ Day of February 1756 assembled all yᵉ Freeholders in the Precinct in yᵉ sᵈ order Mentioned & Processiond & Renewed the Land Marks of every Persons land by Consent of the Parties as followeth Viz.t

The Line Betwext Timothy Ezell & Jaˢ Mason	In Presence of Timothy Ezell, Eppes Moor
The Line Betwixt Jaˢ Mason & Wᵐ More	Jaˢ Heath, Thoˢ Heath John Smith John Dunn
The Line Betwixt Jaˢ Mason Edward Petway & Wᵐ More	
The Line Betwixt Wᵐ More & Edward Petway	
The Line Betwext Wᵐ More & Eppes More	In Presents[sic] of Ditto In Presents of Ditto
The Line Betwext Edward Petway & Eppes More	In Presents of Ditto In Presents of Ditto
The Line Betwixt Eppes Moor & Henry Mitchell	In Presents of Timothy Ezell Eppes Moor
The Line Betwixt Henry Mitchell & Jaˢ Heath	Jaˢ Heath Thoˢ Heath John Smith John Dunn & Henry Mitchell
The Line Betwixt Edward Petway & Jaˢ Heath	In Presents of Ditto
The Line Betwixt Edward Petway & John Smith	In Presents of Ditto
The Line Betwixt John Smith & Thoˢ Heath	In Presents of Ditto
The Line Betwixt Thoˢ Heath & Peter Poytress	In Presents of Ditto
The Line Betwixt Peter Poytress & Edward Petway	In Presents of Ditto

[Procession Masters]
Edward Petway
William Moore

[124]

N° 28 An Account of the Several Lands Procession'd together with ye Particular Names of the Persons Holding Such Lands Respectively and a List of the Persons Present at the time of Processioning each Tract of Land and Renewing the Landmarks Taken by us the Subscribers Pursuant to an Order of the Worshipful The Vestry of Albemarle parish bearing Date the 8th Day of August 1755

Number of Acres	To Whom Belonging	Persons Present at Processioning
545	Thomas Moore	Thomas Moore, Levy Gilliam, John Rachel,
100	Levy Gilliam	Cornelius Loftin, William Loftin,
768	John Rachel	Nathaniel Clanton, John Hargrave, Thomas
480	Cornelius Loftin	Capel, Jones Stokes, Henry Freeman,
385	William Loftin	Robert Land & Curtis Land
190	Nathl Clanton	
574	John Hargrave	
345	Thomas Capel	
500	Jones Stokes	
50	Henry Freeman	[Procession Masters]
225	Robt Land	Robert Webb Junr
215	Curtis Land	Charles Battle
905	Robert Webb Junr	
280	Charles Battle	

N° 29 An Account of the Several Peices[sic] of Land Processioned & the Land Marks thereof Remarked by us the Subscribers pursuant to an Order of the Vestry of Albemarle Parish bearing Date the 8th Day of August 1755 and a List of the Persons present at the time of Processioning each Peice together withe the Names of the Persons owning Such Land Respectively

Names of ye Proprietors		Persons Present at Processioning
John Lambs	Land	Processioned in Presence of Howel Briggs
Howel Briggs	D°	Thos Alsobrook, John Wallace,
John Briggs's	D°	Thos Alsobrook, John Wallace,
John's	D°	Edward Wright D° D°
Thos Alsobrooks	D°	D° D° Howel Briggs, John Wallace
Richd Fitzpatrick's	D°	D° D° D° D°
Wm Hughlins	D°	D° D° D° D°
Edward Wrights	D°	D° D° D° D°
John Wallaces	D°	D° D° D° D°
Saml Maggets	D°	D° Wm Rogers, Thos Alsobrook
Humphrys Bailis's	D°	D° Wm Rogers, Thos Alsobrook
Wm Rogers's	D°	D° Humphry Balis & Ditto

[Procession Masters]
Samuel Maggett
John Alsobrook

[125]

Nᵘ 30 An Account of the Several Lands Processioned and Land Marks Renewed together with the names of the several Persons Owning Such Lands Respectively and a List of every Person Present at the time of Processioning Such Peice of Land taken by us the Subscribers in Obedience to an Order of the Vestry of Albemarle Parish bearing Datae August 8ᵗʰ 1755

Names of the Proprietors of the Several Lands only	Persons Present at Processioning
Part of Timothy Thorps	Timothy Thorp at Processioning Own
Part of John Nanneys	John Nanny
Part of each not being in Our Precinct	Samuel Alsobrook Senʳ
Samuel Alsobrook Senʳ	Samuel Alsobrook Junʳ
Samuel Alsobrook Junʳ	Major Tiller
Major Tillers	Nathaniel Wyche
and Nathˡ Wyches	
a part of John Stewarts the other part not in Our Precinct and also all Our Own	[Procession Masters] James Wyche Joseph Thorp

Pursuant to an Order of the Vestry of Albemarle Parish Dated the 8ᵗʰ Day of August 1755 Wee the Subscribers have assembled the Freeholders within the Precinct Specified by the said Order and have Processioned & the Land Marks Renewed of the Land hereafter Mentioned to Wit Benjamin Harrisons Land, Stephen Hamlins Land, Nathaniel Briggs's Land, Simon Murfees Land, George Briggs's Land, Robert Baleys Land, Nathaniel Davis's Land, William Hicks's Land, Joseph Ellis's Land, Joseph Lanes Land, Henry Sorrons[?] Land, James Turners Land, William Bells Land, Thoˢ Gresswitts Land, John Barkers Land, which Concludes the Precinct Mentioned in the said Order Present at the Processioning Robert Bailey, William Hicks, Joseph Ellis, Arthur Murfee, Nathaniel Briggs, Nathaniel Jones, William Felts, Simon Murfee, Henry Sorron, Joseph Lane, John Long ------ Thoˢ Gresswitt, William Bell, not Present at the Processioning being Remov'd out of the County John Barker, Nathaniel Davis Not present at the Processioning Not Living in the County
March yᵉ 10ᵗʰ 1756   [Procession Masters]   George Briggs & Stephen Hamlin

[126]

At a Vestry Held for the Parish of Albemarle in the County of Sussex at Nottoway Church on the 26ᵗʰ Day of November 1756

Present
The Rev'd William Willie
Thomas Avent   James Gee
James Chappell   Moses Johnson } Gent
Augustine Claiborne & John Mason

Albemarle Parish	Dr	Wt Lbˢ Tobᵒ
To the Revᵈ William Willie as Minister		17,305
To John Tatum as Clerk of Nottoway Church 6 mo		600
To Robᵗ Nicolson as Clerk of Sᵗ Pauls Dᵒ		1,200
To Gregory Rawlings as Dᵒ of Sᵗ Andrews Dᵒ		1,200
To Robᵗ Farrinton as Dᵒ & Sexton of Sᵗ Marks Dᵒ		1,700

To John Denton as Sexton of Nottoway D⁰	500
To John Bain as D⁰ of S¹ Pauls D⁰	500
To Edward Shelton as D⁰ of S¹ Andrews D⁰	500
To Moses Johnson for keeping John Kings lame child a y'	800
To Matthew Whitfield for keeping Rebecca Bird a y'	800
To J' Chappell J' as Clerk of the Vestry	400
To D⁰ for other Services	200
To Edward Walker as Clerk of Nottoway Church 6 Mo.	600
	26305
To 6 per cent for collecting 35952 lb' Tob⁰	2157
	28462
To levied for the use of the Parish	7490
	35952
D⁰ C'	
By 2247 Tithes at 16 lb' of Tob⁰ per Pole	35952

By Consent of the Church wardens it is Ordered that the Sheriff Upon Entering into Bond & Security as Usual Collect from every tithable Person in the Parish 16 Lb' of Tobacco & pay out of the Same According to the above State of the Levy

[127]

Ordered that the Churchwardens pay to the following Persons the Respective Sums Set to their Names Viz'

To William Aldridge as per Account	£0:8:0
To Nath' Bedingfield as per account	2:0:6
To Rich' Reives as per account	1:6:4
To John Denton for Diging a Grave for Mary Delihay a Pensioner	0:1:3

Richard Hay has a greed[sic] with the Vestry to keep David & Sarah Children of Susanna Goff for the Sum of Six pounds fifteen Shillings for the year ensuing finding them Necessaries

Ordered that the Churchwardens pay to Richard Hay the Sum of three Pounds ten Shillings for keeping David & Sarah Children of Susanna Goff Seven Months

Ordered that the Churchwardens pay Six pounds fifteen Shillings & Six Pence for the Several Articles in his account allow'd he giving Bond in ten pound & Security to keep the Bricking & Curb of the Well in repair Seven Years

Ordered that William Rogers & Richard Felts be exempted from Paying their Parish Levies for the future

Ordered that John Knight be paid for keeping Frances Hood one Year According to his Agreement made with M' Robert Jones Jun'

John King Jun' has agreed with the Vestry to keep Frances Hood for the Year Ensuing & find her all Necessaries for five Hundred Pounds of Tobacco

William Aldridge Appeared & Undertaken to Maintain two Children of Mical Odonally, Viz' Hugh & James till the 15th of October Next at the Rate of Nine Hundred pounds of Tobacco Per Year

Ordered that the Churchwardens pay to W'm Renn four pounds for keeping Hugh & James Odonally for the last Ten months

Surry and Sussex Counties, Virginia, 1742-1786 103

The return of Samˡ Maggett & John Alsobrook & Robert Webb & Charles Battle & George Briggs & Stephen Hamlin & James Wyche & Joseph Thorp Processioners Appointed by former Order of Vestry was this Day Made examᵈ Approved & to be Registered

Wᵐ Willie Minʳ
Copy Test Jaˢ Chappell Junʳ Clk Vest.

[128]

In Obedience to an Order of the Worshipful Vestry Held for the Parish of Albemarle in the County of Sussex Dated the eight Day of August 1755 Wee the Subscribers Have met & Processioned all the Lands in Our Precincts & the Land Marks Renewed Belonging to the Proprietors Under Written as in the said Order Expressed

	Proprietors Names	Persons Present
Day	Benjamin Harrison	Lawrence Gibbon
of the	Josiah Smith	Isham Smith
month	Isham Smith	John Wilkerson
March Yᵉ	John Wilkerson	Jaˢ Renn
1ˢᵗ 1756	James Banks	
	Thoˢ Wilkerson	Josiah Smith
	Thoˢ Sykes	Berry Smith
	Richᵈ Pepper	
	Lawrence Gibbons	
2ⁿᵈ day	Wᵐ Yarbrough	William Rachel
	Peter Randolph	William Mitchell
	George Randolph	Thoˢ Mitchell
	Thoˢ Wade	Jaˢ Renn
	Edward Jones	Edward Jones
	Benjamin Bell	
	Thoˢ Mitchell	Wᵐ Yarbrough
	Thoˢ Vines	
	Thoˢ Vaughan	
	Colledge	
18ᵗʰ	John Mitchell	Edward Buckner
	Wᵐ Mitchell	Henry Porch
	David Blanks	John Woodward
	Wᵐ Rachell	Wᵐ Rachell
	Thoˢ Vaughan	Thoˢ Butler
	Jaˢ Porch	Thoˢ Mitchell
	Edward Buckner	David Blanks
	John Woodard	Wᵐ Mitchell Jʳ
		Thoˢ Vines Processioners
		Thoˢ Butler

[129]

At a Vestry held for the Parish of Albemarle in the County of Sussex at Nottoway Church on the 12ᵗʰ Day of April 1757 being Easter Tuesday

Present
The Revᵈ William Willie

Thoˢ Avent   Jaˢ Gee
Jaˢ Chappell   Moses Johnson } Gent
John Mason   Ephraim Parham

Ja^s Gee & Moses Johnson are Appointed Churchwardens for the Year ensuing

Ordered that the Churchwardens pay to the Revd William Willie the Sum of three Pounds eight Shilling & Six pence Out of the Money in their Hands belonging to the Parish

Ordered that the Collector Pay to John Wright 900^{lbs} of Tobacco for Keeping Frances Hood 1 Year

Ordered that the Churchwardens pay to John Earwood the Sum of four Pounds eleven Shillings & eight Pence for keeping Ephraim Muns from the 15th Day of May 1756 till this Day

Ordered that Job Warwick be exempted from Paying his parish Levy for the future

Ordered that Howell Briggs pay to Thomas Cullum the fifty five Shillings in his Hands which has accrued to this Parish from fines & forfeitures

William Willie Min^r
Copy Test Ja^s Chappell J^r Clk Vestry

[130]

At a Vestry held at Nottoway Church for the Parish of Albemarle in the County of Sussex on the 18th Day of July 1757

Present
The Revd William Willie

Ja^s Gee		Moses Johnson	
Ja^s Chappell		Augustin Claiborne	} Gent
John Mason	&	Ephraim Parham	

Maj^r Nicholas Massenburg is Appointed & Elected to Serve this Parish as a Vestry Man instead of Mr Robert Jones Junr who has Resigned his place & Removed out of the Parish & that he Qualify as Soon as Possible to Serve this Parish in that Capacity

Ordered that the Revd William Willie, Augustine Claiborne, James Gee and Nicholas Massenburg or any three of them Examine State & Settle the Several accounts of Churchwardens of this Parish from the Year 1750 to the Year 1756 inclusive in Order to the said accounts being laid before the Vestry for their Approbation

Ordered that the Churchwardens pay to the Revd William Willie the Sum of one Pound Nineteen Shillings Out of the Money in their Hands belonging to the Parish

William Willie Min^r
Copy Test Ja^s Chappell Junr Clk Vestry

[131]

At a Vestry for the Parish of Albemarle in the County of Sussex at Nottoway Church on ye 29th Day of October 1757

Present
The Revd Wm Willie

Ja^s Gee	Moses Johnson	
Augustine Claiborne	John Mason	} Gent
John Edmunds	Ephraim Parham	
& Nicholas Massenburg		

Surry and Sussex Counties, Virginia, 1742-1786   105

Albemarle Parish	Dr	W^t lbs of Tob^o
To the Revd William Willie as Min^r		17305
To Ed^d Walker as Clerk at Nottoway Church		1200
To Robt Nicolson as D^o at St Pauls D^o		1200
To Robt Farrinton as D^o at St Marks D^o		1200
To D^o D^o as D^o at S^t D^o D^o		500
To Gregory Rawlings as D^o at St Andrews D^o		1200
To John Bain as Sexton at St Pauls D^o		500
To Edward Shelton as D^o at St Andrews D^o		500
To William Rigbey as D^o at Nottoway D^o		500
To Moses Johnson for keeping John [King] a lame Child 1 year		800
To Matthew Whitfield for keeping Rebecca Bird 1 D^o		800
To Ja^s Chappell J^r as Clerk of the Vestry		400
To John King J^r for keeping Frances Hood 11 Months		500
To Wm Aldridge for keeping Ja^s Odonally 11 Months		412½
To D^o D^o for keeping Hugh D^o 11 D^o		375
		2392½
To Levied for the Use of the Parish		3022
To the Collector for Collecting 32355 lbs of Tob^o & (?) it away		1941
		32355½
Albemarle Parish	Cr	
By 2157 Taxables at 15 lbs of Tobo Pr Taxable		32355

[132]

Ord^d that James Gee on his entering into Bond & Security to the Vestry of this Parish to be taken by the Clerk of Vestry be Appointed Collector of this Parish for the year ensuing & that he collect & Receive of every Person Chargable therewith the Sum of 15 pounds of Tobacco Per Pole & that he have Authority in case the Said 15 pounds of Tobacco or any Part thereof be Delay'd or Refus'd to Levy the same by Distress & that he pay to each Respective Parish Creditor the Several Sums of Tobacco due to them & that he pay the Tobacco levied for the use of the Parish to the Churchwardens for ye time being

Ord^d that the Churchwardens pay to Wm Connelly the sum of fifty Shillings for finding Tarr & Taring St Marks Church

Ord^d that the Collectors Pay to John Pidington for removing Jane Field 20 miles according to Law

Ord^d that the Churchwardens pay to Ephraim Parham the Sum of Six Shillings & 3 pence for finding Nails & Mending the Pughs[sic] at St Marks Church

Ord^d that the Churchwardens pay to Thos Cullum the Sum of three Pounds for keeping his Son Fredrick & finding him Necessaries the Year Past

Ord^d that Joseph Morriss be exempted from paying his parish Levy for the future

Ord^d that the Churchwardens lay out fifty five Shillings in Cloathing [for] Henry Tudor a Poor Ancient Man

Ord^d That the Churchwardens take care of Daniel & James Odonnally for the Year ensuing

---

Ephraim Parham has a Greed[sic] with the Vestry to keep James Odonnally for the Year ensuing & find him Necessaries for 400 pounds of Tobacco

Ord^d that the Churchwardens pay to Isham Browder the Sum of fifteen Shillings for Transcribing the 39 articles of the Church of England

---

Capt. Samuel Peete is chosen to Serve this Parish as a Vestry Man instead of Mr Ray Briggs who has resign'd his place of Vestry Man & remov'd out of the Parish

The Gen' of the Vestry now Present Subscribed the 39 articles of the Church of England

W'" Willie Min'
Copy Test Ja' Chappell J' Clk Vestry

[133]

1757 Albemarle Parish	Dr
	£ S D
June To Cash Borrowed for the use of the Parish Viz'	
24 £14:11:7 & Dispossed of in in[sic] the Manner following to Wit.	
To paid Rob' Glover	6:15: 6
To paid Nathaniel Bedingfield	2: 0: 6
To paid William Renn	4: 0: 0
To paid Richard Rives	1: 6: 4
To be paid to William Aldridges order to Capt John Mason	0: 8: 0
To the Rev^d M' William Willie as P his acct.	1:19: 0
To paid W'" Connally P order of Vestry	2:10: 0
To paid Isham Browder P Ditto	0:15: 0
To paid Richd Hay	2: 3: 0
To paid Thos Cullum	3: 0: 0
To paid Richd Hay	5:12: 0
To paid John Earwood	5:13: 8
To paid Ephraim Parham	0: 6: 3
To paid John Peter for 17 panes of Window Glass	0:17: 8
Ballance Due to the Parish	37: 6:11
Ballance Due to the Parish	25: 8: 2
	62:15: 1
1757 Albemarle Parish for fines	Dr
To paid Henry Tuder	2:14: 2
To paid Sarah Evans	0: 3: 0
To Peter Smith for his Daughter	0: 1: 9
Ballance Due to the Parish	3:11: 1
	£6:10: 0
Dr Albemarle Parish	
To paid M' Willie	£3:14: 6
To paid Joseph Denton P order John Denton	0: 1: 3
To Repaid in Tob° Levied 3^{lb} a' 14/P C'	0: 0: 5¼
To paid Cap' Mason P' order Vestry in favor M' Willie	3: 8: 6
	7: 4: 8¼
Ballance due to the Parish	18: 3: 5¼
Tob° Levied for the use of the Parish Anno: 1756: lbs Tob° 7490	25: 8: 2
Ballance due to Churchwardens & paid as above 3	
7493	

[134]

Contra Cr	£ S D
By M' Jones P the Hands of M' Willies	15: 0: 0
By Ditto	5: 0: 0
By 1062 lb. Tob° Sold Howel Briggs a' 11/5	6: 1: 2
By 2240 lb. Tob° Sold D8I'(?) John Hays 11/5	13: 1: 4
By 3291 lb. Tob° Peters & Belsheres 14/	23: 0: 9
By Interust[sic] of Money Rec^d to the treasury	0:11:1
	£ 62:15:1

Surry and Sussex Counties, Virginia, 1742-1786

P	Contra	Cr
By the following fines Rec^d Viz^t	£	
of Wm Edmunds for Swearing		0:5:0
of John Wallace for D^o		0:5:0
of Edward Slate for D^o		0:5:0
of Thos Wallace for D^o		0:5:0
of John Adkinson for D^o		0:5:0
of Lucresa Parham for Basterdy		2:10:0
By Samuel Chappell, John Lucas, Wm Conellon, Ja^s Jones		
& an Unknown hand for Swearing 5/each		1:5:0
By Richd Knight & Thos Dowdy 15/each		1:10:0
		£ 6:10: 0
By Ballance Brought from Other side		£28: 8:2

```
Sold as above           6593
paid John Knight         900
errors Excepted         7493
```
March
28th 1758

Ja^s Gee
& Moses Johnson Chwardens

[135]

At a Vestry Held at Nottoway Church for the Parish of Albemarle in the County of Sussex on the 28th Day of March 1758 being Easter Tuesday

Present
The Revd William Willie

Ja^s Gee   Moses Johnson
Howel Briggs   James Chappell } Gent.
Aug:^{e} Claiborne   John Mason
& Nicholas Massenburg

Howel Briggs & Nicholas Massenburg are Appointed Churchwardens for the Year ensuing

James Gee & Moses Johnson late Church wardens this day Rendered their accounts in Vestry which accounts was Examined allowed & ordered to be Registered

Ordered that the Churchwardens Pay to Howel Briggs the Sum of Two pounds fourteen Shillings & Seven Pence out of the Money in their hands Belonging to the Parish

Allowed Matthew Whitfield the Sum of one Pound Nine Shillings & Three Pence for burying Rebecca Bird a pensioner of this Parish

Matthew Whitfield has agreed to pay the Sum of Two pound to the Parish for a Bed & furniture that did belong to said Rebecca Bird

Orderd that the Churchwardens Pay to John Battle the Sum of one Pound Ten Shillings for keeping Edward Facy 7 Months

Order'd that the Churchwardens Pay to Izodoniah a christian[sic] Higgs the Sum of one Pound three Shillings out of the Money in their hands which has accrued to this Parish from fines & forfeitures

Ordered that the Churchwardens pay to Selah Huland the Sum of one Pound three Shillings out of the Money in their Hands which has accrued to this Parish from fines & forfeitures

Ordered that the Churchwardens pay to Sarah Capewell the Sum of one Pound five Shillings & one Penny out of the money in their hands which has accrued to this Parish from fines & forfeitures

[136]

Ordered that John & Joseph Barker be exempted from paying their Parish Levies for the future

Ordered that James Hearn be exempted from paying Parish levy for his Son James

Ordered that the Churchwardens Pay to Augustin Claiborne the sum of four Pounds & that the said Claiborne Lay out the said Money towards Supporting Andrew Kings Children

Ordered tht the Churchwardens pay to Moses Johnson the Sum of three Pounds eighteen Shillings in favour of John Earwood

Wm Willie Min^r
Copy Test Ja^s Chappell Junr Clk Vestry

[137]

At a Vestry Held for the Parish of Albemarle in the County of Sussex at Nottoway Church on the 90th Day of Novr 1758

Present
The Revd Mr Wm Willie

Howel Briggs
Nich^s Massenburg } Chwarden
Ja^s Gee

John Mason
Ephraim Parham } Gent
Aug: Claiborne } Vestry Men

Albemarle Parish	Dr
	N° lb^s Tob°
To the Revd Wm Willie Min^r	17305
To Ed^d Walker Clerk at Nottoway Church	1200
To John Nicolson D° at St Pauls D°	1200
To Amos Love Clerk at St Marks Church from 15th of Decr 1757 to 15th Octr 1758	1000
To Gregory Rawlings Clerk at St Andrews Church	1200
To Richd Wiggins Sexton at Nottoway Church from 15th of Decr to 15th of Octr 1758	412
To John Bain Sexton at St Pauls D°	500
To Ed^d Shelton D° at St Andrews D°	500
To Peter Green D° at St Marks D°	500
To Mr Moses John[son] for keeping John King a lame Child	800
To Mr Ephraim Parham for keeping Ja^s Odonnally 1 y^r	400
To Ja^s Chappell as Clerk of the Vestry	400
To Capt John Mason for overpaid last Year as Collec^r	16

To Wm Briggs for 6 Parish Levies paid in his own Wrong	90
To John Hood for takeing care of Frances Hood	500
To Levied for the Use of the Parish	3955
To the Collec^r for Collecting 31890 lbs of Tob° a^t 6 Pr Cent	1913
	31890
Albemarle Parish Cr	
By 2126 Tithables a^t 15lbs of Tob° Pr Pole	31890

Ord^d that James Gee on his entering into Bond & Security to the Vestry of this Parish to be taken by the Clerk of the Vestry be appointed Collector of this Parish for the Year ensuing & that he collect & Receive of every Person Chargable therewith the Sum of 15 pounds of Tob° Pr Pole or any part thereof be Delay'd or refused to Levy the same by Distress & that he pay to each Respective Parish Creditor the Several Sums of Tob° Due to them & that he pay the Tob° levied for the use of the Parish to the Churchwardens for the time Being

[138]

Ord^d that the Churchwardens lay Put four Pounds two Shillings in Necessaries for Henry Tudor a nantaine[?] Infirm Man & his Children according to Instructions given them this Day

Ord^d that Andrew King, Thos Lashley & John Earwood be exempted from Payment of Parish levy for the future

Ord^d That the Churchwardens Pay to Phillip Harwood ten Shillings for Provision by him purchased for Releif of Alse Felts

Ord^d that the Churchwardens Pay to John Roland on the 15th of March Next Seven Pounds Ten Shillings for keeping & Maintaining John Muns two Years the Compleat

Ord^d that the Churchwardens Pay to Richd Hay Seven Pounds ten Shillings for keeping & Maintaining David & Sarah Goff one Year ending 15th Octr last

Ord^d that the Churchwardens Pay to James Ball Thirty Shillings for keeping Edward Facie to this Day

Ord^d that the Churchwardens Pay unto Thos Cullum Thirty five Shillings for taking care of Fredrick Cullum to ye 22^d of Sepr last

Ord^d that the Churchwardens Pay to Richd Wiggins in Satisfaction of his Acct. eight Shillings

Ord^d that Ten Pounds Current Money be paid to the Revd Mr Willie for the Purchase of two Bibles for the use of Albemarle Parish

Howel Briggs Churchwarden inform'd the Vestry that he contracted with Thos Battail for keeping & Maintaining Ja^s Odonnally at three Pounds fifteen Shillings to commence the 31st of Octr last

Wm Willie Min^r
Copy Test Ja^s Chappell J^r Clk Vestry

[139]

Dr   Albermarle Parish in Account with Howel

1758	To Cash paid the Widow Capell of the fines	£ 1: 5: 0
April 21	To 2^{lb} Sugar for Bell Smith Child	0: 1: 3
June 16	To John Yearwood Paid him	5: 0: 0
	To Ephraim Parham Paid him	0: 1: 3
	To James Carter Paid him	4:10: 0
Novr 9	To the Revd William Willie for Sacramental Elements	6: 0: 0
1759		
Jany 23^d	To John Mason paid him for Barlow	0:12: 6
Feby 18	To Robt Wynne Executor paid him	1: 0: 0
March 16	To Cash paid for 2 Bibles	10: 0: 0
	To Catherine Yearwood p^d her Pr Cap: Gee	2: 0: 0
	To John Pidington 80^{lb} of Tob^o	2: 0: 0
	To John Hood paid him in part for Keeping 2 of John Kings Children a year each from January last	1: 0: 0
April 17	To the Sheriff for Yearwood	1: 1: 0
	To the Revd William Willie for D^o	1:19: 0
H : B	To James Gee paid him	4: 0: 0
	To A Claiborne paid him	6: 0: 0
	To the Revd William Willie paid him	6: 0: 0
	To Howel Briggs paid him	2:14: 7
	To John Battle paid him	1:10: 0
	To Christian Higgs paid him	1: 3: 0
	To Selah Huland paid her of the fines	1: 3: 0
	To Sundrys for Edward Facy	0:17:6½
	To D^o for Alice Felts	0:10:10
	To D^o for Edward Facy	0: 8:2
	To D^o for Alice Felts	0:13:7½
	To D^o for Henry Tuder	4: 2:0
	To 4½ y^{ds} Sheeting for Fanny Hood	0: 9:4
	To Thos Cullum paid him	1:15:0
	To Richd Hay paid him	7:10:0
	To Phillip Harwood paid him	0:10:0
		£ 68: 5:1
	To Ballance Due Pr Contra	0:17:0¾
1759	Dr Fines & Forfeitures	
	To Isaac Robertson paid him Pr Mr Willie	2: 0:0
	To Sarah Capell paid her Pr Moses Johnson	1:10:0
	To Mary Drew paid her Pr Ja^s Gee	1: 5:0
	To Selah Hulin paid her	2: 5:0
	To Anne Gresswitt paid her	1: 5:0
	To John Adkins 30/ & John Underhill 25/	2:15:0
		£ 11: 0:0

[140]

Briggs & Nicholas Massenburg Churchwardens   Cr

1758	By Robt Jones Junr Rec^d of him	10———
June 16	By D^o	5:10: 4
1759		
April 17	By James Gee Rec^d of him for 3022^{lb} of Tob^o a^t Pc^t	30: 4: 4½

H B	By James Gee & Moses Johnson Rec^d of them	21:13: 3¾
H B	By Ballance the Churchwardens	0:17: 0¾
		£ 68: 5: 1
1758	Contra	
	By 4 fines for Swearing	1: 0: 0
	By 4 D^o for Basterdy	10: 0: 0
		£ 11: 0: 0

[141]

At a Vestry Held for the Parish of Albemarle in the County of Sussex at at[sic] Nottoway Church on the 17th day of May 1757

Present
The Revd William Willie

Howel Briggs	Nicholas Massenburg	
Aug^{ne} Claiborne	Ja' Gee	} Gent
Richd Blow	John Mason	
Moses Johnson	Ephraim Parham	

Howel Briggs & Nicholas Massenburg is appointed Churchwardens till Next Easter Tuesday

Howel Briggs & Nicholas Massenburg Churchwardens Rendered their Accounts in Vestry which Accounts wee examined allowed & ordered tbe Registered

Ordered that the Churchwardens Pay to Capt Samuel Peete the Sum of Six pounds Sixteen Shillings & Ten Pence for the cure of Curries Son

William Andrews has agreed with the Vestry to keep Rosannah Dinkins & Maintain her for the Sum of Five Pound Pr Year

Howel Briggs has agreed with the Vestry to let them have Such goods as they shall want on Account of the Pensioners of this Parish at 100 p^r cent advance

Ordered that Timothy Ezell & Joseph Armstrong be exempted from paying their Parish Levies for the future

Ordered that the Churchwardens Pay to Richard King the Sum of Seventeen Shillings Six Pence for Burying Jno King a Pensioner former not being complyed with

Ordered that the Churchwardens pay to Anne Feild the Sum of one Pound five Shillings being a Woman in Necessity Circumstances

Ordered that James Williams be excepted from paying his Parish Levy

Ordered that Matthew Whitfeild be exempted from paying his Parish Levy During his indispossition

A letter of resignation was Received of Capt. Richd Blow as a Member of this Vestry in the following words, May ye 17th 1759 Gentlemen I hereby Resign my place as a member of Albemarle Parish Vestry & do Desire you'd proceed to elect another Member in the Room of Gent.

Your H.ble Servt Richd Blow

To the Vestry of Albemarle Parish

[142]

Mical [Michael] Blow is elected to Serve this Parish as a Vestry Man instead of Capt Richd Blow who has Resigned his place

Henry Harrison is elected to Serve this Parish as a Vestry Man

Lawrence Gibbeons is elected to Serve this Parish as a Vestry Man

Ordered that the Churchwardens pay to Isaac Robertson the sum of two pounds out of the Money in their hands which has accrued to this Parish from fines & forfeitures

Ordered that the Churchwardens Pay to Sarah Capell the Sum of one pound Ten Shillings out of the money in their hands which has accrued to this Parish from fines & forfeitures

Ordered that the Churchwardens Pay to Mary Drew the Sum of one pound five Shillings out of the Money in their hands which has accrued to this parish from fines & forteitures

Ordered that the Churchwardens Pay to Selah Huland the Sum of two pounds five Shillings out of the Money in their hands which has accrued to this parish from fines & forteitures

Ordered that the Churchwardens Pay to Anne Goesswitt the Sum of one pound five Shillings out of the Money in their hands which has accrued to this parish from fines & forteitures

Ordered that the Churchwardens Pay to John Adkins the Sum of one pound ten Shillings out of the Money in their hands which has accrued to this parish from fines & forteitures

Ordered that the Churchwardens Pay to John Underhill the Sum of one pound five Shillings out of the Money in their hands which has accrued to this parish from fines & forteitures

Ordered that John Painter be exempt from paying his Parish Levy for the future

Ordered that the Churchwardens Pay to Matthew Whitfeild the Sum of one pound thirteen Shillings & Seven pence being the Ballance Due to him for keeping Rebecca Bird

Ordered that the Churchwardens & the Revd Wm Willie do agree with workmen to inclose Nottoway Church & Saint Andrews Church with posts & Rails ye inclosure not to be under five feet in heigth[sic] so as not to inclose more than one Acre of Land

Ordered that the Churchwardens leave to the highest Bidder for any term of years not exceeding Seven the Land given to this Parish by Coll: Harrison Reserving Six Acres thereof contegious to Nottoway Church for the immediate use of that Church that they insist & covenanant on the Part of the Lessee in Such Leave for the Building a Dwelling house 20 by 15 feet & leave the same in tennantable Repair

The Revd Wm Willie Decents from the last mentioned Order

Wm Willim Min^r copy
Test Ja^s Chappell Junr Clk Vestry

[143]

At a Vestry Held at Sussex County Courthouse the 15th of June 1759

Present

Moses Johnson
Nic^s Massenburg
Henry Harrison
    Mich^l Blow

John Mason
Ch. Aug: Claiborne Gent
Law^e Gibbons &

The Vestry being met The Revd Mr Wm Willie Appeared & Demanded his Sallary in Tob^o as by the Act of 1748 & the Church wardens having tendered the said Sallary to the said minister in Cash at 2 Pr Pound which he there refused the Vestry now again tendered him the said Sallary at 2 which he again Refused to Receive It's Ordered that the Chwardens tender the said Sallary at 2 Pr Pound to ye said Minister & that they Pay the Same to him taking a Receipt from the Said Minister in the following from June the 15th 1759 Rec^d of the Churchwardens of Albemarle Parish the Sum of One hundred & forty four Pounds four Shillings & two Pence which is Paid me by the Churchwardens as my Sallary for the Year 1758 but Rec^d by me in such a Manner as not to Opperate against me any further than for the Sum aforesaid & Now paid me if I should see fit to bring an Action at Law for a greater Sum not thinking mySelf as minister as aforesaid to Submit to the Late Act of Assembly for Paying off Transfer Debts at 2^d p^r Pound at pay Rec^d by me

                                                                     Wm Willie

Ja^s Gee, Nich^s Massenburg Chwarden
Moses Johnson
John Mason
A. Claiborne
Law^e Gibbons
H. Harrison
Mich^l Blow

                                  Copy Test Ja^s Chappell J^r Clk Vestry

[144]

At a Vestry held for the Parish of Albemarle at Nottoway Church in the County of Sussex on ye 6th Day of August 1759

Present

Nich^s Massenburg
Ja^s Chappell
Ephraim Parham
Lawrence Gibbons
    & Henry Harrison

Howel Briggs
John Mason } Gent
Moses Johnson
Aug: Claiborne

IN pursuance to an Order of Sussex County Court Bearing Date ye 15th Day of July 1759 Directing the Vestry of Albemarle Parish to Divide the same into Precincts for the Processioning of Every Persons Land within the said Parish Wee Do Appoint Robt Nicholson & Wm Hancock to see every Persons Land Processioned & the Land Marks thereof Renewed from Surry County line up Seacock & Tarrapin Swamps to Birchan island Road & up the said Road to the head of Seacock & that they Do assemble all the Freeholders within that Precinct to attend the Performance thereof & that the said Robt Nicolson & Wm Hancock do make a Return to this Vestry an Account of Every Persons Land they shall procession & of every Person Pres^t at the Processioning thereof also of whose Land they shall fail to procession & the Particular Reasons of Such failure & that the Same be Done & Perfomed Between the first Day of November & the last Day of March Next ensuing

Henry Blow & Arthur Smith are appointed to procession from the south side of the Seacock to the head of the Lightwood Swamp & Secaurie Swamp thence to Birchan island Road

Nathl Briggs & Joseph Ellis are appointed to procession from Southampton county line up Assamoosuck Swamp to Secaurie Swamp thence up ye said Swamp to the head thereof

Ja^s Chappell Junr & John Jarrad are appointed to procession from ye Mouth of Secaurie Swamp up Assamoosuck Swamp to the Major Branch up the said branch to Secaurie road by that road to Secaurie Swamp by that Swamp to the Begining

[145]

Nicholas Partridge & Henry Jarrad are Appointed to Procession from ye Major Branch up Assamoosuck Swamp to & including Pettway Johnson Land thence to the head of Copperhawnk Swamp down that Swamp to the Secaurie Road by that Road the head of the Major Branch Down the said Branch to the Beginning

David Jones & Wm Cook are Appointed to Procession from Cooks Bridge a long Cooks Road to Joseph Swamp so to Prince George County line by that Line to Blackwater so to the Beginning

Edward Weaver & John Ogbun are Appointed to Procession from the Governors Road to the Old Parish line all between Assamoosuck Swamp Jospeh Swamp & the old Parish Line

Wm Parker & David Jones Are Appointed to Procession from the Old Parish Down Assamoosuck to Robins branch thence Down Austins Branch to Nottoway River up the River to the Old Parish line by that to the Beginning

Thos Peters & John Chappell are Appointed to Procession all Below Robins Branch & Austins & between Nottoway River & Assamoosuck Swamp to Southampton County Line

Edward Eppes & Thos Adkins are Appointed to Procession from Pettways Mill a long Petways line formerly Harthorns line to the Colledge line a long that line to Jospeh Swamp Down that Swamp to Nottoway River up the River to Jones hole Swamp up that Swamp to the Beginning

Edward Pettway & Wm More are Appointed to Procession all Between Jones hole Swamp the Indian Swamp Nottoway River & Prince George County Line

John Curtis & Joel Tucker are Appointed to Procession Between Monksneck Creek & Stony Creek & up Sappony Creek to Prince George County Line

Richd Hill & John Tyas are Appointed to Procession from Stony Creek up Sappony Creek to Sapony Mill thence to Lewis Parhams Land so Down Nottoway River to the Beginning

[146]

Peter Green & Amos Love are Appointed to Procession from the Plantation of Lewis Parham to Sappony Mill all Between the line that Divides this County & Prince George & up Nottoway River to Harriss Swamp

Isham Smith & Josiah Smith are Appointed to Procession from Harriss Swamp up Nottoway River to the Extent of this County

Robert Webb & Charles Battle are Appointed to Procession Between Rackoon Swamp the Little Swamp & Stokes,s Road

Nathl Parham & Matthew Parham J^r are Appointed to Procession from the Island Swamp to the Old Parrish by that line to the line that Divides this County & Brunswick so to Nottoway River

John Stevens & Wm Ezell are Appointed to Procession Between the Rackoon & Hunting Quarter Swamps out to the Head of Hunting Quarter Swamp

Wm Knight & John Battle are Appointed to Procession all the Land on the East side of Stokes Road Between the line Dividing this County & Southampton County to the Rackoon Swamp

Ja^s Wyche & Joseph Thorp are Appointed to procession all the Land on ye South side of the 3 Creeks Southampton & Brunswick County lines

Nicholas Massenburg & Matthew Wynne are Appointed to Procession from Stokes's Road up Nottoway River to the frying Pan Swamp from the head of the said Swamp a Strait Course to Hunting Quarter Swamp

Samuel Magget & John Alsobrook are Appointed to Procession from the Mouth of Copper hawnk Swamp along the line that Divides this County & Surry County to Birchan island by that Road to Secaurie by that Road to Copper Hawnk Swamp thence to the Beginning

Robt Judkins & John Lambarc Appointed to Procession all Between Blackwater Swamp Copper hawnk Swamp & the old Parish Line

John Barker & Ja^s Busshau Jones are Appointed to Procession from the Mouth of the Old Town Swamp & up that to the head of the Tarr kilmn[sic] Branch Down that to the Mill Swamp to & including Saml Tatums Land thence to the New Road & so to Cooks Road by that to Blackwater & thence to the Beginning

[147]

Willard Roberts & John Toby are Appointed to Procession from Blackwater on the old Parish line by that line to Copper hawnk Swamp up that Swamp to the head thence to the tarr Kill Branch on the Mill Swamp up the said Branch to the Old Town Swamp Down that to the Blackwater so to the Beginning

Thos Mitchell & John Tatum are Appointed to Procession all Between Edward Pettways line formerly Carthorns & the Colledge & the line that Divides this County & Prince George County & Between Joseph Swamp & Jones hole Swamp

Joseph Pidington & Benjamin Hunt are Appointed to Procession all Between Allens line John Pidington line & Robt Jones Junr line & Stokes Road & the Hunting Quarter Swamp

Thos Renn Junr & Wm Bishop are Appointed to Procession all Between Allens line John Pidingtons line Robt Jones line and Stokes's Road & Nottoway River

David Mason & Wm Doby are Appointed to Procession from the Mouth of the Great Swamp to the 3 Creeks & up the 3 [Three] Creeks & up Auterdam [Otterdam] Swamp to Brunswick County Line

Henry Tyler & Thos Pate are Appointed to Procession from ye Great & Down the same to the County line & so to the Poplar Swamp up that to the line Dividing this County & Brusnwick

Hinchea Gilliam & Burrell Gilliam are Appointed to Procession all Between Nottoway River the Rackoon & Hunting Quarter Swamps so a long Loftins Mill Path to the little Swamp Down that to ye Rackoon so to Nottoway River

Cornelius Loftin & Richd Avery are Appointed to Procession up Hunting Quarter Swamp & Little Swamp from Loftins Mill Path to Stokes Road

Thos Parham & Matthew Parham are appointed to Procession from the Indian Swamp to Monksneck Creek & Nottoway River & the line that Divides this County & Prince George County

Robert Pettway & Wm Pettway J^r are Appointed to Procession from the flat swamp up Nottoway to the Mouth of frying Pann Swamp so to the head thereof from thence to Switts's[?] so to the Beginning

[148]

Wm Stuart & Peter Reives are Appointed to Procession from the head of the Frying Pan Swamp to Hunting Quarter Swamp Down that to Island Branch Down that to Nottoway River

Charles Judkins & Silvanus Stokes are Appointed to Procession from the North side of the Spring Swamp up the said Swamp to the County line Down the Rackoon to Stokes's road

Thos Felts & Robt Seat are Appointed to Procession from Stokes Road between the Poplar & Spring Swamps up the said Swamps to the County line

Reubin Baird & Faddy Jarrad are Appointed to Procession from Cooks Road on the New Road by that Road to the Black Swamp Down that Swamp to Pidgeon Swamp up that to Cooks Road Down that Road to the Begining

Hugh Toy & John Baird are Appointed to Procession all the land Between Pidgeon Swamp & Joseph Swamp the Governors Road & Cooks Road

Isaac Seburn is Exempted from Paying his Parish levy for the future

Howel Briggs
& Nich^s Massenburg Chwardens
Copy Test Ja^s Chappell J^r Clk Vestry

[149]

At a Vestry held at Nottoway Church for the Parish of Albemarle in the County of Sussex on the 30th Day of Octr 1759

Present
The Revd William Willie

Howel Briggs	Nicholas Massenburg	
Augustin Claiborne	Moses Johnson }	Gent
Ja^s Chappell	John Mason	
Henry Harrison &	Ephraim Parham	

Albemarle Parish	Dr
	Wt lbs of Tobo
To the Revd Wm Willie 17305	
To Edward Walker Clerk at Nottoway Church	1200
To John Nicholson Do at St Pauls Do	1200
To Amos Love Do at St Marks Do	1200
To Gregory Rawlings Do at St Andrews Do	1200
To Richd Wiggins Sexton at Nottoway Church	500
To John Bain Do at St Pauls Do	500
To Edd Shelton Do at St Andrews Do	500
To Peter Green Do at St Marks Do	500
To Mr Moses Johnson for keeping John King a lame chld 1 year	800
To John Hood for keeping Frances Hood 1 year	500
To Jas Chappell Junr as Clerk of the Vestry	400
To Mary Farringon Exetr of Robt Farrinton Decd	200
To Jas Jones for two Tythes Overcharg'd last Year	30
	26035
To levied for ye use of the Parish	8978
To the collecr for Collecting 37248 lb of Tobo at 6 Pr cent	2235
	37248

Albemarle Parish	Cr
By 2328 Tithables a' 16lb Pr Pole	37248

Ordered that Nicholas Massenburg on his entering into Bond & security to the Vestry of this parish to be taken by the Clerk of the Vestry be Appointed Collector of this Parish for the Year ensung & that he collect & Receive of every Tithable person chargable therewith the Sum of 16 pounds of Tobo Pr pole & that he have authority in case the said Lb of Tobo Pr pole or any part thereof be Delayed or Refused to Levy the same by Distress & that he pay to each Respective Parish Creditor the Several Sums of Tob Due to them that he pay the Tobo levied for the use of the Parish to the Church wardens for the time being

[150]

Ordered that the Churchwardens pay Henry Tudor a Poor infirm Man the Sum of four Pounds

Ordered that the churchwardens Pay Richard Wiggins the Sum of Sixteen Shillings & Six Pence in full of his acct.

Ordered that the Churchwardens let Catharine Earwood a poor woman have three hundred pounds of Pork & four Barrells of Corn

Ordered that the Churchwardens pay to John Hood whatever Appears to be Due to him by Major Massenburgs Book for keeping Drusillah & Rebecca orphan children of John King Decd

William Cox came in Vestry & agreed to keep Drusillah & Rebecca children of John King Decd & find them all neicsaries[sic] for the Year next ensuing for the Sums of Six Pounds

Joseph Armstrong is appointed Sexton at S[t] Andrews church instead of Edward Shelton

Ordered that the Collec[r] pay M[r] Ephraim Parham Seventy five Pounds of Tob[o] for seting up horse Blocks at S[t] Marks Church

W[m] Willie Min[r]
Copy Test Ja[s] Chappell Jun[r] Clk Vestry

[151]

At a Vestry held for the Parish of Albemarle in the County of Sussex at Nottoway Church on the eight Day of April 1760 being Easter Tuesday

Present
The Rev[d] William Willie

Howel Briggs	Nicholas Massenburg	
James Chappell	Moses Johnson	Gent
John Mason &	Augustine Claiborne	

Lawrence Gibbons & Mical Blow is Appointed Churchwardens for the Year Ensuing

Thomas Waller being Recommended to the Vestry by the Rev[d] M[r] William Willie as a Proper Object of Charity it is thereupon Ordered that Major Nicholas Massenburg Put three Pounds fifteen Shillings towards finding the said Waller corn & Meat

Matthew Whitfeild being formerly cleared from Paying his Parish Levy but an Addition being Made to his Estate it is therefore considered & Ordered that the said Whitfeild pay his Parish Levy hereafter

Ordered that the committy Appointed to Examine the Churchwardens Accounts make their Report to the Next Vestry

Ordered thaat the Clerk of the Vestry Write to M[r] Rober[t] Jones Jun[r] to attend the next Vestry held for the parish in Order to make out his Account as Churchwarden

Ordered that the Churchwardens lay Put one pound ten Shillings out of the fines & forfeitures towards Supporting Sarah Capell a poor Woman

Ordered that the Churchwardens lay out Thirty Shillings out of the fines & forfeitures towards Supporting Selah Huland a poor Woman

Ordered that the Executor of Cap[t] James Gee Dec[d] attend the Next Vestry in order to Make out their Accounts & that they have had notis thereof

W[m] Willie Min[r]
Copy Test Ja[s] Chappell Jun[r] Clk Vestry

[152]

Pursuant to an Order of Vestry the 6th Day of August 1759 we the Subscribers have processioned every mans Land & renewed their Land marks in our Precinct from Stokes's Road all Between the Poplar Swamp Spring Swamp to the County Line & had present at the performance of the same every Freeholder in the Precinct Viz: Thomas Felts, Robert Seat, Nathaniel Felts, Joseph Ezell, Phillip Harwood, William Knight, Samuel Stokes, Henry Browns Land not Living in the Precinct, William Brown, Charles Judkins, Samuel Northingtons, Silvanus Bells, Thomas Heath, William Rose, Tho[s] Weathers, William Cragg, William Woodland, John Jennsons, Micajah Winthers, Abel Mabry, John Adkins, Richard Northcross, Coll: Richard Cocke, Isaac Oliver, James Howe, James Stuart,

Surry and Sussex Counties, Virginia, 1742-1786

Timothy Ezels, William Richardson, Thomas Battle, Thomas Ezell, William Harris, John Felts, John Barns. Nathaniel Felts Junr, Thomas Felts Junr, all the Lands in our Precinct have been Peacibly Processioned & the Land marks Renewed by us
N° 1   [Procession Masters] Thomas Felts the Elder
                                                                                                          Robert Seat

Richard Blunts Land Present Richard Blunt, William Briggs, William Gilbert, Hinchea Gilliam, John Edmunds, Thomas Cooper, Patty Lesters Land in Presence of the Same Persons

Part of John Edmunds	Ditto	Ditto
All Frances Willis	Ditto	Ditto
Part of John Tobys	Ditto	Ditto
Thomas Coopers	Ditto	Ditto
William Briggs	Ditto	Ditto
Hannah Moss	Ditto	Ditto
Hinchea Gilliam	Ditto	Ditto
Willute Roberts	Ditto	Ditto

By virtue of the Order of the Vestry hereunto Annext to us Directed we have caused the Several Tracts of Land above mentioned being all contained within our Precinct to be Processioned in our Presence and the lines of the said Land Renewed as is by the said Order Directed
N° 2 Given Under Our hands this 29th Day of February 1760
        [Procession Masters]   John Toby
                                     William Roberts

[153]

In Obedience to an Order of the Worshipful Vestry of the Parish of Albemarle in the County of Sussex Dated August ye 6th Day 1759 Wee the Subscribers have assembled the Freeholders together within the Precinct Specified by the said Order & have Processioned & Renewed all the Land Marks of the following persons to Witt:

January ye 16th Day 1760	We Processioned Drewy Gilliam Benja. Sowsberry Charles Gilliam Edmund Gilliam Thomas Gilliam Ralph Maggee & Our Own John Hargrave Anselin Gilliam	Lands	In Presence of Charles Gilliam Benja. Sowberry Lewis Dunn Anselin Gilliam David Maggee Edmund Gilliam Richard Johnson Charles Gilliam Junr
January 19th 1760	We Processioned Henry Harrison Samuel Peete Richard Felts Thomas Dunn John Dunn James Jones Henry Andrews William Loftin	Lands	Present Richard Johnson Richard Felts John Dunn John Hargave Lewis Dunn Charles Gilliam Anselin Gilliam Drewry Gilliam Charles Gilliam Junr

N° 3
                              Hinchea Gilliam [Procession Masters]
                              Burrell Gilliam

In Obedience to an Order of the Vestry of the Parish of Albemarle in the County of Sussex Bearing Date ye 6 Day of August 1759 Wee the Subscribers have assembled the Freeholdeers together within the Precinct Specified by the said Order & on the third & fourth Days of March Did Procession & the said Land Marks Renew of the Several Tracts of Land hereafter Mentioned to Witt:
Benj: Wickes Land, William Parkers Land, William Allens Land, James Chappells Land, John Cargills Land, James Chappells Junr, James Chappell Min^r Land, William Tomlinsons Land, John Sledges Land, Elizabeth Chappells Land, John Chappells Land, Robert Jones's Land, James Jones's Land & David Jones's Land Present when the above said Tracts of land were Processioned & the Land Marks thereof Renewed James Chappell, James Chappell Junr, David Moss, John Cappell, Robert Jones, James Jones, James Chappell Min^r, John Sledge, William Tomlinson and Peter Doby
N° 4 Certified Under Our hands

            David Jones [Procession Masters]
            William Parker

[154]

By Virtue of an Order of the Vestry of Albemarle Parish Dated the 6 Day of August 1759 as Directed we have Processioned the Lands therein Mentioned & Same Land Marks thereof Renewed as Follows

Lands	Persons Present
John Parham	John Parham
James Parham	James Parham
Charles Leath	Charles Leath
John Heath	Abraham Parham
John Leath	John Leath
Joshua Poytress	Ephraim Rains
Abraham Parham	John Leath Junr
Thomas Parham	
Matthew Parham	

N°   Thomas Parham [Procession Masters]
           Matthew Parham

In Obedience to an Order of the Worshipful Vestry of the Parish of Albemarle Bearing date ye 6th Day of August 1759 Wee the Subscribers did on the 12th & 13th Days of February assemble the Freeholderes within the Precinct Specified by the said Order & did Procession & the Land Marks Renew of the following Tracts of land by Viz^t Richard Parkers Land, Samuel Peetes Land, Thomas Peters's Land, James Renns Land, Lazarus Drakes Land, Henry Harrisons Land, Thomas Hines's Land, John Hines's Land, William Hines's Land, William Hines Junr Land, David Hines's Land, Peter Hines's Land, Richard Hines's Land, William Howels Land, William Edmunds Land, John Chappells Land, Joshua Hines's Land, William Hunts Land & John Edmunds's Land & John Cargills Land [added in a different handwriting]

Present when the above Tracts were Processioned & the Land Marks thereof Renewed Richard Parker, Samuel Peete, James Renn, Lazarus Drake, Henry Harrison, Thomas Hines, John Hines, William Hines, William Hines Junr, David Hines, Peter Hines, Richard Hines, William Howel, William Edmunds, Joshua Hines, John Cargill, John Edmunds, William Hunt
N° 6   Thomas Peters Pro^s Masters
                 John Chappell

[155]

In Obedience to an Order of the Vestry of the Parish of Albemarle in the County of Sussex Bearing the 6th Day of August 1759 Wee the Subscribers have assembled the Freeholders together within the precinct Specified by the said Order & on the Ninth Day of March did Procession & the Land Marks renew of the Several Tracts of Land hereafter Mentioned to Witt John Sledges Land, Reubin Cook Land, Cap' John Mavens Land, Cap' William Halls Land, Alexander Finnies Land, Edward Weavers Land, Cuthbud Staffords Land, John Ogbuns Land, Amos Sledges Land
Present when the above said Tracts of Land were Processioned & the Land Marks therof Renewed
John Sledge, Amos Sledge, Cap' John Mason, Henry Weaver, Edward Weaver, Cuthbud Stafford, John Ogbun,

N° 7 Certified under Our hands Edward Weaver [Procession Masters]
 John Ogbun

By Virtue of an Order of the Vestry of Albemarle Parish bearing Date August the 6th 1759 Wee the Subscribers have assembled the Freeholdeers together within the Precinct Specified by the said Order & have Processioned & Renewed the Land Marks of the Several Persons as follows to Witt
March yᵉ 3ᵈ 1760 Willet Roberts Land, Thomas Lashley Land, John Lashley Land, Walter Lasley Land, Nathaniel Barker Land, Hinchea Gilliam Land, James Barker Land, Benjamin Barkers Land, James Bosau Jones Land, William Cooks Land, Reubin Cooks Land, Henry Barkers Land, Peter Bagley Decᵈ Land, John Barker Land

Present when the abovesaid Land were Processioned Willit Roberts, Nathaniel Barker, James Barker, Benja Barker, Walter Lashley, John Lashley
N° 8 [Procession Masters] John Barker
  James Bojsau[sic] Jones

By Virtue of an Order of the Vestry of Albemarle Parish Bearing Date yᵉ 6ᵗʰ Day of August 1759 Wee the Subscribers have assembled the Freeholders together within the Precinct Specified by the said Order and have Processioned & Renewed the Land Marks of the Several Persons as follows to Witt
March yᵉ 18ᵗʰ 1760 Reubin Cooks, William Cooks, David Jones, John Tomlinson, Benjamin Tomlinson, Charles Gee, Richard Carter, Wyke Hunnicutt, Henry Gee, William Eldrige, William Shands, Adam Heath, William Heath, Thoˢ Young, Nathanˡ Tatum, Thomas Moody
Present when the abovesaid Land were Processioned Adam Heath, Thomas Heath, James Cook, Benjaᵐ Tomlinson, Charles Gee, Richard Carter, Thoˢ Moody, William Shands, Benjaᵐ Figg, Reubin Cook,
N° 9 [Procession Masters] David Jones
  William Cook

[156]

In Obedience to an Order of Vestry Dated August the 6ᵗʰ 1759 Directing us to Procession the Lands in the Precincts laid out to us by the said Order Accordingly on the Seventh & Eleventh & Thirtyfirst Days of March Wee assembled the Freeholders & went in Quiet Procession & Renewed the Land Marks of the following Persons Viz:
The land of Mʳ Robert Jones, The Land of Thomas Mumford, the Land of Thomas Bailey, the land of Mʳ William Willie, the Land of John Pinninton, The Land of Moses Johnson, the Land of M William Allen, The Land of Joseph Pinninton, the Land of John Land, the Land of Ann Dinkins, The Land of Lydia Dinkins

Persons Present
Andrew Troughton   Moses Pinninton   Lewis Johnson

N° 10   [Procession Masters] Joseph Pinninton
                                                              Benjamin Hunt

In Obedience to an Order of the Vestry of the Parish of Albemarle in the County of Bearing Date the 6th of August 1759 Wee the Subscribers have assembled the Freeholders together within the Precinct Specified by the said Order & on the Seventeenth & eighteenth Days of March Did Procession & the Land Marks Renew'd the Several Tracts of Land hereafter Mentioned to Witt Henry Jarrads Land, John Barkers Land, Capt Howel Briggs's Land, Capt James Jones Land, Robert Jones Land, Capt. John Masons Land, Wills Partridges Land, Peter Jones's Land, John Lambs Land, Nicholas Partridges Land, William Briggs's land, William Johnsons Land, Thomas Johnsons Land, Thos Cullums Land not processioned by his refusing to appear on the lines Petway Johnsons Land processioned

Present when the abovesaid Tracts of Land were Processioned & the Land Marks thereof Renewed John Barker, Capt James Jones, Wills Partridge, Robert Jones, James Johnson, Thomas Johnson, Petway Johnson

N° 11   Certified Under Our hands   Nicholas Partridge [Procession Masters]
                                        Henry Jarrad

Pursuant to & Order of Vestry held for Albemarle Parish in the County of Sussex the 8th Day of August 1759 Wee the Subscribers have Processioned & Renewed the Marks of the same according to Order

Persons Land &c	All the Opposite Persons Present
Nathl Hood	Richd Reives
John Spain	James Horn
Peter Reives	Thos Whitehead
William Stuart	Col. Robert Boling
Jn° Anderson Sturdivant	Capt Wm Gilliam
Wm Spain	Robert Newman
Drewry Spain	Susahhan Rottenberry
William Stuart	Sloman Wynne Junr
Matthew Whitehead	Richard Knight
	Howel Briggs line

Test   William Stuart [Procession Masters]
March ye 31st 1760   Peter Reives

[157]

In Obedience to an Order of the Vestry of the Parish of Albemarle in the County of Sussex Bearing Date the 6th Day of August 1759 Wee the Subscribers have assembled the Freeholders together within the Precinct Specified by ye Said Order & on the Seventh & eight Day of March Did Procession & the Land Marks Renew of the Several Tracts of Land hereafter Mentioned to Witt George Briggs's Land, Peter Hines's Land, Nathaniel Briggs Land, Stephen Hamlins Land, Arthur Murfees Land, Joseph Ellis's Land, James Higes [Hix] Land, William Higes Land, Col: Benja: Harrisons Land, James Turners Land, Joseph Hargraves Land, William Hancocks Land, John Barkers Land, Nathl Jones's Land, William Felts Land, Joseph Lanes Land, Ethelred Holts Land, Nathl Davis's Land, Robert Baileys Land

Present when the abovesaid Tracts of land were Processioned & the Land Marks thereof renewed without any Molestation George Briggs, Peter Hines, Nathaniel Briggs, Stephen Hamlin, Arthur Murfee, Joseph Ellis, James Hix, William Hix, James Turner, Joseph Hargrave, William Hancock, Nath' Davis, Nath' Jones, William Felts, Joseph Lane, Robert Bailey

N° 13   Certified Under Our hands   Pro[n] Masters   Nathaniel Briggs
                                                                                  Joseph Ellis

In Obedience to an Order of the Vestry of the Parish of Albemarle in the County of Sussex Bearing Date the 6th of August 1759 Wee the Subscribers have assembled the Freeholders together within the Precinct Specified by the said Order & on the first Day of March Did Procession & the Land Marks Renew of the Several Tracts of Land hereafter Mentioned to Witt William Rogers Land, Umphry Baileys Land, Edward Writes [Wright] Land, Tho[s] Alsobrooks Land, John Alsobrooks Land, Cap' Howel Briggs Land, John Lambs Land, James Whites Land, Samuel Maggots Land

Present when the abovesaid Tracts of Land were Processioned and the Land Marks thereof renewed William Rogers, Umphry Bailey, Edward Write, Thomas Alsobrooke, John Alsobrooke, Cap' Howell Briggs, John Lamb, James White

N° 14   Certified Under Our hands   Samuel Maggot
                                                                     John Alsobrooke
                                                                    Procession Masters

[158]

In obedience to an Order of Vestry of Albemarle Parish bearing Date the Sixth Day of August 1759 we did on the third Day of March 1760 assemble the freeholders within Our Precinct together & did Procession & Renew the Land Marks of James Belsheres, John Mason, John Baird, Hugh Foy & John Wilkerson Present at the time William Shands, Hugh Belsheres, James Belsheres, John Mason we did procession & Renew the Land Marks of Benja: Harrison Dec[d], Nathan Northington, William Shands, William Wilkerson, Cuthbud Stafford & Tho[s] Adkins
Present at the time John Mason, William Wilkerson, & William Riddles, Henry Weaver, & William Bellamy Witness our hands this 4th March 1760

N° 15   Hugh Foy   & Procession
                                                                                 John Baird   Masters

Pursuant to & Order of Vestry held for Albemarle Parish in Sussex County Bearing Date the 6th Day of August 1759 Wee the Subscribers have Processioned & Renewed the Land marks within Our Appointed Precinct belonging to the Persons hereafter Mentioned

Person Lands	Present
Solomon Graves	John Stokes
Rich[d] King	Tho[s] Pinninton
John King	Nath' Holt
William King	Abraham Brown
John Stevens	
Sloman Wynn Jun[r]	Tho[s] Tyas
Matthew Sturdavant	Solomon Graves
John Potts	John King
John Reding	Isham Ezell
John King Jun[r]	Sloman Wynn Jun[r]
John Whitington Jun[r]	John Potts
John Hood	James Williams Jun[r]
William Ezell	Thomas Moore Sen[r]

	Isham Ezell		Hansel Gilliam
	Tho⁵ Moore Sen ʳ		on Rachels line
	John Rachel		
	John Knight		
	James Williams		
	Tho⁵ Pinninton		[Procession Masters]
	John Stokes		John Stevens
	Nathˡ Holt		William Ezell
	Tho⁵ Tyas		
Nº 16	Abraham Brown		March yᵉ 31 1760

[159]

In Obedience of an Order of the Worshipful Vestry of Albemarle Parish Dated 6ᵗʰ Day of August 1759 & to us Directed Wee have on the 7ᵗʰ Day of March 1760 Assembled all the freeholders in the said Precinct & Processioned & Renewed the Land Marks of every Persons Land in the aforesaid Precinct Viz

The line betwixt Timothy Ezell
& James Mason Junʳ
——————
Ditto betwixt James Mason
& William Moore
——————
Ditto Betwixt James Mason
Edward Pettway & Wᵐ Moore
——————
Ditto betwixt Wᵐ Moore
& Edward Pettway
——————
Ditto betwixt Wᵐ Moore
& Eppes Moore
——————
Ditto betwixt Edward Pettway
& Eppes Moore
——————
Ditto betwixt Eppes Moore
& Henry Mitchell
——————
Ditto betwixt Henry Mitchell
& James Heath
——————
Ditto betwixt Edward Pettway
& James Heath
——————
Ditto Edward Pettway & John Smith
——————
Ditto betwixt John Smith & Tho⁵ Heath
——————
Ditto betwixt Tho⁵ Heath & Peter Poytress
——————
Nº 17 Ditto betwixt Edward Pettway & Peter Poytress

In Presence of Timothy Ezell
Frederick Hobbs Eppes Moore
Tho⁵ Heath James Heath
Henry Mitchell John Pettway
& Tho⁵ Floide [?Floyd]

in Presence of Ditto

in Presence of Ditto

in Presence of Ditto

in Presence of Ditto

in Presence of Ditto

in Presence of Ditto

in Presence of Ditto

in Presence of Ditto

in Presence of Ditto

in Presence of Ditto

[Procession Masters]
Edward Pettway
William Moore

In Obedience to an Order of the Worshipfull Vestry of the Parish of Albemarle in the County of Sussex Bearing Date the 6ᵗʰ Day of August 1759 Wee the Subscribers did on the 26ᵗʰ Day of March [1760] assemble the freeholders within the Precinct Mentioned in the said order & did Procession & the Land Marks Renew of the Several Persons

hereafter Named to Witt. John Jarrads, Thomas Wallis's, William Hines Jun[r], Henry Jarrads, James Chappells, John Jones's, James Chappell Jun[r], Howel Briggs's, Benja. Garrisons, John Kennebrough
                        Present
Ja[s] Chappell, Tho[s] Wallis, Sam[l] Chappell, Henry Jarrad, Howel Chappell, John Jones, Howel Briggs & John Kennebrough
N° 18   John Jarrad   Procession Masters
                                               & Ja[s] Chappell J[r]

[160]

An Account of the Several Lands Processioned & Land Marks Renewed together with the Particular Names of the Persons holding Such Lands Respectively & a List of the Persons at the time of Processioning & renewing the Land Marks of each Tract of Land as taken by us the Subscribers in Obedience to an order of the Vestry of Albemarle Bearing Date the 6th Day of August 1759

To whom belonging when processioned		Persons present at Processioning
John Rollings John Morgan		Ja[s] Wyche Ja[s] Sammons
James Sammons Tho[s] Avent		John Samons John Rollings
John Sammons Joseph Thorp		John Dillard Rich[d] Hay
Tho[s] Underwood Gilbert Hay		Lewis Solomon John Whitehorn
Edward Griffin Rich[d] Hay		Edward Griffin Gilbert Hay
Rich[d] Hay J[r] Lewis Solomon	11th Feb	John Thorp Rich[d] Hay Jun[r]
Lewis Solomon Jun[r] Tho[s] Roper	1760	
& the Land of John Lattance		Persons Present 12th Feb 1760
John Roane John Montague		Ja[s] Wyche Lewis Solomon
& Susannah Jones		W[m] Solomon Joseph Thorp
Marmaduke Hamelton John Avent		Peter Avent Rich[d] Barlow
W[m] Solomon Ja[s] Wyche		John Whitehorn & W[m] Barlow
Peter Avent Joseph Thorp	12th Feb 1760	
W[m] Doby David Mason & William Barlow		

                                                            Pro: Masters
                                                         David Mason &
N° 19   W[m] [his X Mark] Doby

By Virtue of an Order of the Worshipfull the Vestry of the Parish of Albemarle Dated the 6th Day of August 1759 & to us Directed we have Agreeable to the Said Order Seen the Lands in the Precinct to us alotted Processioned & the Several Land Marks Renewed in Presence of the Persons hereafter Mentioned

The Proprietors	Persons Present
Joshua Harthorn	W[m] Dunn
John Doby	Nath[l] Mitchell, Christopher Tatum
John Tatum	George Reives, Christopher Reives
Christopher Tatum	Henry Tatum, Joshua Harthorn
Henry Tatum	John Doby, Robert Doby
Augustine Claiborne	Matthew Gibbs, Timothy Reives
Robert Doby	
William Dunn	
Frances Reives	
George Reives	
Sarah Biggins	
Christopher Reives	[Procession Masters]
Tho[s] Mitchel	Thomas Mitchell
Nath[l] Mitchel	John Tatum

Timothy Reives
Matthew Gibbs
John Reives Orphan
N° 20   Feb y^c 22^d 1760

[161]
John Banes Land Present Simon Stacy, John Mongammie, Thomas Tomlinson, William Ellis, John Nicolson, Thomas Broadrig[sic], John Stacy, Benja. Jordan, Wm Roger, Emanuel James, Wm Judkins, John Judkins & John Banes

    John Lambs   Land in Presence of the same persons

Part of John Tobys	Ditto	Ditto
Part of John Edmunds's	Ditto	Ditto
Part of Howel Briggses	Ditto	Ditto
Simon Stacys	Ditto	Ditto
Abner Procters	Ditto	Ditto
Thos Tomlinsons	Ditto	Ditto
John Mongammies	Ditto	Ditto
John Warbintons	Ditto	Ditto
William Ellis	Ditto	Ditto
John Nicolson	Ditto	Ditto
John Stacy	Ditto	Ditto
Wm Blunts	Ditto	Ditto
Benja. Jordans	Ditto	Ditto
William Rogers	Ditto	Ditto
John Gibbons	Ditto	Ditto
Emanuel James	Ditto	Ditto
Robert Judkins	Ditto	Ditto
Wm Judkins	Ditto	Ditto
John Judkins	Ditto	Ditto

By Virtue of the Order of Vestry hereunto annext to us directed wee have caused the Several Tracts of Land above mentioned being all contain'd within Our Precinct to be Processioned in Our Presence & the Lines of the said Land Renewed as is by the said Order Directed Given Under Our hands this 29th Day of February 1760

                                     [Procession Masters]   Robert Judking[sic]
N° 21   John Lamb

In Obedience to an Order of Vestry Dated August ye 6th 1759 Directing us to Procession ye Land in the Precinct laid out to us by the said Order Accordingly on ye 22nd & 23^d days of February we assembled the Freeholders & went in Quiet Procession & renewed the Landmarks of the following Persons Vizt.

                The Land of Coll: Wm Lightfoot
                The Land of Bethel Pare   All the Proprietors Present
                The Land of Nathan Bishop   except Coll: Lightfoot &
                The Land of Anthony Hancock   Richd Jones being present for
                The Land of Morris Zilk   the first Saml Servard & for the
                The Land of David Zilk   Latter Thos Renn Attended
                The Land of John Zilk   by their Appointment
                The Land of John Edwards
                The Land of Wm Bishop
                The Land of Thos Renn
                The Land of Mr Benja Cocke   [Procession Masters]
                The Land of John Pare   Thos Renn
                The Land of Peter Doby   Wm Bishop
                The Land of Benja Hunt
                The Land of Thos Harrison
                The Land of Lambert Zilk
N° 22   The Land of Richd Jones

[162]

In Obedience to an Order of the Worshipfull Vestry of the Parish of Albemarle to us Directed Bearing Date the 6th Day of August Anno Domini 1759 Wee the Subscribers did assemble all the Freeholders within the Precinct by the said Order Mentioned & have Seen the Land Marks thereof Renewed to Witt William Eldridge, Ric^d Reives, Junr, John Reives, Lydia Weathers, Wm Pettway Junr, William Pettway, William Weathers, Edward Pettway, Robert Pettway, Robt Parham, Stith Parham, Sloman Wynne, John Bobbit, Henry Sturdavant, John Wynne, Hollumn Sturdavant, Susannah Rottenberry, William Ecols & Frances Threewitts
Given Under our hands the 25th Day of March Anno Domini 1760

Persons Present when the above Lands were Processioned to Witt,
Richd Reives, John Reives, Sloman Wynne, Matthew Sturdavant, Stith Parham, Robt Parham, Hollumn Sturdavant, John Wynne

N° 23   [Procession Masters]   Robert Pettway
                                                       William Pettway Junr

In Obedience to an order of the Worshipfull Vestry of Albemarle Parish Dated the 6th Day of August 1759 and to us Directed Wee have on the 12th of March 1760 assembled all the Freeholdeers in the Said Precinct & Processioned & Renewed the Land Marks of every person's Land in the aforesaid Precinct Vizt.

Edward Pettways Land		In Presence of Edward Pettway
Peter Harthorns Dec^d	Ditto	Timothy Ezell
The Church Land		Henry Moss
Timothy Ezells	Ditto	Joseph Denton
Jesse Moss's	Ditto	Jesse Moss
Henry Hartwell Marribles	Ditto	William Tomlinson
John Hays Joshua Meachum	Ditto	John Hay
Henry Moss's Edward Lee's	Ditto	Joshua Meachum
Clem^t Hancocks Dec^d	Ditto	John Adkins
Thos Adkins Edward Eppes's	Ditto	Edward Lee
The Revd Wm Willie's Wm Young	Ditto	Henry Porch
Henry Meachums Dec^d	Ditto	
William Tomlinson	Ditto	Given Under Our hands this
William Wills's	Ditto	8th Day of April 1760
John Adkins's	Ditto	[Procession Masters]
Henry Porches	Ditto	Thomas Adkins
N° 24 James Porches	Ditto	Edward Eppes

[163]

In obedience to an Order of Vestry for Albemarle Parish Dated 6th Aughust 1759 Wee have Processioned the lines & renewed the Land Marks as followeth Vizt. Present John Tomlinson, James Tomlinson, William Sandrus Junr, Henry Toy, Wm Harrison &c Processioned the line betwixt William Sandrus Junr & David Jones also between Wm Sandrus & George Bagley In fact Ditto between the said Bagley & David Jones Ditto between the said Jones & Wm Cook Present John Sandrus &c.
Processioned the line between[sic] David Jones & John Tomson formerly Goodwins also between the said Tomson & Nathl Peebles also betwixt Wm Sandrus & John Tomson Ditto between Wm Sandrus & Nathl Peebles also between the said Peebles & Reubin Baird Ditto between ye said Baird & James Tomlinson Ditto between the said Tomlinson & Faddy Jarrad Ditto between the said Jarrad & Nathl Peebles
Present Henry Gee & John Sandrus & Processioned the line between Henry Gee & John

Tomson Ditto between the said Gee & Wm Shands also between the said Gee & Harrison Infant Also between the said Harrison & William Shands Ditto between the said Shands & Nathan Northington
Present John Tomlinson & James Tomlinson Processioned James Tomlinsons New Line Richd Harrisons line formerly Greehills Not to be found

[Procession Masters]   Reubin Baird
                         Faddy Jarrad

N° 25   March ye 1760

In Obedience to an Order of the Worshipful Vestry of Albemarle Parish Dated the 6th Day of August 1759 & to us Directed we the Subscribers having first Summon'd the freeholders with the Precinct in the said Order Mentioned have Processioned & Renewed the Land Marks of every Persons Land within the said Precinct

	Proprietors Names	Persons Present
	Hartwell Marrible	Hartwell Marrible
	William Dancy	Wm Dancy
	Benja: Cocke	Benja: Cocke
	Benja: Weathers	Benja: Weathers
	William Pettway Junr	Wm Pettway Junr
	Thomas Wrenn	Thos Wrenn
	Robert Pettway	Robt Pettway
	William Partin	Wm Partin
	John Clifton	John Clifton
N° 26	Richd Jones	Given Under Our Hands the
	John Mason	1st Day of March 1760
	John Mason Junr	[Procession Master]
	Howel Briggs	Matthew Wynne
	Nicholas Massenburg	Nich^s Massenburg

[164]

In Obedience to an Order of the Worshipful Vestry of Albemarle Parish Dated the 6th Day of August 1759 & to us Directed we have assembled all the freeholders in the Precinct as in the said Order Mentioned & Processioned & the land Mark

Renewed of all the Lines in the said Precinct
The lines Betwixt Peter Poytress & Joel Tucker
& between Joel Tucker & Wm Broadnax
& between Wm Broadnax & Alexander Boling
& between Alexander Boling & John Freeman
& between John Freeman & Robt Wynne Raine
& between Robt Wynne Raine & Alexander Boling
& between John Freeman & John Eckles
& between John Jackson & John Eckles
& between John Freeman & Wm Newsum
& between Thos Wynne & Thos Vines
& between Thos Vines & Wm Malone
The Lines betwixt Geo: Booth & John Malone
& between Geo: Booth & John Curtis
& between Geo: Booth & Wm Malone
& between Wm Malone & John Curtis
& between John Malone & Edward Harper
& between Edward Harper & Richd Huson
& between Richd Huson & David Tucker

In Presence of
    Thos Wynne   John Freeman

John Malone   Peter Winfeild

John Eckles   Robert Jackson
Robert Raine   John Tyas
Wm Malone   Wm Eckles

In Presence of
Wm Malone   Churchwell Curtis
George Parham   George Booth
Edward Harper   John Malone
              David Tucker

Surry and Sussex Counties, Virginia, 1742-1786

N° 27

John Curtis   Processioners
Joel Tucker

In Obedience to an Order of the Worshipful Vestry of Albemarle Parish in the County of Sussex Dated August the 6th 1759 we have peacibly & Quietly Processioned & Renewed all the Land Marks within Our Precinct as to us was directed

Proprietors	Mens Names
Present	
M' Rob' Harrison Isham Smith	M' W'" Yarbrough Tho' Wade
Burwel Banks John Wilkerson	Tho' Wilkerson John Wilkerson
Josiah Smith Tho' Wilkerson	Tho' Bridges Lawrence Gibbons Jun'
Tho' Sykes Mark Harwell	Ditto D° Ditto
Lawrence Gibbons W'" Yarbrough	Ditto D° D°
Tho' Wade Edward Jones	D° D° D°
Henry Broadnax Tho' Vines	Tho' Vaughan John Mitchell
Tho' Mitchell John Mitchell	David Blanks Edward Jones
Tho' Vaughan W'" Mitchell	John Woodard Tho' Mitchell
David Blanks Sam' Mitchell	Tho' Butler Sam' Mitchell
Tho' Butler James Porch	Tho' Butler James Porch
N° 28 Edward Buckner John Woodard	James Buckner John Woodard
	Ditto

Test Isham Smith
[Procession Masters] Josiah Smith

[165]

In Obedience to an Order of the Worshipful Vestry held for the Parish of Albemarle in the County of Sussex Dated on the 6th Day of August 1759 & to us Directed We the Subscribers have met & Processioned all the Lands in Our Precincts belonging to the Proprietors Under written & the Land Marks thereof have Renewed
[Note: It has been impossible to identify the names of the persons present with any given Proprietor, given the manner in which the names are listed]

	Proprietors Names	Persons Present
Day of y° Month	W'" Gilliam Sen' in Presence of Rich'd Hill W'" Wilborn	W'" Wilborn Mich' Hill W'" Wilborn Jn° Hill John Hill
Feb: 20	Michal Hill John Hill	Mich' Hill W'" Wilborn Jn° Hill 1760
	John Tyas W'" Winfeild Sen' W'" Winfield Jun' Rob' Winfeild Peter Winfield John Winfeild	Mich' Hill W'" Wilborn W'" Winfeild Rob' Winfeild Lewis Brown Rob' Winfeild Lewis Brown John Bonner Jn° Malone Jn° Bonner
	George Booth John Malone John Bonner Edward Harper Isaac Rob'son Lewis Brown	John Malone Jn° Bonner Lewis Brown Jn° Bonner Jn° Malone Geo: Boothe Jun' Jn° Malone Jn° Bonner
Feb 21st	Rob' Webb W'" Malone	Jn° Bonner Ed'd Harper Geo: Booth Jn° Malone
	Hamlin Freeman Josiah Freeman	Geo: Booth Isaac Rob'son Ed'd Harper Jn° Bonner Jn° Bonner Jn° Malone
	Jones Freeman John Holts Jos: Richardson Burrell Greene Lewis Parham Nath' Robertson	Jn° Roland Josiah Freeman Jn° Berryman W'" Malone Jn° Berryman Jn° Berryman Jo' Richardson Jn° Berryman Jn° Roland

N° 29	Wm Richardson James Mangum Amos Loves James Mangum	Jn° Berryman Thos Wynne Thos Wynne Ja^s Mangum Wm Richardson Nathl Rob'son Ja^s Mangum Wm Richardson Nathl Rob'son Wm Malone Nathl Rob'son Wm Richardson Ja^s Mangum

[Procession Masters] Richd Hill
John Tyas

Pursuant to an Order of Vestry of Albemarle Parish in the County of Sussex bearing Date the 6th Day of August 1759 we the Subscribers have Processioned the land & Land Marks Renewed within the Precinct Mentioned in that Order in form & Manner as follows to Witt

	February ye 28th 1760	Persons Present
	The land of Thos Oliver	
	The Land belonging to Wm Wynne	Wm Gilliam Wm Oliver
	Three Tracts of land belonging to Richd Jones	Thos Wynne John Wilborn
	The land belonging to John Wilborne	Wm Parham E Parham
	The land belonging to Charles Delihay	
	The land belonging to Ephraim Parham	James Jones Richd Jones Junr
	The land belonging to Wm Oliver	
	February ye 29	February 29th
	The land belonging to Matthew Parham	Ephraim Parham Wm Parham
	The land belonging to Nathl Parham	Ja^s Jones Richd Jones Junr
	The land belonging to Wm Parham	Wm Cryer Wm Hewitt
N° 30	The land belonging to Wm Hewitt	John Hobbs
	The land belonging to John Watkins	
	The land belonging to Isham Smith	
	The land belonging to Francis Eppes	[Procession Masters]
	The land belonging to Burrell Green	Nathaniel Parham
		Matthew Parham

[166]

In obedience to an Order of the Worshipful Vestry held for the Parish of Albemarle in the County of Sussex Dated on the 6th Day of August 1759 & to us Directed we the Subscribers have met & Processioned all the Lands in Our Precinct Belonging to the Proprietors Under written & the Land Marks thereof Renewed

Day of the Month	Proprietors Names	Persons Present
Decr 27th 1759	Mary Farrington	Wm Raney Nathl Raney Nathl Raney
	Edward Powel	Wm Raney Edward Powel Ja^s Cain Junr
	Geo: Randall	Nathl Raney Edward Powel Ja^s Cain
	Ja^s Cain Junr	Nathl Raney Ja^s Cain Burwel Banks
Jan: y^e	Ja^s Cain Senr	Thos Wilkerson Geo: Rob'son
		Geo: Robertson
10th	George Robertson	Burwel Banks Peter Cain Wm Mitchell
1760	Burwel Banks	Wm Mitchell Tad^h[?] Green Ja^s Moss
	Thos Wilkerson	Wm Mitchell Thos Butler Fred: Green
	Elisabeth Burrow	John Kelly Jn° Harrison Thos Huson
	Ja^s Moss	Jn° Kelly Jn° Kelly Mary Jones
	Thos Butler	David Tucker Jn° Kelly Wm Mitchell
March	Wm Mitchell	Peter Cain Fred: Green Peter Cain
ye 20th	Thos Huson	Ja^s Cain Senr Nathl Raney
	John Harrison	Edward Powel Ja^s Cain Junr
21st	David Tucker	Wm Mitchell Fred: Green
	Mary Jones	
	Fred: Green	[Processioning Masters]
	Peter Green	Amos Love

	Peter Cain		Peter Green
	Wm Raney Senr		
N° 31	Ja^s Adam		

An account of the Several lands Processioned together with the Particular Names of the Person holding Such Lands respectively, & a List of the Persons Present at the time of Processioning & Renewing the Land Marks of each Tract of Land as taken by the Subscribers Pursuant to an Order of the Vestry of Albemarle Parish Bearing date the 6th Day of August 1759

To Whom Belonging	when Processioned	Persons Present
John Stuart, Nathl Wyche	25th March	John Stuart Nathl Wyche
John Nanny, Arthur Bass	1760	Joseph Thorp John Nanney
Saml Alsobrook, Joseph Thorp		Saml Alsobrook Maj^r Tiller
Major Tiller, James Wyche & Wm Womack		Wm Womack & Ja^s Wyche

N°32   Ja^s Wyche Pro: Masters
                                                                                      & Joseph Thorp

[167]

Pursuant to an Order of the Vestry of Albemarle Parish Dated the 6th Day of August 1759 Wee the Subscribers have processioned every Mans Land & Renewed their Land Marks in Our precinct from Stoke's road to the head of the spring Swamp so Down the Rackcoon Swamp to Stokes Road excepting William Conneleys Edward Powels & Abel Maberys who would not attend & the reason why they would attend we do not know every Other Mans land in Our Precinct wee have processioned & the Land Marks Renewed & had Precinct [present?] at the Performance of the Same every Freeholder in the Precinct Viz: Henry Brown, Hamlin Stokes Freemans, James Chappell, John Wilborn, Charles Judkins, James Bells, Abraham Browns, Silvanus Stokeses, Thomas Spain, John Owens, William Roland, John Forts, Thos Adkins, Joseph Rolands, Saml Northingtons, Edward Slates, Wm Roses, John Rolands

All their Lands herein Mentioned was Peaciably & Quietly Processioned & their land Marks Renewed by us

                                                 [Procession Masters]   Charles Judkins
N° 33   Silvanus Stokes

Pursuant to an Order of the Worshipfull Vestry of Albemarle Parish Dated August the 6th 1759 we the Subscribers have processioned all the Land within Our Precinct & have Renewed all the Land Marks all the Persons therein being precinct Viz. Robert Webb, Charles Battle, Henry Freeman, Thos Moore, Thos Moore Junr, Joseph Renn, Levy Gilliam, Curtis Land, Robert Land, Jones Stokes, Marcus Stokes Wm Loftin, Mary Clanton, David Pidington, James Cooper & Thos Capell

N° 34   [Procession Masters]   Robert Webb
                                                                                        Charles Battle

Pursuant to the within Order we the Subscribers have processioned all the Lands in the within Mentioned Precinct & Renewed the Land Marks in Company with the Freeholders within the aforesaid Precinct Given Under Our Hands this 22^d Day of March 1760
N° 35   [Procession Masters]   Henry Blow
                                                                                        Arthur Smith

[168]

[These names are presented in sequence as written; the persons present may not be the ones at a particular proprietor's land as processioned].

132   The Vestry Book of Albemarle Parish

Lines Processioned Between	Persons Present	Lines Processioned Between	Persons Present
John Battle Sen[r]	Ja[s] Barns	Charles Sledge	Ja[s] Hubbud
John Battle Jun[r]	John Battle	Matthew Hubbud	W[m] Jelks
John Battle Sen[r]	D[o]	W[m] Jelks	D[o]
John Bradley	Amos Newsum	Matthew Hubbud	
John Battle Jun[r]	Tho[s] Battle	Charles Sledge	D[o]
Ja[s] Stuart	John Battle	Morris Dunn	
John Battle	Ja[s] Barns	Ja[s] Martin	D[o]
Peter Avent	D[o]	Charles Sledge	
John Battle Jun[r]	John Hill	Edward Linsey	D[o]
W[m] Doby	D[o]	Ja[s] Martin	D[o]
Benj: Seburn	D[o]	Ed[d] Linsey	D[o]
George Toy	D[o]	John Morgan	D[o]
John Battle Jun[r]	D[o]	W[m] Sammons	D[o]
John Hill	D[o]	John Morgan	Joel Maclamore
Tho[s] Vinson	D[o]	Rob[t] Sandafer	Bur[l] Maclamore
Joseph Prince	D[o]	Tho[s] Vinson	Benj: Adams
W[m] Battle	Amos Newsum	W[m] Hix	
Tho[s] Vinson	Benj: Seburn	Rob[t] Sandafer	Sam[l] Bulluck
W[m] Battle	Ja[s] Barns	Tho[s] Briggs	
Joseph Prince	Ethel[d] Jelks	John Morgan	D[o]
W[m] Battle	Ja[s] Barns	Sarah Watkins	
Matthew Hubbudd	John Battle	John Morgan	D[o]
Rob[t] Linn	Amos Newsum	Tho[s] Briggs	
Matthew Hubbud	Benj: Seburn	W[m] Hix	
John Hill	Ja[s] Barns	John Bulluck	Joel Maclamore
Tho[s] Vinson	Ethel[d] Jelks	Charles Bulluck	Bur[l] Maclamore
John Bishop	D[o]	Fredrick Flood	Benj: Adams
W[m] Hill	John Battle	Agnes Adams	Tho[s] Adams
John Barns	Rob[t] Linn	John Bulluck	Sam[l] Bulluck
John Bishop	Ethel[d] Jelks	Benj: Hail	D[o]
John Barns	Ja[s] Barns	Tho[s] Adams	D[o]
Amy Bullock	Amos Newsum	Henry Tyler	D[o]
Vol: W[m]son	Sam[l] Bullock	Benj: Hail	D[o]
John Barns	D[o]	Henry Tyler	Bur[l] Maclamore
Amy Bullock	D[o]	Edward Prince	Benj: Adams
Vol: W[m]son	D[o]	John Maclamore Sen[r]	John Pate
Joseph Robork	Benj: Adams	Henry Tyler	
Vol: W[m]son	Tho[s] D[o]	Adam Toy	D[o]
Joseph Ezell	Joseph Prince	Henry Tyler	
Vol: W[m]son	Ardrich Flood	Burrell Maclamore	D[o]
Matthew Hubbud	Joseph Prince	Henry Tyler	
Ethel[d] Jelks	Benj: Adams		

N[o] 36 March 25th 1760   [Processioning Masters]   Henry Tyler
                                                                  Thomas Pate

[169]

In Obedience to an Order of the Worshipful Vestry of Albemarle Parish Dated the 6th Day of August 1759 & to us Directed wee the Subscribers having first Summoned the Freeholders with the precinct in the said Order Mentioned have processioned & Renewed the Land Marks of every Persons within the Precinct

Proprietors Names	Persons Present
Wm Andrews	Wm Andrews
John Pidington Junr	John Pidington
John Pidington	John Pidington
John Bishop	John Bishop
John Clanton	John Clanton
Henry Harrison	Henry Harrison
John Rochell	John Knight
Richd King	Cornelius Loftin
John Knight	Richard Avery
Cornelius Loftin	Wm Rogers
Richd Avery	
Thos Moore Senr	
Wm Rogers	

Given Under our Hands this 1st Day of March 1760

N° 37

[Processioning Masters]
Richard Avary
Cornelius Loftin

[170]

At a Vestry Held for the Parish of Albemarle in the County of Sussex at Nottoway Church on the 12th Day of May 1760

Present
The Revd Mr William Willie

Lawrence Gibbons	Howel Briggs	
James Chappell	Nicholas Massenburg }	Gent.
Ephraim Parham	Henry Harrison	

Ordered that the Churchwardens pay to Peter Smith the Sum of One Pound out of the Money in their hands belonging to this parish for Nursing Amy Smiths Child 9 Weeks & Making a Coffin & Burying the said Child

Ordered that the Churchwardens pay to Isaac Robertson a Poor Ancient Man the Sum of two Pounds

Order that the Churchwardens pay to William Rogers Junr a Poor infirm Man the Sum of three Pounds

Ordered that Howel Briggs Supply Frances Hood a Pensioner with as many Goods as will amount to thirty Shillings

Ordered that the Churchwardens bring Frances Hood to the Next Vestry

William Willie Min^r
Copy Test Ja^s Chappell J^r Clk Vestry

[171]

At a Vestry Held for the Parish of Albemarle in the County of Sussex at Nottoway Church on the 9th Day of June 1760

Present
The Revd William Willie

Law^e Gibbons   Mich^l Blow
Ja^s Chappell   Moses Johnson } Gent.
Howel Briggs   Nich^s Massenburg
       & John Mason

Thirty One[sic] returns of Processioning haveing been Made were this Day Examined & found to be Duly Regestered

Ordered that the Churchwardens find for Edward Carter a Needy infirm & Sickly Man three Barrells of Corn & one Hundred Pounds of Bacon

Ordered Edward Carter be exempted from paying his Parish Levy During his indisposition

Ordered that William Bradley & Thos Alsobrook be exempted from paying their Parish Levies for the future

Ordered that Edward Crosland be exempted from Paying his Parish Levy During his indisposition

This Day John Mason offered his account in Vestry for the Years 1755 & 1756 for which Years he was Collector but the Vestry refused to Receive his Account

Ordered that Edward Facy a Poor infirm Man apply to Capt Howel Briggs for 9 ells of Ozzenbrigge

William Willie Min^r
Copy Test Ja^s Chappell Junr Clk Vestry

[172]

1757 Albemarle Parish to James Gee late Sherriff Dec^d	D^r
To pd the Revd William Willie	17305
To pd Ed^d Walker Clk of Nottoway Church	1200
To pd Robt Nicolson D^o at St Pauls	1200
To pd Robt Farrinton D^o at St Marks	1200
To pd D^o as Sexton at S^t D^o	500
To pd Gregory Rawlings Clk at St Andrews	1200
To pd John Bain sexton at St Pauls	500
To pd Edward Shelton as D^o at St Andrews	500
To pd William Rigbie as D^o at Nottoway	500
To pd Moses Johnson for keeping John King a Year	800
To pd Matthew Whitfeild for keeping Rebecca Bird a Year	800
To pd Ja^s Chappell J^r Clerk of the Vestry	400
To pd John King Junr for keeping Frances Hood a Year	500
To pd Wm Aldridge for keeping Ja^s Odonally 11 Months	412½
To pd D^o for keeping Hugh Odonally 10 Months	375
To levied for the Use of the Parish	3022
To the Collector for collecting 32355lbs Tob^o	1941
To Commission on 169 Tithes	152
To 52 tithes Returned insolvents	780

Surry and Sussex Counties, Virginia, 1742-1786

	33287½
To Ball: as Pr Contra	1648½
	34936
Pr Contra C^r	
By 2157 Tithes 5^{lbs} Pr Poll	32355
By 54 tithes omitted in the list a' 15^{lbs} Tob° Pr Pole	810
By 115 Tithes Unlisted a' 15^{lbs} Tob° Pr Pole	1725
By 6 Pr Cent on 52 Tithes Returned insolvent & twice listed	46
	34936
By Balance Due	1648½

[173]

1758 Albemarle Parish to James Gee late Sherriff Dec^d

To Cash pd Maj^r Nich^s Massenburg for 17305 lb Tob° a' 2^d p^r ll	£ 144: 4: 2
To Cash pd D° for 3955^{lb} Tob° levied for the use of the Parish a' 2^dll	32:19: 2
To Cash pd Ed^d Walker Clk of Nottoway for 1200^{ll} a' 2^d p^r ll	10: 0: 0
To Cash pd John Nicolson Clk of St Pauls for 1200^{ll} a' 2^d ll	10: 0: 0
To Cash pd Amos Love Clerk of St Marks for 1000^{ll} a' 2^d ll	8: 6: 8
To Cash pd Gregory Rawlings Clk of St Andrews for 1200^{ll} a' 2^d ll	10: 0: 0
To Cash pd Richd Wiggins Sexton at Nottoway for 412 at D°	3: 8: 8
To Cash pd John Bain D° at St Pauls for 500 a' D°	4: 3: 4
To Cash pd Edward Shelton D° at St Andrews for 500 a' D°	4: 3: 4
To Cash pd Peter Green D° at St Marks for 500 a' D°	4: 3: 4
To Cash pd Moses Johnson for keeping John King 800 a' D°	6:13: 4
To Cash pd Ephraim Parham for keeping Ja^s Odonally 400 a' D°	3: 6: 8
To Cash pd Ja^s Chappell J^r Clk of the Vestry 400 a' D°	3: 6: 8
To Cash pd Capt John Mason----for 15 a' D°	0: 2: 6
To Cash pd Wm Briggs for 6 Parish levies 90 a' D°	0:15: 0
To Cash pd John Hood for keeping Frances Hood 500 a' D°	4: 3: 4
To Commissions for Collecting 3180^{ll} Tob° a' 6p^r Cent: 19^{ll} w a' 2^d	15:18: 0
To Commission on 525^{ll} Tob° Collected of 35 persons not listed 31^{ll} Tob° @ 2^d	0: 5: 2
To Commission on 134 Tithables error in laying the levy 120^{ll} a' 2^d	1: 0: 0
To 46 insolvent tithes a' 15^{ll} Pr Poll 690^{ll} a' 2^d	5: 15: 0
To 14 Tithes twice listed & overcharg'd D° 210^{ll} a' 2^d	1: 15: 0
To Serving a Writ on Dorothy Brandom by Order of the Churchwardens 24^{ll} a' 2^d	0: 4: 0
	£ 274: 14: 4
To Ball: Due the Parish	12: 12: 2
	£ 287: 6: 4
Pr Contra C^r	
By 2126 tithes @ 15^{lb} Tob° p^r Poll 31890 a' 2^d P^{er} ll	265: 15: 0
By Error in laying the levy 134 Tithes a' 15^{ll} p^r poll 2010^{ll}Tob° a' 2^d p^r ll	16: 15: 0
By 35 Tithes discovered Not listed a' 15^{ll} p^r poll 525 a' 2^d	4: 7: 6
By 46 Tithes returned insolvent a' 15^{ll} p^r pole 690	5: 10: 0
My Commission on that 41¹ a' 2^d	0: 6:10
My Commission on 14 tithes twice listed 12^{ll} a' D°	0: 2: 0
Ball. Due as Pr Contra	£ 287: 6: 4
E. Excepted P Henry Gee Executor	12: 12: 2

[174]

At a Vestry Held at Nottoway Church for the Parish of Albemarle in the County of Sussex on ye 30th Day of December 1760

Present
The Revd Mr Wm Willie

Mich^l Blow	James Chappell	
Howel Briggs	Moses Johnson }	Gent
Ephraim Parham	Nich^s Massenburg	
& Lawrence Gibbons		

Albemarle Parish   D^r

	Wt lbs Tob^o
To the Revd Mr Wm Willie as Min^r	17305
To Edward Walker Clerk at Nottoway Church	1200
To John Nicolson D^o at St Pauls D^o	1200
To Amos Love D^o at St Marks D^o	1200
To Gregory Rawlings D^o at St Andrews D^o	1200
To Richd Wiggins Sexton at Nottoway Church	500
To John Bain D^o at St Pauls D^o	500
To Peter Green D^o at St Marks D^o	500
To Joseph Armstrong D^o at St Andrews D^o	500
To Mr Moses Johnson for keeping John King a lame Child	800
To Ja^s Chappell Junr Clerk of the Vestry	400
To D^o for Services Done	200
To Thos Hines for 3 Levies twice listed last Year	48
To John Pidington for 7 Levies twice listed last Year	112
To John Pidington J^r for 1 levy twice listed last Year	16
To Levied for Supporting Edward Carter a Poor Sickly Man & his Children	700
To John Bain for Services Done at St Pauls Church	150
To Edward Jones for a Levy twice listed last Year	16
	26547
To Levied for the Use of the Parish	9939
To the Collector for Coll:g 38791 at 6 pr. Cent	2305
	38791
By 2403 Tithables a^t 16^{lb} Pr Poll C^r	38448
By Nich^s Massenburg for Ball: on his acct. Due the Parish	343
	38791

[175]

Ordered that Nichols Massenburg on his entering into Bond & Security to the Vestry of the Parish to be taken by the Clerk of the Vestry be Appointed Collector of this Parish for the Year Next ensuing & that he Collect & receive of every Tithable Person Chargable therewith the Sum of 16 pounds of Tobacco Pr Poll or any part thereof be Delayed on Refused to Levy the same by Distress & that he Pays to each Respective Parish Creditor the Several Sums of Tob^o Due to them & that he pay the Tob^o Levied for the Use of the Parish to the Churchwardens for the time being

Ordered that the Chwardens Pay to Thos Huson forty Shillings for keeping & Burying Jamimah Waller a Sickly & infirm Woman

---

Ordered that Edward Meachum be exempted for paying his Parish Levy for the future

---

Ordered that the Chwardens pay to Richd Wiggins five Shillings for cleaning the Well at Nottoway Church & finding a Bucket

Ordered that the Chwardens find 200 pounds of pork for Edward Crosland a poor Cripple man

Ordered that the Chwardens pay to Richd Wiggins three pounds fifteen Shillings for keeping Ja^s Odonnolly 1 Year last October

Ordered that the Chwardens pay to Wm Cox Six Pounds for keeping Drusilla & Rebecca King 1 Year last October

Ordered that the Chwardens Pay to John Moss five Pounds eight Shillings in full of his Account

Ordered that the Chwardens pay to John Roland three pounds fifteen Shillings for keeping John Muns's Children

Ordered that the Chwardens pay to Robt Armstrong four pounds for keeping a child of John Muns's

This Day Henry Gee Rendered his Acct^s in Vestry which Acct^s were Examined allowed & ordered to be Registered

Ordered that the Chwardens pay to the Revd Mr Wm Willie Six Pounds Six Shillings & eight pence in full of his Acc^t

Wm Willie Min^r
Copy Test Ja^s Chappell J^r Clk Vestry

[176]

1760 D^r the Parish of Albemarle to N. Massenburg Sheriff of Sussex
C^r Lb Tob^o

To 38 Insolvents & persons that have Removed out of the the[sic] County Since the Levy was laid Vizt Richd Barlow 1: Thos Bilbro 1: Edward Carter 2: James Cook 1: John Gilliam 2: Wm Green 2: Wm Graves 1: Thos Hood 1: Richd Jones 1: Richd Lanier 1. Wm Lister 1: Robert Morgan 2: Wm Pair 1: Nathan Rogers 1: Ja^s Roper 1. Wm Rawlings 1: Saml Santee 1: Benja: Smith 1: John Underwood 1: Edward Whittington 1: Wm Whittington 1: Robert Whitehead 1: Wm Aldridge 1. Mich^l Exum 1: Thos Browns 1: Ja^s Berkley 1: John Burgess 1: Wm Goging[sic] 1: John Ellis 1: Edward Evinton 1: Semore Mahany 1: Wm Scoging 1: John Verrel 1: Thos Wrenn 1: {216^{lb}:608}

To my commission on Con^r 976 lb Tobo^o	58
To Retry 2 Writs vs Amy Smith for Basterdy	16
To Retry 1 D^o vs Lucy Nunn	8
To Retry 3 D^o vs Lashly	24
To Ballance Due to the Parish	298
1760	1012
By Tob^o Rec^d for 61 Tithables not listed a^t 16^{lb}	976
By a Drawback of Com. on ye Contra 608lbs: Tob^o	36
	1012
By Ballance Due as Pr Contra	298
By Exum, Bartley, & Cook no Insolvents Exclusive of Com:	45
	343

E. E. [Error Excepted] P Nichols Massenburg

[177]

		Dr The Parish of Albemarle to Howel	
1759		To Ballance due of last Settlement	[£] 17: 3
July 20		To 1 Months Board of Jno & D: Odonnally	12: 6
		To 4½ ells Ozzenbrigs for D^o	6: 0
		To Thread 4^d making two shirts 2/	2: 4
		To Cash paid the Sherriff for Earwood	1: 1: -
		To D^o for Peter Smith	4:15: 2
		To D^o Paid Smith	4:10
		To D^o Paid the Sherriff for Richd Hay	2:13: 5
August 2		To D^o Paid Catharine Yearwood in full	11: 8
Sep^t 21		To Paid the Revd Mr Willie for Sacrament^l Elements	6:10
		To Cash paid the Widow King	17: 6
		To Cash paid Matthew Whitfeild	1:10: 7
		To Doct^r Peets Paid him	6:16:10
		To John Roland	0:10: -
Decr 7		To 2 lb Sugar for Amy Smiths Child	1: 4
		To Sundrys Deliver.d by Order of Vestry to Sundry Persons as Pr Capt Briggs's Acct	20: 9: 7½
		To Sloman Wynne paid him for Nursing Sucrese Nun at her Lying in Paying the Midwife &c	2: 6: -
		To 24 Lb Tob^o paid the late Sheriff for executing Writ on D Brandon	4: -
		To Returning 3 writs vs Nun 24th Tob^o	4: -
		To D^o 1 D^o vs Lashley 8th Tob^o	1: 4
		To Cash Paid Thos Battle for keeping Odonally	3:15: -
		To John Hood in full for keeping Kings Childen	5: -: -
			70: 9: -½

	D^r fines & forfeitures	
	To Thos Waller Paid him	3: -: -
	To Cash paid Messrs Gibbons & Blow	7: 8: 9
		10: 8: 9

[178]

	Briggs & Nicholas Massenburg	Cr	[£]
1759	By Cash for Swearing		5: -
	By 1 fine for Basterdy		2:10: -
	By 2 D^o		5: -: -
			£7:15: -
	Carried below		
	By 3955^{lb} Tob^o levied for the Parish		32:19: 2
	By Cor^d. Cash paid Richd Hay being an error		2:13: 5
	By Cor^d 24^{ll} Tob^o paid late Sheriff being an error		4: -
			35:16: 7
	By Ballance Due the Churchwardens		34: 4: 2½
			70: -: 9½

Cor^d	By Sundry fines as above	7:15: -
	By 1 fine for Basterdy	2:10: -
	By Coll: Claiborne Rec^d of him	3: 9
		10: 8: 9

[179]

Albemarle Parish In Obedience to an Order of Vestry of the said Parish Wee the Subscribers did on this Day to wit the 22^d of May 1759 Examine into the Accounts of the Churchwardens of the said Parish to wit Beginning with the Levy of the said Parish laid the 15th of September 1751 which appears as follows

	Accounted for		Levied lb W^t Tob^o
1752	Robert Jones & Robert Wyne Chwardens	22309	21938
1753	Same	1317	1275
1754	Robert Jones & Howel Briggs	1977	none
1755	Same	1827	1809
1756	Thos Avent & Gray Briggs	12	none

Upon which account as above Statd it appers the Ballance Due
to the Parish from Jones & Wynne is   413
              from Jones & Briggs   1975
              from Avent & Briggs   12
                                             2420

It also Appears to us that the following Sums of Money Remain Due to the Parish

	Capt John Mason	[£]	0:16:11
	Howel Briggs		10:15: 9
Mason	Christopher Mason		2: 2:10
&	David Mason		1: 0: 8
Tatum	Daniel Mason		0:16: 9½
Church	David Hunter		16:12: 9
wardens	Mason & Tatum		3: 0: 5
	Jones & Wynne		10: 9: 2½
		£	45:15: 6½

Given Under our hands this twenty first Day of May in the Year of Our Lord One Thousand Seven hundred & fifty Nine & in the xxxij Year of the Reign of King George the Second

                                                          Wm Willie
                                                          A Claiborne
                                                          Nich^s Massenburg

[180]

At a Vestry Held on Nottoway Church for the Parish of Albemarle in the County of Sussex on the 23^d Day of May 1761

Present
The Revd Wm Willie

Aug: Claiborne	Howel Briggs	
Ja^s Chappell	Moses Johnson	
Ephraim Parham	John Mason	} Gent
Nich^s Massenburg	Law: Gibbons	
& Mich^l Blow		

Lawrence Gibbons & Mich^l Blow are Continued Churchwardens till Next Easter Tuesday

---

Ordered that the Chwardens pay to Willam Andrews the Sum of Seven Pounds Ten Shillings for keeping & Maintaining Rosanna Dickings Orphan Child of Thos Dickings one Year & a half

---

Ordered that the Report that the Revd Mr William Willie Augustine Claiborne & Nicholas Massenburg made agreable to an Order of Vestry Bearing Date 18th Day of July 1757 be

Regestered & that the Chwardens do Collect the Several Ballances that Appears to be Due to this Parish by the said Report

Howel Briggs & Nicholas Massenburg who was formerly Chwardens this Day Rendered their accounts in Vestry for the Year 1759 which Acc^{ts} was Examined Allowed & Ordered to be Regestered

Lawrence Gibbons & Mich^l[sic] Chwardens laid their Acc^{ts} before the Vestry for the Year 1760 but they not having Settled with the Collector ordered that the Compleating Examining of the Acc^{ts} be Defered till the Next Vestry

Ordered that the Clerk of this Vestry Notice Howel Briggs & Robert Jons Junr to Appear at the Vestry for laying the Next Levy to Render an Acct of their Churchwardenship the Vestry Objecting to the Acc^{ts} of the said Briggs & Jones laid before Vestry of which they were formerly warned by order of Vestry

[181]

The Revd Wm Willie has Undertaken to find Elements for the Sacrament & Transport the Plate to the Several Churches for which is to have ten pounds Pr Year to commence the Last Easter & to Continue till Next Easter

Ordered that the Chwardens pay to the Rev Wm Willie five pounds four Shillings in full of his acc^t till Last Easter

Ordered that the Chwardens Pay out of the Money in their hands which has Accrued to this Parish from fines & forfeitures to the Several persons hereafter Named the Sums of Money placed against each persons

Name To Witt	
To Edward Crosland	£ 1:10: 0
To Agnes Carter	2:10: 0
To Anne Grosswitt	2:10: 0
To Elisabeth Whitehead	1:10: 0
To Elisabeth Spane	1:10: 0
To Sarah Owen	1:10: 0
To Tabitha Roland	2:10: 0
To Thos Waller	2:10: 0
To Henry Tudor	2: 0: 0
To Ja^s Hearn Junr	2: 0: 0
To the Widow Birdsong	2: 0: 0
To Sarah Capell	1:10: 0
To Isaac Robertson	2: 0: 0
To Selah Huland	1:15: 0
	£ 26: 5: 0

Ordered that Thos Pate be exempted from paying his Parish Levy for the future

Ordered that Saml Stokes be exempted from paying his Parish Levy for the future

David Mason is Elected to Serve this Parish as a Vestry Man instead of James Gee Dec^d & that he Qqualify as Soon as Possible to Serve this Parish in that Capassity

Ordered that Thos Jones on Hardwood [Creek?] be exempted from paying his Parish Levy for the future

Wm Willie Min^r
Copy Test Ja^s Chappell J^r Clk Vest.

[182]

At a Vestry held for Parish of Albemarle in the County of Sussex at Nottoway Church on the 27th Day of Nov. 1761

Present
The Revd William Willie
Lawrence Gibbons   Augustine Claiborne
John Mason   Moses Johnson } Gent
Ephraim Parham   Henry Harrison

Albemarle Parish	D^r	Wt lbs Tob°
To the Revd Mr Wm Willie as Min^r		17305
To Edward Walker Clerk at Nottoway Church		1200
To John Nicolson D° at St Pauls D°		1200
To Amos Love D° at St Marks D°		1200
To Gregory Rawlings D° at St Andrews D°		1200
To Richd Wiggins Sexton at Nottoway Church		500
To John Bain D° at St Pauls D°		500
To Peter Green D° at St Marks D°		500
To Joseph Armstrong D° at St Andrews D°		500
To Mr Moses Johnson for keeping John King a lame Child		800
To Ja^s Chappell Junr Clerk of the Vestry		400
To John Wilkerson for one Levy paid twice		16
To Levied for Making Additions to Nottoway Church & St Marks Church & other Parish Uses		16100
To the Collector for Collecting 440064^{lbs} of Tob° at 6 Pr Cent		2643
		44064
By 2448 Tithables at 18th of Tob° Pr Poll		44064

[183]

Ordered that Ja^s Jones & John Mason the Younger on their entering into Bond & Security to the Vestry of this Parish to be taken by the Clerk of the Vestry be Appointed Collectors of this Parish for the Year Next Ensuing & that they Collect & Receive of every Tithable Person Chargable therewith the Sum of 18 pounds of Tob° Pr Poll & that they have Authority in Case the Said 18 pounds of Tob° Pr Poll or any Part thereof be Delayed or Refused to levy the Same by Distress & that they Pay to each Respective Parish Creditor the several Sums of Tob° Due to them & that they Pay the Tob° Levied for the Use of the Parish to the Churchwardens for the time being

---

Ordered that John Muns & John Bagley be exempted from the Payment of Parish Levy for the future

---

Ordered that John Mason & Augustine Claiborne examine into the Present State of Nottoway Church frame & upon Such Examination to contract with workmen to make all Necessary Repairs to the Present Building & also to Build an addition of Thirty feet long on the North side of the same Weadth[sic] other Dementions & fashion of the Present Building & to take Bond for performance thereof in a workmanlike Manner

---

Ordered that Lawrence Gibbons & Ephram Parham examine the Present State of St Marks Church frame & upon such Examination to contract with Workmen to make all Necessary Repairs to the Present Building & also to Build an Addition of thirty foot long on the North side of the same Weadth other Dementions & fashon of the present Building & to take bond for Performance thereof in a workman like Manner

Ordered that the Churchwardens pay to Moses Johnson three pounds Current Money to be by him laid out in Provisions for Rebecca Pair a poor Old infirm woman of this Parish

[184]

Ordered that the Churchwardens pay to Ann King Widow three pounds current Money for taking care of her child Sarah Ann King till the laying the Next Levy

Ordered that the Churchwardens pay to Ephraim Parham four Pounds six Shillings Current Money to be by him laid out in Provisions for Agnes Carter

Ordered that the Churchwardens pay to Wm Cox Six Pounds for taking care of Drusilla & Rebecca King the last Year

Wm Cox came into Vestry & Undertakes to take care of Rebecca King the ensuing Year for three Pounds to be computed from the last Day of October last

Ordered that the Churchwardens pay to Mary Ezell twenty Nine Shillings for keeping James Odonally 10 Months of the last Year

Wm Willie Min^r
Copy Test Ja^s Chappell J^r Clk Vest.

[185]

D^r the Parish of Albamarle in Account

To Cash paid Capt Gibbons	£ 4: 0: 0
To D^o paid William Willie his Acc^t	6: 6: 3
To D^o paid Wm Cox his Acc^t	6: 0: 0
To D^o paid Richd Wiggins his Claim	3:15: 0
To D^o paid the Widow Moss her Claim	5:14: 6
To Mr Gibbons for the Use of the Parish	16:18: 6
To paid the Widow Birdsong her Acc^t	2: 0: 0
To Mr Gibbons for the use of the Parish	5: 0: 0
To paid William Andrews his Claim	7:10: 0
To paid Mr Wm Willie his Claim	5: 4: 0
To paid the Widow Huland her Acc^t	3: 5: 0
To paid the Widow Moss her Claim	5:12: 6
	£73: 5: 9

E E Pr Mich^l Blow

[186]

With the Churchwardens of ye said Parish for the Years 1760 & 1761

By Cash Rec^d of the late Churchwardens	£ 7: 8: 9
By Cash Rec^d of Thos Wynne for a presentment of the Grand Jury for Profane Swearing	0: 5: 0
By 1090^{lbs} of Tob^o Sold at Auction a^t 18 P^{r}Ct	9:16: 2
By 3050 sold at Auction a^t 17/9 P^r Ct	27: 2: 0
By a fine Rec^d of Sarah Hix for Basterdy	2:10: 0
By a fine on a Presentment of the Grand Jury against James Barns for Swearing	0: 5: 0
By D^o against Henry Harrison for D^o	0: 5: 0
By D^o aganst James Sturdavant for D^o	0: 5: 0
	£72: 8: 8
By Cash of Maj^r Gibbons	0:17: 1
	£73: 5: 9

[187]

1761   The Parish of Albemarle D[r] to Lawrence Gibbons

		£ S D
fines	To Balance Due last Settlement	26: 0: 0
as	To Edward Crosland	1:10: 0
below	To Agnes Carter	2:10: 0
	To Ann Gresswitt	2: 0: 0
	To Elisabeth Whitehead	1:10: 0
	To Elisabeth Spane	1:10: 0
	To Sarah Owen	1:10: 0
	To Tabitha Roland	2:10: 0
	To Tho[s] Waller	2: 0: 0
	To Henry Tudor	2: 0: 0
	To James Hearn Jun[r]	2: 0: 0
	To The Widow Birdsong	2: 0: 0
	To Sarah Capell	1:10: 0
	To Isaac Robertson	2: 0: 0
	To Selah Huland	1:15: 0
		26: 5: 0
	To the Rev[d] M[r] Willie as P[r] Receit	10: 0: 0
	To Cap[t] Jones for £2 for Tho[s] Huson	2: 0: 0
	To Moses Johnson for Rebecca Pair	3: 0: 0
	To Timothy Ezell	1:12: 0
	To William Cox	6: 0: 0
	To Moses Johnson for Sarah Capell	0:10: 0
1761	To Ann King	3: 0: 0
	To Ephraim Parham for Agnes Carter	4: 6: 0
	To Moses Johnson for Sarah Capell	1:10: 0
	W[m] Hix C[r] in William Parhams Store	2: 3: 9
	To Edward Facy C[r] in William Parhams Store	0: 3: 4
		34: 4: 7
	To Ballance Due to the Parish	44: 8: 1
		78:12: 8

[188]

& Mich[l] Blow ——————————   Cr

	[£ S D]
By Tob[o] Sold for the Use of the Parish 10107 [lbs]	
Cap[t] James Jones To 5140 a[t] 14/10	38: 2: 5
M[r] Hunicutt 2514 a[t] 15/2	19: 1: 3
D[o] 845 a[t] 14/10	6: 5: 4
Coll: Massenburg 1608 a[t] 15/	12: 1: 0
	£ 75:10: 0
Rec[d] of Coll: Nicholas Massenburg	3: 2: 8
	78:12: 8

By Contra Ballance	44: 8: 1
By Cap¹ Howel Briggs for Ballance of his Acct. as Churchwarden in 1754	10:15: 9
	£55: 3: 9

Dʳ Brought up	
To Nicholas Massenburg Paid his Acct	7:18: 6
To Cap¹ Briggs Paid him	27:19: 5
To Cash Paid Cap¹ Blow	0:17: 1
To Cash in the hands of Nichˢ Massenburg	4: 2: 6
To Cash Paid Cap¹ Harrison Churchwarden	14: 6: 4
	[£] 55: 3:10

[189]

At a Vestry Held at Nottoway Church for the Parish of Albemarle in the County of Sussex on the 13ᵗʰ Day of April 1762 being Easter Tuesday

Present
The Revᵈ William Willie
Lawrence Gibbons   Mich¹ Blow
Howel Briggs   Moses Johnson }Gent
Nicholas Massenburg   John Mason
& Henry Harrison

John Edmunds & Henry Harrison are Appointed Churchwardens for the Year Next Ensuing

Ordered that the Churchwardens Pay out of the Money in their hands which has Accrued to this Parish from fines & forfeitures to the Several Persons hereafter Named the Several Sums of Money Placed against each Persons Name to Witt

To John Painter	£1: 5: 0
To William Hix	0:10: 0
To Sarah Capell	1: 5: 9
To Tabitha Roland	1: 7: 0
To James Hearn Junʳ	1: 7: 0
To Ann Gresswitt	1: 7: 0
To the Widow Broadribb	1: 7: 0
To the Widow Birdsong	1: 0: 0
	£9: 8: 9

This Day Lawrence Gibbons & Mich¹ Blow brought their Accounts in Vestry for the Years 1760 & 1761 which Accounts were Examined Allowed & Ordered to be Regestered

Ordered that William Rogers & John King be Exempted from Paying their Parish Levies for the future

[190]

Ordered that the Churchwardens Pay to Thomas Alsobrook on Easter Tuesday Next the Sum of Three Pounds for keeping a Orphan Child of Benjamin Whites

Ordered that the Churchwardens pay to Nichˢ Massenburg the Ballance of his Accounts as Collector for the Year 1761

Samuel Harwood came into Vestry & agreed to keep Susannah Painter the Year Next ensung & find her all Necessaries for the Sum of five Pounds

John Doby came into Vestry & agreed to keep Mary Painter the Year Next Ensuing & find her all Necessaries for the sum of three Pounds

Wm Willie Min^r

Copy Test   Ja^s Chappell Junr Clk of the Vestry

[191]

At a Vestry held at Sussex Court for the Parish of Albemarle in the County of Sussex on the 18th Day of Novr 1762

Present
~~The Revd William Willie~~

James Chappell	Howel Briggs
Aug: Claiborne	Nicholas Massenburg
John Mason	Moses Johnson } Gent
Ephraim Parham &	Henry Harrison

Albemarle Parish D^r	Wt lbs Tob^o
To the Revd Mr Wm Willie as Min^r	17305
To Edward Walker Clerk at Nottoway Church	1200
To John Nicolson D^o at St Pauls D^o	1200
To Amos Love D^o at St Marks D^o	1200
To Gregory Rawlings D^o at St Andrews D^o	1200
To Timothy Ezell Sexton at Nottoway	500
To John Bain D^o at St Pauls D^o	500
To Peter Green D^o at St Marks D^o	500
To Joseph Armstrong D^o at St Andrews D^o	500
To Ja^s Chappell Junr Clerk of the Vestry	400
To Sarah Hobbs for 2 Tithes twice listed last Year	36
To the Collector	1475
To levied for the Use of the Parish	315
	26367
By 2397 Tithables a^t 11 Pr Poll	26367

[192]

Ordered that James Jones & John Mason Junr on their entering into Bond & Security to the Vestry of this Parish to be taken by the Clerk of the Vestry to be Appointed Collectors of this Parish for the Year ensuing & that they Collect & Receive of every Tithable Person Chargable therewith the Sum of 11 pounds of Tobacco Pr Poll or any Part thereof be Delayed or Refused to Levy the same by Distress & that they Pay the Tobacco Levied for the Use of the Parish to the Churchwardens for the time being

Ordered that Charles Gilliam Thomas Cullum & John Wynne be Exempted from Paying their Parish Levies for the future

Ordered that the Churchwardens pay to Richard Wiggins twelve Shilling & six pence for keeping James Odonally two Months

Ordered that the following Allowances be made Vizt

To Rebecca Pair	£ 3: 0: 0
To Agnes Carter	6: 0: 0
To William Cox	3: 0:
To Mary Ezell	1: 9: 0
To Timothy Ezell for cleaning Well & Bucket	0: 7: 6
	£ 13:16: 6

That the Said Sums be Paid by the Churchwardens

H Harrison
Copy Test Ja^s Chappell Junr Clk Vestry

[193]

At a Vestry held at Nottoway Church for the Parish of Albemarle in the County of Sussex on the 27th Day of April 1763

Present
The Revd William Willie
Augustine Claiborne   Nicholas Massenburg
John Mason   Howel Briggs } Gents
Henry Harrison   &   David Mason

John Edmunds & Henry Harrison is again[sic] Appointed Churchwardens till Next Easter Tuesday
Henry Gee is elected to serve this Parish as a Vestryman instead of Ephraim Parham Dec^d & that he Qualify to Serve ths Parish in that Capassity[sic] as Soon as Possible
Mr James Chappell having Sent a Letter of Resignation to the Gent. of the Vestry & it being Rec^d Capt. James Jones is Elected to Serve this Parish as a Vestryman in his Stead & that he Qualify to Serve this Parish in that Capacity as soon as Possible
The Revd Mr William Willie having a College Lease for 102 Acres of Land adjoyning the glebe & the present Quantity of land for a Glebe being most of it cut down & worn out & cut to peices much with Swamps & Slashes so as to Render it Upon the whole a Difficult Matter for the Incumbent to make Indian Corn & other Grain and the Said Willie being Willing to take Six pounds eight Shillings his Original Purchase Money for the said Lease Ordered that the Churchwardens Pay the Six pounds eight Shillings to the said Willie & that they procure a new Lease from a Gent of the College for the Said Land for the Lives of three of the most healthy Young persons in their knowledge & that the said Lease be for the Use of the Present Incumbent & his Successiors for the Said three Lives

[194]

Ordered that Henry Mannery be exempted from Paying his Parish Levy for the future

Ordered that the Churchwardens Pay to Agnes Carter the Sum of Two Pounds

Ordered that John Mason & Nicholas Massenburg do agree with a Workman to Build
the Revd William Willie a Garden on the Glebe of the same Dementions as it is now & that they take Bond & Security for the Performance thereof & that it be an Instruction to the said Commissioners to Make use of the Posts & Rails this Day Generously Given to the Parish by Henry Harrison Esqr & now Lying at Nottoway Church & the Pails to be of Cyprus four foot Six INches long & an Inch thick & a good hart Pine Plank at least Nine Inches Wide & Inche & Quarter Prick[sic] thick at the feet of the Poles Round the Garden
Ordered that the Revd Mr Willie lay an Account of the Money in his hands belonging to the Parish that was paid to him by Edmund Ruffin Under a former Order of Vestry

Willliam Willie Min^r
Copy Test Ja^s Chappell Junr Clk Vestry

[195]

At a Vestry held at Nottoway Church for the Parish of Albemarle in the County of Sussex on ye 3rd Day of Jan: 1764

Present
The Revd Mr William Willie

John Mason	Nicholas Massenburg
Howel Briggs	David Mason
Mich^l Blow	James Jones } Gent
Lawrence Gibbons &	Henry Harrison

Albemarle Parish　　　　　　　　　　　　　　　D^r

	Wt lbs Tob^o
To the Revd Mr William Willie Min^r	17305
To Edward Walker Clerk at Nottoway Church	1200
To John Nicolson D^o at St Pauls D^o	1200
To Amos Love　D^o at St Marks D^o	1200
To Gregory Rawlings D^o at St Andrews D^o	1200
To Timothy Ezell Sexton at Nottoway	500
To John Bain D^o at St Pauls D^o	500
To Peter Green D^o at St Marks D^o	500
To William Rogers D^o at St Andrews D^o	500
To Ja^s Chappell Junr Clerk of the Vestry	400
To Swan Prichard as Pr Acct	100
	24605
To the Collector for Collec'g 30719 a^t 6 P^r C^t	1843
To Levied for the Use of the Parish	4271
	30719

Albemarle Parish　　　　　　　　　　　C^r
By 2363 Tithables a^t 13^lb of Tob^o Pr Tithe　　　30719

[196]

Ordered that Maj^r Law: Gibbons on his entering into Bond & Security to the Vestry of the Parish to be taken by the Clerk of the Vestry be Appointed Collector of this Parish for the Year ensuing & that he Collect & Receive of every Tithable Person Chargable therewith the Sum of 13^lb of Tob^o Pr Poll & that he have authority in case the said 13^lb ob Tob^o Pr Poll or any Part thereof be Delayed or Refused to Levy the same by Distress & that he pay the Tob^o Levied for the use of the Parish to be Churchwardens for the time being

Ordered that the Chwardens Pay to Wm Cox the Sum of Forty Shillings

Ordered that the Chwardens pay to Rebecca Pair a poor Ancient Woman the Sum of three Pounds Ten Shillings

Ordered that the Chwardens pay to Elisabeth King A poor Widow Woman the Sum of Three Pounds

Ordered that the Chwardens Pay to Joseph Barker a poor infirm Man the Sum of Three pounds

Ordered that the Chwarens Pay to James Jones the Sum of Forty Shillings for the Use of Elisabeth Whitehead

Ordered that the Chwardens Pay to Mich! Blow the Sum of Thirty Shillings for the of Elisabeth Birdsong

Ordered that the Chwardens Pay to Mich! Blow for the Use of Anne Feilds the Sum of Forty Shillings

Ordered that the Chwardens Pay to Mich! Blow the Sum of Twenty Shillings for the Use of Mary Johnson

Ordered that the Chwardens Pay to David Mason the Sum of Fifty Shillings for the Use of Richd Barlow

Ordered that James Turner be exempted from Paying his Parish Levy for the Future

Ordered that the Chwardens Pay to Agnes Carter the Sum of four Pounds

[197]

The Chwardens having agreed with Thomas Dunn for keeping & Maintaining Sarah Capell an Old infirm Woman at five Pounds Pr Annum & an Allowance as Usual of Twenty Seven Shillings for funeral Charges which Sums Make £4:13:8 She having lived with the said Dunn 8 Months but the Vestry having been informed by Several of their own Members that the said Sarah left effects Sufficient for that Demand & allowance & Thomas Capell son of the Said Sarah being Willing to Pay the said Charge the Vestry thought proper to Refer the said Dunn to the said Thomas Capell

James Chappell Junr Clerk of the Vestry having resigned Edmund Jones is Appointed in his Room & is Ordered to take Charge of the Vestry books & Attend that office

Thomas Vaughan Gent. is elected a Vestry Man for this Parish in the Room of Mr Moses Johnson Dec^d

Ordered that the Collector Pay to James Chappell Junr late Clerk of the Vestry 159^{lb} of Tob^o for Salary not provided & Extraordinary Services

William Bishop having been Appointed Procession Master Accoring to Law but he having Removed Out of the Government since that Appointment William Jones is Appointed in the Room of the said Bishop

                   William Willie Min^r

Copy Test Ja^s Chappell Junr Clk Vestry

[198]

At a Vestry held at Nottoway Church the 24th of April 1764
        Present
      The Reve^d Wm Willie
    Henry Harrison   Howell Briggs
    John Mason   Aug: Claiborne
    Nicolas Massenburg Mical Blow
      & James Jones

  Upon a Motion David Jones was Elected Clerk of the Vestry who will be allow'd the Usial[sic] Salary from this Day
Ordered that John Mason & James Jones Examine into the Regester of this Vestry & the Papers thereunto Belonging & Make Report of the Condition they find the Said Register

Surry and Sussex Counties, Virginia, 1742-1786   149

& papers in & that the S^d Regester be deliver'd to the Clerk
The Following Returns of Land Procession'd in the Parrish[sic] were now Returned &
Amdn'd & Orderd to be Enter'd in the Regester to Wit

In obedience to an Order of Vestry held for the Parrish of Albemarle in the County of
Sussex bearing Date the 5th Day of Sepr 1763 We the Subscribers have Procession'd the
Following Lands & Marks thereof have renew'd

		Persons	Present
Howell Briggs	Timothy Santee		
Samuel Magot	Joseph Petway	Howell Briggs	Benj. Hancock
William Rogers	Buford Pleasant	Samuel Magot	James Clary
Wil^m Carrel	Wm Pleasant	Wm Carrel	Henry Bradley
Thom^s Carrel	Peter Pleasant	Joseph Baley	Benj. Rogers
Jesse Carrel	Mary Nicolson	Edmund Baley	Arthur Smith
Nathan Carrel	Ann Feild	Thos Miers	Benj. Baley
Joseph Baley	Wm Hancock	Bird Clary	
Edmund Baley	Benj. Hancock	Thos Clary	
John Lamb	Nicolas Hancock	Benj. Clary	
Thomas Miers	Wm Bradley	Timothy Santee	
Bird Clary	Henry Bradley	Joseph Petway	[Procession Masters]
Thomas Clary	Mary Hancock	Buford Pleasant	John Presson
Benj. Clary	James Clary	Wm Pleasant	Humphrey Baylis

N° 1

[199]

Pursuant to an Order of Vestry of the Parrish of Albemarle in the County of Sussex
bearing Date the 5th of September 1763 We the Subscribers together with the Freeholders
have Procession'd & renew'd all the Land Marks in the Said Precinct Mention'd To
Wit.————

Persons Land	Processioned	Persons	Present
John Cornwell	Thomas Bryan	Michael Blow	Thomas Masinggill
Michael Blow	Thomas Masinggill	Wm Brittle Junr	James Bane
John Baily	Wm Brown	Henry Blow	Elijah Baley
Henry Blow	Mary Nicolson	Barnaby Baley	Arthur Smith
Barnaby Bailey	John Smith	John Birdsong	Henry Fason
John Birdsong	Elijah Baley	John Freeman	
John Freeman	Arthur Smith	Edward Wootten	[Procession Masters]
Edward Wootten	Henry Fason	Joseph Hix	Arthur Smith
Joseph Hix	Sarah Hartgrave	Thomas Presson	Henry Blow
Thomas Presson	Benj. Baley	Thomas Bryan	March 29th 1764

N° 2

In Obedience to an Order of the Worshipful Vestry of the Parrish of Albemarle in the
County of Sussex Bearing Date the 5th of Sepr 1763 & to us Directed We the Subscribers
have Assembled all the Freeholders together in the Said Precinct & on the 27th Day of
March did Precession & the Land Marks Renew of the Several Tracts of Land hereafter
Mention'd to wit. George Briggs', Peter Hinds, Nathl Briggs, Stephen Hamblins, Charles
Harrison, Joseph Ellis, James Hix, Wm Hix, Joseph Hargrave, Wm Hancock, John Barker,
Nat. Jones, Wm Felts, Maca. Axam, Joseph Land, Dred Holt, James Seward, & James
Turner's

N° 3   Certified under our hands [Procession Masters]
                                                         Nathaniel Briggs
                                                         Joseph Ellis

[200]

In Obedience to an Order of the Worshipful Vestry of the Parrish of Albemarle in the County of Sussex Bearing Date the 5th of Sepr 1763 We the Subscribers have Assembled the Freeholders together within the Precinct Specified in the said Order & and have Precession'd & the Land Marks thereon Renew'd of the Several Tracts of Land hereafter Mention'd to wit. John Jarrads Land, Thomas Wallis's Land, Wm Hind's Land, Henry Jarrad's Land, James Chappell Land, Howell Briggs Land, James Chappell Junr Land, Lucretia Jones's Land, John Hinnibrough's Land, John Jones's Land, the Persons Present when the above Mentione'd Tracts of Land were Procession'd Thomas Wallis, Nics Jarrad, John Hinnibough, John Jones, & Howell Chappell

N° 4   March 1764 Certified under our hands   James Chappell Junr
                                                         John Jarrad

By virtue of an order of the Vestry of Albemarle Parrish Bearing Date Sepr 5th 1763 We the Subscribers have Assemble'd the Freeholders together within the Precinct Specified by the said Order & have Procession'd & Renew'd the Land Marks of the Several Persons as Follows to Wit. Marh 11 1764
Rubin Cook's Land, Wm Cook's Land, David Jones Land, Capt Tomson's Land, Capt Eldridge's Land, Wm Heaths' Land, Gloster Hunnicutt's Land, John Jones Land, John Shand's Land, Rebeckah Heath's Land, Augustine Claiborne's Land, Natha Tatum's Land, Nath Harrison's Land, Charles Gee's Land, Richd Carter's Land, Richd Harrison's Land. Present when the Above Said Lands were Procesion'd Capt Eldredge, Wm Heath, John Clark, Richard Cook, John Jones, Benj. Fig, John Shands

N° 5   [Procession Masters]   William Cook
                                                               David Jones

In Obedience to an Order of the Vestry of the Parrish of Albemarle Bearing Date the 5th of Sepr 1763 John Ogborne the Other Person appointe'd being disabled by a Sad Malady I the Subscriber Did Procession & Renew the Land Marks of John Mason, John Sledge, Amos Sledge, Rubin Cook, Alexander Finnie, William Mason & Edward Weaver & there was Present at the Processioning the 12th of March John Mason, John Sledge, Amos Sledge, Joseph Cook, John Capell & William Mason

N° 6   Edward Weaver Prosn Master

[201]

In Obedience to an Order of the Vestry of the Parrish of Albemarle in the County of Sussex Bearing Date the 5th of Septemr 1763. We the Subscribers have assembled the Freeholders together Within the Precinct Mentioned in the Said Order & on the 26th Day of March Did Procession & the Land Marks Renew of the Several Tracts of Land hereafter Mention'd To Wit. Benj. Wyche's Land, Wm Parker's Land, Wm Parker's Land, Wm Allen's Land, James Chappell's Senr Land, Benj. Chappell's Land, John Sledges Land, Rogr Chappell's Land, John Chappells Land, Rubin Cook's Land, Rogr Jones' Land, James Jones' Land, & David Jones Land
Present when the Above Tracts of Land was Procession'd & the Land Marks thereof Rnew'd Rogr Jones, James Jones, James Chappell, John Sledge, Joseph Cook, James Tomlinson, Henry Weaver, Benj. Wyche, Wm Johnson & Wm Barram

N° 7 Certified Under our hands   [Procession Masters]
                                                  William Parker
                                                  David Jones

In Obedience to an Order of the Worshipful Vestry of Albemarle Parish Bearing Date the 5th Day of September 1763. We the Subscribers have Assembled the Freeholders together within the Precinct Specified in the Said Order & on the 26 & 27 Days of January 1764 did Procession & the Land Marks Renew of the tracts of Land hereafter Mention/d (to Wit) Richd Pookes, Samuel Peete's, Thomas Peters' James Renn's, John Hunt's, John Hind's, Thomas Hind's, Wm Hind's, David Hind's, Richd Hind's, Peter Hind's, Lazarus Drake's, Thomas Clement's, William Edmund's, John Chappell's, Joshua Hind's, John Cargill's, Hannah Howels, John Edmund's, Willi^a Hunts N Part of. Present when the Above said tracts of Land were Procession'd Richd Parker, Samuel Peete, James Renn, John Hunt, John Hind, Thos Hinds, Willi^m Hinds, David Hinds, Richd Hinds, Peter Hinds, Lazarus Drake, Thomas Clements, Wm Edmunds, Joshua Hinds, John Edmunds & Wm Hunt

N° 8 Certified Under our Hands   [Procession Masters] Thomas Peters
                                                                 John Chappell

[202]

In Obedience to an Order of the Worshipfull Vestry of Albemarle Parish Bearing Date 5th Day of Sepr. 1763 & to us Directed. We the Subscribers have on the [21st. ?] Day of March 1764 Assembled all the freeholders & Housekeepers within the Preceint in the said order Mention'd & Processiond all the Lines and the Land Marks Renew'd as Followeth.

[Note: Transcribed and spaced as written]

line Between John Mason &	Present	the line between W^m. Moore	Pros^d. With W^m.
Timothy Ezell D^o. Between	Epps Moore	& Mary Junkins	Moore Henry
John Mason & Edward Petway	Edward Petway	D^o. betw^n. Ep^s. Moore & W^m. Moore	Mitch^l. Thos.
D^o. between W^m. Moore & Edw^r. Petway	Timothy Ezell	D^o. betw^n. Epp^s. Moore & Henry Mitchel	Smith &
N°. 10 D^o. betw^n. Epps Moore & Edwd. Petway	John Edwards	D^o. betw^n. Henry Mitch^l. & James Heath	Thos. Ambross
D^o. betw^n. John Reddin & Edwd. Petway	W^m. Morton	D^o. betw^n. John Reddin & Ja^s. Heath	D^o. with E. Moore
D^o. betw^n. Edwd. Petway & W^m. Pa	Present with W^m.	D^o. betw^n. Ja^s. Heath & Edwd. Petway	Timo^y. Ezell
D^o. betw^n. Edwd. Petway & Pet^r. Poythress	Moore, Edwd. Petway	D^o. betw^n. John Reddin & John Smith	Henry Mitchel
D^o. betw^n. Pete^r Poythress & W^m. Parham	Thos. Smith	& W^m. Parham	& Thos^s. Ambross
	Willi^m. Morton		D^o. with W^m. Moore
	Henry Mitchell		Edward Petway
		William Moore Epps Moore	Henry Mitchel
		[Procession Masters]	Thos. Ambross Willi^m. Morton

152   The Vestry Book of Albemarle Parish

In Obedience to the Worshipfull Vestry of Albemarle Parrish by an Order bearing Date the 5th of Sepr. 1763. & to us Directed We the Subscribers have Mett and Procession'd the Several Lands as Followeth and the Land Marks thereof Renewd.

Proprietors Names	D°.	Persons Present	D°.
Peter Poythress	Thomas Wynne	John Jackson	George Pa
Joel Tucker	Thomas Vines	John Wynne	John Rivers
John Jackson	Willi^m. Malone	George Parham	Thos. Vines
Alex^r. Bowling	George Parham	Peter Winfield	Lewelling Williamson
N°. 11 John Eckles	Robt. Tucker	Thomas Wynne	David Tucker
John Freeman	George Booth	D°.	D°.
William Broadnax	John Malone	John Eckles	Thomas Vines
Andrew King	John Rivers	William Eckles	John Malone
Edward Smith	Thomas Huson	D°.	D°.
Nathan Freeman	David Tucker	Edward Smith	D°.
	James Harrison		David Tucker
		John Curtis	
		Joel Tucker	[Processioners]

[203]

In Obedience to an Order of the Worshipfull Vestry held for the Parrish of Albemarle in the County of Sussex Dated on the 5th Day of Septem^r. 1763 & to us Directed we the Subscribers have Met & Procession'd all the Lands in Our Preceint Belonging to the Proprietors Under Written & the Land Marks Have Renew'd

Day of the Mo.	Proprieters Names		Persons Present.	Persons Present
	Ric^d. Hill	Jo^s. Ingram	W^m. Wilborne, Michal Hill	James Mangam, W^m. Malone
Feby. 25 &27 1764	W^m. Wilborn	Absalom Tyus	W^m. Hill, Michal Hill	W^m. Winfield, Robt. Winfield
	Mical Hill	W^m. Winfield Senr.	W^m. Wilborne, W^m. Hill	Lewis Brown, Robt. Winfield
	Robt. Webb	W^m. Winfield Junr.	W^m. Wilborne, W^m. Malone	Lewis Brown, Jn°. Bonner
	W^m. Malone	Robt. Winfield	Josiah Freeman, Jn°. Beryman	Jn°. Malone, Jn°. Bonner
	Jn°. Beryman	Peter Winfield	Josiah Freeman, Jones Freeman	Jn°. Malone, Jn°. Bonner
	Josiah Freeman	John Winfield	W^m. Malone, Jn°. Beryman	Lewis Brown, Jn°. Bonner
N°. 12	Jones Freeman	George Booth	Jn°. Beryman, Jo^s. Richardson	John Malone, Jn°. Bonner
	John Holt	John Malone	Jn°. Beryman, Burrel Green	John Bonner, Edward Harper
	Jo^s. Richardson	John Bonner	John Beryman, Burrel Green	Edward Harper, John Malone
	Burrel Green	Edward Harper	Jn°. Beryman, Jones Freeman	Jn°. Bonner, Isaac Roberson

Surry and Sussex Counties, Virginia, 1742-1786   153

Ephraim Parham	Isaac Roberson	Burrell Green, Jno. Beryman	Edward Harper, Jno. Bonner
John Curtis	Lewis Brown	Amos Love, Jo^s. Ingram	John Bonner, John Malone
James Mangam		Ephraim Parham, W^m. Malone	
Amos Love		Josep Ingram, W^m. Raney	

Rich^d. Hill
George Booth
[Procession Masters]

In Obedience to an Order of Vestry held for the Parrish of Albemarle in the County of Sussex Dated ye 6 Day of Augt. 1763 and to us Directed we the Subscribers have met & Processed all the Lands in our Preceint Belonging to the Propritors under written and the Land marks thereof Renew'd.

Propriters Names	D^o.	Persons Present	D^o.
W^m. Raney Senr.	Thos. Butler	Nat. Raney, George Rand^h.	D^o.
Amy Farringt^n Orphan	W^m. Mitchel	D^o.	Tom^s. Butler, Fed^k. Green
Edward Powell	Federick Green	D^o.	William Mitchel
George Randolph	Peter Green	Geo^e. Rober^n. Ja^s. Cain J^r.	Dav^d. Tucker, John Kelley
James Cain S^r.	Mary Jones	W^m. Raney, James Cain	John Kelley Jo^s. Dameron
N°. 13 James Cain Junr.	David Tucker	D^o.	David Tucker
Peter Cain	John Kelley	Geo^e. Randolph, Na^l. Raney	George Randolph
Isham Cain	W^m. Gillium	D^o.	George Roberson, D^o.
George Roberson	John Wilkerson	D^o.	James Cain
Burwell Banks	W^m. Raney Junr.	Geo^e. Ran^h., Geo^e. Rober^n.	W^m. Mitch^l., Fed^k. Green
Thos. Wilkerson	W^m. Burrow. Dec^d.	D^o.	Thomas Huson
Elizabeth Wilkerson	John Harrison	D^o.	David Tucker, Jo^n. Kelley
Maj^r. Lawr^e. Gibbins	Thomas Huson	D^o.	
James Moss		Fed^k. Green, W^m. Mitch^l.	

Amos Love
Peter Green
[Procession Masters]

[204]

In Obedience to an Order of the Worshipfull Vestry of Albemarle Parrish Bearing Date the 5th Day of Sepr. 1763 we the Subscribers have Processioned all the Lands in the Said Order Mention'd & Renew'd the Land Marks in Presence of the Persons in the List Below.

To Whome Belonging	When Procesion'd	Persons Present at Processioning
Thomas Moore Senr.		Thomas Moore Senr.
Thomas Moore Jn^r.	March 9th 1764	Thomas Moore Junr.
Levy Gillium		Levy Gillium
Jones Stoaks		Jones Stoaks
Henry Freeman		Henry Freeman
Joseph Renn		Joseph Renn
N°. 15 Curtis Land		Curtis Land
Marcus Stoaks		Robt. Land
Robt. Land		W^m. Loftin
William Loftin		David Pennington
Mary Clanton		Charles Battle
David Pennington		Thomas Capel
Charles Battle		Cornelius Loftin
Thomas Capel		
Curnelius Loftin		
John Southard		
Robt. Webb		Robt. Webb Procession Masters
Procession Masters		Jam^s. Cooper
Jam^s. Cooper		

Pursuant to an Order of the Vestry of Albemarle Parrish in the County of Sussex Bearing Date the 5th of September 1763 we have Procession'd the Lands and the Land Marks have Renew'd of the Land Mention'd in that Order the Persons Present are as Follows.

		Persons Present	D^o.
The Land of Thomas Oliver	The Land of John Wadkins	Willium Gillium	
The Land of W^m. Gillium	The Land of W^m. Hewet	James Jones	Frances Epps
The Land of W^m. Oliver	The Land of Isham Smith	John Wilborne	William Fire [sic]
The Land of Rich^d. Jones J^r.	The Land of Frances Epps	Thos. Wynne	
The Land of Thos. Wynne	The Land of Burwel Green	Richard Jones J^r	
N°. 16 The Land of John Wilborne	The Land of Mathew Parham S^r.	Charles Dilliha	
The Land of W^m. Parham J^r.	The Land of Mathew Parham J^r.	Peter Threewitts	
The Land of W^m. Parham	The Land of Nat^l. Parham		
The Land of Peter Threewitts			

William Parham
Nathaniel Parham
[Procession Masters]

[205]

A List of the Several Lands Procession'd and Land Marks Renew'd in the Preceint Alloted to Nicholas Massenburg and Mathew Wynne.

Lands Procession'd	Persons Present	Lands not Procession'd
Hartwell Marrables's	Nic^s. Massenburg	A line Between Hartwell Marrable
Benjamin Cocke's	Mathew Wynne	& Benjamin Weathers A line Between
Part of Benj. Weather's	William Partin	B. Weathers & W^m. Petway &
Nic^s. Massenburg's	Banister Shackelford	Nicolas Massenburg a line
John Mason's Junr.	John Clifton	Between W^m. Petway &
x James Glovier's	James Glovier his own	Nico . Massenburg...
N°. 19 James Chappell's		
Thomas Wren's	Nic Massenburg	The S^d. H. Marrable, B. Weathers
W^m. Jones's	Mat Wynne	& W^m. Petway not being Present
John Wathers	William Partin	to see the Same Preform'd
Howell Briggs	William Jones	
John Clifton's	John Clifton his own land	
W^m. Partin's		
Anne Lilley's		
John Mason's		

In Obedience to an Order of the Worshipfull Vestry of Albemarle Parrish bearing Date the 5th of Sepr. 1763. We the Subscribers have Procession'd and Renew'd the Land Marks of the Several Lands in the said Preceint as Above. Given under our hands the 26 of March 1764.

                                                  Nicolas Massenburg
                                                Matthew Wynne
                                                [Procession Masters]

John Bane's Land. Present Simon Stacy, Thomas Tomlinson, W^m. Nicolson, Emanuel James, William Ellis, John Stacy, William Judkins, Robt. Judkins, John Judkins, Abner Proctor, William Rogers, John Gibbins & John Banes.

John Lambs	Land	in the Presence of the [Fol.?]	W^m. Nicolsons	Land	in the Presence of the [illeg.]	
Part of Mary Tobys	D^o.	D^o.	John Stacy's	D^o.	D^o.	
Par. of Jo^s. Edmunds	D^o.	D^o.	Part of W^m. Blunt's	D^o.	D^o.	
Par. of Howell Brigg	D^o.	D^o.	W^m. Rogers	D^o.	D^o.	
Simon Stacy's	D^o.	D^o.	John Gibbins's	D^o.	D^o.	
N°. 21 Thos. Tomlinson's	D^o.	D^o.	Emanuel James	D^o.	D^o.	

John Montgomery's	D°.	D°.	Rob¹. Judkins	D°.	D°.
John Warburton's	D°.	D°.	John Judkins	D°.	D°.
Wᵐ. Ellis's	D°.	D°.	Wᵐ. Judkins	D°.	D°.

By Virtue of the Order of Vestry of Albemarle Parrish Bearing Date the 5th of Sepr. 1763 & to us Directed we have [illeg.] the Several Tracts of Land above Mention'd being all Contain'd within our Preceint to be Procession'd in our Presence & the lines of the s^d. Land Renew'd as is by the s^d. Order Directed Given under our hands this 20th Day of March 1764.}

John Lamb
John Nicolson
[Procession Masters]

[206]

An Account of the Several Lands Procession'd & the Land Marks Renew'd in the Preceint whereof Rich^d. Avary and Cornelius Loftin are Appointed.

Lands Procession'd	Lands Procession'd	Persons Present	Persons Present
Jesse Williamson's	Anne King's	Henry Harrison	John Clanton
John Pennington's Junr.	Wᵐ. Rogers's	William Andrews Junr.	William Andrews
John Bishop's	Mary Rochel's	Jesse Williamson	Arthur Williamson
John Pennington's Carp^r.	Jordon Knights	Marcus Pennington	Marcus Pennington
Rich^d. Avery N°. 29 Wᵐ. Andrews's	Thoˢ. Morris' Cornelius Loftin's	Jesse Rogers John Rochel	Jesse Rogers John Rochel
Arthur Williamson's Federick Parker's	John Clanton's Henry Harrison's	the First Day	Jorden Knight the Second Day

In Obedience to an order of the Worshipfull Vestry of Albemare Parrish Bearing Date the 5th of Sep⁻. 1763. We the Subscribers have Procession'd & Renew'd the Land Marks of the Several Lands in the said Preceint as above Given under our Hands the 30th March 1764.

Rich^d. Avery
Cornelius Loftin
[Procession Masters]

In Obedience to an Order of the Worshipfull Vestry of the Parish of Albemarle bearing Date the 5th Day of Sep⁻. 1763. We have Assembl'ed the Freeholders within the Precinct in the said Order Mention'd & have seen the Land Marks thereof Renew'd (to wit) the line between Nico⁻. Massenburg & Lidia Weathers, Between Nico^s. Massenburg & John Reives, Between Massenburg & Thomas Cureton, Between Cureton & John Reives, Between Reives & Wᵐ. Petway Junr., Between Thomas Cureton & W. Petway Junr., Between W. Petway Junr. & W. Petway, Between Petway & W. Weathers, Between Weathers & Edward Petway, Between Weathers & Rob¹. Petway, Between Rob¹. Petway & Edward Petway, Between Rob¹. Parham & Rob¹. Petway, Between Rob¹. Petway & Stith Parham, Between Robt. Parham & Stith Wynne. The Aforesaid lines was Procession'd in the Presence of Stith Parham, Stith Wynne and William Weathers.

Nº. 31   The Following Lines was Procession'd in the Presence of Henry Sturdivant, James Glovier, Rob¹. Wynne, William Sturdivant, John Wynne & John Sturdivant (to Wit). The Line Between John Bobbit & Hollom Sturdivant, Between Hollom Sturdivant & Henry Sturdivant, Between Henry Sturdivant & Susannah Rossenbery, Between Rob¹. Wynne & Stith Wynne, Between Rob¹. Wynne & Hollom Sturdivant, Between Susannah Rossenbery & Threewits, Between Threewits & Stark, Between Stith Wynne & John Wynne, Between John Wynne & John Wynne Junʳ., Between John Wynne & Mathew Wynne, Between James Glovier & Stith Wynne, Between John Wynne Junʳ. & John Sturdivant, Between John Sturdivant & Howell Briggs, Between Brigg & Mathew Wynne, Between Henry Sturdivant, Edward Ecols, Between John Mason & Mathew Wynne, Between John Wynne & James Glovier, Between Glovier & Rob¹. Wynne in Witness Whereof We have Hereunto Set our hands this 24ᵗʰ Day of April 1764.

Rob¹. Petway
William Petway
[Procession Masters]

[207]

By Virtue of an Order of the Vestry of Albemarle Parrish Dated Sepʳ. 5ᵗʰ. 1763. and to us Directed We have Processiond the Lands therein Mentiond & the Same Land Marks thereof have Renew'd as Follows.

Persons Lands	Persons Lands	Persons Present	Persons Present
Charles Leath	Wᵐ. Wilkerson's	Charles Leath	Abram Parham
30. Mathew Parham Jʳ.	John Adams	John Parham	
John Parham's	Abram Parham	John Leath	
John Leath's	Mathew Parham Sʳ.	John Leath	Thoˢ. Parham
James Parham	Thomas Parham	Wᵐ. Wilkerson	Mathew Parham

In Obedience to an Order of the Worshipfull Vestry of Albemarle Parrish Bearing Date the 5ᵗʰ Day of Sepʳ. 1763. We the Subscribers Persuant thereto have Procession'd all the Lands in the said order mention'd & Renew'd the Land Marks thereof in Presence of the Several Persons as Below.

To Whome the Lands Belongs	W. Perfᵈ.	Persons Present at Processioning
Charles Judkins, James Chappel Jnʳ.	Maʳ 12	Charles Judkins, Charles Dº. Jnʳ., Isham Gillium
Isham Gillium, Abram Brown, James Bell, Silvanus Stoaks, John Willis, John Samuel Roland son of Joseph Rowland Deceasᵈ.	1764	Abram Brown, John Owen, Benj. Dº., David Dº. William Rowland Samuel Northinton, Thomas Spain, Silvanus Stoaks
John Fort, Sam⁻. Northington & Wm. Rose	Maʳ. 19	Webb Roland, Thoˢ. Adkerson, John Adkerson,
33. Thoˢ. Adkerson, Edward Powel, Abel Mabry, John Adkerson, Collo . Richᵈ. Cocke, Isaac Oliver, Edward Slate.	1764	William Green, John Powel, & John Willis

William Green, Susannah Knight
Widow, Jacob Jones, Webb Rowland orph^n. of John Rowland Decea^{sd}., Benj$^.$. Owen, W^m. Rowland, David Owen, John Owen & Thomas Shane.

James Bell
& Nat^l. Holt
Proces$^.$. Masters

In Obedience to an Order of the Vestry of the Parrish of Albemarle in the County of Sussex bearing Date the 5th Day of Sepr. 1763. We the Subscribers have Assembled the Freeholders together within the Preceint Specified by the Said Order and on the 19th. Day of Febuary 1764 Did Procession & the Land Marks Renew the Several Tracts of Land hereafter Mention'd (to Witt) William Sanders's Land, David Jones's Land, James Jones's Land, William Cook's Land, William Even's Land, John Sanders's Land, 34 John Gary's Land, Fadde Jarrad's Land, Fed Andrew's Land, William Harrison's Land, John Tomson's Land, William Strange's Land Procession'd. Present When the Above Tracts of Land Were Procession'd & the Land Marks Renew'd W^m. Sanders, David Jones, James Jones, W^m. Cook, W^m. Evens, John Sandres [sic], John Gary, Fadde Jarrad, Fed Andrews, John Tomson, William Shands.

Certified under our hands

William Harrison Procession Masters
Fadde Jarrad

[208]

At a Vestry held for the Parrish of Albemarle in the County of Sussex, the 21 of April 1767.

Present

The Rev^d. M^r. W^m. Willie   Nicholas Massenburg
John Cargil   James Jones
John Mason   Henry Gee
Davis Mason   & Augustin Claiborne Gen^n.

Augustin Claiborn and David Mason are Appointed Curch Wd^n. till Easter Teusday Next.

Or'^{d} that the C:W Pay to the Rev'^{d}. W^m. Willie ten Pounds for Providing Elements for the Sacrament.

This Day David Mason and James Jones Late C:W Rendered their Acct in Vestry Which Were Examined and Order to be Regestered.

This Day John Cargil late C:W Rendered his Acc^t. in Vestry Which was Examined Allowed and Or^d. to be Regestered.

Or^d That the Ch.W^d. Pay to David Mason late Church War^d. £ 22.10.11 Which Appears to be Due to him by his Acc^t. Rendered this Day.

Or^d that the Ch:W^d. pay John Knight forty Shillings.

Or^d that the Ch:W^d. pay to William Rives for Burying John Bagley £ 1.7.6. also 20/ for having the S^d. Bagley 3 Months.

Or'^{d} that the Ch:W^d. Lay Out £3 in Nesseries for the support of Lucrecia Sammons and her Children till the Laying of the Next Levy.

Or^d that Joseph Blaton be Exexpted from paying Parish Levy for the futer.

Or^d that the Ch:W^d. Lay out £5 in Nesaseries for the Use of Thomas Cooper & family.

Or^d That the Several Collectors of the parish of Albemarle that has not Already Rendered Acc^t. with the Ch:W^d. make up their Acc^t. with the Present Ch:W^d. According to Law.

Or^d That the former Order for Renting the Church Land be Discharg'd.

W^m. Willie Minis^{tr}.

David Jones Clk Vestry

[209]

	Albemarle Parrish	D^r.
1764	To laid out in Provisions for Richard Barlow	£ 2..10..=
	To D^o. in D^o. for Thos. Waller	1..15..=
	To D^o. for Frances Aldredge's Wife & Children	1..5..=
Sepr. 20	To Paid Joseph Barker an Allowance from the Parrish	3..=..=
1765		
Febu^r. 7	To Paid Edward Prince & Henrietta Aldredge for keeping Frances Aldredge's 5 Children 2 Months & 18 Days. at £10= p Annum}	2..6..=
	To Paid James Hern for keeping his Son	5..=..=
	To Paid Samuel Harwood Due to him Easter 1764	5..=..=
	To Paid Capt. Mical Blow for Mary Johnson	1..=..=
	To Paid W^m. Carrel p Order	6..9..=
	To Paid Agnis Carter as p Order Sepr. 1763	2..=..=
	To Paid D^o. as p Order Janu^r. 1764	4..=..=
	To Paid John Doby for keeping Mary Painter Due Easter 1764	3..=..=
	To Paid the Rev^d. M^r. W^m. Willie for Providing the Elements &c for the Use of the Parrish Due Easter 1764 }	10..=..=
	To Paid Anne Gesswit	1..10..=
		£ 48..15...
	To Paid a Lawers fee & Tax of a Writ the Parrish Agst. Roberts	=..16..3
		49.11.3
	To Balance as p C^r. in the Amount of 1765	9..12..1
		£ 59..3..4

[210]

	p Contra		C^r.
1764	By Mary Felts for a Bastard		£ 2..10..=
June	By Nathl. Newsum for Profane Swearing		=..5..=
Augt. 17	By 4059 ^{lb} Tobacco Levied Last Levy & sold as Follows Viz.		
	2743 lb a^t 12/	£ 16..9..2}	
	807 a^t 11/4	4..11.6}	23..19..2
	509 a^t 11/6	2..18..6}	
	4059	}	
Novr. 16	By James Cain Junr. for Profane Swearing		=..5..=
	By a Ballance Due to this Parrish on a Bond from Capt. James Jones		2..13..1
	By a Judgment Obtain'd for this Parrish against Willit Roberts In trust from 6. Jany. 1763 till Paid		25..5..=
			2..14..11
	By 97 lb Tobacco Cost of the Suit a^t 2^d		=..16..2
	By a Lawers fee		=..15..=
			£ 59..3..4

David Mason Church Warden

[211]

	Albemarle Parrish	D^r.
March 1765	To Paid Agnis Carter her Allowance from the Parrish	£ 6..=..=
	To Paid the Clk of Sussex his Ticket for 162 lb Toba^o. a^t 15/	1..4..4
	To Paid the She^f of Sussex 32^{lb} Tob^o. the Par^o. Ag^t. Roberts	=..4..9½
	To Paid Mary Ezell	1..7..=
	To Paid out in Provisons for Hannah Rose	1..15..5
	To Paid out in D^o. for Richard Barlow by Order of Vestry	3..=..=
	To Paid Bathia Barlow keeping a Small Child of Rich^d. Bar^{lw}. Mon. at 40/ p Annum}	=..13..4
	To Paid Rebeccah Pair by M^r. Jesse Williamson	2..10..=
	To P^d. John Knight part of his charge for Repairing S^t. And^s. Church	8..=..=
	To Paid W^m. Colston as p Order Last Levy	8..=..=
	To Paid the Rev^c. M^r. W^m. Willie for Providing the Elements & for the Sacrament &c for the Parrish to Easter 1765}	10..=..=
	To Paid D^o. for Repairs Done on the Glebe Barn	1..=..=
	To P^d. Donald Macanish as p Order last Levy	14..15..6
	To P^d. Jam^s. Cain Junr. for keeping W^m. Delihay till the Levy 1765	2..10..=
	To P^d. Saml. Harwood for keeping Painters Child Due Easter 1765	5..=..=
	To P^d. Peter Green, Thimothy Ezell, W^m. Rogers & John Bane Sexton 100 lb Tob. for Their Allowance made them Last Levy a^t 15/ p C.}	3..=..=
	To P^d. David Jones J^r. as p Order April 1765	2..1..3
	To P^d. John Doby for keeping Mary Painter Due Easter 1765	3..=..=
	To P^d. Jones Stoaks as p Order December 1764	1..18..4
	To P^d. Anne Lilley as p Order Decr. 1764	2..=..=
	To P^d. Tabitha Roland as p Order Decr. 1764	2..=..=
	To P^d. Mathew Whitfield	2..=..=
	To P^d. Joseph Denton for Rebeccah Davis	3..=..=
	To P^d. Timothy Ezell	=..7..6
	To P^d. W^m. Carrel for keeping John Hulin	4..3..4
1766 Mar^h 31	To P^d. Co^l. Mass^r. [Massenburg] 212 ^{lb} Tob^o. the Rent of the Collage Tene^t. Poss^d. by M^r. Willie a^t 15/	1..11..9½
	To P^d. Frances Threewits for 100 ^{lb} of Bacon for the Use of Elizabeth King a^t 5^d.	2..1..8
	To P^d. the Widow Carter as p Order at the laying of the Levy in Novr. 1765	3..=..=
	To P^d. John Hood as Ex^r. of John King Dec^d. for 200 lb Pork found Anne King in the Year 1763	2..=..=
	To P^d. Jam^s. Hern for keeping his Son for the Year 1765 & till Easter 1766	5..=..=
	To P^d. Joseph Prince for Services as p Acct.	2..7..=
	To P^d. Solomon Graves for 2 Barrels Corn for Widow King a^t 10/	1..=..=
	To P^d. W^m. Ezell for 64 lb Pork for D^o. a^t 2^d. in 1765	=..10..8
	To P^d. Lewis Solomon for keeping Nat Barlow 1 Year Ending August 1766	3..10..=
	To P^d. Ben. Owing for Repairing S^t. Andrews Church Plastering	=..12..6
	£	111..5..3

[212]

	p Contra	C^r.
1765 Aug^t.	By Levied for the Use of the Parrish last Levy 10184 lb. Tobacco & Settled with the Collector a^t 15/ p C.}	£ 75..6..1 ¼
	By the Reve^d. M^r. W^m. Willie in Part of the Money he Retain'd from M^r. Ruffin for the Use of the Parrish	1..=..=
	By Balance Due to this Parrish as p Acct of 1764	9..12..1
1767. March 2nd. By Ballance as p Debit		25..12..=¾
		£ 111..10..3

April 21. 1767. Albemarle Parrish to David Mason	D^r.
To Balance as p Acc^t. Settled this Day	£ 25..12..=¾
By M^r. Cargill this Day	3..1..1 ¼
	£ 22..10..11

E E p David Mason

[213]

D^r.	Albemarle Parrish in Accompt	
1766	To Cash Paid William Colston for keeping Man, 1 Child	£ 6..=..=
	To Cash Paid the Reve^d. W^m. Willie	5..=..=
	To Cash Paid Thos. Cooper	5..=..=
	To Cash Paid Collo. Massenburg for 212 ^{lb} of Tobacco for the Rent of the Collage Place	1..16..6¼
	To Cash Paid M^{rs}. Earwood	2..=..=
	To Cash Paid William Jones for 25^{lb} of Bacon a^t 6^d. for the Use of M^{rs}. Carter	=..12..6
	To Cash Paid James Cain for keeping W^m. Dilihay	5..=..=
April 21st	To Paid Major Mason	3..1..1¼
1767		£ 28..10..2

At a Vestry held for the Parish of Albermarle in the County of Sussex the 19th Day of August 1767.

Present
The Rever^d. M^r. W^m. Willie

Augustin Clairborn	Henry Harrison
David Mason	James Jones
Howell Brigg	John Cargill
Nicolas Massenburg	John Mason

No. 1xx In Pursuance to an order of Sussex County Court Bearing Date July Court 1767 Directing the Vestry of Albemarle Parish to Divide the Same into Precents for the Processioning Every Persons Land within the s^d. Parish We do Appoint Humphry Balis & Bird Clary. to See Every Persons Land Procesnd & the land marks thereof Renew'd from Surry County line up Secock and Tarripin Swamps to Burchant Island Rhoad & up the s^d. Rhoad to the head of Secock & that they assemble all the Freeholders within the s^d. Preceint to Attend the Performance thereof & that the Said Humphry Balis & Bird Clary do make Return to this Vestry of Every Persons Land they Shall Procession & of Every Person Present at the Processiong thereof also of whose land they Shall fail to Procession & the Particular Reason of Such Failure & that the Same be Done & Perform'd between the first Day of November & the last Day of March next.

2x x Henry Blow & Arthur Smith are App^d. to Proces^n. from the South side of the Secock to the head of the Lightwood Swamp & Secawrie ~~illegible~~ Swamp to Burchant Island Rhoad.

3x x Nat Briggs & Joseph Ellis are App^d. to proces^n. from Southampton County line up Assam^k. Swamp to Secawrie Swamp Up the S^d. Swamp to the head

[Note: Second x is below first as if checking off that entry]

[N.B. the bottom of this page is dog-eared, but there only appears to be one word missing, as opposed to an entire line of writing]

[214]

To Whom the Land belongs	When. Proce^s.	Persons Present
Benjamin Rogers, John Alsobrook, Samuel Magot	March 23rd 1768	Reubin Rogers Benjamin Rogers Samuel Magot John Alsobrook [Procession Masters]

By virtue of an Order of the Vestry of Albemarle Parish bearing Date August. 19th. 1767 we the Subscribers have Assembled the Freholders together within the Preceint Specified by the Said Order and have Processioned and Renew'd the Land marcks of the Several Persons as Follows to Witt— Willot Roberts Land, Patrick Lashley Land, William Lashley Land, Harmon Bishop Land, Pettway Johnson Land, John Gilliams Land Fromerly Samuel Tatums, Nathaniel Barkers Land, James Boiseau Jones Land, James Barker's Land, David Jones Land, James Cooks Land, Foster Cooks Land, Henry Bark[er], Rhubin Cooks Land, Benjamin Hills Land, Drury Barker.

Present when the above said Land were processioned Willott Roberts, Hinchie Gilliam, Patrick Lashley, William Lashley, Harmon Bisshop, Henry Barker, James Barker, David Jones, James Cooke, Drury Barker, Henry Cooke, Holmes Jones, Benjamin Roberts.

James Boiseau Jones
Nathaniel Barker
[Procession Masters]

In Obedience to an order of the Vestry of Albemarle Parish in the County of Sussex Dated the 19th Day of August. 1767 and to us Directed. we have seen the Several lines in the Preceint in the S^d. Order Mention'd Procession'd & the Land Marks thereof have Renew'd the land of M^r. John Veril or we have not Procession'd because he would not attend the Due notis was by us Given him.

Proprietors Names	Persons Present
Col^o. Aug$^-$. Claiborne, Henry Tatum, Robt. Doby, John Doby, Mary Tatum, Elizabeth Hawthorne. W^m. Dunn, Timothy Reives, Nat. Mitchel, John Raines, John Pettway, John Reives, Edwd. Walker, George Reives, Christopher Reives.	Nat. Mitchel, John Raines, John Pettway, Tim. Reives, Henry Tatum, Thos. Young, Nat. Tatum, Aug$^-$. Claiborne Senr. , Robt. Doby, John Doby, Isham Hawthorne, Joshua Doby George Reives Christopher Reives Pro. Masters

March the 1. 1768   N°. 24

Surry and Sussex Counties, Virginia, 1742-1786   163

[215]

In Obedience to an Order of Vestry of Albemarle Parrish Bearing Date the 19th Day of August 1767 We the Subscribers Did Assemble the Freeholders within our Preceint on the 21st Day of Febuary & Procession & Renew the Land Marks of John Sledge, Amos Sledge, Rich^d. Cook, Thomas Johnson, William Mason, John Mason, Elisa . Finnie, John Mason Junr., Edward Weaver & Edward Weaver Junr. and there was Present at the Doing the Same John Sledge. Amos Sledge, Rich^d. Cook, William Mason, Simon Stacy Junr. and William Clifton. Witness our hands this 31st Day of March 1768.

Edward Weaver Senr. }
Edward Weaver Junr. }
[Procession Masters]

Pursuant to an Order of Vestry Dated the 19th Day of August 1767. We the Subscribers have Procession'd & Renew'd the Landmarks of Every Persons lines in our Precinct.

Lines Processioned between	Persons Present	Lines Proces^d. between	Person Present
Natha . Newsum		Thos. Addams	
Jones Glovier		Benj . Hill Senr.	
Trubel Hix		Henry Tyler	Adam Ivey
Richard Hays	Benjamin Adams	Thos. Addams	Henry Tyler
Thos. Addams	Charles Sledge	Henry Tyler	Burwell Macklemore
Robt. Lynn	Edward Prince	Benj . Hill Senr.	Hery [sic] Tyler
Thos. Dowdy	Rich^d. Hays	Benj . Hill Senr.	
Robt. Lynn	Benj Fedder	Benj . Hill Junr.	
Matthew Hubert	Thomas Pate Junr.	John Hill	
William Seborn	Morris Dunn	Benj . Hill Junr.	
Matthew Hubert	Thos. Sammons	Edward Prince	Done
Morris Dunn	Natha . Newsum	John Hill	March 20. 1768
John Morgin	Charles Knight	Henry Tyler	
William Sammons	Henry Tuder	Edward Prince	
Charles Sledge	Adam Ivey	Thos. Pate Senr.	
Morris Dunn	Burwell Macklemore	Edward Prince	
Edward Lundy		Thos. Pate Junr.	
Morris Dunn		Henry Tyler	
Benj . Hill		Joel Macklemore	
Jones Glovier		Henr[y] Tyler	
Thos. Addams			
Benj . Hill	Benj . Hill Junr. [&]	William Seborn	
Henry Tyler	Refused to Attend	the Processioning	
Thos. Addams			Henry Tyler
Henry [Tyler?]			John Pate
Benj. [Hill?]			[Procession Masters]
Jones Glovier			
[Benj . Hill?] Senr.			

[216]

In Obedience to an Order of the Worshipfull Vestry of the Parrish of Albemarle in the County of Sussex Bearing Date the 19th Day of August 1767 We the Subscribers Persuant to the Said order have Procession'd all the Lands in the Preceit Mention'd in the Said Order & Renew'd the land Marks thereof in Presence of the Several Persons Whose names are under Written.

To Whome the Land Belongs	When Procession'd	Person Present at the Processioning
William Shands, Francis Rosers, Nat^r. Harrison, John Mason, James Belsches, Hugh Ivey, Nat^r. Dunkin, John Adkins, John Mason Junr. & John Baird	Febuary the 19 & 20 1768	John Mason, James Belsches, John Mason Junr., John Baird, Austin Shands, John Shands, Henry Ivey, Daniel Ivey, W^m. Baird & Stephen Baird Hugh Ivey Nathan$^-$. Dunkin Pro. Masters

In Obedience to an Order of the Worshipfull Vestry of Albemarle Parrish bearing Date the 19th Day of August 1767. We the Subscribers have Processioned all the lands in the Said Order Mention'd & Renew'd the land marks thereof in Presence of the Several Persons Hereafter Named.

Proprietors of the Lands
Maj^r. John Masons, Jesse Jones, Peter Jones, Lawrance Smith, M^{rs}. Mary Partridge, William Johnson, Pettway Johnson, & Nicolas Partridge.

Persons Present
Peter Jones, Jesse Jones, William Johnson & Daniel Turner

Nicholas Partridge
Pettway Johnson Pro.
Masters

In Obedience to an Order of the Worshipfull Vestry of Albemarle Parrish bearing Date the 19th Day of August 1767. Wee the Subscribers have Processioned and Renew'd the land marks of the Several Persons within the Preceit in the Said Order Mentioned & in Presence of the Several Persons hereafter Named.

The Proprietors of Land	When Procession'd	Persons Present
Federick Fort, John Barns, Samuel Bullock, John Battle j^r., Thos. Williamson, Vallintine Williamson, Nicho^s. Jarrad, Benja$^-$. Harrison [of] Brunswick	11th March 1768	Federick Fort, Samuel Bullock, J^r., Thos. Williamson, Benj$^-$. Seeborne, Rubin Baird, Thomas Dowdy, Robt. Lynn
Charles Stuart & James Stuart, Benjamin Seeborn, Rubin Baird, Thomas Dowdy, Robt. Lynn, John Bishop of Prince George, Nathan Northington and James Barns	12 March 1768	James Barns Nathan Northington Processioners

Surry and Sussex Counties, Virginia, 1742-1786   165

[217]

In Obedience to an Order of Vestry Dated 19th of August 1767 Directing us to procession in the Preceint laid out to us by the Said Order Accordingly we the 24 of November We Assembled the Freeholders and went in Quiet Possession & Renewed the Land marks of the following Persons to Witt.

The Land	of	W^m. Johnson
The Land	of	M^r. Allen
The Land	of	John Pennington
The Land	of	John Land
The Land	of	Joseph Pennington
The Land	of	Joshua Pennington
The Land	of	Thomas Bayley
The Land	of	Capt. John Walker

By us
John Pennington
Benjamin Hunt
[Procession Masters]

In Obedience to an Order of the Worshipfull Vestry of Albemarle Parrish Bearing Date the 19th. Day of August. 1767. We the Subscribers have Processioned all the Lands in the Said Order Mentioned & Renew'd the Land Marks thereof in Presence of the Several Persons hereafter Mentioned.

Proprietors of the Land	When Processiond	Persons Present
Capt. Howell Brigg's, Peter Jones, Jesse Jones, Maj^r. John Masons, Capt. James Jones, Jehugh Barker, M^r. Robert Jones, the Land belonging to the Estate of Edmend Jones Dec^d., Henry Jarrard, & Jesse Jones's.	March 21 1768	Capt. Howell Briggs, Maj^r. John Mason, Jehugh Barker, Capt. James Jones, Robt. Jones & Peter Jones. Henry Jarrad Jesse Jones Processioners

In Obedience to an Order of the Worshipfull Vestry of the Parrish of Albemarle in the County of Sussex bearing Date the 19th Day of August 1767. to us Directed We the Subscribers have Processioned all the Lands in the S^d. Order Mention'd and Renew'd the Land marks thereof in Presence of the Persons herein Mention'd.

To Whome the Land belongs	Proformed.	Persons Present
Lewis Johnson, Marcus Stoaks. Henry Freeman, Robt. Webb, Thos. Moore, W^m. Moore, Levi Gillium, Joseph Renn, belonging to the Estate of John Southworth, Robt. Land, Curtis Land. Bird Land, Curnelus Loftin, W^m. Loftin. David Pinnington, Thos. Capel, Charles Battle, James Cooper, Belonging to the Estate of Natha^l. Clanton	March the 9th 1768	Lewis Johnson, James Hern, Henry Freeman, Thos. Moore, W^m. Moore, Levi Gillium, Joseph Renn. Robt. Land, Curtis Land. Bird Land, Cornelus Loftin, W^m. Loftin, David Pennington, Thomas Capel, Charles Battle

Robert Webb
[Procession Masters]
James Cooper

[218]

In Obedience to an Order of the Worshipfull Vetry of Albemarle Parrish bearing Date the Nineteenth Day of August. 1767. We the Subscribers have Procession'd and Renew'd the Land Marks of the Several Persons within the Preceint in the Said Order Mentioned & in the Presence of the Several Persons hereafter Named.

The Proprietors of the Land	When Performed	Persons Present
Joseph Thorp, Major Tiller, Thomas Wommock, James Day Ridley, Seymore Powell, Peterson Thorp, Nathaniel Wych, John Stuart, James Wych Orphan of James Wych Dec^d. & John Alsobrook, Orphan of Samuel Alsobrook Dec^d.	March 16 1768	Thomas Wommock, Arthur Bass, Major Tiller, Joseph Thorp and Lewis Thorp Nathl. Wyche and John Stuart

In Obedience to an Order of Vestry hereunto Annax'd We have Assemble'd the freeholders and have Seen all the Lands processioned in our preceint & the Land Marks thereof Renew'd.

Proprietors Names

Rich^d. Hill, W^m. Wilburn, Mical Hill, Robt. Webb. Josiah Freeman, Thomas Wynne, Burwell Green, John Holt, William Mangum, James Mangum, John Curtis, John Dillihay, Amy Ferrington, Joseph Ingram, Ephraim Parham, George Booth, William Wingfield Senr., William Wingfield Junr., Rebeccah Tyus, Peter Wingfield, John Wingfield, Joseph Richardson, Robt. Wingfield, John Bonner, John Malone, Nathaniel Malone. Isaac Robertson, Thomas Saunders

Person Present

William Wilburn, John Berriman, Jones Freeman, Mical Malone, W^m. Wilburne, John Freeman, John Berryman, Jones Freeman, John Holt, Jones Freeman, John Holt, Burwell Green, John Holt, Jones Freeman, Burwell Green, Jones Freeman James Mangum, Mical Malone, Ephraim Parham, Jo^n. Curtis, Joseph Ingrum, James Mangum, John Curtis, W^m. Raney, W^m. Raney, John Dillihay, Ephraim Parham, James Mangum, John Holt, Joseph Ingrum, John Malone, W^m. Wingfield Junr., Joseph Richardson, Jo^n. Wingfield, Joseph Richardson, Peter Wingfield, W^m. Wingfield & W^m. Wingfield Junr., Joseph Richardson. John Wingfield, Peter Wingfield, Joseph Richardson, Peter Wingfield, John Wingfield, William Wingfield J^r., Peter Wingfield, John Malone, Thos. Saunders, John Bonner, Thos. Saunders, John Malone. John Bonner, John Bonner, Thos. Saunders, John Malone, John Bonner

Richard Hill
&
George Booth
[Procession Masters]

[219]

In Obedience to an Order of the Worshipfull Vestry of Albemarle Parish bearing Date the 19th Day of August. 1767. We the Subscribers persuant to the s^d. order have procession'd all the lands in the s^d. order Mention'd & Renew'd the Land Marks thereof in Presence of the Several persons hereafter Named.

The proprietors of the Lands	When Perform'd	Persons Present at Processioning
Nat. Felts j^r., Willm. Richardson, John Rowland, John Barns, John Felts, Willm. Harris, Thos. Ezell, John Ezell, Nic˙. Jarrad, Rich^d. Stuart, the Land belonging to the Estate of James Stuart De^d., Col. Rich^d. Cocke, Rich^d. Northcross, Abel Mabry, Isacck Oliver, John Adkinson, Mical Weathers, Thos. Ezell J^r. & George Ezell.	11th March 1768 & 12th March 1768	John Rowland, John Felts, Willi^m. Harris, Thos. Ezell, John Ezell, Thomas Ezell J^r., Rich^d. Northcross & John Adkinson. William Richardson Nathaniel Felts Ju^r} Proce

In Obedience to an [Order] of the Worshipfull Vestry of Albemarle Parish in the County of Sussex Bearing Date the 19 Day of August 1767. We the Subscribers have Procession'd all the Lands in the Said Order Mention'd and Renew'd the land Marks thereof in Presence of the Parties herein Mention'd.

To Whom the Land belongs.	When Perform'd	Persons Present at Processioning
Thomas Nusum		Henry Tyler
Gregory Rawlings	February 28th	George Hogwood
Jesse Newsum	1768	Daniel Harwood
Henry Manry		Joel Cornett
Belonging to the Estate of Ed˙. Long	1st Day	Jonah Cornett
Sampson Newsum		
Benjamin Newsum		
William Prince		
Joel Cornett		Henry Tyler
John Myrick		W^m. Myrick
Belong˙. to the Estate of Ro^l. Bullock		Phillup Harwood J^r.
Henry Tyler	2^d. Day	Daniel Harwood
Belon˙. to the Estate of W^m. Night		Charles Barrum
Thos. Barham		Thos. Barrum
Phillip Harwood		Joel Cornett
William Longbottom		Jonah Cornett
Charles Barhah [sic]		

Thomas (his "T" mark) Newsum
Gregory Rawlings
[Procession Masters]

[220]

In Obedience to an Order of the Worshipfull Vestry of the Parish of Albemarle bearing Date the 19th Day of August 1767 we the Subscribers Did on the 29. of February & the 1st Day of March 1768 Assemble the freeholders within the Preceint Specified by the S^d. order & Did Procession & the Land marks Renew'd of the following Tracts of Land.

Richard Parker's	Land	David Hind's	Land
Thos. Clement's	Land	Rich^d. Hind's	Land
Thos. Peter's	Land	William Edmunds	Land
X Samuel Peete	Land	Peter Hind's	Land
John Hunt's	Land	John Chappell's	Land
James Renn's	Land	Joshua Hind's	Land
John Hind's	Land	Hannah Howell's	Land
Thos. Hind's	Land	John Cargill's	Land
Lazerus Drak's	Land	John Edmund's	Land
William Hind's	Land	& William Hunt's	Land

Present when the above Tracts of Land were Procession'd & the Land Marks thereof Renewed.
Richard Parker, Thomas Clements, Thomas Peters, John Hunt, James Renn, John Hinds, Thomas Hinds, Lazerus Drake, W^m. Hinds, David Hinds, Richard Hinds, William Edmunds, Peter Hinds, John Chappell, Joshua Hinds, Hannah Howell, John Edmunds, & William Hunt. Certified under our Hands.

Thomas Peters
John Chappell
[Procession Masters]

In Obedience to an Order of Vestry to us Directed bearing Date the 19th Day of August 1767. we have Renewed the Land Marks and Processioned the Lands of John Zells, Present John Zells Junr. and of Morres Zells present Morres Zells & of Nathan Bishop present Nathan Bishop, & of Colo$^`$. Rich$^d$. Cocke present Richard Marks y Order of Colo$^`$. Rich^d. Cocke & of John Pair present John Pair & of William Hancock present W^m. Hancock, & of the Estate of Collo$^`$. William Lightfoot Dec$^d$. present John Soan Marston by of the Executors & of Isaac Bendall present Isaac Bendall, & of David Zells present Morres Zells by order of David Zells & of Lambert Zells Dec$^d$. present Morres Zells Executor & of Joshua Moss Present Joshua Moss & of Benj$^`$. Hunt present Benjamin Hunt & of James Fawn present James Fawn & of we the Suscribers being present Witness our hands this Sixteenth Day of May one thousand Seven Hundred & Sixty Eight.

Thomas Wren
William Jones
[Procession Masters]

[221]

In obedience to an Order of the Worshipfull Vestry of the Parish of Albemarle bearing Date the 19th Day of August 1767 being Directed to David Jones and Benjamin Wyche to Procession a certain Preceint as by the S^d. Order may Appear but the Said Wyche being Dead before the Service was Performed I the I the [sic] Subscriber Surviveing Procession master Did on the 28th & 29th Days of March 1768 Procession & the Land marks thereof Renew of the Several Tracts of Land hereafter Mentioned in Presence of the following Persons.

Surry and Sussex Counties, Virginia, 1742-1786

Lands Processioned	Persons Present	Land not Processioned
David Jone's, James Jone's, Robert Jone's, William Willcock's, Rich^d. Cook's, John Sledge's, Allen Jone's, John Mason Senr., Benjamin Chappells, James Chappells, James Chappell Junr., James Chappells Senr., John Cargills & Par of William Allens	Robert Jones Thos. Adkins W^m. Willcocks John Sledge James Chappell J^r.	A line between W^m. Allen & William Parker, A line Between William Parker & Elizabeth Wyche The S^d. W^m. Parker, W^m. Price & W^m. Johnson Overseer for the Widow Wyche not being Present to See the Same Performed. David Jones } Procession Master

In Obedience to an Order of the Worshipfull Vestry of Albemarle Parish Bearing Date the 19 Day of August, in the Year of our Lord one Thousand Seven Hundred & Sixty Seven we the Subscribers have Procession'd & Renew'd all the Lands in the Said order Mentioned the Land marks thereof Renewed in Presence of the Several Person hereafter Named.

Whose Lands Processioned	When Performed	Persons Present
To wit the land of John Knight, hinchey [sic] Gilliam, Capt Henry Harrison, John Clanton, Arthur Williamson, Jesse Williamson, William Andrews, John Cargill Joseph Pennington, John Bishop, Macus Pennington, Capt. Richard Avery, Ann king, Jurdan Knight, William Rogers, Cornelious Loftin, Mary Rochel, William Moore	1768 Feb^r. 7 Febr^r. 10	To wit present John Cargill, Marcus Pennington, Arthur Williamson, John Clanton, William Rogers, Cornelious Loftin, Hinchey Rochel, Cyrill Avary, William Andrews, Richard Avary, Jesse Williamson Marcus Pennington, William Andrews, Cyril Avary, Cornelious Loftin, Jurdan Knight, John Clanton, Arthur Williamson, William Rogers, Joseph Pennington, Hinchey Rochel, Richard Avary, Jesse Williamson

Richard Avary
Jesse Williamson
[Procession Masters]

[222]

In Obedience to an Order of Vestry held for the parish of Albemarle in the County of Sussex bearing Date the 19th Day of August 1767. We the Subscribers have Processioned the Lands & Renewed the Land Marks of all the Lands within the Preceint for which the Said Order was made as by the same is Directed & as by the following Return may Appear which we have Sign'd this 30th. Day of March 1768.

Proprietors of Land thir Names	Whom Present
Richard Blunt	
John Edmunds	
The Estate of John Irby, Dec^d. now in the Possession of his Relict Mary Irby	
The Estate of W^m. Briggs Dec^d. Now in Possion of Mary Bonner & Lawrance Smith in Right of his wife	Hinchia Gillium, John Garland Lawrence Smith & John Irby
The Estate of W^m. Gilbert Dec^d. now In Possion [sic] of Joanna Moss	
Thomas Cooper	N.B. Thomas Cooper present at Processiong his own Land
Hinchia Gillium	& Part of Mosses, Brigg's &
Willirt Roberts	Irby's
The Estate of Andrew Lester Dec^d. Now in Possion of John Garland in Right of his wife	
Benjamin Roberts Infant	Richard Blunt
John Irby Infant	J. Edmunds
	[Procession Masters]

In obedience to an Order of the Worshipfull Vestry of Albemarle Parish Bearing Date the 19th Day of August 1767 We the Subscribers Did on the 24th Day of March 1768 Assemble the freeholders within the Preceint Specified in the S^d. Order & Did Procession & the Land marks thereof Renew of the following Tracts of Land to Witt Howell Briggs Land, James Chappells Land, Henry Jarrads Land, William Hines Land, Thos. Willises [sic] Land, John Kennebroughs Land, James Chappells Junr. Land, Howell Chappells Land, James Turners Land, Lucretia Jones Land, William Turners Land & Edmunds Turners Land. Present when the Above mentioned Tracts of Land were Processioned Henry Jarrad, James Chappell, Thos. Wallis, Nicholas Jarrad, Howell Chappell, Henry Chappell, W^m. Hines. Witness our Hands this 24th Day of March 1768.

Ja^s. Chappell Junr.
Ja^s. Turner
[Procession Masters]

[223]

In Obedience to an Order of Vestry of Albemarle Parish in Sussex County bearing Date the 19 Day of August 1767. to us Directed we have [View'd?] & Renew'd the land marks in our Precints Viz.

December 21 1767. Present		December 22. 1767. Present	
We Renew'd lands of	James Roberson	We Renew'd the land of	John Malone
Peter Pothress	John Eckels	George Booth	George Parham
Joel Tucker	Fed Freeman	John Malone	Robt. Tucker
John Jackson	Thos. Vines	George Parham	David Tucker
James Robersons	W^m. Malone	Robt. Tucker	Thos. Huson
John Eckels	John Freeman	John Rivers	Thos. Wynne
John Freeman	Thomas Wynne	Jurkins Hunt	Thos. Vines
W^m. Malone	Frances Jackson	Thos. Hasons [Huson?]	
Thomas Vines		Edward Harpers Est.	
Thos. Wynne			
Elizh [sic] Boling			

W^m. Broadnax   Joel Tucker
                                                    John Freeman
                                                    [Procession Masters]

In Obedience to an Order of the Worshipfull Vestry of Albemarle Parish in the County of Sussex bearing Date the 19 Day of August 1767. we the Subscribers have Assembled the Freeholders together & Procession'd all the lands in the Said Order Mention'd & Renew'd the Land marks thereof in Presence of the Several Persons hereafter Mention'd

Proprietors of the Lands	When Procession'd	The Persons Present
Colo. Augustin Claiborne		David Jones, James Jones,
Nat. Harrison	March 4, 1768	Benjn. Figg, W^m. Evens, John
Capt. John Tomson,		Sandrus, John Shands,
David Jones		Augus^n. Shands, John Gary,
James Jones, Benjn. Figg		W^m. Harrison, Fadde Jarrad,
W^m. Evens, John Sandrus		Federick Andrews, John
John Gary, Fadde Jarrad		Tomlinson, James Cook,
Federick Andrews		John Bigins. Certified under
William Harrison		our hands

                                                    Fadde Jarrad
                                                    Federick Andrews
                                                    [Procession Masters]

In Obedience to an Order of Vestry Held for the Parish of Albemarle in the County of Sussex the 19th Day of August 1767. We the Subscribers have Assembled all the Freeholders in the Preceint and have Seen all the Persons Land Procession'd and the Land Marks Renew'd the 7th 8th and 9th Days of March 1768.

George Briggs, Nat. Briggs, Stephen Hamblin, Joseph Ellis, Nat. Jones, Bartholomew Batts, Jesse Hargrave, James Turner, John Birdsong, Michael Axum, Joseph Lane, W^m. Felts, Robt. Baley, W^m. Hix, Etheldred Davis, James Hix Who were all Present at Doing the Same.

                                                    Joseph Ellis
                                                    Nathaniel Briggs
[224]   [Procession Masters]

By virtue of an Order of the Vestry of Albemarle Parish Dated the 19 of August 1767 and to us Directed we have Procession'd the Lands therein Mention'd & the Same Lands Markes Thereof have Renew'd as Follows Viz.

Lands..	Lands..	Persons Present	Persons Present
Charles Leath	Matthew Parham	James Parham	Stith Parham
James Parham	John Leath	John Addams	William Leath
John Addams	Matthew Parham j^r.	John Leath	P
W^m. Wilkerson	John Parham	John Parham	Thos. Parham
Frances Haddon	Thos. Parham	Matthew Parham j^r.	Abram Parham
William Leath	Abram Parham	Abram Parham j^r.	Proces^n. Masters

In Obediance to an Order of Vestry of Albemarle Parish in Sussex County Bearing Date ye 19th Day of August 1767. to us Directed we have Vewed & Renew'd all the Land Marks in our Preceint According to Order.

March ye 10th 1768　　　Present　　　　　March ye 11 1768　　　Present
We Renewd the　　　Willium Mitchel　　We Renewd the Land　　David Tucker
Land Marks
of Amy Ferington　　James Cain　　　　Marks of　　　　　　Daniel Mitchel
Edward Powel　　　Ephraim Pa　　　　John Ferrington　　　Rich^d. Jones
William Raney Senr.　George Randolph　Peter Green　　　　　Thos. Huson
James Cain Junr.　　Thos. Butler　　Fed Green　　　　　　John Harrison
George Randolph　　Thomas Hunt　　　Wyat Harpers Est.　　Joseph Ingrum
Peter Cain　　　　　& Nat. Raney　　　Rich^d. Jones　　　　W^m. Burrow
James Cain　　　　　--------------　　David Tucker　　　　& John Kelley
George Roberson　　　　　　　　　　　John Kelley
W^m. Gilliums Estate　　　　　　　　　Thomas Huson
Burril Banks Dec^d.　　　　　　　　　John Harrison
John Woodward　　　　　　　　　　　Rich^d. Carter
John Wilkerson　　　　　　　　　　　Daniel Mitchel
Lawrance Gibbons　　　　　　　　　　& W^m. Mitchel
Thomas Burrow
William Burrow
James Moss　　　　　　　　　　　　　　　　　　　　　　　Frederick Green
Thos. Butler　　　　　　　　　　　　　　　　　　　　　　Peter Green
& Thos. Hunt　　　　　　　　　　　　　　　　　　　　　[Procession Masters]

[225]

In Obedience to an Order of the Vestry of Albemarle Parish Bearing Date the 19th of August 1767. and to us Directed we have Assembled the Freeholders & Renew'd All the Land Marks in our Preceint According to the Aforesaid Order To wit

The Land Marks of Colo^r. Nico^	　　　John Wynne
Massenburg
Thomas Curtland　　　　　　　　　　　John Wynne Junr.
Lidia Weathers　　　　　　　　　　　Mathew Wynne
William Pettway Junr.　　　　　　　　Henry Sturdivant
William Pettway　　　　　　　　　　　Rachel Tenning
W^m. and John Weathers　　　　　　　　John Bobbit
Edward Pettway　　　　　　　　　　　James Glovier
Robt. Pettway　　　　　　　　　　　Hartwell Marrible
Stith Parham　　　　　　　　　　　　John Threewit
Robt. Parham　　　　　　　　　　　　Charles Sturdivant
Holemn Sturdivant
Stith Wynne

Present Holemn Sturdivant, John Wynne j^r., Stith Wynne, Thos. Sturdivant, Charles Sturdivant, William Weathers and John Sturdivant.
　　　　　　　　　　　　　　　　　　　　　　　　　　　William Pettway Junr.
　　　　　　　　　　　　　　　　　　　　　　　　　　　　　　　Stith Parham
　　　　　　　　　　　　　　　　　　　　　　　　　　　　　[Procession Masters]

Surry and Sussex Counties, Virginia, 1742-1786

With Submission to Order of Vestry bearing Date 19th Day of August 1767 We the Subscribers has Procession'd & Renew'd the Land marks in the Preceint According as the Order Directed to wit

Propriators March 24 1768}	People Present	Propri. March 25 1768	People Present
John and [sic] Sturdivant	John A. Sturdivant	Rob¹. Numans	John Cocks
Wᵐ. Spane	Wᵐ. Spane	Robert Wynne	Jesse Sturdivant
Joseph Dennis	Joseph Dennis	Wᵐ. Sturdivant	Wᵐ. Spain
Nathaniel Hood	Nathaniel Hood	Wᵐ. Cocks	William Reives
John Cocks	John Cocks	Propriators . 26	People Present
John Hardy	Wᵐ. Reives	Moses Knight	Moses Knight
Wᵐ. Reives	Richard Hill	Willᵐ. Sturdivant	Willᵐ. Sturdivant
Richard Hill	James Horn	John Sturdivant	John Sturdivant
James Horn			
	Jeasent [adjacent] Lines Mʳ. Gray Briggs Mʳˢ. Cary -- no Appearance.	Done P	& Concluded by us William Stuart John Harday [Procession Masters]

[226]

In Obedience to an Order of the Vestry of Albemarle Parish in the County of Sussex Dated the 19th Day of Augt. 1767. and to us Whose Names are hereunto Subscrib'd Directed we have Procession'd the Several lines of the Different Tracts or Parcels of Land in the Preceint by the Said Order Express'd & the land Marks thereof have Renew'd, a part of the line between the Church land & that Land purchas'd of Frances Mabry by Peter Hawthorn Decᵈ. Excepted which neither we nor any that attended the Processioning Could find.

Propritors Names	Persons Present	
Henry Porch	Bridges Porch	Order N°. 9
Lucy Adkins widow of	Henry Moss Jʳ.	N.B. Since we
Thoˢ. Adkins Decᵈ.		clos'd the Procession
Charles Gee		ing we are inform
	Prdges [sic] Porch	ed from Gᵉᵒ. Reives
Halcott Pride	Henry Moss jʳ.	by Mʳ. Willie that
Joshaua Mechum	Joshua Meachum	the uper line of
Sarah Edwards	Lemmon Shele for Mʳ.	the Church land
Hartwell Marable	Pride	Passes thro͞. the
Hugh Belsches	Wᵐ. Tomlinson	corn field belonging
Ezell an Infant	Banks Meachum	to the land of John
Edward Epps		Hawthorn an Infant
Church Land	the former Six & Mʳ. Willie	& that the line trees are all cut Down
John Hawthorn an Infant	the former Seven &	tho we found trees
Edward Pettway	Hugh Belsches	Chop'd along the Corn
Glebe land		Field fence.
Revᵈ. Wᵐ. Willie		

Banks Meachum
W^m. Tomlinson
Henry Moss
John Adkins

Bridges Porch
Henry Moss J^r.
Joshua Meachum
W^m. Tomlinson
Banks Meachum

Done this 23rd Day of March A.D. 1768
by John Adkins
Henry Moss Proces˜. Masters

[227]

1768
March
14

By Virtue of an Order of the Vestry of Albemarle Parish bearing Date August 19th 1767. we the Subscribers have Assembled the Freeholders together within the Precint Specified by the S^d. order and have Procession'd and Renew'd the Land Marks of the Several Persons as Follows to wit --
Rubin Coocks Land, Foster Cooks Land, James Cooks Land, Capt. John Thompsons Land, Colo˜. Augustine Claiborne Land, William Shands Land, David Jones Land, William Eldridge Land, Rebeccah Heaths Land, William Heaths Land, William Heaths Junr. Land, Thomas Tatums Land, Frances Rogers Land, Glaster Hunnicutts Land, Richard Carters Land, Charles Gees Land, Richard Harrisons Land.
Present when the above Said Land were Procession'd John Jones, James Cook, John Clark, James Granthum, Mark Heath, John Heath, William Heath Ju^r., Jesse Gee, Holmes Jones, Glaster Hunnicutt, Richard Carter, Augustine Shands.

David Jones
W. Eldridge
[Procession Masters]

In Obedience to an Order of the Vestry of Albemarle Parish in Sussex County Bearing Date ye 19th Day of August 1767 to us Directed we have Vew'd & Renew'd the Land marks in our Precint as followeth.

March y^e. 8. 1768
The Land of W^m. Gillium Dec^d.
W^m. Oliver – Robt. Owen
Richard Jones, Thomas Wynne
John Wilborne
James Jones
Robt. Jones
John Sturdivant
William Parham Junr.
Peter Threewitts
Nat. Parham
and Webb Roland
Present
Frances Epps
Richard Jones
Robert Jones
Thomas Wynne
W^m. Oliver

March y^e. 9. 1768
The Land of Frances Epps
William Hewett Dec^d.
William Parham Senr.
Burrel Green
William Green and
Matthew Parham
Present
Frances Epps
John Hobbs
John House
& Richard Jones
The Lands of Isham Smith and John Wadkins Not Renew'd there being no Person Present to see the Land marks Renew'd The Legal Notis Given

Surry and Sussex Counties, Virginia, 1742-1786   175

John Sturdivant
Peter Threewitts and   James Jones
Burrel Wilborne   Nat. Parham
                                          [Procession Masters]

[228]

In Obedience to an Order of the Worshipfull Vestry of Albemarle Parish bearing Date the nineteenth Day of August 1767 we the Subscribers have Processioned and Renew'd the Land Marks of the Several Persons within the Precint in the Said Order Mention'd & in Presence of the Several Persons Hereafter Named.

The Proprietors of the Land	When Perform'd	Persons Present
The Land belonging to the Estate of James Stuart Dec^d., David Masons, Nathan Northington, John Whitehorn, Lewis Thorp, James Wych Orphan of James Wych Dec^d, Joseph Thorp, Henry Gee, Ric^d. Hay & Thomas Griffis Orpan of Edward Griffis Dec^d.	26 Febu$^-$. 1768	Capt. Nat. Wych, Joseph Thorp, John Whitehorn, Rich^d. Hay, Nathan Northington, John Morgin, James Sammons. Thos. Avent & Willm. Solomon Nathan Northington, James Sammons, John Morgin, Joseph Thorp, Thos. Avent, Rich^d. Hay & John Whitehorn.
The Land belonging to the Orphans John Sammons Dec^d., John Morgan, John Roland, James Sammons & Thomas Avent	27 Febu$^-$. 1768	David Mason & Henry Gee Processioners

In Obedience to an Order of the Worshipful Vestry of Albemarle Parish in the County of Sussex Bearing Date the 19th Day of August 1767 to us Directed We the Subscribers have Procession'd all the Lands in the S^d. Order Mention'd & Renew'd the Land marks thereof in Presence of the Parties herein Mention'd.

To Whom the Land belongs	When Procession'd	The Persons Present
Charles Mabry		Charles Mabry
John Battle	March 28. 1768	John Battle
William Moss	the first Day	John Moss
John Richardson		John Richardson
Benjamin Arrington		Benjamin Arrington
William Richardson		Richard Rawlings
George Long		Benjamin Richardson
Thomas Newsum		Samuel Harwood
Gregory Rawlings		Benjamin Phips
Belon$^-$. to the Estate of John Southwort		Richard Barlow
Thomas Dunn	The 2^d Day	Benjamin Phips
Richard Rawlings		Samuel Harwood
Benj$^-$. Phips		John Manry
Henry Manry		Thomas Peoples
Benj$^-$. Richardson		George Haywood
William Brown		
John Austin Finnia		

Belong'. to the Estate of Ric^d.
Rose
Belo'. to the Estate of Joshua
Pritlow
Charles Judkins

      his
Thomas "X" Dunn
     mark
George Long
[Procession Masters]

[229]

With Submission to an Order of Vestry Bearing Date 19th Day of August 1767 – We the Subscribers has procession'd and Renew'd the Land Marks on the Preceint According as the Order Directed to wit

Febu'. 22. 1768 Propriators	People Present	27th Propriators	People Present
Sarah Moore	James Cocks	Soloman Graves	John Potts
Sarah Stoaks	James Williams Ju'.	Elizabeth King	Edward Davis
John Stoaks	Charles Williams	Ann King	James Williams j'.
Young Stoaks	Young Stoaks	Peter Knight	Charles Williams
Thomas Pinnington	Thos. Pinnington	Ebenezar Shairmon	Ebenezar Shairmon
Nat. Holt	Nat Holt	John Hood	Thomas Hood
Abram Brown	Abram Brown	Barham Moore	James Cocks
Silvanus Stoaks	Thos. Adkins	Hinchia Rochel	Thomas Adkins
Thomas David	Edward Davis	William Ezell	William Th^o. Pinnington
Orphan of Thos. Tius Dec^d.	Thomas Hood	Isham Ezell	William Cocks
Benj'. Evens	John Potts	Marcus Stoaks	
26th Propriators	People Present		
Thomas Adkins	Thomas Adkins		
Robt. Whitehead	James Cocks		
John Potts	John Potts		
Matthew Strudivant	Young Stoaks		
James Williams	Charles Williams		
James Williams j'.	James Williams j'.	Done & Concluded	by us
James King	Edward Davis		p Soloman Graves
William Cocks	William Cocks		William Ezell
Thomas Stoaks	Ebenezar Chairman		[Procession Masters]
	Howel Pinnington		
	Thomas Hood		

[230]

        Albemarle Parish   D^r.

April	To Balance Due to David Mason as p Acc^t. Renderd this Day	£ 22..10..11
21	To Paid Lucrecy Sammons as p Order of Vestry	3..0..0
1767	To P^d. John Woodward for keeping Wilkersons Child 1 Yr. Ending 8 July 1767	5..0..0

To P^d. the Rev^d. M^r. Willie a ballance Due 1766 £5 ~ To P^d. D^o. Due Easter 1767	15..0..0
To P^d. D^o. for Providing Neceseries for the Use of Thos. Cooper & family	5..0..0
To P^d. Willi . Colston for keeping Mangums Child Due. 1767	5..0..0
To P^d. Tabithy Roland for 3 barrels of Corn Allow'd her by the Vestry a^t 10/.	1..10..0
To P^d. Willi . Rives for Bureing [sic] &c John Bagley	2..7..6
To P^d. Rebeccah Pair as p Order of Vestry	2..10..0
To P^d. Richard Hay Ju^r. as p D^o.	0..15..0
To P^d. Peter Zell as p D^o.	2..10..0
To P^d. Edward Wooton as p D^o.	1..5..0
To P^d. Capt. Richard Hill for John Owen	3..0..0
To P^d. John Knight as p Order of Vestry	2..0..0
To P^d. Edward Prince for keeping Hix's Child 1 Year as p Order Vestry	5..0..0
To P^d. Rich^d. Hill for Robt. Whitehead for 300 lb Pork Allow'd by Vestry No^m. 1766	3..0..0
To P^d. Drewry Zell in Part for keeping Kathrin Yearwood as by Contract of the late Church Wardens at 40/. p Annum	0..10..0
To P^d. Mary Hix in part of £5~ All^r. at Laying the Levy 1766 it being Suff [sufficient]	3..10..3
To P^d. Hannah Rose in Part of £5~ Allow^d. her at Laying the Laying the [sic] Levy Novr. 1766 it being Sufficient	3..8..10
To P^d. Thos. Waller for Sundreys found him by Capt Gee it being 9/ over what was Allow'd by Order of Vestry Novr. 1766.	3..9..0
To P^d. Thos. Adams for Provisions Provided for Mary Adams by Order of the Late Church Wardens	0..10..10½
To P^d. Willi . Solomon for keeping Nat. Barlow 1 Year Ending 1 Augt. 1767 by Contract of the late C. Wardens	3..10..0
To P^d. Matthew Hubbard for taking Care of Nat. Barlow & Releasing the Parish from any ruther Expence.	7..0..0
To P^d. Henry Tacon for the Use of Eliz . Birdson as p Order Vestry 1765	3..0..0
To P^d. D^o. for D^o. as p Order of Vestry 1766	4..0..0
To P^d. Doctor Ridley for Sallavating [sic] Mark Underwood by Contract of Capt. Gee as p Order Vestry }	5..0..0
To P^d. Thos. Waller as p Order of Vestry Octo^r. 1767	3..0..0
To P^d. Anne Barr for keeping & Burying Frances Ham	1..12..6
To P^d. John Potts for keeping S^d. Ham by Contract of the late C.Ward.	1..0..0
To P^d. W^m. Loftin for 3 Barrels of Corn for the Use of Mary Southworth as p Order of Vestry 1766	1..10..0
To P^d. Joseph Renn for keeping John Renn Due Octr. 1767 by Contract	4..0..0
To P^d. John Pinnington for keeping Frances Ham by Contract of the Late Church Wardens	0..10..0
To Lay'd out in Necesaries for Mary Hix as p Order Vestry Octr 1767	2..0..0
To P^d. Capt. Charles Briggs for Drewry Zell his Ballance for keeping the Widow Yearwood	1..10..0
To P^d. William Colston as p Order of Vestry 1765 for keeping Mangums Child the Same having been Omited	5..10..0

Feb~ 1768	To P^d. the Rev^d. M^r. W^m. Willie for Providing the Elements &c for the Parish to Easter 1768	10..0..0
	To P^d. D^o. for a Bushel of Wheate for the Use of Thomas Cullum by Order of the late C^Wardens	0..4..0
	Carried Over	£ 144..3..10½

[231]

	Brought Over	£144..3..10½
	To P^d. Capt. Charles Briggs for Sundreys Providing for Anne Gaswit [Gresswit] by Order of the late Church Wardens	1..14..8½
	To P^d. Arthur Williamson on Acc^t. of Patty Gillium as p her Order & his Receipt	3..0..0
	To P^d. Solomon Graves on Acc^t. of an Allowance to Agnis Carter by Order of Vestry	3..0..0
	To P^d. D^o. for 4 Bushels of Wheat for the Use of the S^d. Carter by Order of the Late Church Wardens a^t 3/.	0..12..0
	To P^d. M^r. Charles Battle for 300 lb Pork for the Use of the Widow Southworth as p Order Vestry 1766	2..14..0
	To P^d. the Widow Sammons as p Order of Vestry Octr. 1767	1..5..0
	To P^d. Thos. Coopers Order to M^r. George Kerr for Sundreys for Thomas Cullum	3..17..6
	[Land]	£ 160..7..1

To P^d. Colo~. Massenburg as agent for Collage for the Tenement Possesed by M^r. Willie 212 lb Tobacco
To P^d. M^r. Hugh Belsches for Repairs at Nottoway Church in 1767.
    100 lb Tobacco

[232]

Albemarle Parish   C^r.

April 22 1767.	By M^r. John Cargill as late Church Warden for a fine he Omited in his Acc^t. Return'd to the Vestry of this Day.		£ 0..5..0
Augu^st 20	By 19973 lb Tobacco Levied at the Last Levy and Sold 19661 lb as Follows Viz		
	3596	a^t 16/1	£ 28..18..5
	2189	a^t 16/8	18..4..10
	3232	a^t 16/-	25..17..1½
	5038	a^t 16/4	41..2..10½
	1599	a^t 16/2	12..18..6
	1403	a^t 16/7	11..12..8
	2604	a^t 16/3	21..3..1½
	19661		£ 160..2..6½
	212 P^d. Colo~. Massenburg as p Debit		
	100 P^d. M^r. Belsches as p Debit		
	19973		
	March 28th 1768.		
	By Ballance Due as p Debit		£ 0..4..6½
			£ 160..7..1

Albemarle Parish Debit brought Over   £ 160..7..1

March 28 1768
  To Balance Due to D. Mason as p Contra   £ 0..4..6½

  E.E. p

  Aug. Claiborne
  David Mason   Church Wardens

[233]

At a Vestry held for the Parish of Albemarle in the County of Sussex the 19th Day of October 1768.

Present
The Rev^d. M^r. William Willie

Augustin Claiborne	Mical Blow
David Mason	Henry Gee
John Mason	William Blunt
James Jones	

Albemarle Parish	D^r. lb of To^o.
To The Rev^d. M^r. Willie as Minister	17305
To John Veril Clk of Nottoway Church	1200
To John Nicolson Clk of St Pauls D^o.	1200
To George Randolph Clk of St Marks D^o.	1200
To Gregory Rawlings Clk of St Andrews D^o.	1200
To Joseph Denton Sexton of Nottoway Church	500
To John Bane Sexton of St Pauls D^o.	500
To W^m. Rodgers Sexton of St Andrews D^o.	500
To Peter Green Sexton of St. Marks D^o.	500
To the Clk of the Vestry	400
To Edward Walker for one Months Service as Clk	100
To William Brittle over P^d. in his Levy	12
	24617
To the Sheriff's Comision for Collecting 45900 lb of Tobac^o a^t 6½	2754
	27371
To Levied for the Use of the Parish	18529
	45900
The Parish C^r.	
By 2550 Tiths a^t 18 lb Tobacco p Poll	45900

The following Allowances is Order'd to be made the following Persons Plaes'd against Each Person Name

To Humphrey Balis as p Acc^t.	£ 1..12..5
To Capt. Howell Briggs for Joseph Clark	=..18..=
To William Rodgers from this time	3..=..=
To Thos. Cooper	4..=..=
To Thos. Cullum	3..=..=
To Robt. Whitehead	2..10..=
To Mary Southward	2..=..=

To Patty Gillium	2..=..=
To Tabithy Rowland	1..10..=
To John Woodward for Wilkersons Child	4..=..=
To Franklin Clark for keeping Eliza". Birdson	3..=..=
To Rebeccah Pair	3..=..=

[234]

To Samuel Bullock for keeping Cupel Hixes Child	£ 3..=..=
To Thos. Waller & family	3..=..=
To Charles Delihay for keeping W^m. Delihay Due Next November	4..=..=
To Levy Gillium for keeping John Renn	3..=..=
To Sarah Owen	3..=..=
To James Hern for the Ensuing Year	3..10..=
To Doc^r. Ridley as p Acc^t. Balance of his last Years Acc^t.	7..5..9
To W^m. Hix for keeping Ann Greswit	3..18..=
To Samuel Stoaks for the Ensuing Year	2..10..=
To Lucrecy Sammons.	1..10..=
To Edward Wooton for keeping Green fields one month	=..10..=
To Ann Barr for Buriing [sic] Catron Earwood	1..7..6
To John Land for Buriing Ed^d. Loy'd a poor Man of this Parish & keeping him 3 Weeks in his Sickness	1..17..6

The Vestry taking into Consideration that the Present Church being to Small it is Agre^d. on that the Addition of 30 foot out on the North Side of the Church & in Equal Width of the Old be forthwith built and that The Rev^d. M^r. Willie, Augustin Claiborne & Nicolas Massenburg or any two of them Contract with Some Person or Persons for the Same.

Or^d. That the Ch⁻. Wardens pay to the Reve^d. M^r. Willie Ten Pounds for Providing Elements for the Sacrament.

William Willie Minister

At a Vestry held for Albemarle Parish at Nottoway Church May 6 1769

Present
The Reve^d. M^r. W^m. Willie

Augustin Claiborne & David Mason Church Wardens
John Mason, James Jones
Henry Gee & Lawrance Gibbons J^r.} Vestrymen

Or^d. that 10/. /in the poor found/ were in Aug^n. Claiborne hands be Paid to the Use of Thos. Cullum to buy him Some corn by M^r. Willie.

Church Wardens Render'd Acc^t. of last Levy by which a Ballance Due Church Wardens of £24..18..6¼ which was Read Examined & Approved of & Order'd to be Registerd.

Augustin Claiborne & David Mason Elected Church Wardens.

William Willie Minister

[235]

	Albemarle Parish	D^r.
August 1768	To balance Due to David Mason as p Acc^ت. Easter 1768	£ =..4..6½
	To P^d. Thos. Barham for 3 Barrels of Corn for the Use of Saml Stoaks [a^t] 7/6	1..2..6
	To P^d. Charles Sledge for 1 Barrel of D^o. for D^o.	=..7..6
	To P^d. Pettway Johnson for 3 Barrels of Corn for the Use of Thomas Cullum's Family a^t 7/6	1..2..6
	To P^d. D^o. for 200 lb Pork for D^o. All^d. at the Levy 1767 a^t 16/8 [C?]	1..13..4
	To P^d. Mary Southworth as p Allow^e. at laying the levy 1767	2..=..=
	To P^d. William Colson as Ord$^-$. at D^o.	3..=..=
	To Paid Patty Gillium as p D^o.	3..=..=
	To P^d. John Delihay for keeping W^m. Delihay last Year	7..=..=
	To P^d. Lam^l. Bullock for keeping Tubal [sic] Hix's Child one Year Ending 25th Sepr. 1768 }	2..10..=
	To P^d. Thos. Cooper as p Allowance at last Levy	4..=..=
	To P^d. John Woodard for keeping Wilkerson's Child last Year	4..=..=
Nov^r.	To P^d. Rebeccah Pair as p Allowance as last Levy	2..=..=
	To P^d. Capt. Rich^d. Hill for Robt. Whitehead	2..=..=
	To P^d. Lewis Johnson for Provisions found for Jam^s. Herns Family	=..13..1½
Jany. 1769	To P^d. Rebeccah Pair an Allowance made her in 1765 Which became Due in 1766	2..10..=
March	To P^d. M^r. Humphrey Balis as p Order last Levy for Provisions found for William Rodgers	1..12..6
	To P^d. John Bane for Services Done at S^t. Pauls Church	1..=..=
	To P^d. Thos. Waller as p order at the Last Levy	3..=..=
	To found him 4 Y^{ds}. of planes [sic] Over & above his Allowance a^t 2/6	=..10..=
	To P^d. Levy Gillium as p order last Levy	3..=..=
	To P^d. Lucrecy Sammons as p D^o.	1..10..=
	To P^d. Samuel Stokes as p D^o.	2..10..=
	To P^d. Rebeccah Pair as p Levy 1768	3..=..=
	To P^d. Capt. Jones as p ord^r. from Edward Wooton as p Allowa^e. last Levy 10/ & a further Charge for keeping Green Fields Subsequent to the Said order	=..14..6
Ma^{ch}. 28 1769	To P^d. Peter Green for Services at S^t. Marks Church	2..10..=
Ap^l 20	To P^d. Joseph Ellis for Frankling Clark for keeping Eliza$^-$ Birdsong in 1768	3..=..=
		£ 59..10..6

[236]

1768	p Contra	C^r.
Aug^t	B[y] 3753 lb of Tobacco Rec^d. of Capt. James Jones Collector & Sold upon an Average a^t 18/4¼	£ 34..11..11¾
Ma^h. 28 1769	By Balance as p Debt Due to Da^d. Mason	24..18..6½
		£ 59..10..6

David Mason
for
Claiborne & Mason } Church Wardens

[237]

At a Vestry Held for Albemarle Parrish at Nottoway Church the 18th Day of October 1769.

Present
The Reve^d. M^r. William Willie Minister

Augustin Claibrone & David Mason Churchwardens
John Mason, Michael Blow, James Jones & Henry Gee.

The following poor were Duly considered & the Allowances to Each of there names Set Down allowed for there Support this Present Year /To wit/

	£	
To Thomas Cooper		4..=..=
To Robt. Whitehead		2..10..=
To Mary Southworth		3..=..=
To Patty Gillium		3..=..=
To Tabithy Rowland		1..10..=
To John Woodward for keeping Wilkersons Child		4..=..=
To Frankling Clark for keeping Eliz^h. Birdsong		3..=..=
To Rebeckah Pair		3..=..=
To Thomas Waller		3..=..=
To Henry Harrison for keeping John Renn		3..=..=
To James Hern		5..=..=
To William Hix for keeping Ann Gresswitt		3..10..=
To Samuel Stoakes		2..10..=
To Natha^l. Holt for keeping one of Benj^a. Nusums Children		3..=..=
To Thos. Barham for another of Nusums D^o.		3..=..=
To Geo^c. Long J^r. for another of D^o. & he agrees to take the Child Appren^{ed}. on the Year		3..15..=
To Michael Blow for keeping Green Fields		2..15..=
To Nathaⁿ. Felts		4..=..=
To Joseph Clark		2..10..=
To Howell Briggs for a Barrel of Corn for Joseph Clark		=..8..6
To John Alsobrook for 30 ^{lb} Bacon found D^o.		=..12..6
To Charles Gillium		5..=..=
To George Rieves for Seting Seats at Nottoway Church		1..15..~

Order^d that the Church Wardens Contract with Some Person to Board Elizabeth Bailey the Ensuing Year.

Order^d that Nicolas Massenburg, John Mason, Augustin Claiborne or any two do Contract with a Workman to Repair the Gleab Garden blown Down by the Last Great Tempest.

[238]

Then the Vestry Proceeded to Lay the Parish Levy (to wit)

Albemarle Parish	D^r.	W^t lb Toba^o
To the Reve^d. M^r. Willie		17305
To John Nicolson, Clark [clerk] of St Pauls Church		1200
To George Randolph, Clark of St Marks D^o.		1200
To Joseph Denton, Sexton of Nottoway Church		500

To John Bane D°. of St Pauls D°.	500
To William Rodgers D°. of St Andrews D°.	500
To Peter Green D°. of St Marks D°.	500
To the Clark of the Vestry	400
To Henry Porch for one Levy Over Paid Last Year	18
To John Dunn D°. 1767	20
To Levied for the Use of the Parish	26807
To the Colec^r. Commision on 52180 of Tobacco a^t 6 p	3130
	52180

p Contra   C^r. W^t lb Tobacco

By 2609 tiths at 20 ^{lb} Tobacco p Poll   52180

Order$^{'d}$ That the Sheriff upon Giving bond Collect the Parish Levy According to the above State and it is
an Instruction to the Church Wardens that they Advertise a Sale of the Tobacco and after Receiving it from the Sheriff Sell the Same themselves for the most to be got for for [sic] it.

Orde^d that the Church Wardens pay M^r. Willie £ 12~~~ for finding Element for the Sacrament.

The Vestry agrees with Augustin Claiborne to let him have a Pew in the New building aded [sic] to the Church of Nottoway he the S^d. Claiborne Paying to John Peter What Ever Sum M^r. Willie Shall AdJudge the building the Said Pew is worth to go to the Credit of the Parish in the Undertaking of the Said building & the Said Claiborne is to have an Absulate Right to the S^d. Pew to him & to his heirs he & they keeping the Same in Repair for Ever.

William Willie Minnister [sic]

[239]

	Albemarle Parish	D^r.
June	To ballance Due David Mason p Aco^t. Rend^d in Vestry 6th of May 1769	£ 24..18..6½
1769	To P^d. for 38½ ^{lb} of Bacon for M^r. Charles Gillium by Instructions from the Vesy a^t 5^d	=..16..½
	To P^d. Thos. Moore for one Barrel of Corn bought for M^r. Charles Gillium	=..8..4
	To P^d. Messrs. Jesse & Arthur Williamson for James Hern in Part of his Allowance for the Year 1767. the Same being Omited to be Levied for him	1..10..=
	To P^d. James Hern the Residue of his Allowance for the Year 1767. as by Order of Vestry 1768.}	3..10..=
	To P^d. Thos. Cooper as p Allowance at Laying the Levy 1768	4..=..=
	To P^d. the Reve^d. M^r. William Willie for Providing the Ele^{ts}. &c for the Parish to Easter 1769 }	10..=..=
	To P^d. D°. for Providing a New Surplis & Making the Same	5..10..=
	To P^d. Ann Barr for burying Kathrin Yearwood	1..7..6
	To P^d. D°. for keeping Silvia Newsums Child one year Ending June 25th 1769.	3..=..=

	To P^d. Messrs. Purdie & Dixon for advertising the leting the Repairs a^t Not^y. Church	=..5..=
	To P^d. John Alsobrook for 74 ^lb Bacon for the use of Joseph Clark a^t 4^d.	1..4..8
	To P^d. Henry Nicolson for 200 Herrings [a^t] 4/ & for Some bacon [a^t] 1/6 for the [use] of Joseph Clark	=..5..6
	To P^d. M^r. Humphrey Bailis in Part of W^m. Rodgers Acc^t. Allowed at the Laying the Levy in 1768.	1..5..3½
	To P^d. the Clark of Sussex 81 ^lb Tobacco a^t 2^d	=..13..6
	To P^d. Thos. Cullum as p Allowance at Laying the Levy 1768	3..=..=
	To P^d. Capt. Jones for 2 Barrels of Corn as a Further Allow^e. to the S^d. Cullum a^t 7/6	=..15..=
	To P^d. Pettway Johnson for 2 Barrels of Corn for the S^d. Cullum a^t 7/6	=..15..=
	To P^d. Capt. Howell Briggs as p Levy 1768	=..18..=
Augt. 1769	To P^d. Robt. Whitehead as p D^o.	2..10..=
	To P^d. Mary Southworth as p D^o.	2..=..=
	To P^d. Patty Gillium as p D^o.	2..=..=
	To P^d. Timothy Rowland as p D^o.	1..10..=
	To P^d. John Woodward as p D^o.	4..=..=
	To P^d. Charles Delihay for keeping his Bro^r. William Due Novem^r. 1768	4..=..=
	To P^d. John Owen as p Allowance for his Mother and for burying her as She did not Live the Year out	3..=..=
	To P^d. Doc^r. James Day Ridley as p Allow^e. at Laying the Levy 1768	7..5..9
	To P^d. W^m. Hix as p D^o. for Ann Greswitt	3..10..=
	To John Land as p State of the Levy	1..17..6
	To P^d. Frederick Andrews for 12 Tobacco Orderd to be Remited for a Tithable over Listed a^t 15/11.}	=..1..11
	To P^d. Colo^n. Massenburg for the Collage Rent for the use of the Minister 212 ^lb Tobacco a^t 15/11. }	1..13..9
	To P^d. Peter Green for a Second Repair done at S^t. Marks Chappell by Order of M^r. Lawrence Gibbons Junr. }	=..10..=
	£	98..1..3½

[240]

	Debit Brought up	£ 98..1..3½
	To P^d. John Knight for Repairs Done at S^t. Andrew Chappell in Part of his Demand & It's Submited to John Peters Whether he Deserves More	2..6..=
1770	To P^d. Geo^r. Long Junr. as p Allowance at Laying the Levy Octr. 1769	3..15..=
	To P^d. John Peters in Part for the Repairs at Nottoway Church	62..10..=
	To P^d. Nat. Flets [Felts] as p D^o.	4..=..=
	To P^d. Samuel Stoaks as p allowance at Laying the Levy 1762	2..10..=
	To P^d. Burrel Macklemore for Mary Southworth as p Allowance at Laying the Levy 1769	3..=..=
	To P^d. Thos. Waller as p D^o.	3..=..=
	To P^d. Lamuel Bullock for keeping Hix's Child due Sepr. 1769 & Allowed in the State of the Levy 1768 }	3..=..=

To P^d. Doc^r. James Day Ridley in Part of his Bond Against James Hern as Orderd by the Vestry		7..10..=
To P^d. Messrs. Briggs & Blow for Stephen Hamblin for keeping Anne Gresswitt 2 Years to witt 1766 & 1767 }		6..=..=
To the Tax of a Writ ags^t. Ezell		=..1..3
		£195..13..6½

		p Contra	C^r.
Augt 1769	By 17302 ^{lb} Tobacco Rec^d. of the Collector or Accounted with me for and Sold and Accounted for at the Following Rates Viz		
	1492 lb Tobacco	a^t 19/.	£ 13..12..9
	2851	a^t 15/.	21..7..6
	2556	a^t 15/1	19..3..6
	2556	a^t 15/.	19..1..4
	1278	a^t 15/3	9..14..10½
	2261	a^t 16/10	19..=..7
	644	a^t 18/6	5..19..3½
	4224	a^t 15/11	35..12..3¾
			£ 143..12..1¾
	By a Fine for Basterdy Rec^d. from Nancy Hix in 1769 }		2..10..=
	By a Fine Omited to her Accounted for in last Acc^t. Render'd		2..10..=
April 14 1770			£ 146..12..1¾
	By Ballance Due to David Mason as p Debit		49..1..4¾
			£ 195..13..6½

[241]

At a Vestry Held for the Parish of Albemarle in the County of Sussex the 17th Day of April 1770.

Present
The Reve^d. M^r. W^m. Willie,

Augustin Claiborne, David Mason, C.Wardens,
John Mason, James Jones, Henry Gee & Lawrance Gibbons, Junr. Gen⁻.

Augustin Claiborn & David Mason are Appointed Church Wardens till Easter Tuesday Next.

Robt. Jones is Elected a Vestry Man in the Room of John Edmunds Dec^d.

This Day Augustin Claiborne & David Mason Late Church Wardenes Render'd their Acc^t. in Vestry which were Examed Allow'd & Order'd to be Regester'd, by which a Ballance appears to be Due to David Mason of £49..0..1¾.

Orderd that the Church Wardens Pay to Thos. Cullum for the Use of himself and Family out of the fines & Forfitures Accrued to this Parish 30/.

Orderd that it be an Instruction to the Collector of the Parish Levy that he Receive from Debtors in the last Levy for theis Parish at the Rate of Twenty Shillings p Hundred it being the Opinion of the Vestry that it will be more Equal & Just to set a price for all Tobacco payable for the Parish use / the Ministers Salary Excepted / than to Leave it to the Colectors to Set a Price & Depend upon a price the Tobacco may Sell for to Regulate the Price for Debtors to pay that Cannot Provide Tobacco Some Inconveniences & Losses to the parish being Sensibly felt in the last Levy by that Pernicious Custom & the Collector is to Acc^t. with & pay the Church Wardens the Tobacco or money as they Receive According to the Sence and Meaning of this Order.

Orderd that James Hern be Exempted from paying Parish Levy for his Son Federick Hern he being infirm

W^m. Willie Min^r.

[242]

At a Vestry Held for the Parish of Albemarle in the County of Sussex the 19th Day of September 1770.

Present
The Reve^d. M^r. William Willie

Augustine Claiborn & David Mason C.Wardens,
Howell Briggs, James Jones, Henry Gee, William Blunt,
Lawrance Gibbons Junr. & Robert Jones Gen˜.

It Appearing that there are Several Debts due to the Parish from Several Church Wardens prior 1759. to this Time Orderd that the Present Church Wardens be Instructed to call the Several former Church Wardens & Collectors to Acc^t. for the Several Ballances that Appear to be due for the Same & in case they Refuse that then they are to bring Suit against them for the Same.

Orderd that the Church Wardens be instructed to pay the Present Sheriff the Quitrents of 100 Acres of Land Whereon Nottoway Church now Stands for the Year 1769.

Thos. Vaughan Gen˜. Collector of the Parish Levy for the Year 1765 & 1766. this Day Renderd Acc^t. thereof which were Sworn to Examed & Approv`d & Orderd to be Regestered Twenty Seven Pounds of Tobacco Due to the Parish.

Orderd that the Clk of the Vestry do Transmit to the Church wardens a copy of Thos. Vaughan Gen˜. his Acc^t. this Day Renederd in Vestry & that the S^d. C:Wardens be instructed to Employ a proper Officer to Collect the ballances due from the Several Insolvants.

Orderd that the C:Wardens be instructed to Lease the Land whereon Nottoway Church now Stands for the Term of five Years Reserving to the present incumbant of the Glebe Land of the S^d. Parish a Right to git Rail Timber off the S^d. Land for the use of the Said Glebe.

Capt. Howell Briggs personally appear'd in Vestry & Resign'd his Office as a Vestryman of the Parish which is orderd to be Regestered.

Orderd that Major Richard Blunt be Appointed a Vestry man in the Room of Capt. Howell Briggs who has Resigned.

W^m. Willie Min^r.

[243]

At a Vestry Held for the Parish of Albemarle in the County of Sussex the 16 Day of November 1770.
Present
Augustine Claiborne, & David Mason, C Wardens,
James Jones, Henry Gee, Henry Harrison, Mical Blow,
Lawrance Gibbons Ju^r. & Robt. Jones G .

The Vestry Proceeded to Lay the Parish Levy to witt

Albemarle Parish	D^r. W^t. lb of Tobacco
To the Rev^d. M^r. W^m. Willie as Minister	17305
To Thos. Eskrage [sic] Clk. of Nottoway church	1200
To John Nicolson Clk of S^t. Pauls D^o.	1200
To George Randol [sic] Clk of S^t. Mrks D^o.	1200
To Nat. Holt Clk of S^t. Andrews D^o.	1200
To Joseph Denton Sexton of Nottoway Church	600
To John Bane Sexton of S^t. Pauls D^o.	500
To Peter Green Sexton of S^t. Marks D^o.	500
To W^m. Rodgers Sexton of S^t. Andrews D^o.	500
To the Clk of the Vestry	400
To W^m. Rodgers for Over Listed in 1767	12
	24617
To the Collectors Com . a^t 6 p Cent	1933
	26600
To Levied for the Use of the Parish	6460
	33060
The Parish C^r.	
By 2735 Tiths a^t 12^{lb} Tob^o. p Poll	33060

[244]

The following Allowances is Orderd to be Made the following Persons

To Thos. Cooper & family	£ 5..0..0
To Robt. Whitehead	2..0..0
To John Woodward for Wilkersons Child	4..0..0
To Frankling Clark for keeping Elizabeth Birdsong	4..0..0
To Rebeckah Pair	3..0..0
To Thos. Waller	3..0..0
To James Hern for his Son James Hern	5..0..0
To W^m. Hicks for Anne Gresswitt	4..0..0
To Nat. Felts for Hickes Child	3..0..0
To Patty Gillium	2..0..0
To Mary Southworth	2..0..0
To John Delihay for keeping W^m. Delihay	4..5..0
To James Turner Senr. for keeping Eliz . Baley	4..0..0
To Thos. Cullum	5..0..0
To Peggy Jones	2..0..0
To Charles Gillium	4..0..0

To Henry Harrison for Providing Elements for the Sacraments to   8..0..0
Commence from Easter Next

Orderd that the Collage Lease that was Purchasd for the Ease of the Gleab be Sold by the Present Church Wardens for the Use of the Parish Giving Such Credit as theay [sic] the Church Wardens Shall think Proper.

Ord'. that Cap'. Mical Blow Contract with Some person to keep Elizabeth Baley the Ensuing Year.

Ord'. that Cap'. James Jones Contract with Some Person to keep W^m. Bane the Ensuing Year.

Aug'. Claiborne
&
David Mason   Ch. Wardens

[245]

At a Vestry Held for the Parrish of Albemarle in the
County of Sussex the 2^d Day of April 1771

Present
The Reve^d. M^r. W^m. Willie.

Nicholas Massenburg	William Blunt
James Jones	Lawrance Gibbons j^r.
Henry Gee	& Robt. Jones Gen'.

Nicho^s. Masenburg & Lawrance Gibbons jun^r. are Elected Church Wardens till Easter Tusday Next

Ord.   That the Present C:Wardens Call the former Church Wardens to an Acc^t.

Ord   That the C:Wardens pay to Donald Macanish £ 12..18 for Rebuilding the Garden for the Glebe

Ord   That the C:Wardens pay to W^m. Blunt £ 1..3..6 in full of his Acc^t. for neseries [sic] found Joseph Clark.

Ord   That the C:Wardens pay to Robt. Wynne Ranes £ 1..2..6 for Repairing S^t. Marks Church.

Ord   That the C:Wardens provide for Joseph Clark 8 Bushels of Corn

Ord   That Capt. James Jones provide for Joseph Blaton 2 Barrels of Corn

Ord   That the C:Wardens Enquire into the Curcumstances of Susan^h Rae & make her Such Allowance as they Shall think Proper.

Whereas There was an Order of Vestry held at the Court House the 16 Day of November 1770 that Capt. Henry Harrison Should provide the Elements for the Sacrament for £8.... to which he agree'd.

Ord.   That the S^d. Order be Discharg'd

Ord.   That Howell Jones & W^m. Mason on there Entering into Bond & Security to the Vestry of this Parish to be taken by the C:Wardens be Appointed Collectors of this Parish for the Present Year & that they Collect & Receive of Every Tithable person Charagable therewith the Sum of Twelve pounds of Tobacco p Poll & that they have Authority in case the S^d. 12^{tb}. of Tobac^o p Poll or any Part thereof be Detain'd or Refus'd to Levy the Same by Distress & that they pay to Each Respective parish Creditor the Several Sums of Tobacco Due to them & that they pay the Tobacco Levied for the Use of the parish to the C:Wardens for the time being & that it be an Instruction to the S^d. C:Wardens that they Advertise the Sale of the Tobacco & after Receiveing it from the Sheriff Sell the Same themselves for the most that Can be had for it Either for Ready Money or Short Credit as to them Shall Seem most Convient. Upon a Motion made by M^r. Robt. Jones one of the Gen`. of the Vestry it is considerd that the Allowance made to Robt. Whitehead by the Reason of the Largness of his family is to Small it is therefor Or'd that forty Shillings more be Allowed him.

W^m. Willie Minister

[246]

At a Vestry Held for the Parish of Albemarle the 1 Day of October 1771

Present
The Reve^d. M^r. Willie   Mical Blow
Nicholas Massenburg   James Jones
Augus`. Claiborne   W^m. Blunt
David Mason   & Ric^d. Blunt Gen`.

In pursuance to an Order of Sussex County Court bearing Date July Court 1771 Directing the Vestry of Albemarle Parish to Divide the Same into preceints for Processioning Every Persons Land within the Said Parish.

N°. 1

We do Appoint Humphry Balis & Benjn. Clary to See Every Persons Land Procession'd & the Land Marks thereof Renewed from Surry County line up Seacock & Tarripin Swamp to Burchant Island Road & up the Said Road to the head of Seacock & that they Assemble all the Freeholders within the S^d. Preceint to Attend the performance thereof & that the S^d. Humphry Bailis & Ben`. Clary do make Return to this Vestry of Every Persons land they Shall Procession & of Every Person Present at the Processioning thereof & of Whose land they Shall fail to Procession the Reason of Such failure & that the Same be Done & perform'd between the first Day of November & the last Day of march nex.

2   Arthur Smith & Edward Wooton are App^d. to Proces`. from Seacock up Snake branch to the head from thence to Secorries Down Secorries to Burchant Island Road So to the Beginning.

3   Henry Blow & W^m. Brittle are App^d. to Proces` from the Sou^h. Side of Seacock to the head of the Lightwood Swamp & to the head of Seecorries Swamp to a branch Called the winding branch from that branch to the head of Snake branch Down that branch to Seacock So to the beginning.

4   Nat Briggs & Joseph Ellis are App^d. to proces` from Southampton County line up Atsamosauk Swamp to Secawry Swamp up the S^d. Swamp to the head thereof.

5   James Turner & Howell Chappell are app^d. to Proces`. from the mouth of Secawry Swamp up the Atsamosauk to the Majors Branch up that branch to the Secawry Road by the S^d. Road to Secawry Swamp by the S^d. Swamp to the beginning.

6   David Jones & W^m. Eldredge are App^d. to Proces`. from Cooks bridge along Cooks Road to Joseph Swamp So to prince George County line by the line to black water Swamp So to the beginning.

[247]

7x	Edward Weaver & Edward Weaver j^r. are App^d. to proces$^`$. from the Governors Road to the Old Parish line all between Atsamosauk Swamp, Joseph's Swamp & the Old Parish Line
8 x	David Jones & James Peters are App^d. to Proces$^`$ from the old Parish line Down Atsamosauk Swamp to Robins Branch So Down Austins branch to Nottoway River up the River to the old Parish line by that to the beginning.
9x	Thos. Peters & John Chappell are app^d. to Proces$^`$. all between Robins branch, Austins branch, Nottoway River, Atsamosauk Swamp and Southampton County line
10 x	John Adkins & Henry Moss are App^d. to proces$^`$. from Pettways mill Along Pettways line formally Hawthon's line to the Collage line Along that line to Josephs Swamp Down that Swamp to Nottoway River up the River to Jones Hole Swamp So to the beginning.
11 x	Hugh Belsches & Edward Pettway are App^d. to proces$^`$. all between Jones Hole Swamp, the Indian Swamp, Nottoway River and prince George County line
x 12	John Freeman & Joel Tucker are App^d. to proces$^`$. Between Monks Neck Creek, Stoney Creek & Up Sapony Creek to Prince Geo$^`$. County line
13x	Rich^d. Hill & George Booth are App^d. to proces$^`$. from Stoney Creek up Saponey Creek to Sapony Mill thence to Epharm Parhams line So Down Nottoway to the beginning
14x	Peter Green & John Malone are App^d. to proces. from Epharm Parhams line to Sapony Mill all between the line that Divides this County & Dinwiddie & up Nottoway River to Harries Swamp
15x	Isham Smith & W^m. Yarbrough are App^d. to proces$^`$. from Harries Swamp up
16x	James Cooper & Joseph Renn are App^d. to proces$^`$. between Rackoon Swamp, Little Swamp & Stoakes Road
17x	Nat$^`$. Parham & Rob$^t$. Jones are App$^d$. to proces$^`$. from the Island Swamp to the Old Parish line by that line to the line that Divides this County & Brunswick So to Nottoway River
18x	Solomon Graves & Cudburth Stafford are App^d. to proces$^`$. from Stoakes
19x	Nat$^`$. Wych & John Stewart are App$^d$. to proces$^`$. all the Lands on the South Side of the 3 Creeks Southampton & Brunswick County lines.
20x	Nicolas Massenburg & Matthew Wynne are App^d. to proces$^`$. from Stoakes Road up Nottoway River to the Frying pan Swamp from the head of the Said Swamp a Straight Course to the Hunting Quarter Swamp.

[248]

21 x — Edward Cross & John Alsobrook are App^d. to proces˜. from the mouth of Copperhawnk Swamp along the line that Divides this County & Surry to Burchant Island Road by that Road to Seacawry Road by that Road to Copperhawnk Swamp So to the beginning,

22 x — John Lamb & Simon Stacy are App^d. to proces. all Between Black Water Swamp, Copperhawank Swamp & the Old Parish line all Except the Lands of W^m. Blunt, W^m. Nicolson & Thos. Tomlinsons

23 x — James Bois˜. [Boisseau?] Jones & Nat. Barker are app^d. to Proces. from the mouth of the Old Town Swam up that to the head of the Tarr Kiln branch Down that to the mill Swamp & Including John Gilliums formally Tatums Land So to the new Road & So to Cooks Road by that to black water So to the beginning.

24 x — David Mason & John Whitehorn are App^d. to proces˜. from the the [sic] mouth of the Great Swamp to the 3 Creeks & up the 3 Creeks & Auter Dam Swamp to Brunswick County line;

25 x — George Rieves & Christopher Rieves are App^d. to proces˜. all between Edward Pettways line formally Harthorns line & the Collage line & the line that Divides this County & Prince George, Josephs Swamp & Jones Hole Swamp

26 x — John Pennington & Thomas Bayley are App^d. to proces˜. all between Allens line, John Penningtons line, John Berrimans line, Stoakes Road & the Hunting Quarter Swamp.

27 x — Thomas Renn & John Zells are App^d. to proces˜. all between Allens line, John Penningtons line, John Berrimans line, Stoakes Road & Nottoway River

28 x — Richard Blunt & W^m. Nicolson are App^d. to proces. from Black on the Old Parish line by that to Copperhawnk Swamp by that Swamp to the head, So to the Tarr Kiln branch on the mill Swamp up that to the Old Town Swamp Down that to black water, so to the beginning including W^m. Blunts, W^m. Nicolson & Thos. Tomlinsons Land

29 x — Henry Harrison & Anselm Gillium are App^d. are [sic] proces˜. all between Nottoway River, the Hunting Quarter & Rackcoon Swamps So Along Loftins mill Path to the Little Swamp Down that to Rackcoon Swamp So to Nottoway River

x 30 — Jesse Williamson & Arthur Williamson are App^d. to proces˜. up Hunting Quarter Swamp to Little Swamp from Loftins mill Path So to Stoakes Road

31 x — Thos. Parham & John Parham are App^d. to proces˜. from the Indian Swamp to Monks neck Creek, nottoway River & the line that Divides this County & Prince George County

[249]

x 32 — W^m. Pettway & Stith Parham are App^d. to Proces˜. from the flat Swamp up Nottoway River to the mouth of Frying Pan Swamp so to the head of it from thence to threewitts so to the beginning

33 x		John Wynn & W^m. Sturdivant are App^d. to Proces⁻. from the head of frying pan Swamp to Hunting Quarter Swamp Down to Island Branch down that to Nottoway River
34 x		James Bell & Nat. Holt are App^d. to Proces⁻. from the north Side of the Spring Swamp up the S^d. Swamp to the County line so Down the Rackcoon to Stoakes Road – Except so much as is App^d. Sam⁻. Northington & Webb Roland
35 x		Samuel Northington & Webb Roland are App^d. to Proces⁻. from Thomas Adkins line thence by David Owens to the Rackoon Swamp up the S^d. Swamp to Brunswick County line so along the S^d. line to the Spring Swamp so to the beginning being the Uper Part of Bell & Holt's Preceint
36 x		Fadde Jarrad & Federick Andrews are App^d. to Proces⁻. from Cook Road on the new Road by that Road to Black Swamp Down that to pegian [Pigeon] Swamp up that to Cooks Road Down that Road to the beginning
37 x		Hugh Ivey & Nat⁻. Dunkin are App^d. to proces⁻. all between Josephs Swamp & Pigion Swamp the Governors Road & Cooks Road.
38 x		Henry Jarrad & Jehu Barker Senr. are App^d. to proces⁻. frome Majors branch up Atsamosauk Swamp to Jones Church Road by that Road to Secawry Road by that Road to the Majors Branch So to the beginning
x 39		Nicolas Partridge & ~~Phillip~~ Johnson are App^d. to proces⁻. from Jones Church Road up Atsamosauk & including Pettway Johnsons Land thence to the head of Copperhawnk Swamp by that to Secawry Road by that Road to Jones Church Road so to the begin⁻.
40 x		George Long & Charles Long are app^d. to proces⁻. all between Rackoon Swamp Southampton line Butt's Road & Stoake's Road
41 x		Benja⁻. Addams & John Pate are App^d. to proces⁻. from the poplar Swamp near Bullocks to Wyches Road to the Great Swamp by that to Southampton line by that line to the poplar So to the begin^g.
42 xx		Phillip Harood [Harwood] & Charles Barham are App^d. to proces⁻. between Butt's Road the Poplar swamp Southampton County line and Stoakes Road
43		James Barns & Nathan Northington are App^d. to proces⁻. from the poplar Bridge up the South branch to Brunswick County line by that line to the great Swamp by that to Wyche's Road by that to the beginning
44 x		Thos. Felts & W^m. Rose are App^d. to proces⁻. from the Poplar at Mical Weather's along a Path that leads from Weather's to Abel Mabry's on the Spring Swamp Down the Spring Swamp to Stoake's Road by that to the poplar Swamp So to the beginning.

[250]

x 45		William Richardson & Nat⁻. Felts are App^d. to proces⁻. from the Path that leads from Mical Weathers's to Abel Mabrys on the Spring Swamp up the S^d. Swamp to Brunswick County line by that to the South branch Down the Same to the fork So up the North Prong to Mical Weather's.

Ord   That John Smith be Exempted from paying Parish Levy for the future.

Ord   That Thos. Woodham be Exempted from paying Parish Levy for the future.

The following Allowances is Order'd to be made the following persons Place'd against Each Persons name to Witt

To William Rodgers	£ 2..=..=
To Thos. Cooper	5..=..=
To Robt. Whitehead	2..=..=
To John Woodward for keeping Wilkersons Child	4..=..=
To Frankling Clark for keeping Elizabeth Birdsong	4..=..=
To W^m. Partin for keeping Rebeccah Pair to commence from 15 Oc^r. 1771	6..=..=
To Thomas Waller	3..10..=
To James Hern for his Son James	5..=..=
To W^m. Hicks for keeping Ann Gesswitt	4..=..=
To Patty Gillium	2..=..=
To the C:Wardens to be Layd out in Nes^s for Joseph Clark	5..=..=
To Mary Southwort	2..=..=
To Benjamin Wilburn for keeping W^m. Delihay	5..=..=
To The Rev^d. M^r. Willie for Sacramental Elements	12..=..=
To Joseph Lane for keeping Elizabeth Bayley Due 1 De^r. 71	4..15..=
To James Bane for keeping his Bro$^-$. W^m. for the present Year	3..=..=
To Peggy Jones	2..=..=
To David Mason late CWarden balance Due to him	21..7..1
To Charles Gillium	2..=..=
To Charity Clifton	2..=..=
To Thomas Cullum	6..=..=
To Joanna Moss	2..15..=
To James Bane for keeping his Brother W^m. the Ensu^g Yr	3..10..=
To Anne Lilly for keeping Silve Nusums Child	3..=..=
To William Lamb for 2 Setts of horse blocks at S^t. Pauls Ch	=..5..=
	£ 112..2..1

[251]

Then the Vestry Proceeded to Lay the Parish Levy...to Witt

Albemarle Parish	D^r.	W^t lb Tob^o.
To The Reve^d. M^r. W^m. Willie as Minister		17305
To Thos. Eskarge [sic] Clark of Not^{ty} Church 8 months		800
To M^r. Baird Clk of D^o. 2 months		200
To M^r. Williams Clk of D^o. 2 months		200
To John Nicolson Clk of St Pauls Church		1200
To George Randal Clk of S^t. Marks D^o.		1200
To Nat^l. Holt Clk. of S^t. andrews D^o.		1200
To Joseph Denton Sexton of Nottoway Church		600
To John Bane D^o. of S^t. Pauls D^o.		500
To Peter Green D^o. of S^t. Marks D^o.		500
To William Rodgers D^o. of S^t. Andrews D^o.		500
To the Clark of the Vestry		800
To the late Collectors M^{ess}. Mason & Jones		903

To Levied for the Use of the Parish	21282
To the Collet Comission on 50202 lb Toba°. at 6 p Com.	3012
	50202

	Albemarle Parish	C^r.
By 2789 Thiths at 18 ^{lb} Tobacco p Poll		50202

Order'd that that [sic] the Succeeding Sheriff on there giving Bond & Securrity to the Vestry of this Parish to be taken by the Church wardens be appointed Collector of this Parish for the present Year and that they Collect & Receive of Every Tithable Person Chargeable therewith the Sum of Eighteen Pounds of Tobacco p Poll & that they have an Athority in case the said Eighteen Pounds of Tobacco p Poll or any Part thereof be Delay'd or Refus'd to Levy the Same by Distress & that they Pay to Each Parish Creditor the Several Sums of Tobacco Due to them & that they pay the Tobaco Levied for the use of the Parish to the Church wardens for the time being & that it be an Instruction to the Said Church wardens that they Advertise the Sale of the S^d. Tobacco & after Receiving of it from the Sheriff Sell the Same themselves for the most that can be had for it Either for Ready money or Short Credit as they Shall think most Convient.

Ordered that the Church Wardens Apply to James Stuarts Executers to be Reumburst £2. Paid by the Late Church Wardens for John Bush and in case of their Refusing payment thereof to Bring Suit for the Same.

This Day David Mason and Augustine Claiborne Late Church Wardens Rendered their Accompt in Vestry Which were Examined Allowed and Ordered to be Regestered by Which Accompt there Appears to be Due to David Mason £21..7..1.

[252]

William Mason and Howell Jones Collectors of the Parish Levy for the years 1770 a[nd?] 1771 this Day Rendered their Accompt thereof which were Sworn to Examined and Approv'd and Ordered to be Regestered Ballance Due to the Collectors 903^{lb} of Tobacco.

W^m. Willie Minister

William Willie Min^r

	Albemarle Parish		D^r.
August 1770	To Ballance Due to David Mason as Church Warden as p Acc^t. Rendered Easter Tuesday 1770	}	£ 49..1..4¾
	To 2 Barrels of corn for the use of old William Rose and family a^t 10/		1..=..=
	To paid Thos. Tomlinson for fish for Joseph Clark found him in 1769		=..4..6
	To paid Benjn. Adams for 7½ Bushels of Corn for the use of Mary Adams and Her Children	}	=..15..=
	To paid Frankling Clark for Keeping Elizabeth Birdsong Due November 1769 (by W^m. Mason)	}	3..=..=
	To paid Capt. Hill for Thomas Davis for the S^d. Davis's Keeping Newsums Child Paid by W^m. Mason	}	3..=..=
	To Paid Charles Delihay for keeping his Brother W^m. p^d. by D^o.		4..=..=
	To paid Nathaniel Holt for Keeping Benjn. Newsoms Son Holliday 1 year and 2 Months a^t £3. p Annum	}	3..10..=
	To paid Thos. Holt for keeping Ben^n. newsoms son Crawford 1 year	}	3..=..=

Surry and Sussex Counties, Virginia, 1742-1786

To paid Charles Gilliam as p Order Vestry 1769	5..=..=
To paid Patty Gilliam as p D°. D°.	3..=..=
To Paid William Colson for Keeping John Renn two months and 11 Days a¹ £5 p year }	=19..8½
To P^d. James Herns Order to James Jones it being the Said Herns Allowance Due Easter 1770 }	5..=..=
To P^d. John Delihay for keeping W^m. Delihay Due Novem^r. 1770	4..5..=
To P^d. John Ellis for Frankling Clark for keeping Eliz^h. Birdsong Due November 1770 }	3..=..=
To Paid Pettway Johnson as p his Acc^t. for Sundreys found Thomas Cullum & Family for the year 1769 & Spring 1770 }	6..3..5
To P^d. W^m. Sammons as p Acc^t. for taking Care of Rich^d. Barlow in his Sickness & Burying him after his Death }	2..7..6
To P^d. the Reve^d. M^r. Willie for Providing Elements for the Sacrament to Easter }	12..=..=
To Paid James Turner as p Order Vestry Novem^r. 1770	4..=..=
To P^d. D°. a Subsequent Acc^t. on Acc^t. of Elizabeth Bayley	=..14..2
Carried over £	114..=..8

[253]

Debit brought Up £	114..=..8
To P^d. John Peters the Ballance Due from the Parish for Services and Repairs at Nottoway Church }	55..10..=
To P^d. Nat^l. Holt for puting up Seats at S^t. Pauls Church	2..=..=
To P^d. Thos. Coop as p Levy 1769	4..=..=
To P^d. Robt. Whitehead as p D°. D°.	2..10..=
To P^d. John Woodward as p D°.	4..=..=
To P^d. Rebecca Pair as p D°.	3..=..=
To P^d. Capt. Harrison as p D°. / by Howell Jones	3..=..=
To P^d. W^m. Hicks for keeping Ann Gresswitt as p levy 1769	3..10..=
To P^d. Thos. Barham for keeping Benjn. Newsums Child as p Levy 1769	3..=..=
To P^d. Thos. Massengill for keeping Green Fields as Levied to Capt. Blow 1769	2..15..=
To P^d. Capt. Briggs by Geo^n. Kerr for Acc^t. of Joseph Clark as p Levy 1769	2..10..=
To P^d. D°. by D°. on his own Acc^t. as p Levy 1769	=..8..6
To P^d. John Alsobrook for Bacon for the Use of Joseph Clark as p Levy 1769	=..12..6
To George Rieves as p Levy 1769	1..15..=
To P^d. James Renn for keeping his Bro^r. John Renn one Year End^g. Febu^y. 1771	5..=..=
To the Clark of Sussex 144 lb. Tobacco a¹ 2^d.	1..4..=
To Robt. Whitehead as p Levy 1770	2..=..=
To Thos. Waller as p D°.	3..=..=
To P^d. James Hern as p D°.	5..=..=
To P^d. Nat^l. Holt as p D°.	3..=..=
To 2 Barrels of Corn Bou^t. for the Use of Mary Wilborne in the Year 1771	1..=..=

To Sundry Neceries of Cloathing & Beding Provided for John Bush	2..=..=
To Sundreys Provided for Elizabeth Spain	2..=..=
To 13 Y^{ds}. of Holland Provided for M^r. Willie for a Surplice at S^t. Pauls Church a^t 3/6 Sterling p Y^d. 62½ p Cent	3..13..11¼
To P^d. John Knight a Ballance for Repairs at S^t. Andrews Church	1..=..=
To P^d. Jos`. Denton Sexton of Nottoway Church by Direction of the Vestry for Extrodiny Services 100 lb Tobacco a^t 17/	=..17..=
Tobacco P^d. for the Parish out of the Depossitum of the Levy 1769	232..6..7½
To Witt. 350 To John Verel as Clk. of Nottoway Church 762 to Thos. Eskarge [sic] as D^o. at D^o. 212 To Col^o. Massenburg as agent for the Collage 1200 to Nat`. Holt & to the Estate of Gregory Rawlings Dec^d. the S^d. Holt & Rawlings as Clk of S^t. Andrews Church Total 2524	
May 1771 To Ballance Due David Mason as p Contra	£ 21..7..½

[254]

Augt 1770	p Contra	C^r.	
	By 26307 lb of Tobacco Levied for the Use of the Parish and Sold 24283 as Follows		
Viz^t.	3187 Sold to George Kerr	a^t 17/	27..1..9½
	4841 D^o. to Howel Jones	a^t 16/9	40..10..10
	4459 D^o. to D^o.	a^t 17/1	38..1..9
	3065 D^o. to D^o.	a^t 16/10	25..15..11
	4034 D^o. to Maj^r. Williamson	a^t 17/	34..5..9
	4697 D^o. to George Kerr	a^t 18/	42..6..6½
	24283		
	By an Errow [sic] in Addition of the Levy 1769 of 100 lb Tobacco	a^t 17/	=..17..=
	By the Rev^d. M^r. Willie an Abatement on Acc^t. of his Not Adminis`. the Sacrament at one Quarter of the Year		2..=..=
			£210..19..7
May	1771 By Ballance Due as p Debit		21..7..½
			£ 232..6..7½

E E p David Mason
For Claiborne & Mason Church Wardens

At a vestry held for the Parish of Albemarle in the County of Sussex the 21st Day of April 1772

Present

The Rev`. M^r. Willie	David Mason
Augustine Claiborne	William Blunt
John Mason	Richard Blunt
James Jones	& Robert Jones Gen^t.

David Mason and William Blunt are Appointed Church Wardens till Easter Teusday Next

Nathaniel Harrison, Richard Parker and George Rives are Elected Vestry men in the Room of Nicholas Massenburg and Henry Harrison Deceas'd and Henry Gee Who has Remov'd out of the Government

Agree'd by the Vestry to give W^m. Hites Wife £10. for keeping Joshua Cottons 2 youngest Children and Providing Choaths [sic] and all other Necessaries for the Same to be Paid to the Rev. M^r. Willie and James Jones to be by them Layed out Occationly for the Use Aforesaid

Ordered that the Rev. M^r. Willie provide for Joshua Cottons Wife During life or Present Illness Such Nesaceries as She Shall have Occation of ———

Ordered that the Church Warden provide for Henry Porch 2 Barrells of Corn

Ordered that the Church Wardens provide for Elizabeth Blaton 2 Barrells of Corn

Ordered that Benjamin Owen be Exempted from paying Parish Levy for the futer

W^m. Willie Rector

[255]

In Obedience to an order of the worshipfull Vestry of Albemarle Parrish bearing Date the 1st Day of October 1771 We the Subscribers have Processioned all the Lands in the Said Order mention'd & Renew'd the Land marks thereof as by the Said Order is Directed.

Proprieters of the Lands	Persons Present at Prosessioning
Mary Nicholson, Harris Nicholson, Elizth. Clary, Joseph Bayley. Nathan Carrel, Edmund Bailey, W^m. Carrel, Thimothy Sante, Joseph Glovier, Capt. Howell Briggs, Mary Clary, Saml. Maggot, John James, Beauford Pleasant, Benja. Rogers, John Preson, Sterling Pettway, Mary Hancock, Thos. Hancock, Nicho^s. Hancock, James Clary, Henry Bradley, Henry Andrews, Benja. Hancock, Humphry Baylis & Benja. Clary.	Joseph Bayley, Harris Nicolson, Nathan Carrel, Edmund Bailey, Mark Carrel, Thimothy Sante, Joseph Glovier, Howell Briggs, Nicho^s. Hancock, John Hancock, Thos. Hancock, John Clary, Benja. Hancock, George Pleasant, Sterling Pettway, James Clary & John Nicolson Humphry Baylis Benja. Clary Procession Mas

In Obedience to an Order of the worshipfull Vestry of Albemarle Parrish bearing Date the first Day of October 1771 We the Subscribers have Processioned all the Lands in the S^d. order Mentioned & Renew'd the Land Marks thereof.

Owners of the Land	Persons Present at Processioning
Nicholas Jarrad, Richard Stewart, W^m. Conelly, Charles Stewart, Rich^d. Cocke, Thos. Llewellin, Isaac Oliver, Rich^d. Northcross, John Adkinson, Abel Mabry, Michail Weathers, W^m. Richardson, John Rowland, Nath`. Felts, James, John Felts, W^m. Harrison, Thos. Ezell, Thos. Nusum, Jacob Nusum. Thos. Ezell Junr.	William Richardson, Nat. Felts, John Rowland, John Felts, W^m. Harriss, Thos. Ezell, Nicholas Jarrad, W^m. Collins, Rich^d. Northcross & John Adkinson William Richardson } Nathaniel Felts } Processioners

In Obedience to an Order of the Worshipfull Vestry of Albemarle Parish in the County of Sussex bearing Date the first Day of October 1771 We the Subscribers have Assembled the Freeholders & have Processioned all the Lands in the S^d. order Mentioned & Renew'd the Land marks thereof in Presence of the Several Persons here Mentitioned

Proprietors of the Lands	When Procession'^{d}	the Persons Present
Colonel Augustin Claiborne, Natha^l. Harrison, Willison Shands, Capt. John Thompson, David Jones, James Jones, John Clark, Sarah Evens, John Gary, John Sandress, Fady Jarrad, Frederick Andrews, William Harrison	March the 23 & 24 1772	David Jones, James Jones, Travis Griffis, Natha`. Harrison, W^m. Shands, John Clark, John Sandress, Fady Jarrad, Frederick Andrews, W^m. Harrison, not Present John Gary & Capt. Thompson was Sick but Desird we would Procession their Land

Certified under our hands
Fady Jarrad
Frederick Andrews
Procession Masters

[256]

In obedience to an Order of the Worshipful Vestry of the Parish of Albemarle bearing Date the 1. Day of Octo^r 1771 We the Subscribers Did on the 24.25 & 26 Days of February 1772 assemble the Freeholders within the Preceint[sic] Specified by the S^d Order & Did Procession & the Land Marks Renew'd of the Following Tracts of Land

Richard Parkers, Thomas Clements, Thos Peete, Thomas Peters, Wm Hines Senior, Wm Hines Minor, Wm Hines Junr, Thomas Hines, Lazarus Drake, Wm Edmunds, The Land of John Edmunds Dec^d, John Chappell, Joshua Hines, John Cargill, Hartwell Hines, Hannah Howell, Wm Hunt ——————
Present when the Above Tracts of Land were Processiond & the Land marks thereof Renew'd Richd Parker, Thos Peters, Wm Hines Senr, Wm Hines Minor, Lazarus Drake, Wm Edmunds, Wm Hines Junr, John Chappell, Hartwell Hines, William Hunt
Certified under our Hands

[Procession Masters]
John Chappell
Thos Peters

In Obedience to an order of the Vestry of Albemarle Parish in the County of Sussex Dated the first Day of Octo^r 1771 & to us whose names are hereunto Subscrib'd [and] Directed we have Procession'd the Several Lines of the Defrant[sic] Tracts of Land in the Preceint by the S^d Order Express'd[sic] & the Land Marks thereof have Renew'd

Proprietors Names	Persons Present
Lucy Adkins Widow of Thom^s Adkins Dec^d	Henry Moss Junr
Henry Moss Junior	James Epps
Charles Gee	Peter Porch
Herbert Claiborne lately	the three above &
Joshua Meachum & Halcott Pride	Hubert Claiborne
Thos Whitfield	Wm Tomlinson
Hartwill Marrable	Banks Mechum
James Ezell Infant	Henry Moss Junr James Epps
Sarah Edwards widow of John Edwards	Peter Porch Banks Mechum
Church Land	Edward Epps Wm Tomlinson
Hugh Belsches	the Six above & Mr Willie
John Harthorn in[sic] Infant	Mr Willie
Henry Porch	Edward Epps
Henry Moss	Henry Moss Junr
Glebe Land	Mr Willie Henry Moss Junr
Revd Wm Willie	Mr Willie Edward Epps
Edward Epps	Henry Moss Junr
Banks Mechum	William Tomlinson
John Adkins	Edward Epps
William Tomlinson	William Tomlinson

Done 26 & 27 Day of March A.D. 1772

Process Mas^r
John Adkins
Henry Moss

[257]

In Obedience to an Order of the Worshipfull Vestry of Albemarle Parish bearing Date the 1st Day of Octo 1771. The Subscribers with Capt Thomas Parham was therein Appointed to Procession the Lands in the S^d Order Mention'd but owing to the Indisposition of the S^d Thos Parham & his Death the Execution of the Land Order hath been complyed with the Subscriber & the Land Marks in the Said Preceint Renew'd

To Whom the Land belongs	When Processioned	Persons Present
Capt Thos Parham, Matthew Parham	25 of March 1772	Matthew Parham Junr
Abram Parham, Francis Haddon		John Leath Leath
Matthew Burge, Wm Wilkerson, John Adams		Abrams Parham
John Heath, Urpley Heath		William Leathers
James Parham, John Leath Wm Leath		William Wilkerson &
Matthew Parham & J. & John Parham		John Adams
		John Parham } Procession Mtr

In Obedience to an order of the Vestry of Albemarle Parish Dated the 1 Novem^r 1771. we the Subscribers on the 10 and eleventh of February Assembled the Freeholders in our Preceint and went in Quiet Procession & Procession'd and Renewed the Land of Harbert[sic] Claiborne Present Thom^s Hobbs, Overseer, the Land of Wm Jones Present Porch[sic] Henry Porch by Order --- The Land of Thomas Wren Present Thos Wren, the Land of Isaac Bendol, the Land of Henry Moss present Gabrial Moss by Order, the Land of Nathan Bishop Present Nathan Bishop, the Land of Wm Hancock, The Land of John Walker & Wm Hunt Present Thos Wren by Order of John Walker, The Land of Henry Porch Present Henry Porch, the Land of Joshua Moss Present Joshua Moss, The Land of Morris Liles Present Moses Liles, the Land of John Liles Present John Liles, the Land of Ann Wren present Morris Liles, Execu^r, The Land of John Pair Present John Pair, the Land of Thom^s Harrison by Processioning Other Lines Overseed it The Land of William Lightfoot Infant Present Samuel Seward

[Procession Masters] Thos Wren & John Liles

200   The Vestry Book of Albemarle Parish

In Obedience to an Order of the Vestry of the Parish of Albemarle in the County of Sussex bearing Date the 1st Day of Octor 1771 we the Subscribers have Assembled the Freeholders together within the Preceint Specified by the S^d order & on the tenth of March Did Procession & the Land Marks Renew of the Several Tracts of Land hereafter Mention'd to Witt Peter Jones Land, Mary Jones Lands, Major John Masons Land, Nicolas Partridge Land, Nicholas Partridge Junr Land, James Johnsons Land, Wm Johnsons Land, Pittway Johnsons Land. Lawrence Smith Land not Procession'd by not attending Present when the Above S^d lands were Procession'd & the Land Marks thereof Renew'd Peter Jones, James Johnson, David Mason, Pettway Johnson Present

Certified under our hands   Proc^n Mas^r Nicholas Partridge
                                                              Wm Johnson
[258]

According to Order of the Worshipfull Vestry Held for Albemare[sic] Parish in the County of Sussex the first Day of October 1771 We the Subscribers have Processioned and Renew'd the Land marks in the preceint the Order Directed to Wit Beginning March 2d 1772

Beginning on the Lands Marks of   People Present
Lewis Johnson, Nathaniel Stoaks Orphan   Lewis Johnson, Nathaniel Holt
Nathaniel Holt, William Thos Pennington   William Thos Pennington
Abraham Brown, Silvanious Stoakes   James Williams, Edward Daviss
John Tyus Orphan. Thomas Daviss   John Spain, William Roland
James Spain, Benjamin Evens
March 3rd 1772 The lands of
Robert Whitehead, William Stuart   John Hood Edward Daviss
David Woodrouff   David Graves William Clifton
March 6 1772 The Lands of the
Orphan of Thomas Adkins, James Williams   John Hood Charles Williams
Charles Williams, Matthew Sturdevant   Ebenezer Shearman David Graves
John Hood, Cudburth Stafford   William Clifton, William,[sic]
                                                Thos Pennington
Thomas Adkins, William Pair
Ebenezer Shearman, Hinche Rochel
Barham Moore, Isham Ezell
John Rochell
March the 7th 1772 the lands of   John Hood
Ann King, Elizabeth King, Thomas Moore   Ebenezer Shearman
Ann King, Solomon Graves, John Cargill

                finished and Concluded be[sic] the Subscribers
                     [Procession Masters] Solomon Graves
                              Cudburth Stafford

In Obedience to an Order of the Worshipfull Vestry of Albemarle Parish bearing Date the 1st Day of October 1771 We the Subscribers have Processioned all the lands in the Said Order mentioned and Renew'd the land Marks thereof as By the S^d Order Directed

Owners of the Land   Persons present at Processioning
The lands belonging to the Estate of   Samuel Seward. Joseph Hoomes
Wm Lightfoot Esqr Deceas^d, Colo. Wm Allen, Wm Johnson John Land, John Moore
Wm Johnson, John Land, the Orphan of   Thomas Eskridge, Wm Andrew
Thomas Dickens Deceased, John Pennington   John Berriman & Mr John Cargill
Thomas Eskridge, Wm Andrews, Thomas Bailey
John Berryman, Mr John Cargill
                                                John Pennington
                                                Thomas Bailey Processioners

[259]

In Obedience to an Order of the Worshipfull Vestry of Albemarle Parish bearing Date the 1st Day of Octr 1771 The Subscribers Hath Processioned all the Lands in the P. Order Mentioned and Renew'd the Land Marks thereof as by the P. order is Directed

Owners of the Land	Persons at the Processioning
Holloday Fort, Robert Seat	Holloday Fort Robert Seat
Maj^r Wm Brown, John Judkins, Joshua Smith	Joshua Smith, Silvanus Bell
Sillvanus [Bell], Daniel Epps	Daniel Epps, Abel Mabry,
Samuell Northington, Abel Mabry	Absolum Underwood, Burrel
Absolum Underwood, Wm Richardson	Felts (son of Thomas),
Wm Woodland, Thomas Weathers	William Woodland
Thomas Felts, Christopher Stoaks	Christopher Stoaks
and Wm Rose	
	Processioner William Rose

N B Thomas Felts Died before the Processioning was made

Sussex County Albemarle parish In Obedience to an order of Vestry Bearing Date the 1st of October 1771 to us Directed we have processioned the Lands and Renew'd the land marks of Willut[sic] Robarts, Jno Hinchia, and Wm Gilliam Infants, Wm Briggs, Joanna Moss, Jno Irby, Thomas Edmunds, Thomas Cooperer[sic], Thomas Tomlinson, William Nicolson, William Blunt, Andrew Lister and Richard Blunt or at least so much thereof as was contained in our Said Order present Benj. Roberts, Hichia Gilliam, Lawrence Smith, Thomas Cooper, Jno Irby, Wm Irby, Thos Tomlinson, Wm Blunt

March 30th 1772 [Procession Masters] William Nicolson
Richard Blunt

In Obedience to an Order of the Worshipfull Vestry of the Parish of Albemarle in the County of Sussex Bearing Date the 1st Day of October 1771 We the Subscribers persuant to the Said Order Did on the 2nd Day of March 1772 Procession all the Lands in the Preceint Mentioned in the Said Order & Renewed the land Marks thereof in presence of the Several pesons Whose names are Underneath

To Whom the Land belongs	Persons present at the Processioning
Robert Jones, John Mason, James Jones	Robert Jones, James Jones
Henry Jarrad, Jehu Barker, Jesse Jones Dec^d	Howell Briggs, Peter Jones
Howell Briggs, Peter Jones & John Lamb	& John Jarrad

Processioners Jehu Barker
Henry Jarrad

[260]

By Virtue of an Order, of the Worshipfull the Vestry of the Parish of Albemarle Dated the 1st Day of Octo^r 1771, and to us Directed we have Agreable to the Said Order Seen all the lands in the Preceint to us alloted processioned and the Several Land Marks renewed. in presence in presence[sic] of the persons thereafter Mentioned —

The Proprietors	The persons Present.
Wm Dunn, Henry Tatum, Mary Tatum	William Dunn, Henry Tatum,
Elizabeth Hawthorn, John Doby	Thomas Young, John Doby,
Robert Doby, Col. A. Claiborne	Robert Doby, John Hawthorne,
John Rives, John Petway, Frances Epps	John Petway, Timothy Rives,

Thomas Mitchell, Wm Bishop Peter Ivy Junr, Peebles Lells[sic]
John Mitchell, Timothy Rives
Christopher Rives, George Rives

George Rives } Pro. masters
Christopher Rives
March 27th 1772

By Virtue of an Order of the Vestry of Albemarle Parish Dated Octo^r 1st 1771 and to us Directed we have processioned the lands therein Mentioned and the Same land Marks thereof Renew'd as follows ——

Lands Processioned   Persons Present
Stith Parham J^n, Jno Sturdivant   Stith Parham J^r John Sturdivant
Moses Knight, James Cocks   Moses Knight, James Cocks
William Reeves, Nathaniel Hood,   William Reeves, Nathaniel Hood
Joseph Dennies, Jno Anderson Sturdivant   Jno Anderson Sturdivant
Isham Whitehead, Robert Wynne, Green Hill   Isham Whitehead, Robert Wynne
Robert Newman, William Sturdivant, Jno Atkins Green Hill, Robert Newman
James Horn, William Cocks, Jno Hardy   William Sturdivant
William Speirs, William Stuart J^r
Markus Gilliam

Process. by
Jno Wynne &
William Sturdivant

In Obedience to an order of the Worshipfull Vestry of Albemarle Parish in the County of Sussex Bearing Date the 1st of Octob. 1771 We the Subscribers perusant to the S^d Order have processioned all the Lands in the Preceit Mentioned and Renewed the Land Marks In presence of the persons Mentioned

Proprietor of the Land   When Perform'd   Persons Present

John Mason, John Sledge   John Mason, John Sledge
Thomas Johnson, William Willcocks   March 7th   Thomas Johnson, Richard
                                                         Cook, Richard Cotton,
Richard Cook, John Austin Finnie   1772   William Weaver
Richard Cotton, Edward Weaver,
Edward Weaver, Junr
                                                         Edward Weaver
                                                         [Procession Master]

[261]

In Obedience to An Order of the Worshipfull Vestry of the Parish of Albemarle bearing Date the 1st Day of October 1771 We the Subscribers Did on the Twenty Seventh Day of February 1772 Assemble the Freeholders Within the Preceint Specified by the Said Order and Did Procession and the Land Marks Renew of the following Tracts of Land Jesse Wallis, James Chappell Senior, James Chappell, Junior, John Kennebren, Thomas Brian, Nicholas Jarrad, William Hines, James Turner, Howell Chappell, Present when the Above Tracks of Land were Processioned and the land Marks thereof Renew'd Jesse Wallis, James Chappell Senior, James Chappell Junr, John Kennebren, Thomas Bryan, Nicholas Jarrad, William Hines

Certified under Our hands
Howell Chappell
James Turner } Proc. Masters

Surry and Sussex Counties, Virginia, 1742-1786   203

John Bains Land, Present Simon Stacy, William Ellis, Caleb Ellis, William Jordan, Robert Judkins, William Judkins, Stephen Andrews, Thomas Gibbons

John Baines	Land in the presence of the Same Persons	
John Lambs	D°	D°
Simon Stacys	D°	D°
Part of Howell Brigges	D°	D°
Part of Wm Ellis	D°	D°
William Judkins	D°	D°
Robert Judkins	D°	D°
Part of Caleb Ellis	D°	D°
Part of Thomas Gibbons	D°	D° and a line between them in Dispute
Emanuel James	D°	D°

Holt Prides Land Not Processioned no body being present to Shew the Lines
John Montgomaries not Processioned there being no person to Shew the line
By Order of Vestry hereunto annexted[sic] to us Directed we have Caused the Several Tracts of land Above mentioned being all Contained within Our preceint to be Processioned in our presence and the lines of the Said land Renew'd as is the Said Order Directed Given under Our hands this 20th Day of April 1772

        John Lamb [Procession Masters]
        Simon Stacy

In Obedience to an Order of the Worshipfull Vestry of Albemarle Parish in the County of Sussex Bearing Date the 1st Day of October 1771 We the Subscribers persuant to the Said Order have Processioned all the lands in the Preceint Mentioned and Renewed the Land Marks thereof in Presence of the Several persons whose Names are Underneath

To Whom the Land Belongs	When Performed	Persons Present
Benjamin Rogers, Humphrey Bailis		Benjamin Rogers, Humpery Bailis
Samuel Magot, Benjamin Hancock	April 7th	Samuel Magot, Howell Briggs
James White, John Alsobrook	1772	Benjamin Hancock, James Waite
Howell Briggs		

        John Alsobrook Pro. Master

Edward Cross the Other Procession Master Moved Out of the Preceint Last fall

[262]

In Obedience to an Order of the Worshipfull Vestry of the Parish of Albemarle in the County of Sussex Bearing Date the 1st of October 1771 We the Subscribers persuant to Said Order have Processioned all the lands in the Preceint Mentioned and Renewed the land Marks thereof In presence of the Several persons Whose names are Underneath

To whom the land belongs	Persons Present at the Processioning
Wm Shands, Francis Roser,	William Shands, William Shands, Jun[r]
Nathaniel Harrison, John Mason,	Nathaniel Harrison, Peter Cole Harrison
James Belsches, Hugh Ivoy,	James Watkins, Jesse Ivoy, John Mason,
Nathaniel Dunkin, John Adkins,	Daniel Ivoy, Stephen Baird, Richard Ivoy
John Mason, Jun. and John Baird	

        Hugh Ivoy Proces. Masters
        Nathaniel Dunkin

In Obedience to an order of Vestry, Held for the Parish of Albemarle in the County of Sussex the first Day of Octo[r] 1771 To us Directed We the Subscribers have Processioned and Renewed the Land marks then then[sic] the Preceint the Order Directed To wit. 16. March 1772

Beginning on the land marks of
William Oliver, Sam¹ Gilliam Orphan
of Wᵐ Gilliam, John Anderson Sturdivant,
Benjⁿ Tyus, Estate of Richard Jones
Estate of James Jones, Burwil Willborne,
Benjᵃ Wilborne, Robert Jones, Peter Threewitts

Persons Present
William Oliver, Anderson Sturdivant
John Anderson Sturdivant,
Benjᵃ Tyus, Burwill Willborne
Peter Threewitts

17ᵗʰ March 1772 the lines of
Nathaniel Dunn, Nathaniel Parham,
Mathew Parham Jun.
David Orvin on Wᵐ Roland
11ᵗʰ of April 1772 the lines of
Burwil Green, William Green, Mʳ Hewit,
John Batts

Persons Present
Peter Threewitts, Mathew Parham Sen.
Mathew Parham Sen
Nathaniel Durgn[sic]
Persons Present
James Bilbro and Semore Parvell

Finished and Concluded by
Nathaniel Parham
Robert Jones [Procession Masters]

[263]

In Obedience to an Order of the Worshipfull Vestry of the Parish of Albemarle in the county of Sussex Bearing Date the 1 Day of October 1772[sic] We the subscribers persuant to the Said Order have Processioned all the Lands in the preceint Mentioned and Renew'd the Land Marks thereof In presence of the Several persons Whose Names are Underneath.

To Whom the land belongs
Charles Judkins, Thomas Pridlow, George Mosley, Robert Armstrong, Benjamin Graves, Richard Rawlings, Charles Long Drewry Clanton, Mary Southward, George Long John Meglemry, Mary Moss, John Hargrove, Charles Mabry, Ben. Arrington William Barker, Thomas Newson Sarah Rawlings, Benjamin Phips, Benjamin Richardson, Henry Manry, Samuell Harwood, William Brown, Mary Knight John Long

Persons Present at the Processioning
Charles Judkins, Charles Blizard
Benjamin Graves, Richard Rawlings
Drury Clanton, John Moss,
John Hargrove, Charles Mabry
Benjamin Arington
Howell Rawlings, Benjamin Phips
Benjamin Richardson, John Manry
Samuel Harwood, Thomas Worpole

Proces. Masters
George Long
Charles Long

When Performed March 17ᵗʰ 1772

In Obedience to an Order of the Worshipfull Vestry of Albemarle parish in the County of Sussex bearing Date the 1ˢᵗ Day of October 1771 We the Subscribers perusant to the said Order Did on the 26ᵗʰ and 29ᵗʰ Days of February 1772 Procession all the lands in the Preceint Mentioned in the Said Order and Renew'd the Land Marks thereof in presence of the Several persons Whose Names are Underneath

To Whom the land belongs
David Jones, James Peters, James Jones
William Willcox, Richard Cook, Part of
John Sledge's, Allen Jones of North Carolina
Benjamin Chappell Decᵈ, Nathaniel Doby
James Chappell, James Chappell Jun.
John Cargill, William Allen, James Speed
Elizabeth Wyche and part of Hartwell Hines,
and Robert Jones

Persons present at the Processioning
James Chappell, James Chappell Jun'
James Jones, Robert Jones, John Sledge
Daniel Turner, Thomas Adkins,
Natha. Doby, John Hoomes
and James Speed

Procession Masters
David Jones
James Peters

Surry and Sussex Counties, Virginia, 1742-1786   205

In Obedience to an Order of the Worshipfull Vestry of the parish of Albemarle in the County of Sussex Bearing Date the 1st Day of October 1771 We the subscribers persuant to the Said Order hav processioned all the Lands in the Preceint Mentioned and Renewed the Land Marks therof in presence of the Several persons Whose Names are Underneath.
                    Performed March the 17th 1772

To Whom the Land belongs   Persons Present
James Lashley, Willert Roberts, Benjamin   Drury Barker, Benjamin Hill, James
Roberts, Hermon Bishop, William Lashley   Gilbert, Henry Barker, William
Henry Barker, James Barker Deceased   Lashley, Benjamin Roberts, Avires
Lawrence Smith, James Gilbert, John   Bishop, Patrick Lashley, Hinchey
Gilliam Junr, Holmes Jones, Henry Cook   Gilliam, Willert[sic]
Benjamin Hill, Drury Barker, John   Roberts, Henry Cook,
Gilliam, James Boiseau Jones,   Jesse Barker
Nathaniel Barker
                    James Boiseau Jones   Proces. Masters
                    Nathaniel Barker

[264]

In Obedience to an Order of Vestry Held for the parish of Albemarle in the County of Sussex The first Day of Oct. 1771 We the Subscribers hath Seen Every persons land Processioned and the Land Marks thereof Renew'd between the Rackoon Swamp, Little Swamp and Stoak's road and that the following Freeholders was present

Barham Moore	Land	Processioned	William Moores	Land	Processioned
Henry Freeman	Ditto	Ditto	John Rochell	Ditto	Ditto
Lewis Johnson	Ditto	Ditto	Harmon Webb	Ditto	Ditto
Robert Land	Ditto	Ditto	Levi Gilliam	Ditto	Ditto
Thomas Moore	Ditto	Ditto	Bird Land	Ditto	Ditto
Curtis Land	Ditto	Ditto	Robert Land Junr	Ditto	Ditto
William Lofling	Ditto	Ditto	William Loftin Jr	Ditto	Ditto
Burrel Lofling	Ditto	Ditto	Mary Clantons	Ditto	Ditto
Charles Battles	Ditto	Ditto	Thomas Capel[sic]	Ditto	Ditto

          Witness Our hands James Cooper and Joseph Renn

In Obedience to an Order of the Worshipfull Vestry of the Parish of Albemarle in Bearing Date the 1st Day of Octor 1771 We the Subscribers Persuant to the sd Order have Procession'd all the Lands in the Sd order Mentioned & Renew'd the Land Marks therof in Presence of the Person in the List Below   Performed 23 March 1772

To Whom Belonging   Persons Present at Processioning
James Chappell, Isham Gilliam   Mr Charles Judkins, Do Junr, Isham
Abraham Brown, James Bell   Gilliam, Abraham Bottom, Wm Brown
Cisla Stoaks, Abraham Bottoms   Son of Abraham Brown, Thos Spane
Thos Spain, John Owing and   & David Owing
David Owing
                    James Bell
                    Nat. Holt   Procession Masters

In Obedience to an Order of Vestry of Albemarle Parish Bearing Date the first Day of October 1771 we the Subscribers have Procession'd all the Lands in the sd Order Mention'd & Renew'd the Land Marks Thereof
                    When Perform'd 26 & 27 March 1772
Owners of the Land   Persons Present at Procession
William Barham, Henry Manery, Thos   George Hogwood, Jonas Cornet
Nusum, the Orphans of Gregory Rawlings   Wm Barham, William Prince
Jonas Cornet, the Orphans of John Jones Lewis Nusum, Benja. Bullock,

Lewis Nusum, William Prince, Wm Myrick   William Knight, Thomas Barham
the Orphans of Robt Bullock,   Daniel Harwood
Henry Tyler, Charles Barham
the Orphns of William Knight
Philip Harwood, William Longbottom   Processioners
William Brown, Benja. Barham   Philip Harwood &
   Charles Barham

[265]

In Obedience to an Order of the Worshipfull Vestry of Albemarle Parish Bearing Date the 1st Day of Octo^r 1771. We the Subscribers have Procession'd all the lands in the S^d Order Mention'd & Renew'd the Land Marks Thereoff as by the Said Order is Directed

Owners of the Land   Persons Present at Processioning
Thos Adams, Frederick Fort, John Sands   Thomas Adams, Frederick Fort, Nat.
Nusum, Thomas Williamson   John Sands, Nat. Nusum, Thomas
Barns, Benjamin   Williamson, John Rivers, Benj.
Seaburn, John Battle Junr, John Battle,   Seaburn, John Battle, Junr,
Nicholas Jarrad, Richd Stewart, Charles   Rubin Baird and Robert Linn
Stewart, Rubin Baird, Nathan Northington
& Robert Linn
   Processioners
   Nathan Northington
   James Barns

In Obedience to an Order of the Worshipfull Vestry of the Parish of Albemarle in the County of Sussex Dated the first Day of October 1771 the Subscribers being Appointed with Henry Harison Dec^d Who Died since the Date of the Order of Vestry & before the lands hereafter Mention'd were Processioned have Assembled the Freeholders together within the Preceint Specified by the Said Order & have Procession'd & Renew'd the land Marks of the Following Persons to Witt

The Names of Whose lands Procession'd   Whom Present & Attended
March 30th Henry Harrison Dec^d John Simon's   Wm Hancock, Henry Andrews
1772 Samson Collier, Benj. Serewsbury[sic]   Samson Collier, Benjn Serewsbury
Waddle Johnson, Charles Battle   Waddle Johnson, Charles Battle
Hinchey Gilliam, John Dunn   Hinchey Gilliam, John Dunn
Henry Andrews, Lewis Dunn   Henry Andrews, Lewis Dunn
William Loftin Junr, John Knight   Did not attend being indisposd
Frederick Loftin, Richd Felts   John Knight, Frederick Loftin
Drewy Magee, Robt Magee   Richd Felts, Drewry Magee
John Hairgrove, Edmund Gilliam   Robt Magee, John Hairgrave
Charles Gillium, Patty Gillium   Edmund Gillium, Charles Gillium
Sarah Gillium, Anne Magee   Wm Colson, William Magee
Anne Hutchings   Epharaim Hutching

   Procession'd agreable to the above Order by Anslem Gillium

[266]

At a Vestry held for Albemarle Parish the 15th day of July 1772

   Present
David Mason
William Blunt   }   Gentlemen Church Wardens
John Mason   Augustine Claiborne
Richard Blunt   Robert Jones &
Lawrence Gibbons jun   Gent. Vestrymen

Nathaniel Harrison and George Rieves Gent. lately elected into Vestry having taken the usual Oaths to his Majesty's Person and Government the abjuration Oath and repeated and Subscribed the Test in the Court of this County as Appears by Cerificate and Now in Vestry having Subscribed to be Conformable to the Doctrine and Discipline of the Church of England did thereupon take their Seats in Vestry Accordingly————————

Upon a Motion, the Vestry took into consideration the inconveniences attending the congregation usually at St Marks Church in this Parish occasioned not only by the small size of the said Church but also by the Ruinoous condition the said Church is in and thereupon it was————————
Resolved that a new Church be built as near as conveniently may be to the Spot the present Building Stands on that the Same be a wooden Building underpined With Bricks done in neat and Workman like Manner and of the Diemensions following (that is to say) Seventy feet long and thirty feet Wide and twenty two feet Pitch with a Gallery in the west end thereof, that the Pews and all and every of the inside work and the Decorations thereof and of the outside be perform'd according to a plan to be designed prepared and laid Down by the Church Wardens for the time being that the Whole inside or so much thereof as is Usual be neatly lathed and plaistered and that David Mason and William Blunt Gen^t Church Wardens with Robert Jones jun. and Lawrence Gibbons Gen^t or any three of them be and prehereby[sic] appointed a committee to contract for carrying this resolution into execution in haveing the said Church compleatly finished within two years from the time the same Shall be undertaken for complying with which and all others matters and things relative to the Said Building the Said Committee are injoined to take bond with Good and Sufficient Security, and the Said committee are instructed to make as great advantage from the present Church by a Sale thereof to the undertaker of the new Church in Ease of the parish as may be: and it is further Resolved that the payments to the person or persons undertaking to perform the Said Building be as followeth (that is to say) one half of the consideration be paid out of and at the finishing of the Collection of the Levy of this Parish next after the said Building shall be lett and Undertaken and the other Moiety half part or residue out of and at the finishing of the Collection next after the Said Church so to be built, Shall be compleatly finished and received by the Vestry of the Said Parish for the time being————————
On a Motion Made the Vestry took into Consideration whether to repair or rebuild the front part of Nottoway Church would be most beneficial to this Parish and after a debate it was Resolved that the present front Part of the Said Church is by means of the Rotten condition thereof not worth the Expence of repairing and therefore that the same be taken Down and Removed and that the present new building be raised fifteen Inches higher from the ground than the same is now placed and that a New bulding of the same Size and Dementions of the present form Building as do part Neatly Lathed & Plastered be erected and built upon a foundation or underpinning of Bricks of the <u>lenth</u> as the present Underpining and that the Said New Building so to be built be 15 Inches higher Pitch's than the present old building so as to make the tops of the Pews - of the whole Church range on the Top or upper parts thereof as its purposed that the Pews of the Present old Building Shall be placed in the New and that the Whole Inside Work with the decorations and Ornaments thereof of the outside be contrived and performed according to a plan designed formed and laid Down by the Church Wardens of the Parish for the time being in Doing which particular regard is to be had to the Seats in the Pews so as the Same be full 14 Inches wide and David Mason and William Blunt Gen^t Church Wardens John Mason Augustine Claiborne and Nathaniel Harrison Junr or any three of

[267]

Them be and they are hereby Appointed a committee to Contract for carrying this resolution and every part thereof in due execution by having the Said Church Compleatly finished Within Two Years from the time the same shall be let and Undetaken for complying with Which and all Others Matters and thing relative to the said Building the

Said Committee are Enjoyned to take Bond with Sufficient Security and the Said Committee are instructed to make as Great an advantage from the present old Building so as aforesaid to be taken Down by Selling the Same to the Undertaker of the New, in East of the Parish, as may be and it is further Resolved that the payments to the person or persons undertaking to perform the said Building be as followeth (that is to say) one moiety or half part of the consideration be paid to such undertaker Out of and at the finishing of the Collection of the Levy of the parish next after the Said Building Shall be let and Undertaken and the Other Moiety or half part or Residue be paid out of and at the finishing of the Collection next after the Said Church shall be Compleatly finished or built and receiv'd by the Vestry of the Said parish for the time being

David Mason
William Blunt
Church Wardens

At a Vestry Held for the parish of Albemarle in the County of Sussex the 29th Day of September 1772

Present
The Revd Mr Willie
David Mason William Blunt Church Wardens, Augustine Claiborne
John Mason Robert Jones & George Rives Gent^n

Albemarle Parish	D^r	W to Tob^o
To the Reve^d Mr Wm Willie Minister		17305
To the Clk of Nottoway Church		1200
To John Nicolson Clk of St Pauls Do^o		1200
To the Clk of St Andrews D^o		1200
To the Clk of St Marks D^o		1200
To Rebecca Denton Sexton a Nottoway D^o		600
To John Bane D^o at St Pauls D^o		500
To Wm Rodgers D^o at St Andrews D^o		500
To Peter Green D^o at St Marks D^o		500
To the Clk of the Vestry		400
To Levied for the Use of the Parish		41430
To the Collector for Collection a^t 6 Pr		4215
		70250
Albemarle Parish	Cr	
By 2810 Tiths	a^t 25lb tobacco P Poll	70250

[268]

The following Allowances is Ordered to be made the following persons to Wit

To the Revd Mr Willie for providing Elements for the Sacrament	12 = =
To William Rogers	2 = =
To Thomas Cooper	5 = =
To Robert Whitehead	2 = =
To John Woodard for Wilkersons Child	2 = =
To Frankling[sic] Clark for Elizabeth Birdsong	4 = =
To Thomas Waller	3.10 =
To James Hern for keeping his son James	5 = =
To Mary Southard	2 = =
To James Bane for keeping his Brother William Bane	3.10 =
To Peggy Jones to be Lay'd out by the Church Wardens	2 = =
To Charles Gilliam	2 = =
To Thomas Cullum	6 = =
To Joanna Moss	2.10 =

To Benjamin Barham for keeping Sarah Nights Child	4 = =	
To Mary Finnie	2 = =	
To Doctor Thomas Peet as Pr Acct.	= 10 =	

Ordered that the Church Wardens Examine as Acct. of Pettway Johnson When Produced pay the Said Johnson the Ballance Due to him ———————————

The Comissioner appointed to Contract for rebuilding the front part of Nottoway Church now report to the Vestry that they had Considering the large sum the new Church to be built at S¹ Marks went at and the bad prospect of a Crop of Tobacco Occasioned by the present Draught Contract for the Said front building to be finished Within thre years instead of two Years and proportioned the payments to the undertaker so as the same be paid Out of three Levies instead of two as Directed by the order made at last Vestry on Consider Whereof the Vestry (now) greatly Approve of this Conduct of the comissioners and Do Confirm the Same ————————————

Wm Willie Rector

[269]

At a Vestry held for the parish of Albemarle in the County of Sussex the 16th Day of June 1773

Present
David Mason   Richard Blunt
William Blunt   Robert Jones
Augustine Claiborne   Lawrence Gibbons Junr   Gent.
John Mason Senr

Michael Blow and Lawrence Gibbons Junr Gen^t are appointed Church Wardens till Easter tuesday Next

Ordered that the Church Wardens Give Notice to John Peters the Undertaker to sink a well and brick the same to be finished according to agreement in two Months from this day or a Suit Shall be brought against him for the Same.

This day David Mason and William Blunt late Church Wardens Rendered their Accompt [account] as well of the tobacco as of the fines &c in Vestry which were Examined Allowed and Ordered to be Registered by which a Ballance appears from David Mason to be Due to the Parish of £2:6:6½

It Appearing to the vestry that William Blunt Gen^t late Church Warden paid for the use of Joseph Clark £4:8:1 which was omitted to be Charged in Masons and Blunts General accompt[sic] and the further Balance of 1/3½ Due to the Said year William Blunt Amounting to £4:9:4½ Ordered that the succeeding Church Wardens pay the same out of the sales of Tobacco the present Year

Ordered that Nathaniel Wyche Gentleman be Appointed Collector of the parish Levy for the preset Year and that he Give bond and Security to the Church Wardens for the Due Execution of the Same

Ordered that David Mason pay unto Mr Hugh Belches £5 = = being a Balance Due to Wm Hite for keeping Joshua Cottons Children til Easter 1773 and that so much of the former Order Directing the same to be paid the Revd Mr Willie and Capt. James Jones be Discharged

Ordered that Webb Land be exempted from paying parish Levies During his Inability

Ordered that William Hite be paid £10 = = out of the Sale of the parish Tobacco that Shall be levied in the next Levie for his Keeping Joshua Cottons two Children one Year from Easter last and that the said Sum be paid to David Jones for the purpose aforesaid

---

David Jones Jun' this day Declared his Desire of not Continuing Clerk of the Vestry of This Parish Therefore it is Considered that John Nicolson be appointed to Succeed him in that office

Ordered that John Mason Jun' be Desired to Provide Necessarys for Jane Scoggin Widow for the Support of the Said Janes Children for one Year from this time who is to be paid out of the Next Levies to the Amount of £10 = = if necessary

---

[270]

Lawrence Gibbons Jun' Gentleman Church Warden in 1771 With Coll. Massenburg This Day Rendered an Accompt of what money Came into his hands and the manner he had Applied the same and it Appearing that there is a Ballance of £3:2:6 Due to him it is Ordered that the Said Ballance be paid him by the Present or Future Church Wardens When the Money is in their hands

---

Ordered that Nathaniel Harrison Gen' Administrator of Henry Harrison Deceas'd and Wm Blunt Gen' an Executor of John Edmunds Whose testator and Intestate have failed to Render their Account as Church Wardens of this Parish Formerly be Cited to make up the Accompt at the next Vestry and that the Clerk of the Vestry have them with a Copy of this Order

                        Lawrence Gibbons Jun' C W

1771 The Parish of Albemarle   Dr
    To Lawrence Gibbons J' Church Warden
    To paid Robert Whitehead by Order Vestry   £ 2: 0: 0
    To paid Robert Wyne Raines by D^o 1: 2: 6
    To one Horse for Charles Dillehay   5: 0: 0
                                                    £ 8: 2: 6
    Pr Contra   Cr
    By Cash Received of Col^o Massenburg   £ 5: 0: 0
            E Excepted Lawrence Gibbons Jun'

[271]

Albemarle Parish   D^r
August 1772   £

To paid the Revd Mr Wm Willie for Sacramental Elements to Easter 1771	12 = =
To Paid D^o for D^o ---------- to Easter 1772	12 = =
To paid D^o for Making a Surplice for St Andrews Church	1.10 =
To paid D^o for Neccesarys for Joshua Cottons Wife	11 = 3
To paid D^o for the Repairs Done to the Surplice at St Marks	5 = =
To paid Wm Rogers as Pr Levie 1771	2 = =
To paid Thomas Cooper as Pr D^o	5 = =
To paid Robert Whitehead as Pr D^o	2 = =
To paid John Woodard for Keeping Wilkersons Child as Pr D^o	4 = =
To paid Wm Mason for Woodard for keeping Wilkersons child in 1770 he not being Paid in 1771 by the Preceeding Church Wardens	3 = =
To paid Wm Partin for keeping Rebeckah Pair one Month and 21 days at £6 Pr Annum	17 = =
To paid D^o as Usual for Burying &c	1.17 6
To paid Thomas Waller as Pr Last Levy	3.10 =

Surry and Sussex Counties, Virginia, 1742-1786

To paid James Hern as Pr Last levy	5	=	=
To paid Wm Colson for Patty Gilliam as Pr D^o	2	=	=
To paid Mary Southworth as P D^o	2	-	-
To paid Benjn Wilborn for keeping Wm Dillahay at the Rate of £5 Pr year as Pr Levie	4	=	=
To paid D^o for Burying Wm Dillahay	. 1	7	6
To paid Peggy Jones as Pr Levie 1771	2	=	=
To paid Charles Gilliam as Pr levie 1771	2	=	=
To paid Charity Clifton as Pr D^o	2	-	-
To paid Anne Lilly for Keeping Newsoms Child Due Augt 1771	3	=	=
To paid D^o - - - - - for D^o as Pr levie - - - - - -Due Augt 1772	3	=	=
To paid Charles Judkins for a Causeway over the branch to the Spring at St Andrews Church	1	7	6
To paid 2½ barrels Corn found Peter Smith by Order of Col^o Massenburg in 1771	1	5	=
To Sundrys Provided for Peter Smith by Directions of the Vestry in 1772	2	=	=
To paid John Knight as Pr Acco^tt for Repairs at St Andrews Church by Order of the Late Church Wardens	3	15	=
To paid for two Barrels Corn for Henry Porch	1	5	=
To Paid the Reve^d Mr Willie in Part for Wm Hiters wife for keeping Joshua Cottons Children	5	=	=
To Balance Due David Mason as Pr State of Levie 1771	21..7..1		
To Paid Thos Waller as Pr Levy 1772	3.10	=	
To P^d the Re^d Mr Finning for corn & Meet for John Bush in 1771 & 1772	1.15	=	
To P^d Mr Ric^d Blow for Wm Hix for keeping Amey Gresswitt 3 Months & 11 Days at £4 Pr Annum	1..2	5	
To P^d D^o for Buring Mrs Gresswitt	1	7	6

[272]

D^o Brought up

To 7 Yards of Dowles M^m Wm Blunt P^d Maj^r Briggs & Blow for Wm Hicks on acc^t of the S^d Gresswitt 2/ Pr Yard	£ 0.14..0
To P^d Edward Prince for keeping Seloy[sic] Hix by order of Mr Gibbons as Pr Acct &c	1.13..4
To P^d Joseph Renn for keeping John Renn on a Year by Agreem with the Church Wardens	7.. 0..0
To P^d the Ex^r of Thos Davis a Ballance Due for keeping Silvia Nusums Child in the Year 1771	2.. 0..0
To P^d John Pain for keeping his Mother in 1771	3.. 0..0
To P^d Capt Wm Blunt as Pr Order of Vestry April 2 1771	1.. 3..9
To P^d Wm Hicks by Capt Blunt as Pr Levy 1771 for keeping Ann Gresswitt	4.. 0..0
To P^d Frankling Clark for Mrs Birdsong P^d by D^o	4.. 0..0
To P^d James Bane in Part for keeping his Brother by D^o	2.. 5..0
To P^d Jed. Hines for keeping John Renn in 1771 by D^o	5.. 0..0
To P^d Wm Lamb as Pr Order Vestry Oc^r 1771 by D^o	0.. 5..0
To P^d John Bane for Services at St Pauls Church by D^d	2.15..6
To P^d Thos Cullum as Pr Levy 1771 by D^o	6.. 0..0
To Sundreys found Joseph Clark P^d by Capt Blunt in Part of his allowance in 1771	1.13..0
To P^d James Bilbrow for half a Barrel of Corn in 1772 for Charles Delihay	0.. 6..0
To P^d Capt Thos Moore for corn & Bacon found Geo. Mosleys wife & Children in 1772	1.. 0..0
To P^d Thos Adkins for 2 Barrels of Corn for Eliz^h Blaton by C^t Blunt	1.. 5..0

To P^d the Agent for the Collage 212^{lb} Tobacco for the Tenament for the Use of the Minister a^t 16/ by Capt Blunt	1.13.11
To P^d Burwell Roland for 200^{lb} Pork for his Mother Tabitha Roland a^t 21/6	2..3..0
To Paid Samson Nusum for Provisions for Benj. Nusums Children in 1769	0.11..4
To P^d the two Printers for advertising the sale of the Parish Tobacco Each 7/	0.14..0
To P^d D^o for twice advertising the leting[?] of the Churches in this 7/ each	0.14..0
To P^d David Owing for 200^{lb} Pork for Eliz^h Roland	2..3..0
To P^d Mr Belsches for Hite	5..0..0
1773 To Laid out in corn Bacon &c for the support of John Booch an aged & infirm Person	2.10..0
	£ 178..4.10

E. E. Pr David Mason
for Mason & Blunt Ch W[ardens]

[273]

Albemarle Parish   Cr
Augt By 21282 lb of Tobacco Levied last Levy & Sold as Follows to Witt

1772	2244	a^t	16/8	£ 18.14..0
	2638	a^t	16/4	21.10.10
	2106	a^t	16/7	17..9..3¾
	1914	a^t	16/6	15.15..9¼
	2153	a^t	16/6	17.15..2¾
	2098	a^t	16/9	17.11..4¾
	2804	a^t	16/4	22.17.11¾
	2664	a^t	16/6	21..1..6
	2106	a^t	16/6	17..7..5
	555	a^t	16/6	4..8..0
	21282			£ 175..10..3

May 31	By a Fine Rec^d for Profane swearing in May 1772	0..5..0
1773	By 4 fines Rec^d for Profane Swearing this Present Month	1..0..0
By a fine Rec^d for Bastardy in 1772		1..0..0
By a fine Rec^d of Lucy Gilliam for Profane Swearing		0..5..0
		£ 178..0..3

E. E. P David Mason
for Mason & Blunt C Wardens

[274]

At A Vestry held for Albemarle Parish the 20th day of Octr 1773

Present
The Revd William Willie   Augustine Claiborne
Michael Blow   Richard Parker
Laurence Gibbons   Robert Jones J
James Jones   George Rieves
Richard Blunt

The following Allownaces is ordered to be made to Wit.	£ S D
To the Revd William Willie for provideing Elements 3 Sundays omitted	10..0..0
William Rogers	2..0..0
To Thomas Cooper for the support of his Wife	5..0..0
To Robt Whitehead	2..0..0
To John Woodward for Wilkinsons Child	2..0..0

Surry and Sussex Counties, Virginia, 1742-1786   213

Franklin Birdson for Elizabeth Birdsong	4..0..0
Thomas Waller	3.10..0
James Hern, to be provided by the Ch. Wardens	5..0..0
Mary Southald	2..0..0
James Bane for keeping his Brother William	3.10..0
Peggy Jones to be laid out by the Ch. Wardens	3..0..0
Charles Gillam	4..0..0
Elizabeth Gillam	6..0..0
Joanna Moss	3.10..0
Benjamin Barham for keeping Sarah Nights Child	4..0..0
To Mary Finnie	3..0..0
To Joseph Lane for keeping Eliz^a Bailey 4 Mo	1..11..0
Funeral Expenses for D^o	1..9..0
Wm Hite for keeping Joshua Cottons Children £10 £3 p^d by the Ch. Wardens	7..0..0
Martha Gilliam	2..0..0
Aron Sillis for keeping Silviah Newsums Child	2..0..0
William Horne for keeping & Burying Robt Newsam	1.10..0
Jane Pair a poor Woman with Eight Childen	10..0..0
John Curtis a poor Man with 10 Children he being 76 yr^s of age & had the s^d Children in 12 years	5..0..0
Edward Smith for keeping Mary Butler	3..0..0
Widdow Blaton	3..0..0
Benjamin Graves for keeping Tubert Hicks's Child as Pr agreement with Ch. Wardens	6..0..0
Carr^d up	£ 105..1..8

[275]

At a Vestry held for Albemarle Parish the 20th day of October 1773

Present
The Revd William Willie   Augustine Claiborne
Michael Blow   Richard Parker
Laurence Gibbons   Robert Jones J
James Jones   George Rieves
            Richard Blunt

Albemarle Parish D^r	ll W^t Tob^o
To the Revd William Willie Minister	17305
To John Nicholson Clerk of St Pauls Church	1200
To the Clerk of St Andrews Church	1200
To the Clerk of St Marks Church	1200
To Rebeccah Denton Sexton of Notway Church	600
To John Bane Sexton of St Pauls Church	600
To William Rogers Sexton of St Andrew Church	600
To Peter Randolph Sexton of St Marks Church	500
To David Jones Clerk of the Vestry	400
To Thomas Eskridge Clerk of Notway Church for 9 Months	800
To Benjamin Baird for D^o 2 Mo	200
	24405
To levied for the use of the parish & paying the collect^r	87595
	111990

Albemarle Parish Cr		ll W^t Tob^o
By 2800 Tythables a^t 40 Pr Tythe		112000

or at 12/6 Pr C^t by rule of Vestry, according to late Act. of Assembly
Mr William Dunn appointed Vestryman in the room of Capt James Jones who this day resigned that office
Ordered that George Wilson be Exempted from paying parish Levy

William Willie Rector

Brought up	£ 105..1..8
To Ballance due Laurence House 1st payment	78..0.11½
To ballance due Jno Woodward	27..9.10¾
To other Moiety for L. House	194..17..6
To Jno Woodward 2^d payment	58 .. 6..8
	£ 463 .16..8½

[276]

At a Vestry held at Notway Church for Albemarle parish 17th Novr 1773

Present

The Revd William Willie	John Mason
Laurence Gibbons	William Blunt
Augst Claiborne	Robert Jones, &
David Mason	George Rieves

Ordered that James Jones is appointed to collect the parish Levys on his giveing Bond & Security as usual, & that the Bond be lodg'd with the Clk of Vestry

It appearing tha there is a deficiency of Money ariseing from the sales of the Tob^o at the last Levy to answer the engagements of the parish. Ordered that the Ch. Wardens borrow a Sum of money on Int. not exceding one hundred pounds to answer the s^d deficiency

Ordered that the Revd William Willie, David Mason, Richd Blunt, Richard Parker examine the vestry Books & make report to the next Vestry the condition they find them in ————

William Willie, Rector

[277]

At a Vesty held at Notway Church for Albemarle Parish ye 20th Ap^l 1774

Present
the Revd William Willie

John Mason	George Rieves
Augst Claiborne	Robert Jones } Gent
David Mason	Richard Parker

Hugh Ivy undertakes to diet lodge & take care of Thomas Musselwhite a poor infirm man till the laying of the next Levy on his remaining at his House at ten Shillings Pr Month

William Dunn appeared in Vestry & undertakes to supply Eliz^a Anderson Widdow with necessarys to the amt. of £5 — which sum the Vestry ingage he shall be repaid & if he advance the cash to allow him Interest

Surry and Sussex Counties, Virginia, 1742-1786   215

William Dunn lately elected into this Vestry now appearing & refuseing to act in that
office, in the room of whom Henry Gee is elected, George Booth in the room of Nathaniel
Harrison out of the parish, & John Peter in the room of Richard Blunt Dec^d

The Church Wardens failing to appear to render their Acct^s it is order'd that they attend at
the next Vestry to perform the same, also that all collectors do then appear that have
failed to render acct^s
Also which Vestry is to be held the day before July Court

It appearing that John Peter has nearly finished his undertaking the new building to
Notway Church, and the well, The coping & the pews & the doors & remaining yet to be
done, nor can the same be safely done till the front building is raised, the Vestry do
therefore receive the S^d building as the same is do he[sic] & no farther
                                                                William Willie Rector
[278]

At a Vestry held at Notway Church for Albemarle Parish ye 20th July 1774

                        Present
                   the Revd William Willie
        Robert Jones   Michael Blow
        Augst Claiborne   William Blunt } Gent.
        David Mason   Laurence Gibbons &
        John Mason   George Rieves

Michael Blow & Laurence Gibbons late Church Wardens rendered Acc^{ts} of their
proceeding for 1773. ballance due to the Parish £2.5.6½ which being rec^d & approved of
by the Vestry, Ordered to be regestered[sic]

John Cargail Ex: of Nicholas Massinburgh late Church Warden render'd his Acc^t & a
ballance due to the Parish of £2.7.11 which being rec^d & Approved of by the Vestry
Ordred to be registred.

Ordered that it be an instruction to the ChWardens that they advertise in the Gazettees the
day of sale of the Tob^o to be sold the present year for the use of the parish, and that they
sell the same as follows, one moiety for ready payment & the other upon credit till the 25th
of Ap^l 1775, taking Bond with sufficient Security for such payment to be made in
Ap^l

Ordered that Edward Prince, Henry Credle, James Samman & James Bane be exempted
from payment of Parish Levy in future

Order'd that the Ch Wardens pay Laurence Gibbons Junr £4-0-0 for keeping Patty Atkins's
Child & the Sd Gibbons undertakes to keep the s^d Child the ensueing Year a' £4-0-0

Order'd that Thomas Musselwhite be exempt from payment of Parish Levy till the
recovery of his health

Order'd that the Ch Wardens lay out 40/ for the use of Unity Waller wife of Thos Waller
an infirm Woman
                                                                William Willie, Rector

[279]

1773 Albemarle Parish   Dr   £   S   D
To Cash p^d the Revd William Willie   12..0..0
To Laurence House   112.10.7½

To Thomas Coopers	5..0..0
To Franklin Clark	4..0..0
To James Hern	5..0..0
To Mary Southald	2..0..0
To James Bane	3.10.0
To Charles Gilliam	2..0..0
To Thomas Cullam	6..0..0
To Joseph Lane	4.15.0
To William Hicks	2.14.3
To William Hite	3..0..0
To Martha Gillan	2..0..0
To Susan Lilly	2..0..0
To John Woodward, Carpenter	30.16.9¼
To Laurence House	4..0..0
To Charles Williams for Jane Pair	1.10.0
To Charity Clifen	2..0..0
To Joshua Moss	2.10.0
To William Blunt, Order	4..9..4¼
To Cash spent in selling Tobacco	0.10.0
To Sundrys bought for William Ramsey, Orphan	1..0.10
To Jn° Blow for keeping & Doctoring Wm Ramsey 6 weeks	=..13..0
To p^d Laurence House by Laurence Gibbons	77.10..0
To p^d John Woodward by D°	2..0..0
To p^d Doct^r Pete for himself & for Mary Finnie by D°	2.10.0
To p^d William Rogers by D°	2..0..0
To p^d Robert Whitehead by D°	2..0..0
To p^d Laurence Gibbons Junr his ball^a as Pr Ord. Vestry in 1772	3..2..6
To laid out in provision for Elizabeth Rowland	2..0..0
To p^d Petway Johnson as Ballance due him on old acct. Pr Acct. of Thomas Culham p^d by D°	4..5..6
To p^p the Revd William Willie Pr D° for Peggy Jones	2..0..0
To p^d John Woodward, Carpenter	27..9..10¾
July 20th 1774	£ 339..17.8¾

Michael Blow
Laurence Gibbons Junr Ch Ward^s

[280]

1774 Pd Contra Cr	£ S D
By 4130 ll Tob° sold for the use of the Parish	240..3..3¼
By Cash borrowed of the Revd Wm Willie for the use of the Parish	52..0..0
By D° of Petway Johnson for the use of the Parish	50..0..0
	£ 342..3..3¼

Michael Blow
Laurence Gibbons Junr Ch Wardens

[281]

1774 Albemarle Parish Dr	£ S D
May 25th To ½ Barrel Corn to Thomas Cooper	0..6..3
To a Rent of a Colledge Tenement 212 ^{ll} Tob° at 16/11	1.15.11
To the cost of Lease for ditto	0.15..0
Aug 15th To Nathaniel Felts 2 Bushels wheat a^t 4/1	0..8..0
To Cash p^d for corn for ditto	0.12.6
To Charles Gilliam p^d him	4..0..0
To Thomas Cooper p^d him	4.13.9
To John Delehay for keeping William Delehay	0.18.0

To Petway Johnston for Thomas Cullam	0..5..0
To Donald Mc Kenish for the Glebe Garden	12.18.0
To Peggy Jones p^d her	2..0..0
To Cash p^d Susannah Bay 15/1 D^o 15/	1.10.0
Sep. 19th To Cash p^d for 200^{ll} pork for Joseph Clark	2..0..0
To D^o for 2 Barrels corn for D^o	1..5..0
To Cash p^d Joseph Clark for cleaning ye Church Yard	0..6..6
To Patty Gilliam p^d her	2..0..0
To Thomas Davis for keeping Newsums Child	3..0..0
To Cash p^d Mary Southworth Pr C. Gilliam	2..0..0
To D^o p^d Laurence Gibbons Junr for Thos Delehay	5..0..0
To p^d Robert Whitehead by Laurence Gibbons	2..0..0
To p^d Robert Wynne Raines by D^o	1..2..6
July 20th 1774 £	53.11.5

[282]

1774 P	Contra	Cr	£ S D
Jun 20th By Cash for a fine for Swearing			0..5..0
By Messrs Williamson for 1074^{ll} Tob^o	16/2		8..3..7
By D^o for 1006	16/		8..0..11
By Addam Fleming for 1044	16/9		8.14.10½
By D^o for 1070	16/11		9.17.11
By D^o for 1005	17/2		8.12..6½
By D^o for 1022	16/10		8.12..7
By overcharge for p^d L. Gibbons for Whitehead & Robt Raney			3..2..6
		£	55.19..4

Pr John Cargail Ex^r of
Nicholas Massenburgh   Laurence Gibbons Junr

[283]

At a Vestry held for Albemarle Parish at Notway Church 14th Decr 1774

Present
The Revd William Willie, Rector, Robert Jones, Ch Warden
John Mason, Augustine Claiborne, Michael Blow, William Blunt
Laurence Gibbons Junr, George Booth & George Rieves, Gent ---

Ordered that Hugh Belches be appointed Clerk to this Vestry in the room of John Nicholson -------------------

The Vestry then proceeded to lay the Parish Levy as follows to wit ---

Albemarle Parish Dr	ll W^t Tob^o		
To the Revd William Willie his Sallery	17305		
To the Clk^s of all the Churche's their Salery's	4800		
To the Sextons of ditto	2100		
To the Clk of the Vestry his Salery	500		£ S D
	24705 a^t 2d		205.17..6
For the support of Thomas Cooper & Wife very infirm people			8..0..0
For John Alsobrook for burying Joseph Clark			1..7..6
William Rogers & Wife			5..0..0
Robert Whitehead			2..0..0
Charles Gilliam			4..0..0

Sarah Heron Widow of William	5..0..0
Mary Heron Widow of James	8..0..0
For the support of Joshua Cottons Children	10..0..0
John Curtis	5..0..0
Jane Pare & Children	6..0..0
Thomas Waller	5..0..0
Jane Scoggin	6..0..0
Elizabeth Belighton	2..0..0
Benjamin Barham for keeping Knights Child	4..0..0
Mary Southworth	2..0..0
Charity Clifton	2..0..0
Joanna Moss	3..0..0
William Partin for the entertainment of Jones Stokes ye preceeding y^r	3.12.0
Franling Clark for d^o Elizabeth Birdsong	4..0..0
Hugh Ivie for d^o y^t Thomas Musselwhite	3.19.5
Elizabeth Anderson	3..0..0
For the Revd Mr Fennon for support &c Jno Bush & family 3 yrs as Pr acct.	17..3..5
For the support of ditto	3..0..0
For the last payment to Jno Woodward for building Notway Ch	58..6..8
For Jno Jones for drawing 2 plans at building d^o	17..6
For Elizabeth Roland a poor Woman	2..0..0
For answering the future contingent charges of the Parish	20..0..0
Carr^d forw^d	£ 390.14.0

[284]

Debit brought Forward	£ 390:14: 0
For George Rieves for cleaning the Ch Yard	9: 0: 0
For the Sheriffs Com. for collecting £420:0:0	25: 0: 0
	£ 416: 3: 0

By 2800 Tithables at 3/ or 24^{lb} Tob^o at the option of the payor according to Law   420..0..0

Ordered that the Ch Wardens pay unto the Revd William Willie Rector of this parish for finding the Elements for the Communion to Easter 1775   12..0..0

Ordered the Money allow'd in the above state of the Levy for Cottons Children be paid to Hugh Belches for that up, That for Jane Scoggin to be paid to John Mason Junr for that up.

Ordered that the Ch Wardens pay to Edward Smith for the support of Mary Butler the ensuing year   3: 0: 0

Ordered that James Jones Gent. Sheriff, be appointed collector of the above Levy and after giving Bond & Security for the same, that he collect according to the above state of the Levy

The Vestry being informed that in one of the two Wrightings found among the papers of Hartwell Marrable, perporting his last Will there is a considerable Legacy devis'd in some manner to this Parish & that the contest arising on those wrightings now lay before the Court of this County———————
Ordered that the Ch Wardens employ an Attorney to speak in the s^d contest in support of the right the Parish has under the s^d Wills

William Willie Rector

[285]

At a Vestry held for Albemarle Parish at Sussex Court House 20th Ap^l 1775

Present
Robert Jones & Richard Parker, Ch Wardens, David Mason, George Rieves, William Blunt, George Booth, John Peters & Michael Blow, Gent. Vestry

Ord^d that David Mason & George Rieves, Gent. be appointed Ch Wardens for the present Year

Ord^d that the Ch Wardens pay Mary Hern Five pounds which was omitted to be levy^d in the year 1773

The Collector for this Parish appear'd in Vestry and inform'd the Vestry that he has collected a very Inconsiderable quantity of Tob^o for the use of the Parish & that there are no probability of collecting a sifficient quantity to pay the Ministers Salery, Therefore it is Ordered that the present Ch Wardens purchase the Tob^o for the Minister agreeable to the Act of Assembly in that case made & provided —

It appearing to the Vestry that Richard Blunt dec^d was appointed with the Revd William Willie & David Mason to examin the Vestry Books
Ord^d that William Blunt be appointed in the room of Richard Blunt dec^d to examin the s^d Books

James Jones Collector for this parish in the Year 1774. This day appear'd in Vestry & render'd his acct. which was exam^d, sworn to & order'd to be register'd and there appear'd to be a ballance of 2/1½ due to the s^d collector which is ord^d to be p^d him

It appearing to the Vestry that at the last Levy laid for this parish there was £8.. only levy'd for the use of Mary Hern's Family & that it will prove insufficient, it is therefore order'd that the Ch Wardens make her the further allowance of £2.. for the present year

David Mason
George Rieves Ch Ward^s

Albemarle Parish to James Jones Sheriff			Dr			£ S D
To Benjamin Arrington remov'd to Carrolina 3 Levy's at		5/1				0.15..0
To William Andrews	2 ditto	10/1	Richd Adkins	1 d^o	5/1	0.15..0
To Hartwell Battle	1 d^o	5/1	Thos Broadrib	1 d^o	5/1	0.10..0
To Thomas Booth	2 d^o	10/1	William Cain	1 d^o	5/1	0.15..0
To Mathew Careless	1 d^o	5/1	James Cook	1 d^o	5/1	0.10..0
To William Dabney	1 d^o	5/1	Wilson George	1 d^o	5/1	0.10..0
To John Heath	3 d^o	15/1	Ja^s Hatt Junr	1 d^o	5/1	1..0..0
To Saml Judkins	1 d^o	5/1	Joell Knight	1 d^o	5/1	0.10..0
To Eph^m King	1 d^o	5/1	Daniel Lee	1 d^o	5/1	0.10..0
To John Long	1 d^o	5/1	Lewis Morris	1 d^o	5/1	0.10..0
To Michael More	1 d^o	5/1	Solomon Porch	1 d^o	5/1	0.10.0
To Jno Redwood	1 d^o	5/1	William Rieves	1 d^o	5/1	0.10.0
To John Sturdivant over Listed 1 Pole						0..5..0
To Thomas Smith removed to Surrey				1 d^o	5/1	0..5..0
To Robert Tuder				1 d^o	5/1	0..5..0
			Acc^t carr^d over		£	8..0..0

[286]

Albemarle Parish Dr to James Jones Sheriff £ S D
To ballance brought forward   8..0..0
To John Tuder 1 pole 5/1 Howell Tatum 1 d° 5/1 0.10..0
To David Thweat 1 d° 5/1 Isham Underwood 1 d° 5/1 10.10..0
To John Underhill Jun' Dec^d 2 d° 10/1 0.10..0
To William Wooten 1 d° 5/1 Benj^m Williams 1 d° 5/1 0.10..0
To Elijah Whitfield 1 d° 5/1 John Washer 1 d° 5/1 0.10..0
To Benjmain Watkinson 1 d° 5/1 John Gilliam 1 d° 5/ 0.10..0
To Barnabas Bailey over Listed 1 d° 5/1 James Ezell 1 d^d 5/1 0.10..0
To Robert Mitchel 0..5..0
 11.15..0
To Commissions on £10 at 6 Pr C^t 0.12..0
 £12..7..0

D° Albemarle Parish Cr
By Commissions on £11 15 at 6 PC^t 0.12.10¼
By Supernumries as follows Viz^{cr}
Isack Bendoll 1 Tythe 5/1 Edmund Bailey 1 d° 5/1 0.10..0
Joseph Bailey 1 do° 5/1 James Clary 1 d° 5/1 0.10..0
Benjamin Fauson 1 d° 5/1 Edmund Gilliam d° 5/1 0.10..0
Joseph Glover 3 d° 15/1 William Heath Junr Decd 7 d° 35/1 2.10..0
John Hargroves Senr 1 d° 5/1 Samuel Jones 5 d° 25/1 1.10..0
Eliz^a Johnston 1 d° 5/1 John Kelley 2 d° 10/1 0.15..0
Timothy Rieves 5 d° 25/1 John White 2 d° 10/1 1.15..0
Benjamin Wilbourne 1 d° 5/1 Samuel Harwood 6 d° 30/1 1.15..0
John Sledge 1 d° 5/1 0..5..0
By overcharg'd for Ephraim King 5/1 d° Michael More 5/1 0.10..0
By d° John Redwood 5/1 By Commissions on £11 a^t 6 P^{ct} 12/1 0.17..0
 £12..4.10¼ £11.19.10

[287]

At a Vestry held for the Parish of Albemarle in the County of Sussex the 20th Day of Decr 1775

Present

The Revd William Willie, Rector, George Rieves, Genl Ch Warden, John Mason, Augustine Claiborne, Michael Blow, William Blunt, & John Peters, Vestrymen

In pursuance to an order of the Court of this County directing the processioning of the Lands in this County agreeable to the Act of Assembly in that case among other things made and provided, the Vestry proceeded therein as to layng of the precincts & appointment of processioners, Verbatim as to the last appointm^t except as follow, to wit,

We do appoint William Wilson Michael Blow Nathaniel Briggs & Joseph Ellis to see every persons Land processioned and the land marks thereof renew'd from Southamton County up Atsamosauh Swamp to Secawry Swamp up the s^d swamp to the head thereof, and that they assemble all the freeholders within the S^d Presinct to attend the performance thereof, and that the s^d Nat. Briggs & Joseph Ellis do make return to the Vestry of every persons land they shall procession & of every person present at the processioning thereof also of whole land they shall fail to procession & the particular reason of such failure and that the same be done & perform'd between the first day of November & the last day of March __ [the purpose of the + notation is not given]
V N° 1————James Turner & Howell Chapel are appointed to procession from the mouth of Secawry Swamp up the Atsamosak swamp the Maj^r branch, up the s^d branch to Seacory road, by the s^d road to Secowry Swamp, by the s^d Swamp to the beginning __ N°

+ 2————William Mason & John Jones are appointed to procession from Cooks Bridge, along Cooks road to Joseph Swamp so to Prince George Cot^y line, by that line to Blackwater Swamp so to the beginning

+ 3————John Mason Junr & Edward Weaver are appointed to procession from the Govourners road to the old parish line all between Atsamosauk Swamp, Joseph Swamp, & the old parish line.

+ 4————James Chapel Junr & James Peters are appointed to procession from the old parish line, down Atsamosak Swamp to Robins branch, so down Austins branch to Notway River, up the River to the old parish line by that to the beginning

[288]

+ 5————Thomas Peters & John Chapel, are appointed to procession all between Robins branch, Austins branch, Notway River, Atsamosauk Swamp and Southamton County Line

+ 6————John Adkins & Henry Moss, are appointed to procession from Petway Mill along Petway line formily Harthorns line to the Colledge line, along that line to Joseph Swamp, down that Swamp to Notway River, up the River to Jones hole Swamp so to the beginning

+ 7————Hugh Belches & John Petway, are appointed to procession all between Jones hole Swamp, the Indian Swamp, Notway River & Prince George County line

+ 8————James Hall & John Eacols are appointed to procession between Monks neck Creek, Stony Creek & up Sappony Creek to Prince George Cot^y line

9————Thomas Saunders & George Booth are appointed to procession from Stony Creek, up Sappony Creek to Sappony Mill, thence to Ephram Parhams line so down Notway River to the beginning

+10————William Parham & John Milone, are appointed to procession from Ephram Parhams to Sappony Mill, all between the line that divides this County and Dinwiddie & up Notway River to Harries Swamp

+11————Isham Smith & William Yarbrough are appointed to procession from Harries Swamp, up Notway River to the extent of this County

+12————James Cooper & Joseph Renn are appointed to procession between Rackoon Swamp, little swamp & up Stoake's Road

+13————Nathaniel Parham & Robert Jones are appointed to procession from the Island Swamp to the old Parish Line by that line to the line that divides this County & Brunswick so to Notway River

+14————Solomon Graves & Cud'[Cudworth] Stafford are appointed to procession from Stoake's between Rackon Swamp and Hunting Quarter swamp so up the head line of the s^d Hunting Swamp

+15————Lewis Tharp & John Stewart are appointed to procession all the Lands on the South side of the Three Creeks Southamton & Brunswick Cot^y lines

+16————William Moreing & Mathew Winne are appointed to Procession from Stoake's Road up Notway River to the frying pan Swamp, from the head of the s^d swamp a streight course to the hunting Quarter Swamp

+17————Nicholas Wilson & John Alsobrook, are appointed to procession from the mouth of Coperhank Swamp along the line that divides this county and Surrey to Burchan island Road, by that Road to Seacury road, by that Road to Coperhank Swamp, so to the beginning

[289]

+18————John Lamb & Simon Stacy are appointed to procession all between Blackwater Swamp, Coperhank Swamp & the old parish line

+19————James Bois^u Jones & Nathaniel Barker are appointed to Process^n from the mouth of the old Town Branch Swamp up that to the head of the Tar kiln branch down that to the Mill Swamp and including John Gilliums, formily Tatams land so to the new

Road and then to Cooks Road by that to Black water so to the beginning
+20----------Thomas Vent & John Whitehorne are appointed to procession from the mouth of the great Swamp to the Three Creeks & up the three Creeks & Outer dam Swamp to Brunswick County Line
+21----------William Dunn & George Rieves are appointed to procession all between Edward Petways Line, formally Harthons Line & the Collage line and the line that devides this County & Prince George Joseph Swamp & Jones hole Swamp
+22----------John Carter & Thomas Bailey are appointed to procession all between Allens Line, John Pinningtons line, John Berrymans line, Stoake's road & the Hunting Quarter Swamp
+23----------Thomas Renn & John Yells are appointed to procession all between Allen line, John Pinningtons line, John Berrymans line, Stoake's road and Notway River
+24----------Laurence Smith & William Nicholson are appointed to procession from Blackwater on the old parish line, by that to Coperhank Swamp, by that Swamp to the head, so to the Tar kiln Branch on the Mill Swamp, up that to the Old town Swamp, down that to Blackwater, Including William Blunt, William Nicholson & Thomas Tomlinson's Lands
+25----------Lewis Dunn & Austin Gillium are appointed to procession all between Notway River, the Huntington[sic] Quarter, & Rackoon Swamps & along Loftins Mill path to the little swamp, down that to Rackoon Swamp so to Notway River
+26----------Jesse Williamson & Arther Williamson are appointed to procession up Huntington Quarter Swamp to little Swamp from Loftins Mill path so to Stoake's Road

+27----------Stith Parham Junr & John Parham are appointed to procession from the Indian Swamp to Monks Neck Creek, and Notway River and the line that devides this County and Prince George County
+28----------Benjamin Weathers & Stith Parham are appointed to procession from the flat Swamp up Notway River to the mouth of Frying pan Swamp so to the head of it, from thence to Threeits[sic] so to the beginning

[290]

+29----------John Wynn & Willam Sturdivant are appointed to procession from the head of Frying pan Swamp to Hunting Quarter Swamp, down that to Island branch, down that to Notway River
+30----------James Bell & Nathaniel Holt are appointed to procession from the North side of the Spring Swamp up the s^d Swamp to the County line so down the Rackoon to Stoake's Road except so much as is app^d Saml Northington and Webb Roland
+31----------Faddy Jarrot & Fredrick Andrews are appointed to procession from Cooks road on the new road by that road to black swamp down that to pegion Swamp, up that to Cooks road down that road to the beginning
+32----------Hugh Ivy & David Mason Junr are appointed to procession all between Joseph Swamp, Pegion Swamp, the Governers road & Cooks Road
+33----------Henry Jarrad & Nicholas Jarrad are appointed to procession from the Majors branch up Atsamosauk swamp to Jones Church road by that Road to Secaury Road, by that road to the Maj^r Branch so to the beginning
+34----------Nicholas Partrige & Petway Johnston are appointed to procession from Jones Church road up Atsamosank and including Petway Johnstons land thence to the head of Coperhank Swamp by that to Secaury Road by that to Jones Church road so to the beginning
+35----------George Long & Charles Long are appointed to procession all between Rackoon Swamp, Southampton Road line, Butt's road & Stoke's Road
+36----------Fredrick Ford & John Pate are appointed to procession from the Poplar Swamp near Bullocks to Wyches road, by that to the great swamp, by that to Southamton line, by that line to the poplar, so to the beginning
+37----------Daniel Harwood & Charles Barham are appointed to procession between Butt's road, the poplar swamp, Southamton County line & Stoake's road

+38————James Barnes & Nathan Northington are appointed to procession from the poplar Bridge up the south branch to Brunswick Cot^y line, by that line to the great swamp, by that to Wyches road, so to the begining
+39————Thomas Felts & William Rose are appointed to procession from the poplar at Michael Weathers along a path that leads from Weather's to Abel Mabrys on the Spring Swamp, down the Spring Seamp to Stoake's road, by that to the Poplar swamp, so to the beginning
+40————William Richardson & Nathaniel Felts are appointed to procession from the path that leads from Mical Weather's to Abel Mabry's on the spring swamp up the said swamp to Brunswick Cot^y line, by that to the south branch, down the same to the fork & up the north prong to Mical Weathers
+41————Henry Blow & William Brittle are appointed to procession from the south side of Seacock to the head of Lightwood Swamp & to the head of Scacory Swamp to a branch called the winding branch from that branch to the head of Snake branch, down that to the Seacock
+42————[Note: this number is listed at bottom of the page, as has been done with the earlier page breaks; however, there is no entry for this number on the following page and the following page, number 291, as numbered, appears out of sequence.]

[291]

2d That the Ch Wardens pay unto Charles Gillam £ 4:0:0 Pr Year for keeping Fibby Gillam a young child 2 years & 7 months
3d That the Ch Wardens pay unto Elizabeth Cullam £6:0:0 for the year 1774

William Willie Rector

At a Vestry held for the Parish of Albemarle at the Courthouse in the County of Sussex the 18th day of July 1776
Present
Auguston Claiborne, David Mason, William Blunt, Michael Blow, Richard Parker, John Mason, George Rieves, & Henry Gee Genl Vestrymen

Ord^d that David Mason & George Rieves be appointed Ch Ward^s for this parish
Ord^d that Hugh Belches, Auguston[sic] Claiborn & Henry Moss or any two of them do superintend the building of Notway Ch.
Resol^d that the Revd Mr William Andrews be rec^d as Rector of Albemarle parish in this County upon the special conditions that he accommodate himself at his own expence with a House to reside in, till Miss^{rs} Willie our late incumbants widdow removes from the Glebe, which is expected at Xmas, and also that he will submit to be upon the same foundation with the rest of the Clergy in this Government as the common wealth of Virginia & that the Ch. Wardens
write to Mr Andrews the contents of this resolution and request him to remove [to the parish and perform devine service in this parish as soon as possible

David Mason
George Rieves Ch Ward^s

[292]

In Obedience to an Order of Vestry To us Directed Bearing Date the [torn] of December 1775, We have Assembled the Freeholders & Processioners and Renew'd the Land marks of the Following Lines The Persons Present To Witt

Beginning on the Land mark of William Olivers	March 16th 1776	Persons Present William Oliver

Capt. William Gilliam Estate
Benja Tyus
Capt Henry Gee
Burwel Wilborne
Benja Wilborne
John Anderson Sturdivant
James Spain
Robert Jones
Peter Threewitt
Nath{a} Dunn
Nath{a} Pareham
Benja Owin

Anderson Sturdivant
Benja Tyus
Miles Spain
Burwel Wilborne
Peter Threewitts
Nath{a} Dunn

March 19 1776
The Landmarks of
John Batt
Susanah Parham
Mathew Pareham
Burwill Greens Estate
William Green
Mrs Hewitt

Persons Present
Joseph Dennis
John Davis
Jesse Smith
James Chamlis
Frederick Owin
Natha{l} Dunn
Thomas Pareham

Finished and Concluded this 19th Day of March 1776

Robert Jones
Nath{a} Pareham

[293]

John Bains Land Present Stephen Andrews, William Ellis, Thomas Tomlinson, Robert Judkins, William Judkins, William Jordan, Caleb Ellis, Emanuel James, William Nicholson & John Bain

John Lamb — Land in the Presence of the same persons

Part of John Irby	D{o}
Simon Stacy	D{o}
Part of Howel Briggs Dec{d}	D{o}
Thomas Tomlinsons	D{o}
Stephen Andrews	D{o}
William Ellis	D{o}
Part of William Nicholsons	D{o}
Robert Judkins	D{o}
William Judkins	D{o}
William Jordan	D{o}
Caleb Ellis	D{o}
Thomas Gibbons	D{o}
Emanuel James	D{o}

John Montgomery not Present no person to Show the line By virtue of the order of Vestry hereunto anexted[sic] to us directed we have caused the several Tracks of Land where mentioned being all Contain'd within our Precinct to be processioned in our Presence and the lines of the said Lands Renew'd as by the said order Directed Given Under our hand this 21st Day of March 1776

John Lamb
Simon Stacy

[294]

At A Vestry Held for the Parish of Albemarle at the Court House in the County of Sussex April 18th 1777

Col° Augustine Claiborne, Col. Henry Gee, Col° Micol Blow, Robert Jones, Richard Parker, George Rieves, William Blunt Gent. Vestrymen
William Lamb appointed Clk. of this Vestry
M' Hamilton Jones in behalf of the Extaire[sic] of the late Revd Mr William Willie late Minister of ths Parrish appear'd in Vestry and Demanded the arrears of Salary due to the s^d Willie at the time of his Decease which happened on the 3rd of April 1776 which was for one year & Six months — whereupon the Vestery entered upon fully unto the Situation of Trade at Present the advanced price of 30/ & 40/ Pr Cent paid for Tob° the great Scarcity of that Comodity so as to render it almost impracticable to Collect so as to pay off so heavy a debt in Tob° thought it most prudent & advisable to enter enter[sic] into agreement to pay off the said Debt at amortisation Cash and there upon it was an dualy[sic] agreed between the s^d Jones in behalf of the s^d Extria[sic] & this Vestery that the s^d year & half sallary shall be paid off in money as Speedy as possible at twenty two and sixpense PCent in consequence of which agreement the Vestery proceed to lay the levy as follows

Viz. Albemarle Parrish Dr	lbs. wt. Tob°
To Salary due to Mr Willie from 15th Octr 1774 to the 15 Oct° 1775	17305
To d° from the 15 Oct° 1775 to the 3^d of April 1776 when the s^d Willie Dec^d	8652
To the present Incumbent in prepartion from the 1 Oct° 1776 to 1 Jan 1777 3 mo.	4326
To John Nicholson Clk. of St Pauls Ch. his Sallery from 15 Oct° 1775 to the 1 January 1777. 26 months & half	2650
To Robt Mcgee Clk. of St Andrews same time	2650
To Peter Randall Clk of St Marks same time	2650
To Benjamin Baird Clk of Nottaway same time	2200
To adm^r of Rebecca Denton late Sexton of Nottoway Ch	725
To James Wiggins Sexton of St Pauls Ch	635
To Peter Rand all d° St Marks	1085
To Wm Rogers late d° of St Andrews 1½ years	750
To Wm Longbottom present d° of d° for 8 mo.	338
To John Nicholson late Clerk Vestery	833
	44794
The above 44794 discharged at 22/6 PCent	
To raise money to disch. the money debt or the bal.	44099
Struck see forward £204..3..2	
To raise money from Tob° at 12/6 to Discharge the above 44794 at 22/6	80627
	124726
To 6 PrCent for Collecting 124726 is	7483
Cr	132209
D° 2200 Tithables at 60 lbs. Tob° or the same in [torn] Cent at the option of the payer	132000

[295]

David Mason by letter Resign'd his Seat as a Vestery man of this Parrish, John Mason of Sandy hill Elected in the Room of David Mason, (Ordered that Wm Blunt & John Mason be app^d. Ch. wardens for the year Ensuing from this day The Following allowance for the Support of the poor & Indigent to the first day of January 1777, are made with to be levied in the following State

Wm Rogers	£ 10.16..4
Thomas Cooper	8..1..4

Robᵗ Whitehead	4..6..4
Franklyn Clark for Elisabeth Birdsong	5..0..0
Thomas Waller	5..0..0
Thomas Moor for maintaining James Hearn & abed	8..5..0
Jane Davis for D⁰ D⁰ 5 mo⁵ aᵗ 7/ Pyear	3..0..0
John Alsobrook for Burieng Joseph Clark	1..7..0
The Estate of Wᵐ Wilie[sic] for providing Element	12..0..0
Robᵗ Magee for Charles Gilliam	8..0..0

[296]

At a Meeting of the Vestry of Albemrle Parish on Tuesday 29ᵗʰ of June 1779
Present
Augustine Claiborne, Henry Gee, John Mason Sen.,
George Booth, George Rives, Nath. Dunn, and Jn⁰ Mason

Ordered that Jn⁰ Massenburg be appointed Clk to this Vestry in the room of Wᵐ Lamb who is discharged from that office

The following allowances were made to the poor & Indigent To the first of January last aᵗ the Parish of Albemarle to Answer the contigent charges of the Poor & indigent

£ 3666
234
£ 3900

By 2600 Tiths   aᵗ 30/ or 15ll Tob⁰   £ 3900

Ordered that Jn⁰ Massenburg be appointed Collector of the above levie & that the Collect 30/ or 15ˡᵇ Tob⁰ for each Tiths

Order'd that Aug. Claiborne employ an attorney to prosecute the Bonds of Lawrance Nouse [House] & Jn⁰ Woodward upon undertaking to Build Notway & Sᵗ Marks Churches

A Copy Test   George Booth
Jn⁰ Massenburg Clk. Vestry   Jn⁰ Mason   } CW

[Note: pages 297-300 dim and badly damaged; processioning appointments for precincts 1-23 are missing and the names of those entered are in a different and unfamiliar handwriting from the appointment descriptions]

[297]

24 X Jn⁰ Carter & Jn⁰ Hawthorn are appointed to procession all between Allen line, Penningtons, Hartwell Marrablle's line, Stoake's road & Notway River
25 X David Mason & Wᵐ Nicholson are appointed to procession from Black Water
26 X Anslum Gilliam & Jn⁰ Peters are appointed to procession between Notway River, Hunting Quarter & Rackoon swamp along Loftins Mill path to the little Swamp down that to Rackoon Swamp so to Notway River
27 X Jn⁰ Clanton & Cyril Avary are appointed to procession up Hunting Quarter Swamp to Little Swamp from Loftins Mill path so to Stoake's Road
28 X Robert Tucker & Jn⁰ Parham are appointed to procession from the Indian Swamp to [illeg.] Neck Creek of Notway River the line that divides this County from P. George County
29 X Augustin Ogborn & Kith Parham are appointed to procession from the Flatt Swamp up the Notway to the Mouth of the Frying pan Swamp so to the head of it
30 X Jn⁰ Sturdivant & Wᵐ Sturdivant are appointed to procession from the head of the Frying pan Swamp to hunting Quarter Swamp down that to Island ~~Branch~~ Swamp down

that to Notway River
31 X Nathl Holt & Jn° Judkins are appointed to procession from the ~~mouth~~ North side of the Spring Swamp up the said Swamp to the County line so down the Rackoon to Stoake's road except that appointed to Wm Stewart & Benj Gunn
32 X Faddy Jarratt & Jn° Gary are appointed to procession from Stoake's Road on the new Road by that Road to Black Swamp down that to pigion Swamp up that to Cooks road down new Road to the beginning
33 X Aug. Shands & Daniel Ivey are appointed to procession all between Josephs & Pigeon Swamp the Governors Road and Cooks Road
34 X L Henry & Nichl Jarratt are appointed to procession from the Major branch up Asamosack to the Jones Church road by that road to Seacury road by that road to the Maj^r branch to the beginning
35 X Dan^e[sic] Smith & Nich^l Partridge are appointed to procession from Jones Church Road up Asamorack & including Petway Johnsons Land thence to the head of Coperhank Swamp by that Swamp Road by that to Jones Church road so to the beginning
36 X Chas Judkins & C W Long are appointed to procession all between Rackoon Swamp Southamton line Butts Road and Stoakes Road

[298]

37 X Jn° & Richd Mason are appointed to procession from the Poplar Swamp near Bullocks to Wyche's road by that to the great Swamp by that to Southamton line by that line to the Poplar so to the beginning
38 X Daniel Harwood & Jn° Massenburg are appointed to procession between Butts Road the poplar Swamp Southampton County line & Stoakes road
39 X Wm Thorn & Richd Stewart are appointed to procession from the poplar Bridge up the south Branch to Greenville County line by that line to great Swamp by that to Wyche's road
40 X Joel Adkins & Abel Mabry are appointed to procession from the Poplar at Michael Weathers along a path that leads from Weathers to Abell Mabrys from the Spring Swamp down the Spring Swamp to Stoakes road up that to the poplar Swamp so to the beginning
41 X Richd Northcross & Th° Ezell are appointed to procession from the path that leads from Michael Weather, Abell Mabrys on the Spring Swamp up the Swamp to Greenville County line By that to the South Branch down that to the Fork & up the North prong to Michael Weathers
42 X Wm Brittle & Mich^l Blow are appointed to procession from the south side of Seacory to the head of Lightwood Swamp & to the head of Seacock Swamp to the Branch called the winding Branch from that Branch to the head of Snake Branch down that to Seacock
43 X Wm Kinart J^r and Benj^a Gunn are appointed to procession from Joel Adkinses[sic] line thence by David Owens line to the Rackoon Swamp up s^d Swamp to Greenville Ct^y line along line to the Spring Swamp so to the beginning
44 X Wm T. Pennington & Clemant Hartley are appointed to procession and renew the land marks of all the lands within the following District to wit beginning at David Graveses[sic] line to the [word left out] and Joseph Hartleys line on Graveses mill pond thence along s^d line to the head of the north prong of the double branch near s^d Hartley thence down s^d branch to Andrewses Mill thence down s^d Run to the Rackoon swamp to the mouth of the great branch of the Rackon Swamp up that branch to Robt Joneses line thence along s^d line to James Spains line and along s^d Spains line to the Hunting Quarter Swamp thence along s^d swamp to the beginning
The Vestry now proceds to lay the levy for 1783 and made the following allowances to the Poor of this Parish up to the 25th of No^v 1784
To wit
Dr   Albemarle Parish
1783   To Mary and Eliz^a Rogers   £ 6..0..0
        To James Hern   10..0..0

To Charles Gilliam	10..0..0
To Phebe Shands	6..0..0
£	32..0..0

[299]

Debit Continued [edge of page torn]	£	[torn]
1783 To Thomas Waller		[torn
To Robt Bonds for Knights Child		8..0 = "
To Jane Pair		5..0 = "
To Peter Zell		5..0 = "
To Richard Adkins		3..0 = "
To James Sammons for his son		4..= =
To William Caudle		8..= = "
To Widdow Owen of Jno Owen Dec{d} for his children		3..0 = "
To Eliza Rowland widow of Joshua Rowland Dec{d}		3..0 = "
To Mary Felts for Mr Worrick		5..0 = "
To Richard Scogin		3..0 = "
To William Saunders		3..0 = "
To Adam Ivey as Pr Acct for provisions furnish'd Hanah Prince		0.10 = "
To Robt Anderson for Mrs Jones for Her Child as Pr Acct		8..4..0
To Richd Blow & Co as Pr acct ags{t} Jno King one of the Poor		2.16..9
To the Clk of Vestry		6..0..0
	£	105.11..4
To the Colc{t} 6 PrC for collecting ~~£ 105:11:4½ £140~~		8: 4: [torn]
	£	113.11..4
To answering contingent charges		26..4..7
Cr by 2800 Titheables a 1/ P Poll	£	140..[torn]

David Mason   Church W.

[300]

[Note: page badly worn and torn]
[torn] Vestry held for the Parish of Albemarle at Sussex Court House
[torn] 19th 1784[sic]

Present

David Mason	Nathaniel Dunn	
Robt Jones	Geo. Rives	Gent. Vestrymen
Wm Richardson	Jesse Williamson	
George Boothe	John Mason	
Nat. Newsom	Ben. Lanier	

Order'd that David Mason & Nathaniel Dunn be continued as Churchwardens the Present year from Ester[sic] Tuesday Last until the next Ester Tuesday.

The Vestry Proceeded to oversee several returns of Processioners
    Wm & John Sturdavant
    Wm Stewart jr & Ben Green
    Hen{y} Moss & Morris Giles
    Richd & Thomas Mason
    Wm Graves & Barham Moore
    John Carter & Jno Hawthorne
    Wm Chambliss & Robt Jones
    Abel Mabry & Joel Adkins
    Jno Judkins & Nat{l} Holt
    Mical Blow. Wm Brittle

Charles Judkins John Long
John Whiteledon[sic] R^d Stuart
Wm T. Pennington Clint Hartley
David Mason H[illeg.] Marrable
Wm Lanier & Simon Stacy
Faddy Jarratt Jn° Gary
Nathan Headley Jn° Jones
Thomas Adkins Edmund Moss
Thos Ambrose Ed: Smith
Geo: Rives Wm Dunn
Nat Dunn Henry Parsons

[Note: Written on the side of this page "To be returned to Genl W. B. Shands Jerusalem Southampton Co when directed. Left by Federal Soldiers]

[301]

At a Vestry held for the Parish of Albemarle in the County of Sussex the 20[?] Day of March 1780[sic] at the Court House

Present
George Booth & Jn° Mason Churchwardens
Robert Jones, George Rives, Henry Gee, Lawrence Gibons, Nath. Dunn
and John Peters

In persuance to an order of Sussex County Court bearing date Feb 7 Court, directing the processioning all the Lands in this County, The Vestry proceed therein as to Laying of the precincts & appointment of processioners, as the [illeg.]ment except as Follows to Witt

[Precinct numbers were indicated at the end of each entry, rather than the beginning]
X 1 We do appoint Nathl Briggs & Edwin Ellis to see every persons Land processioned & the Land markes thereof renewed from Southampton County line up Assimosack Swamp to Secawry swamp up the said swamp to the head thereof, and that they assemble all the Freeholders within the said precinct to attend the performance thereof ant[sic] that the said Nath. Briggs & Edwin Ellis do make a return to the ves. of every persons Land they shall procession & of every person present at the process...thereof also of whose Land they shall fail to procession & the particular reason of their failure & that the same be done & peform'd between

---
X 2 Ordered that James Burns & Howell Chappell be appointed to procession from the mouth of Secaury up the Assimosack swamp the Maj. Branch, up the said Branch to Secaury Road by the said Road to Secaury swamp by the s^d swamp to the beginning

---
X 3 Wm Mason & James Jones are appointed to procession from Cooks Bridge along Cooks road to Joseph Swamp so to Prince George County line by that line to Black Water Swamp so to the beginning

---
X 4 John Mason Ju. & Jn° Weaver are appointed to procession from the Governors road to the old Parish line all between Ajoin'd sacks swamp Joseph Swamp & the old parish line

---
X 5 James Chappell & Mch^l Bailey are appointed to procession from the old Parish line down Asemosack Swamp to Robins branch so down Austins Branch to Notoway River up the River to the old parish line by thus to the beginning

---
X 6 Jn° Chappell & Richd Parker are appointed to procession all below [illeg.] branch, Austins branch, Notoway River Assamosack swamp & Southampton County line

[302]

X 7 Jn° Adkins & Henry Moss Sen' are appointed to procession from Belches' Mill along Belches line to the Colledge line along that line line[sic] to Joseph Swamp so to the beginning

X 8 Hugh Belches & Jn° Pettway are appointed to procession all between Jones hole swamp, the Indian Swamp Notoway River & P. George County line

X 9 James Hall & Jn° Eccols are appointed to procession between Monks Neck Creek, Stoney Creek & up Sapponey to P. George County line

X 10 Thomas Sanders & Mich¹ B Malone are appointed to procession from Stoney Creek up Sapponey Creek to Sapponey Mill thence to Ephraim Parhams line so down Notoway River to the beginning

X 11 Wm Parham & Jn° Malone are appointed to procession from Ephraim Parhams to Sapponey Mill all between the line that divides this County & Dinwiddie & up Notoway River to Norris Swamp

X 12 Isham Smith & Wm Yarbrough are appointed to procession from Norris Swamp up Notoway River to the extent of this County

X 13 Joseph Wren & Flood Nicolson are appointed to procession all beween Rackoon Swamp, little Swamp & Stoakes road

X 14 Nath¹ Parham & Robert Jones are appointed to procession from the island Swamp to the old Parish lines by that line to the line that divides this County of Brunswick so to Notoway River

X 15 ~~Thomas Gravely~~ Wm Graves & Barham Moore are appointed to procession from Stoakes road between the Rackoon Swamp & Hunting Quarter Swamp so up the said Hunting Quarter Swamp

X 16 Denis Thorp & James Wyche are appointed to procession all the Lands on the South side of the three Creeks to Southampton & Brunswick lines

X 17 Matthew Wynne & Hartwell Marrable are appointed to procession from Stoakes Road up Notoway River to the Frying pan Swamp from the head of the said swamp a straight course to the Hunting Quarter Swamp

X 18 Nicholas Wilson & John Alsobrook are appointed to procession from the mouth of Coperhank Swamp along the Line that divides this County and Surry to Burchin Island road by that Road to Secaury Road by that Road to Coperhank Swamp so to the beginning

[303]

X 19 John Lamb & Simon Magy[sic] are appointed to procession all between Black Water Swamp Coperhank Swamp & the old Parish line

X 20 James Rois Jones & Nath¹ Barker are appointed to procession from the mouth of the old Town Swamp up that to the head of the Tar Kiln Branch Down to the Mill Swamp & including Jn° Gilliams formerly Tatums Land so to the new Road & then to Cooks road by that to Black Water so to the beginning

X 21 Thomas Avant & Jn° Whitehorn are appointed to procession from the mouth of the great Swamp to the three Creeks & up the three Creeks & Auter Dam swamp to Brunswick County line

X 22 Wm Dunn & George Rives are appointed to procession all between Edward Pettways line formerly Harthons lines & the Colledge line & the line divides this County & P George Joseph's & Jones hole Swamp

X 23 John Carter & Thos Bailey are appointed to procession all between Allens line Jn° Pennington line Hartwell Marrable line Stoakes road & ~~Notoway River~~ the Hunting Quarter swamp

X 24 Thomas Wren & Morrice Liles are appointed to procession between Allens line Jn° Pennington line Hartwell Marrable line Stoakes road & Notoway River

X 25 Lawrence Smith & Wm Nicolson are appointed to procession from Black Water on the old Parish line by that to Coperhank Swamp by that Swamp to the head so to the Two Kids Branch on the Mill Swamp up that to the old Town Swamp down that to Black Water Including Wm Blank Wm Nicolsons and Thos Tomlinsons Land

X 26 Lewis Dunn & Jn° Peters are appointed to procession all between Notoway River the Hunting Quarter & Rackoon Swamp along Loftins Mill path to the little Swamp down that to Rackoon Swamp so to Notoway River

X 27 Jesse & Auther Williamson are appointed to procession up Hunting Quarter Swamp to little Swamp from Loftins Mill path so to Stoakes road

X 28 Robert Tucker Jun. & John Parham are appointed to procession from the Indian Swamp to Monks Neck Creek & Notoway River & the line that divides this County and P. George County

X 29 Benj. Weathers & Stith Parham Sen. are appointed to procession from the Fla[t] Swamp up Notoway River to the mouth of Frying pan Swamp so to the head of it from thence to Threewitts so to the beginning

X 30 John Wynne & Wm Studivant Jn° are appointed to procession from the head of the Frying pan Swamp to Hunting Quarter Swamp from that to Island Branch down that to Notoway River

[304]

X 31 Nathl Nott & Jn° Judkins are appointed to procession from the North side of the Spring Swamp up the said Swamp to the county line so down the Rackoon to Stoakes Road except so much as is appoined Saml Northington and Webb Roland

X 32 Faddy Jarrett & ~~Fredk Andrews~~ Jn° Gary are appointed to procession from cooks road down the new road by that road to Black Swamp down that to Pegion Swamp up that to cookes road down that road to the beginning

X 33 Hugh Ivey & ~~Nicolas Jarrat~~ Nathaniel Dunn are appointed to procession all between Joseph and Pegion Swamp to the Governours road & Cooks road

X 34 Henry Jarrat & Nicholas Jarrett are appointed to procession from the Maj. Branch up Asemosaack Swamp to Jones Church road by that road to Secury road up that road to the Maj. Branch so to the beginning

X 35 Pettway Johnson & Nicholas Partridge are appointed to procession from Jones Church road up Asamosack & including Pettway Johnsons and thence to the road of Coperhank Swamp by that to Secaury Road by that to Jones Church road so to the beginning

X 36 George Long & Charles Long are appointed to procession all between Rackoon swamp Southampton lines Ritts road & Stoakes road

X 37 Fredk Fort & John Pate are appointed to procession from the popler Swamp near Bullocks to Wyches road by that the great Swamp by that to Southampton line by that line to the popler so to the beginning

X 38 Daniel Harwood & Charles Barham are appointed to procession between Butts road & the poplar Swamp, Southampton County line & Stoakes road

X 39 Nathl Newsom & Morledge Jones are appointed to procession from the poplar Bridge up the South Branch to Brunswick County line by that line to the great Swamp by that to Wyches road so to the beginning

X 40 Wm Roes & Abell Mabry are appointed to procession from the popler at Michael Weathers along a path that heads from Weathers to Abell Mabrys on the spring Swamp down the spring swamp to Stoakes road by that to the popler swamp so to the beginning

X 41 Wm Richardson & Nathl Felts are appointed to procession from the path that leads from Michael Weathrs to Abell Mabrys on the spring Swamp up the s^d swamp to Brunswick County line by that to the south Branch down that the fork & up the north spring to Michael Weathers

[305]

X 42 Henry Blow & Wm Brittle are appointed to procession from the south side of Seacock to the head of Lightwood Swamp & to the head of Seacock Swamp to the Branch called the winding Branch from that Branch to the head of Snake Branch down that to Seacock

Order that the Following allowances be made to the following Persons Vizt.

	£	
To Francis Hadon for Jones Stoakes	272..3.=	
To Geo Booth for Stoakes Coffin	20..	
To Peter Liles for keeping Sally Jones a orph^d Child till 25th Dec next	125..	
To Peter Liles for his Daughter	125..	
To Edward Pate for keeping Molly Jones an orphan Child	100	
To Sarah Barham for her Son	200	
To Ann Curtis for keeping 3 children	100	
To Susanna Roland for keep^g 3 d^o	125	
To Mary Felts & Martha Gilliam each £20	40	
To Sarah Hern for keeping James Hern	200	
To Mary Rogers	120	
To Robert Whitehead	300	
To Thomas Waller	120	
To Susanna Rollings	100	
To Ann Painter	100	
To Sarah Anderson	150	
To Levie Gilliam for Jones Stoakes 3 mo.	27	
Wm Stewart for Phebe Shands	150	
To James Sammons for his Son a Lunatick	120	
To Richard Adkins	150	

To Edward Smith for Mary Butler	150
To Charles Gilliam	150
To Phebe Roland for her children	150
To Mary Shell	120
To John Hill for ~~Mary~~ Suder	80
To Clk. Vestry his Salary	120
	£ 3414..3
To the Collecters Commission	[illeg.]

Ordered that Samuel Santee be exempt from pay. Parish Levie in future
Carter Land Sen. be exempt for ditto
Thos Hood   ditto   Cr
James Cockes   ditto   By 2290 Tiths at 30/
Thos Mustlewhite   ditto
Timothy Santee   ditto

[306]

At a Meeting of the Vestry of Albemarle Parish at Sussex Court House the 29th of April 1780[sic]

Present
George Booth & Jno Mason C.W.
Henry Gee, Nathl Dunn, Robt Jones, George Rives,
Jno Peters, Laurance Gibbons and Michael Blow, Gent.

Jno Mason Appeared in vestry & resind'd[sic] a C.W.

Ordered that Nathl Dunn & George Booth be appointed Church Wardens for the ensuing Year

Ordered that Jno Mason pay to Wm Graves the sum of 102 pounds for 5 Bar^{ls} Corn & 93^{lbs} Pork found Mary Rogers

Orderd that Mrs Mary Parkes be allowed 4 pounds for Boarding & Buring[sic] Wm Coggin
Ordered that the Church Wardens agree with some person for keeping of Thomas Bain
Ordered that the further allowance of 50 pounds be paid to Sarah Hern
Ordered that William Sanders and James Turner be discharged from paying their Parish Levies
Ordered that Abram Brown be paid 50 pounds for keeping Jones Stoakes 7 Months

Test   George Booth
Jno Massemburg Clk   Jno Mason   } Ch W

At a Meeting of the Vestry of Albemarle parish A Sussex Courthouse the ~~7~~ 9th of Jan. 1782
Present
George Booth & Nathl Dunn C.W.
Nathl Newson, Gray Judkins, Robt Jones, George Rives,
Jesse Williamson, Jno Mason, Wm Richardson

Or[sic] Sterling Harwell, Benjamin Lanier, Nath. Dunn are chosen Vestrymen insted of Henry Gee, Wm Mason & Flood Nicholson

Order'd that Nathl Dunn & Sterling Harwell be appointed Church wardens for one Year
Nath Dunn   C.W.
Sterling Harwell

[307]

At a Meeting of the Vestry of Albemarle Parish at Sussex Courthouse Jany 25th 1782

Present Nathl Dunn C. W., George Booth, Robt Jones, John Mason, Jesse Williamson, Nathl Newsom, Wm Richardson, George Rives & Benjn Lanier Gent.

Ordered that the Following allowances be made to the poor & Indigent untill the first of January 1783

	£	
To Mary & Eliz^h Rogers		13
To Sarah Hern for keeping James Hern 1 Year		10
To Fred^k Hern for d^o James Hern for year ensuing		10
To Nathl Holt for d^o Mary Shell from July 80 till 83		7. 10
To Charles Gilliam for 2 Years		20
To Phebe Shands......ditto		20
To Thomas Waller......ditto		20
To Hanah Prince...... 1 Yer		10
To Sarah Barham for her son 2 Years		10
To Jane Pare for 2 Years		10
To Edward Smith for Keeping Mary Butler last Year		7
To Thos Bailey for Keeping his Mother the ensuing Year		5
To Mrs Hite W^o of Wm Hite Sen for Keep. 2 Ch. 2 Years		8
To Peter Sills for Daughter 2 Years		20
To Richard Adkins 2 Years		20
To Susanna Roland & 3 Ch. 2 Years		10
To Eliz^h Roland for 2 Years		5
To Sarah Anderson 2 Years		10
To The Clk for his services 2 Years		8
To Answer Contingent charges of the parish		11.10
	£	235. =
6 PCt. for Collecting		15
Cr by 2500 Tiths at 2/. Specia a Tith	£	250

Ordered that Robt Land, Morrice Dunn, Charles Wood and Wm Sammons be exempt from paying parish levies for the future

Recorded by   Nathl Dunn Ch. War.
Jno Massenburg Clk   Ster^g Harwell

[308]

At a Meeting of the Vestry of Albemarle Parish Easter Thursday At Sussex Courthouse April 2nd 1782

Present Jno Mason, Jesse Williamson, Robt Jones, Gray Judkins, Sterling Harwell, George Rives, Nathl Dunn, Nathl Newsom & William Richardson Gent———

Col. David Mason is appoint'd a Vestry man in the room of James Jones who resind

Ordered that Sterling Harwell & Nathl Dunn be apinted[sic] Church Wardens for the ensuing Year

Wm Blunt & Jno Mason C. Wardens return^d there Acc^t to Vestry for 1776 & Order'd to be recorded

Ordered that Benjn Cooper be allowed the sum of five pounds

Dr Capt Richd Parker Shf of Sussex for the Year 1776
In Acc^t with Wm Blunt & Jno Mason C.W.

			[£] 825
To Tob^o Levied for the use Alb^e Parish 132.000 a^t 12/6			
By Paid Est. of W. Willie as P Rect.			363..8..=
d^o Revd Wm Anderson			48.13..=
Jno Nicholson	Clk		39..3..7½
Robt Magee	Clk		29.16..3
Peter Randal	D^o		29.16..3
Benjn Baird			24.15..=
Adm. Rebecca Denton			7.18..5½
James Wiggins			7..2.10
Peter Randal Sexton			12..4..=
Wm Rogers	D^o		8..8..9
Wm Longbottom	D^o		3.14.11
Wm Rogers	D^o		10.16..4
Thomas Cooper			8..1..4
Robt Whitehead			4..6..4
Franklin Clark			=..=..=
Thomas Waller			5.11..4
Thomas Moore			8..5..=
Jane Davis			3..=..=
Jno Alsobrook			1..7..=
Charles Gilliam			8..=..=
Matthew Wynne for C.C.			=.11..=
Joanna Moss			6.10..=
Jno Blow			1..=..=
James Bain			5..=..=
James Sammons			2..=..=
D^r. Tho. Teete/Lanier & Hood			9..2..=
Sarah Hunt			4..7..=
Richd Parker			=.17..6
James Wiggins			=..3..4
Lawrance Gibbons			6..=..=
Wm Hite Sen.			17..3..4
Richd Blow for Hite			1.10..=

[309]

Brought Forward			683.15.11
To Tob^o amount Brought up	825		
To Ball. due shf as P Contra			52..1..2
		£	878.11..2

	By	Edward Smith	6.10..=
		By Ben^t Barham	8.13..4
		Sarah Anderson	10..=..=
		Eliz^h Anderson	5..8..=
		John Bain	2.10..
		Walter Peter	96..4..8
		Simon Stacy	5.12..7
1779 March 10th		Wm Hite Jun.	3..=..=
To Col^o Claiborne Chargd		Jesse Hargrave	2.11.10
his Acct	5..4..7	Wm Nicholson College rent	4.14.10

	829..1..2
To Cash in full 46.16..7	
£ 52.11..2 By Your Com{n} for Collect'g	
at 6 PCt	49..0..=
	£ 878..11..2
By Ball. due Cap/ Parkerson a settlement 5th Feby 1779	52.11..2

Test   Nath Lann
Jno Massenburg Clk   Sterling Harwell C Wardens

At a Vestry held for Albemarle Parish at Sussex Court House on Wednesday the 22d January 1783.

Present Nath Dunn C Warden, David Mason, Robert Jones, George Rives, Jesse Williamson, Benjamin Lanier & John Mason Vestrymen ⎯⎯⎯⎯⎯

The following allowances were made to the poor & Indigent to the 1st January 1784 as follows. Vizt ⎯⎯⎯⎯⎯

	£	
To Mary & Elizabeth Rogers		6..
Frederick Hern for James Hern		10..
Mary Shell		5..
Charles Gilliam		10..
Phebe Shands		5..
Thomas Waller		6..
Robert Bonds for Knights child		5..
Jane Pare		5..
Wm Hite for Cottons Children		6..
Peter Liles		5..
Richard Adkins		6..
Sarah Anderson		5..
Thos Cooper for Son Benjn		5..
James Sammons for his Son a Lunatic		8..
Wm Fires for his Daughter		8..
Wm Carroll Senr		8..
Widow Owen (of Jno Owen decd for her children)		8..
Ann Meacham		8..
	[£]	102..

[310]

	£	
Amount brought over		102..
To Elizabeth Rolans		3..
		105..
The orphans of Patrick Lashley		
To the Clk for his Salary		4
To Harwell Hines P Acct for keeping & burying John Renn		2..
To Doctor Thomas Peete for Jno King P Acct		8..0..
	£	119.12..
To Shf Com P on [Acct] 4 Pct		8..8..
Cr ~~By 2800 tithables a{t}~~	£	128.10..

Cr By 2800 Tythables a{t}   4 PT or 6th Tob{o}   £ 140..
                                                                           £   12

The following Persons discharg'd from paying Parish Levy to witt
    Robert Linn, Benjn Richardson, & Joseph Morris
                         Nathl Dunn
                         Ster{n} Harwell } C.W.

At a Meeting of the Vestry of Albemarle Parish at Sussex Courthouse 22 Augt 1783

Present Sterling Harwell & Nathl Dunn C W, David Mason, George Rives, George Booth, Robt Jones, John Mason, Nathl Newsom, Jesse Williamson, Gray Judkins & William Richardson Vestry men

Col^n David Mason appointed C Warden in ~~the room~~ sted of Capt Ster^g Harwell who resind
Order'd that all the Ch. Wardens & Collectors to this Parrish of Albemarle heretofore make up their Acct according to law & return them to next Vestry on Monday 22^n Sep. & that a failer[sic] of there [sic] comply therewith will induce the Vestry to proceed with requre[sic] therein————————
Order'd that the Clk do Write to the different Ch Wardens of & Collector & give them proper notice

      David Mason
      Nathl Dunn Church Wardens

[311]

[Note pages 311 & 312 are faded and difficult to read; the names of precinct appointees were added in a different and unfamaliar handwriting in very bold ink]

At a Vestry held for Albemarle Parish at Sussex Courthouse on Mondy 22nd of December 1782

Present David Mason, George Rives, John Mason, Benjamin Laniar, William Richardson, Robt Jones and Jesse Williamson Vestrymen Wm Massenburg appointed Clerk for the Day

In pursuance of an order of Sussex Court Bearing date June Court 1783[sic] directing the processioning all the Lands in this County, the Vestry proceeded therein as to Laying of the precincts & appointment of processioners as the last appointment except as Follow & To Wit

We do appoint John Irby & Edwin Ellis to see every persons Land processioned & the Land Marks thereof renewed from Southampton County line up Assamosack Swamp to Secaury swamp up the said Swamp to the head thereof & that they assemble all the freeholders within the said precint to attend the performance thereof and that the said Irby and Ellis do make a return to the Vestry of every persons Land they have procession & of every person present at the processioning there also of whose Land they shall fail to procession and the perticular reason of such failure and that the same be done and record the first Monday in March next
X 1 ———— [Precinct numbers are noted in the original after the precinct description]
Ordered that James Turner and Howel Chappell be appointed to procession from the mouth of Secaury up the Asaimosack Swamp to the Maj^r Branck up the said Branch to Secaury Road by the said Road to Secaury Swamp by the said Swamp to the beginning
X 2 ————————
Nathan Heath and Jno Jones are appointed to procession from Cooks Bridge down Cooks Road to Joseph Swamp so to Prince George County line by that line to Black Water Swamp so to the beginning
X 3 ————————
Nathl Dunn and Henry Parsons are appointed to procession from the Governors Road to the old Parish line all Between Assamousack Swamp, Joseph Swamp & the old Parish line

X 4 ———————
James Chappell & Mich^l Bailey are appointed to procession from the old Parish line down Assamoosack Swamp to Robins Branch so down Austins Branch to Notway River up the River to the old parish line by that to the beginning

X 5 ———————
John Chappell & Richd Parker are appoitntd to procession all between Robins Branch Austins Branch Notoway River Assamosack Swamp & ye Southampton boundary

X 6 ———————
Thos Adkins & Edmund Moss are appointed to procession from Belches Mill Belches line to the Colledge line along that line to Joseph Swamp so to the beginning

X 7 ———————
Thos Ambrose & Edward Smith are appointed to procession all between Joseph Hole Seamp the Indian Swamp Notoway River & P. George County line

X 8 ———————
James Hall and John Echols are appointd to procession all between Monks Neck Creek Stoney Creek & up Saponey to Dinwiddie County line

X 9 ———————
Seymour Powell & Mich^l Malone are appoiinted to procession from Stoney Creek up Sapponey Creek to Sapponey Mill thence to Ephraim Parham's line & down Notoway River to the beginning

[312]

X 10 ———————
T Huron & Jno Malone are appointed to procession from Ephraim Parhams to Sapponey Mill all between the line that divides the County of Dinwiddie and up Notoway River to Harris Swamp

X 11 ———————
[illeg.] Smith & Law: Gibbons are appointed to procession from Harris Swamp to Notoway River to the Start of the County

X 12 ———————
[illeg.] Loftin & David Renn are appointed to procession all between Rackoon Swamp and little Swamp to Stoakes road

X 13 ———————
Wm Chambliss & Robt Jones are appointed to procession from mouth of the Hand Swamp to the old parish line by that line to the line that divides his County and Greenville so to Notoway River

X 14 ———————
Wm Graves & Barham Moore are appointed to procession from Stoakes Road between the Rackoon Swamp & Hunting Quarter Swamp so up the said Swamp

X 15 ———————
Lewis Thorp & Arthur Ross are appointed to procession all the lands on the South Side of the three Creeks to Southampton & Greenville lines

X 16 ———————
David Mason & Nathl Marrable are appointed to procession from Stoakes Road up Notoway River to the Frying Pan Swamp from the head of the said Swamp a straight course to the Hunting Quarter Swamp

X 17 ———————
Nich^ls Wilson & Jno Alsobrook are appointed to procession from the mouth of Coperhank Swamp along the line that divides this County & Surry to Burchin Island Road up that Road to Secaury Road by that road to Coperhank Swamp so to the Beginning

X 18 ———————
Wm Lamb & Simon Stacey are appointed to procession all between Black Water Swamp Coperhank Swamp & the old parish line

X 19 ———————————
James R Jones & Nath' Barker are appointed to procession from the mouth of the Old Town[?] Swamp up that to the head of the Tar Kiln Branch down to the Mill Swamp including Jn° Gilliams formerly Tatums and so to the new Road & then to Cooks road by that to Assamosack so to the beginning
X 20 ———————————
L Avent & Thos Whitehorn are appointed to procession from the mouth of the Great Swamp to the Three Creeks & up the Three Creeks & Auter Dam Swamp to Greenville County line
X 21 ———————————
Wm Dunn & Geo Rives are appointed to procession all between Edward Pettways line formely Hawthorns and Belches line & the Colledge line & the line divides P George Joseph & Jones Hole Swamp
X 22 ———————————
Henry Moss & Morris Zills are appointed to procession all between Allens line Jn° Pennington line Hartwell Marrable line & the Hunting Quarter Swamp
X 23 ———————————
[Note in the March 1780 list of precincts to be processioned there were 42 precincts listed]

[313]

[date of entries not given and this page torn on right edge]
David Mason C: Warden laid before the Vestry a Letter from Matthew Dance Ext of Wm Castleer[sic] who was one of the Securities for Jn° Woodw[ard] for the rebuilding of Nottoway Church Praying a Longer time for the completion of the same, the Vestry having taken the same under consideration have agreed to indulge him untill October next provid[ed] some person will undertake the same in a reasonable time, if not the Chur[ch] Wardens is Order'd to Prossecute a Suit against Woodward &c in Dinw[iddie] Court

Ordered It appearing to the Vestry that Mark Underwood is in Danger of Loosing one of his legs from a bad ulcer its Therefore Order'd, that David Mason Wm Richardson & Nat Newsom contract with the Surgeon to affect the cure ———————————

Order'd that David Mason & Jesse Williamson be appointed to examine as to Robert Lands family and make such provison as appears Necessary ———————————

Order'd George Rives & Nat° Dunn be appointed to examine into State & Condition [two words marked out] of Phebe Shands and if they find Five Pounds is not Sufficient to Support her infirmity then make such allowance as shall appear reasonable ————:

Order'd that George Hogwood be allow'd Three Pounds to be laid out by C. Wardens

Order'd that Sarah Smith be allow'd Three Pounds ———————————

That upon the Examination of the Parish acc^t returned by James Jones D^r to David Mason & Geo: Rives Church Wardens in the year 1775 it appears that the s^d sheriff accounted with the s^d Church Wardens for only 2632 Tr. at 24 Lb Tob. P/Poll or 3/. that upon the Examination of Acct we find that is Deficiency. of 168 Tit^e at 3/ Am^t £25..4/. and after Deducting his Com. on D° find the ballance of £23.13.10 due to the Parish which is Order'd that he Pay the same to the C. Wardens with In^t from Aug. 1775.

David Mason & George Rives CW returned their Acc^t and there remaind still a Ballance from David Mason C. Warden which he is Order'd to pay to the Church Wardens, which is £39.13/. it appearing that he render'd his Acc^t in April 1777 and not attended to by the Vestry and not liable to pay Interest ————

Wm Massenburg D^r under Geo Booth Gent Shf app^d in Vestry & render'd his Audit of collection in 1780 Levied for 1779 in which there is a ballance due from him of £2226.18 in paper Curr^y which is to be settled at 250 for 1. amounting to £8/18.0 which sum they are directed to pay the present CWardens———————————— Int to be pd of the above ball. from June 1780————————————

Geo. Booth & Jno Mason CW ret.^{d} their Acc^t including for 1779 & 1780. in Vestry in which there is a ballance of of £87 and 2 paper Acct which is to be sealed and he fin'd £14..7..4. Specie due s^d Mason which is to be p^d him with Int from the June 1780————————

[314]

John Massenburg D^r under Richd Parker ret^d his Acct. for 1777 collected in 1778 in which there is a ballance due of £93.14..1½ paper curr'y which is to be settled at 22 for 1. to be paid CWardens £4..5..2————————
John Massenburg D^r under Wm Blunt Gent Shf ret^d his Acct. for 1779 in which there is a ballance due of £1555.5..7 paper curr'y. which sum is to be settled at 75 for 1. is £20.14..8 — to be p^d to the present CW. [settle] above sums to be p^d with Int. from Dec. 1780.————————
[Ord]'d that the Churchwardens pay John Bonner the sun of Thirty two pounds eight shillings & ten pence with Interest on the same from July 19. 1779.————————
Ord'd that the Exers of Capt. J Wyche or Collectors under him, Capt. R Parker and Robert Jones CWardens Jr. Parker as of 1777 James Jones Collector. make up their Acct. before David Mason, Jesse Williamson & Geo. Rives or any 2 also Mich^l Blow & Law. Gibbonds j^r their Acct. as C Warden

          David Mason
          Nathl Dunn   CW

[315]

At a Vestry held at Sussex Court house for Albemarle Parrish the 17 day of Nov. 1784

        Present
    David Mason & Nath. Dunn C.W.
John Mason, George Booth, Robt Jones, Jesse Williamson & George Rives

Ordered that the Following allowances be made to the Poor & indigent

	To Mary Rogers Including the Expense of Buring[sic] Eliz^h Rogers	£6 ----
	James Hern	8 ----
1. ✓	Charles Gilliam	10 ----
1. ✓	Thomas Waller	6 ----
9..	Robt Bonds for Knights Ch^d	8 ----
	Peter Sills	2 ----
1.	Richard Adkins	2 ----
✓	William Carrel	4 ----
✓	Widow of Jno Owen for her Ch^d	3 ----
	Eliz^h Roland	3 ----
✓	William Sanders	3 ----
	Prudence Jones as P Acct.	4.17--
	James Cockes	8 ----
		67 17--
	Clk Vestry John Massenburg	4 ----
	To CP C^t for Collecting £105	7$^t_6$.17$_6$.-
	By 2800 tith[es]. a^t 9^d P poll	£ 105

Rob'. Jones & Richard Parker Church wardens render'd there Acc' for the Year 1773 Examined & order'd to be recorded

John Massenburg resinde's as Clk to this Vestry

Ordered that William Massenburg be appointed Clk to this Vestry in the room of John Massenburg as he has resind[sic]

      David Mason
      Nath' Dunn } Ch. Wardens

[316]

~~At a meeting of a Vestry at Sussex Court House of Albemarle Parish on Monday the 4th April 1785~~

At a meeting of the Vestry of Albemarle Parrish at Sussex Court House on Monday the 4th April 1785.

Present the following Gentlemen. Vizt.
George Rives, Nathaniel Dunn, George Booth, David Mason, William Massenburg, Benj^a Lanier and John Massenburg Gen.^{men} who being Elected Vestrymen agreeable to an Act of Assembly for Incorporateing the Protestant Episcopal Church. who having taken their Seats in Vestry do hereby Subscribe to be conformable to the Doctrine Discipline and Worship of the Protestant Episcopal Church. Viz.' [signed]
    David Mason George Booth
    Nath' Dunn   John Massenburg
    George Rives Wm Massenburg
    Benj^a Lanier

The Vestry then proceeded to Appoint a Clerke and have appointed Ben. Baird Clerk, who is to act in future.
Ordered that Colo. David Mason and Captn Nath. Dunn be appointed Church Wardens for the present year.
Ordered that Colo. David Mason and Colo. George Rives be appointed Deputies to meet in Convenison agreable to an Act. entitled an Act for Incorporateing[sic] the Protestant Episcopal Church
      David Mason
      Nath' Dunn C W

At a meeting of he Vestry of Albemarle Parish, at Nottaway Chuch on 20th September 1786. Present/
    David Mason CW George Booth
    George Rives   John Massenburg
    Benjamin Lanier Wm Massenburg &
    John Mason   Jesse Williamson

Robert Jones and John Howell Briggs have taken their seats in vestry, do subscribe to be conformable to the Doctrine, Discipline and worship of the protestant episcopal Church—

[317]

[signed] Robert Jones   John H. Briggs
   Jesse Williamson John Mason

  The vestry having taken into consideration the state of a suit now depending against John Woodward &al; and the said Woodward app^g and engaging to commence the Repairs to Nottaway Church in the space of one month from this Date, and to complete the same on or befoe the last day of July next ensuing --- The vestry are of Opinion that

the said Woodward shall be indulged til the lst mentioned period, and that David Mason be desired to instruct the Attorney prosecuting the said suit to permit it to stand continuied, until he receive Instructions, again to proceed.
Ordered that ~~Colo. David Mason and~~ Capt.ⁿ House be directed that he is to finish the Church of S¹ Marks by the last day of July next ensuing the vestry declaimining to indulge him till that time and no longer — and that Colo. David Mason make him acquainted with the Same.
                    [signed] David Mason } Church Warden

[npn (318)]

[Note this page is bound as the first page of the Parish Vestry Book, though the date follows the disestablishment of the Church of England, see date 1787. It is thought it was inscribed there to utilize the blank frontspiece of the Parish Vestry Book]

Att. A Meeting of the Overseers of the poor for the County of
Sussex on Satturday the 28th day of April 1787

Present
George Reives, Mason Harwell, Law[rence] Smith, Isham Gilliam & David Mason Gent¹

The Overseers of the poor ~~of Sussex County~~ proceeded to the Choise of a Clerk have apointed Person Wᵐson [Williamson] Clerk to the overseers of the poor of the said County They then proceeded to take Under theire Considerations an Act to amend the Act Instituted an Act to provide for the poor of the several Counties within this Commonwealth and to make the following allowances that is to say[sic]

	£	
Mary Rogers	5	----
James Hern to be paid	9	----
Thomas Waller & Wife	6	----
Robert Bonds for Henry Knight	6	----
Peter Sills	5	----
Richard Adkins to be paid Isham Gilliam	6	----
William Carrell	6	----
Elizabeth Owen (W) of Jnº for Keeping her Children	3	----
Tabitha Roland	2	----
John Prince for keeping Sarah Warrick (2) Years	7	----
Mary Shearman to be paid Isham Gilliam for Corn	3	----
Burw[ell] McLimore for keeping Ann McLimore Child	5	----
Lewis Underwood	2	----
Robert Land for the support of his Children Susanah & Isham	5	----
William Judkins for son Nicholas self & Wife	6	----
Mary Wade to be paid Mason Harwell	3	----
Mildred Johnson to be paid Law. Smith	2	10--
John Cooper to be paid ditto	5	----
Orphans of David Jones Jʳ decᵈ to be paid ditto	6	----
	£ 92	10--
Shff Comⁿ for Collect £112.10.6 aᵗ 6 Pr	6	15--
To a deposition in the hands of the shff	13	1
To the Clerk [illeg.]		
Sussex County Dr	£ 112	16--
To Amt. for the support of the poor aᵗ 6 [no further designation]		
	£ 112	16--
Contra Cr	£ 112	10--

[bottom of page torn]

APPENDIX
Will of the Reverend William Willie

Transcribed from a copy of the original will as entered in the Sussex County Will Book C, following 15th May 1777. William Willie (nephew) qualified as Executor July 1788, Sussex County Court.

May Court M D C C L xxvii

In the name of the everblesed, misterious and adorable trinity Amen William Willie of the parish of Albemarle in the county of Sussex, Clerk being in a valetudinary[sic] state; but of sound judgment and memory and considering that it is appointed for all men to die and that tho' this thing be certain, the time is uncertain do make and ordain this my last Will and testament and I do declare that I firmly and Stedfastly believe the articles of the Christian faith as contained in holy scripture and collected in that Simbol of faith, called the apostles Creed, according to their true and genuine meaning, My soul I firmly believe and hope, at its departure from the body will be received under the guardianship of holy Angels and preserved from evil spirits till its reunion with the body; which at the second coming of our blessed redeemer Jesus Christ, the righteous, will be raised up with power to behold forever the face of god in the glories of Jesus Christ, my body I desire may be buried according to the decent rites of our holy Church and as to other matters at the discretion of my Executrix hereafter mentioned. as to what Estate or worldly goods it hath pleased Almight god to bestow upon me (after my debts and funeral charges are paid) them I dispose of in manner followig Vizt--

First I give and bequeath to my Godson Willie Jones my Pebblestone sleeve buttons set in gold and a mourning ring with this motto inscribed, in Christ solo Salve,- and Circumscribed with my name, age, day and year of my decease.

Also I give unto Allen Jones, Brother of Willie, a mourning ring with the motto's aforesaid.

Also I give to my friend, James Belches a mourning ring with the above motto:

Also I give to my Nephew William [Willie], Watchmaker my plain gold sleeve buttons, my gold watch a mournig[sic] ring with the above motto's and my negroe boy Regulus.

Also I give to my Neice Jacobina [Willie] a mourning[sic] with the above motto's, a Spinnet, my negroe girl Leonora and such apparel as my Executrix shall think proper.

Also My will is that my Executrix hereafter mentioned do give to each of ten poor children in the parish of Albemarle as it now stands two years Schooling amd to enable her so to do I give her twenty five pounds to be immediately raised out of my estate.

Also I give and bequeath to my loving and dearly beloved Wife, Elizabeth, the Gold watch she now wears such of my books as she shall choose and also these following Pieces of plate Vizt: a tea pot, a milk pot, sugar dish, twelve table spoons, one Soup spoon, twelve tea spoons and tongs a scolloped waiter a Sauce boat and pint Cup without a handle and also one hundred pounds to enable her to fit up houses for her reception if she shall be obliged to remove from the place where I now live I also give to my Wife, during her natural life the use of all the rest of my estate, that I now am, or shall be possessed of or have right to at my death of what sort or quality soever. real & personal and that the word use above mentioned may be not misunderstood, my meaning is that if any money be due to me by bond, note, account &tc. or if any Salary be due, above what is sufficient to pay my debts funeral charges and legacies aforesaid — Then the money arising from such be put to interest and that interest be to the use of my wife, as aforesaid. What of my estate shall remain after the decease of my wife, I desire may be sold for money, and the money arising from such sale, together with the money at interest (if any such be) be equally divided among my Sister Isabel, Wife of James Forbes of Aberdeen, my Nephew William and my Neice Jacobina share and share alike, but if my Sister Isabel shall die before my wife, then her share to be equally divided among her children. But again if my Nephew and Neice above named should not be willing that my negroes and other estate be exposed to sale, then my Will is, that after the decease of my wife aforesaid, that the estate remaining be duly and exactly inventored and justly valued by three of the most sensible and knowing Gentlemen of the county of Sussex or elsewhere to be nominated and appointed by the said court, that the whole be equally divided between my said Nephew & Neice in such manner as they shall agree but if they cannot agree then the division to be made by the Gentlemen aforesaid and that my said Nephew and Neice do, within eighteen months after the decease of my wife pay unto my sister foresaid or her children one third part of the value of my estate aforesaid. This I think is clear and explicit and cannot be misunderstood. I also give to my wife amouring[sic] ring and those I wear.

Lastly I do hereby nominate and appoint my loving, dutiful and dearly beloved wife, Elizabeth Executrix of this my last will and testament and my Will is that she give no Security for discharging the said office (except in the case of marriage) after the decease of my wife I do appoint my Nephew & Neice aforenamed to succeed my Wife in the further execution of my Will, according to the true intent and meaning thereof and that they give proper security at my death I desire there may [be] an Inventory but no appraisement of my estate. Written with my own hand dated, signed and sealed this eighteenth day of May in the year of our lord one thousand seven hundred and seventy three and in the sixty second year of my age.

Wm Willie, {Seal}

At a Court held for Sussex County the 15th day of May 1777 the last Will and Testment of William Willie, Clerk deceased, was presented into court by Elizabeth Willie, Widow and relict of the said deceased and executrix there in named who made oath thereto as the law directs and there being no subscribing witnesses to the said Will and testament the court proceeded to take depositions in support of the validity thereof. And first Augustine Claiborne being first sworn on the Holy Evangelists of almight god deposeth and saith that he the deponent was intimately acquainted with the said Willie in his lifetime and had been upwards of thirty years and well knew his writing and doth verily believe that the writing produced as the last Will and testament of the said Willie (which he the deponent hath carefully looked over, is wholly writ by his own hand. Also Thomas Peete, being first sworn in like manner deposeth and saith that he the deponent was well acquainted with the said William Willie in his life time and also with his writing and that he hath looked over the said last Will and Testament now produced and does verily believe the whole thereof was writ by the said Willie's own hand. Also William Mason being first sworn in like manner deposeth and saith that he was well acquainted with the said William Willie in his life time and also with his hand writing and that he does verily believe that the said last Will and Testament so as aforesaid produced which he hath looked over was wholly writ by the said William Willies own hand. Also James Belches being first sworn in like manner deposeth and saith that he the deponent was intimately acquainted, both with the said Willie, in his life time, and his handwriting and that he hath carefully looked over the said last Will and Testament and doth verily believe that the same is wholly writ by the said Willies own hand. And also Hugh Belches being in like manner first sworn saith that he the deponent was intimately acquainted with the said Testator Willie in his life time and also with his writing and having looked over the Will and Testament now produced does verily believe that the same was wholly writ by the said Willies own hand. Whereupon it is ordered that the said last Will and Testament and the depositions afore taken be recorded. And on the motion of the said Elizabeth Willie who made oath as the law directs, certificate is granted her for obtaining a probate thereof in due form.

Test

William Claiborne jun' C. S. C.

Sussex County Will Book C, May 1777. pp.242-243; Sussex County Will Book D, July 1788, p. 517.

INDEX

NFN No first name given; NLN No last name given

Adam
  James 131
Adams
  Agnes 132
  Benj: 132
  Benjamin 12, 45, 97, 98, 163, 194
  John 157, 199
  Mary 177, 194
  Thomas 132, 163, 177, 206
Addams
  Benjamin 192
  John 171
Addison
  Allen 14
  Thomas 14
Adkerson
  John 157
  Thomas 157
Adkins
  Elizabeth 37
  Henry 70
  Joel 227, 228
  John 59, 60, 70, 92, 110, 112, 118, 127, 164, 174, 190, 199, 203, 221, 230
  Lewis 65
  Lucy 173, 199
  Richard 219, 228, 232, 234, 236, 240, 242
  Robert 37
  Thomas 13, 14, 35, 70, 71, 92, 114, 123, 127, 131, 169, 173, 176, 192, 199, 200, 204, 211, 229, 238
Adkinson
  John 107, 167, 198
Aldredge
  Frances 159
  Henrietta 159
Aldridge
  Francis 97, 98
  William 102, 105, 106, 134, 137
Alfin
  Jones 60
Allen
  John 12, 18
  Mr. 165
  nfn 115
  William 64, 91, 93, 94, 120, 121, 150, 169, 200, 204
Allmond
  Edward 38
Alman
  Edward 13
Alsobrook
  John 69, 73, 84, 100, 103, 115, 123, 162, 166, 182, 184, 191, 195, 203, 217, 221, 226, 230, 235, 238
  Samuel 17, 36, 69, 101, 131, 166

Alsobrook
  Thomas 16, 69, 100, 123, 134, 144
Ambrose
  Thomas 229, 238
Ambross
  Thomas 151
Anderson
  Elizabeth 214, 218, 235
  James 29, 30, 34, 52, 78, 79, 82
  Mr. 72
  Robert 228
  Sarah 232, 234-236
  William 235
Andrew
  Fed 158
Andrews
  David 18, 95
  Frederick 171, 184, 192, 198, 231
  Fredrick 222
  Henry 43, 119, 197, 206
  John 21, 22
  Stephen 203, 224
  Willam 139
  William vi, 13, 43, 111, 133, 142, 156, 169, 200, 219, 223
Andrus
  Benjamin 72
  David 37
  William 89
Armstrong
  Joseph 111, 118, 136, 141, 145
  Robert 137, 204
Arnold
  Elisabeth 48
  Elizabeth 33, 46, 51, 57
Arrington
  Benjamin 175, 219
Atkins
  Elizabeth 18
  John 35, 44, 89, 202
  Lewis 65
  Patty 215
  Robert 18
  Thomas 44, 89
  William 14
Avant
  Thomas 231
Avary
  Cyril 226
  Richard 13, 156
Avent
  John 8, 12, 27, 45, 56, 58, 69, 125
  L 239
  Peter 27, 45, 56, 58, 69, 97, 125, 132
  Thomas 1-4, 7, 11, 19, 21, 22, 24, 26, 33, 45, 47, 49, 52, 54, 69, 79, 81, 87, 88, 97, 98, 101, 103, 125, 139, 175

Avery
  Richard 27, 43, 56, 85, 89, 116, 133, 156, 169
Axam
  Maca 149
Axum
  Michael 171
Bagley
  George 127
  John 141, 158, 177
  Peter 27, 56, 59, 71, 84, 121
  William 71
Bailey
  Anselm 18, 37
  Barnabas 220
  Barnaby 149
  Edmund 197, 220
  Elizabeth 182, 213
  Joseph 220
  Michael 229, 238
  Philip 36
  Robert 101, 122
  Thomas 93, 121, 200, 222, 231, 234
  Umphry 123
  Walter 18
Bailis
  Humphrey 184, 203
  Humphry 100
Baily
  John 149
Bain
  James 67, 235
  John 57, 77, 78, 80, 81, 86, 87, 102, 105, 108, 117, 134-136, 141, 145, 147, 224, 235
  Thomas 233
Baines
  John 203
Bains
  John 203
Baird
  Benjamin 213, 225, 235, 241
  John 54, 71, 83, 116, 123, 164, 203
  Mr. 193
  Reubin 71, 116, 127, 128
  Rubin 164, 206
  Stephen 164, 203
  William 164
Baker
  James 38, 61
Baley
  Barnaby 149
  Benj. 149
  Edmund 149
  Elijah 149
  Elizabeth 187
  Joseph 149
  Philip 12
  Robert 171
  Walter 7, 26

Balie
  Phillip 62
  Thomas 62
Balis
  Humphrey 95, 179, 181, 189
  Humphry 161
Ball
  Benjamin 42
  James 109
  [-?-] 9
Banc
  James 149, 193, 208, 211, 213,
    215, 216
  John 160, 179, 183, 187, 193,
    208, 211, 213
  William 188, 193, 208, 213
Banes
  John 126, 155
Banks
  Burril 172
  Burwel 129, 130
  Burwell 153
  James 14, 17, 35, 42, 66, 91, 103
Barham
  Benjamin 206, 209, 213, 218,
    235
  Charles 167, 192, 206, 222, 232
  Sarah 232, 234
  Thomas 167, 181, 195
  William 205
Barker
  Benjamin 46, 121
  Drury 162, 205
  Henry 13, 59, 121, 162, 205
  James 121, 162, 205
  Jehu 60, 96, 192, 201
  Jehugh 165
  Jesse 205
  Joel 16, 18, 23, 24, 28, 29, 42,
    46, 48, 49
  John 13, 27, 39, 59, 84, 96, 101,
    108, 115, 121, 122, 149
  Joseph 16, 108, 147, 159
  Nathaniel 121, 162, 191, 205,
    221, 230, 239
  William 38
Barlow
  Bethia 160
  Nathaniel 160, 177
  nfn 110
  Richard 11, 69, 98, 137, 148,
    159, 160, 175, 195
  Samuel 87, 89
  Thomas 25
  William 11, 17, 22, 23, 25, 36,
    125
Barnes
  James 223
  John 97
Barns
  James 132, 142, 164, 192, 198,
    206
  John 96, 98, 119, 132, 164, 167
Barr
  Ann 180, 183
  Anne 177

Barradall
  Mr 4
Barram
  William 150
Barron
  Edmund 87
Bartley
  nfn 137
Bass
  Arthur 131
  James 45, 98
  John 11, 45, 77
  Samuel 45, 72, 85, 88
  William 69
Batt
  John 224
Battail
  Thomas 109
Battle
  Charles 17, 27, 41, 55, 70, 84,
    100, 103, 115, 131, 154, 165,
    178, 206
  Hartwell 219
  John 8, 11, 27, 41, 44, 55, 61, 84,
    96-98, 107, 110, 115, 132,
    164, 175, 206
  Thomas 11, 61, 95, 119, 132, 138
  William 97, 98
Battles
  Charles 205
Batts
  Bartholomew 171
  John 204
Bay
  Susannah 217
Bayley
  Elizabeth 193, 195
  Joseph 197
  Thomas 165, 191
Baylis
  Humphrey 149, 197
Beddingfield
  Thomas 4, 13, 29
Bedingfield
  Nathaniel 102, 106
Belches
  Hugh 209, 217, 221, 223, 230,
    244
  James 243, 244
Belighton
  Elizabeth 218
Bell
  Benjamin 69, 103
  Burrel 71
  Burrell 89
  Hannah 70
  James 70, 89, 131, 158, 192, 205,
    222
  John 14, 27, 44
  Landon vi
  Phebe 71
  Sillvanus 201
  Silvanus 118
  Thomas 26, 54
  William 67, 101

Bellamy
  Mrs 95
  William 123
Bellemy
  John 77
Belsches
  Hugh 173, 178, 190, 199
  James 164, 203
  Mr. 178, 212
Belsheres
  Hugh 123
  James 123
  nfn 106
Bendall
  Isaac 168
Bendol
  Isaac 199
Bendoll
  Isack 220
Berkley
  James 137
Berriman
  John 166, 191, 200
Berryman
  John 129, 166, 222
  Beryman
  John 152
Biard
  John 71
Biggins
  Sarah 62, 125
Bigins
  John 171
Bilbro
  James 204
  Thomas 137
Bilbrow
  James 211
Bird
  Jones 46
  Rebecca 78, 80-82, 86, 102, 105,
    107, 134
  Rebeckah 57
  Robert 17
Birdson
  Franklin 213
Birdsong
  Elisabeth 148, 226
  Elizabeth 177, 180-182, 187,
    193-195, 208, 213, 218
  John 67, 149, 171
  Mrs 211
  Widow 140, 142-144
Bishop
  Avires 205
  Harmon 162
  Hermon 205
  John 89, 96, 132, 133, 156, 164,
    169
  Nathan 126, 168, 199
  William 12, 36, 61, 93, 115, 126,
    148, 202
Bland
  Colonel 12, 45
  Theodorick 14, 68

Surry and Sussex Counties, Virginia, 1742-1786   247

Blank
  William 231
Blanks
  David 103, 129
Blaton
  Elizabeth 197, 211
  Joseph 158, 188
  Widdow 213
Blizard
  Charles 204
Blow
  Henry 67, 83, 114, 131, 149, 162, 189, 223, 232
  John 216, 235
  Majr. 211
  Mical 112, 113, 118, 134, 136, 139, 142, 144, 147, 148, 159, 179, 187-189, 225, 227
  Michael 149, 182, 185, 195, 209, 212, 213, 215-217, 219, 220, 223, 233, 240
  Mr. 138
  Richard 7, 20, 24, 26, 28, 54, 58, 67, 77, 111, 112, 211, 228, 235
Blunt
  Captain 9
  Richard 1-4, 7, 13, 16, 20-23, 28, 42, 119, 170, 186, 189, 191, 196, 201, 206, 209, 212-215, 219
  William 42, 126, 155, 179, 186, 188, 189, 191, 196, 197, 201, 206-209, 211, 214-217, 219, 220, 223, 225, 234, 235, 240
Bobbit
  John 127, 157, 172
  Thomas 93
Boling
  Alexander 65, 89, 128
  Elizh 170
  Robert 63, 68, 122
Bolling
  Alexander 15
  Robert 15, 37, 39, 40, 95
Bonds
  Robert 228, 236, 240, 242
Bonner
  John 39, 68, 90, 129, 152, 166, 240
  Mary 170
Booch
  John 212
Booge
  Mr. 2
Booth
  George 37, 39, 65, 68, 89, 90, 128, 129, 152, 153, 166, 170, 190, 215, 217, 219, 221, 226, 228, 229, 232-234, 237, 240, 241
  Thomas 75, 219
Bottoms
  Abraham 205
Bowen
  John 89

Bowling
  Alexander 152
Bradley
  Henry 95, 149, 197
  John 37, 62, 92, 95, 97, 132
  William 37, 95, 134, 149
Bradly
  Parsons 68
  William 18
Brandon
  D 138
Brewer
  Thomas 12, 61, 93
Brian
  Thomas 202
Bridges
  Thomas 36, 129
  William 15, 40, 44
Brigg
  Howell 155, 161, 165
Brigges
  Howel 90
Briggs
  Capt. 72, 73, 195
  Captain 138
  Charles 177
  George 7, 18, 26, 54, 58, 67, 83, 101, 103, 122, 149, 171
  Gray 60, 82, 87, 88, 95, 139, 173
  Howel 2, 24, 27, 28, 42, 51, 56, 58, 60, 63, 75, 76, 80-82, 86-88, 95, 100, 106-111, 113, 116, 118, 122, 123, 125, 126, 128, 133, 134, 136, 139, 140, 144-147, 224
  Howell 7, 16, 18, 20, 22, 26, 37, 39, 40, 42, 44, 46, 48, 81, 96, 104, 148-150, 155, 157, 170, 179, 182, 184-186, 197, 201, 203
  John 100, 241
  Majr. 211
  Mary 60
  Mr 4
  Nathaniel 18, 67, 101, 114, 122, 149, 162, 171, 189, 220, 229
  nfn 138
  Thomas 43, 65, 80, 98, 132
  William 7, 13, 27, 60, 96, 109, 119, 122, 135, 170, 201
Brittle
  William 67, 149, 179, 189, 223, 227, 232
Broadnax
  Edward 37, 89
  Henry 129
  William 65, 128, 152, 171
Broadrib
  Thomas 219
Broadribb
  Widow 144
Broadrig
  Thomas 126
Brooks
  Peter 97

Browder
  Isham 105, 106
Brown
  Abraham 43, 70, 89, 124, 131, 200, 205
  Abram 157, 176, 233
  Henry 14, 44, 89, 118, 131
  James 40
  Lewis 90, 129, 152, 153
  Mary 41, 44, 70, 95
  Thomas 137
  William 11, 67, 118, 149, 175, 201, 204-206
Browne
  Abraham 65
Bryan
  Edward 67
  Thomas 68, 149
Buckner
  Edward 42, 69, 103, 129
Bullock
  Amy 132
  Benjamin 205
  Jeremiah 12, 45, 72, 97, 98
  John 98
  Lemuel 181, 184
  Martha 95
  Robert 11, 41, 61, 167, 206
  Samuel 132, 164, 180
Bulluck
  Charles 132
  John 132
  Samuel 132
Burge
  Matthew 199
Burgess
  John 137
Burgis
  Thomas 58
Burgiss
  Thomas 74, 76
Burnet
  Thomas 15
Burns
  James 229
Burrough
  Thomas 35
Burrow
  Elisabeth 130
  Thomas 91, 172
  William 91, 153, 172
Burrows
  Thomas 66
Bush
  John 194, 196, 211, 218
  Nicholas 18
Busshau
  James 115
Butler
  George 11
  John 11
  Mary 213, 218, 233, 234
  Thomas 14, 22, 35, 42, 55, 66, 69, 84, 91, 103, 129, 130, 153, 172

Cain
  James 8, 14, 17, 27, 35, 66, 91,
    130, 153, 159-161, 172
  Peter 91, 131, 153, 172
  William 219
Capel
  Thomas 41, 100, 154, 165, 205
Capell
  John 150
  Sarah 110, 112, 118, 140, 143,
    144, 148
  Thomas 70, 131, 148
  Widow 110
Capewell
  Sarah 108
Caponell
  Thomas 17
Capp
  William 37
Careless
  Mathew 219
Cargail
  John 215, 217
Cargil
  John 158
Cargill
  John 18, 64, 94, 120, 151, 161,
    168, 169, 178, 198, 200, 204
  Mr. 161
  nfn 38
Carlile
  Samuel 11, 45
Carlisle
  William 29
Carrel
  Jesse 149
  Nathan 149, 197
  Robert 37
  Thomas 149
  William 95, 149, 159, 160, 197,
    240
Carrell
  William 242
Carril
  John 25
Carrill
  William 18, 37
Carroll
  William 236
Carter
  Agnes 140, 142, 143, 146, 148,
    159, 160, 178
  Agnis 178
  Edward 134, 136, 137
  James 11, 14, 41, 61, 70, 87, 95,
    110
  John 70, 91, 222, 226, 228, 231
  Mrs. 161
  Richard 1, 7, 16, 35, 66, 90, 121,
    150, 174
  Widow 160
Carthorn
  nfn 115
Caudle
  William 228

Chairman
  Ebenezar 176
Chambliss
  William 228, 238
Chamlis
  James 224
Chappel
  James 4, 28, 157
  Samuel 38
Chappell
  Benj. 150
  Benjamin 169, 204
  Elisabeth 94
  Elisha 64
  Elizabeth 120
  Henry 170
  Howel 125, 237
  Howell 150, 189, 202, 220, 229
  James 3, 7, 18, 19, 21-24, 26, 33,
    38, 39, 46-49, 51-54, 57-60,
    64, 77-82, 85-90, 94,
    101-109, 112-114, 116-118,
    120, 125, 131, 133-137,
    139-142, 145-148, 150, 155,
    169, 170, 202, 204, 205, 221,
    229, 238
  John 94, 114, 120, 150, 151, 168,
    190, 198, 221, 229, 238
  Roger 150
  Samuel 18, 107, 125
  Thomas 64
Claiborne
  Augustine 22, 34, 44, 53, 54, 57,
    58, 62, 79, 81, 86, 88, 92,
    101, 104, 107, 108, 110, 111,
    113, 116, 118, 125, 139, 141,
    145, 146, 148, 150, 158, 162,
    171, 174, 179-183, 185-189,
    194, 196, 198, 201, 206, 208,
    209, 212-215, 217, 220, 223,
    225, 226, 244
  Coll 235
  Coll: 138
  Herbert 199
  William 244
Clairborne
  Augustine 161
Clanton
  Drewry 204
  John 13, 89, 133, 156, 169, 226
  Mary 131, 154, 205
  Nathanel 58
  Nathaniel 13, 43, 56, 70, 85, 100,
    165
  Richard 13, 43
Clapp
  Thomas 37
Clark
  Franklin 180-182, 187, 193-195,
    208, 211, 216, 218, 226, 235
  John 73, 150, 174, 198
  Joseph 57, 76, 179, 182, 184,
    188, 193, 195, 211, 217, 226
Clary
  Benj. 149
  Benjamin 95, 189, 197

Clary
  Bird 149, 161
  Elizabeth 197
  James 149, 197, 220
  Mary 197
  Thomas 18, 95, 149
Clement
  Thomas 168
Clements
  Benjamin 18
  Thomas 151, 198
Clifen
  Charity 216
Clifton
  Charity 193, 211, 218
  John 128, 155
  William 40, 41, 163, 200
Clinch
  Joseph 15
  Mr. 74
Coates
  Mary 87
Coats
  John 17, 39, 63, 64
  Mary 50, 59, 74
Cocke
  Benja: 128
  Benjamin 126, 155
  Mr. 73
  Richard 118, 157, 167, 168, 198
  Thomas 2
Cockes
  James 233, 240
Cocks
  James 176, 202
  John 173
  Rubin 174
  William 173, 176, 202
Coffin
  Stoakes 232
Coggin
  William 233
Coles
  Mary 33
Collier
  John 14
  Samson 206
Collins
  William 198
Colson
  William 181, 195, 206, 211
Colston
  William 160, 161, 177
Concllon
  William 107
Conelly
  William 198
Connally
  William 105, 106
Con["]
  Alexs 9
Cook
  Foster 162, 174
  Henry 205
  James 121, 137, 162, 171, 174,
    219

Surry and Sussex Counties, Virginia, 1742-1786

Cook
  Joseph 150
  nfn 137
  Reuben 13, 16, 66
  Reuhin 59, 61, 64, 90, 96, 121, 150
  Richard 150, 163, 169, 202, 204
  Rubin 150, 162
  William 16, 26, 54, 58, 59, 63, 66, 71, 80, 83, 90, 95, 114, 121, 150, 158
Cooke
  Reuben 38
Coop
  Thomas 195
Cooper
  Benjamin 235, 236
  James 11, 41, 61, 131, 154, 165, 190, 205, 221
  John 242
  Thomas 28, 48, 50, 74, 86, 119, 158, 161, 170, 177-179, 181-183, 187, 193, 201, 208, 210, 212, 216, 217, 225, 235, 236
Cornet
  George 11, 41, 95
  Jonas 205
Cornett
  Joel 167
  Jonah 167
Cornit
  George 61
Cornwell
  John 149
  Samuel 18, 37
Cotes
  Joseph 96
  Mary 48
Cotten
  David 78
Cotton
  Joshua 197, 209-211, 213, 218
  nfn 218, 236
  Richard 202
Cox
  Lenda 50
  Widow 48, 74
  William 117, 142, 143, 146, 147
Cragg
  William 14, 44, 70, 118
Credle
  Henry 215
Cripps
  William 18
Crosland
  Edward 134, 137, 140, 143
  Frances 24
  Mary 50
  Widow 74
Cross
  Edward 191, 203
Crossland
  Frances 33
Cryer
  William 130

Culham
  Thomas 216
Cullam
  Elizabeth 223
  Thomas 216, 217
Cullum
  Fredrick 105, 109
  Israel 60
  Thomas 60, 79, 82, 85, 88, 96, 104-106, 109, 110, 122, 145, 178-181, 184, 185, 187, 193, 195, 208, 211
Cumboe
  nfn 95
Cureton
  Thomas 156
Curtis
  Ann 232
  Churchwell 128
  John 15, 37, 55, 65, 75, 84, 89, 114, 128, 152, 153, 166, 213, 218
Curtland
  Thomas 172
Dabney
  William 219
Dain
  Mary 66
Dameron
  Joseph 153
Dance
  Matthew 239
Dancy
  William 128
Dansey
  William 44
Danzy
  William 88
Darling
  John 71
David
  Thomas 176
Davis
  Edward 176
  Etheldred 171
  George 38
  Hugh 14
  Jane 226, 235
  John 17, 35, 66, 73, 224
  Mr 9
  Nathaniel 67, 101, 122
  Priscilla Shepherd vi
  Rebeccah 160
  Sarah 48, 49, 51, 78, 80
  Thomas 33, 47, 80, 194, 200, 211, 217
  Virginia Lee Hutcheson vii
Dean
  Mary 16
Deford
  Edmund 46
Delahay
  Mary 4, 9
Delehay
  Charles 67
  John 216

Delehay
  Thomas 217
  William 216
Delehays
  Mary 59
Delihay
  Charles 90, 94, 130, 180, 184, 194, 211
  John 181, 187, 195
  Mary 59, 102
  William 180, 181, 184, 187, 193-195
Deloch
  Thomas 18
Deloncy
  Lewis 2
Delony
  Mr. 23
Delshay
  Mary 87
Dempsey
  nfn 42
  Patrick 14, 42
Dennies
  Joseph 202
Dennis
  John 69
  Joseph 173, 224
Dento
  John 80
Denton
  John 81, 86, 102, 106
  Joseph 92, 106, 127, 160, 179, 182, 187, 193, 196
  Rebecca 208, 225, 235
  Rebeccah 213
Dickens
  Joshua 91
  Thomas 200
Dickings
  Alexander 12
  Rosanna 139
  Thomas 139
Dickins
  Alexander 36
Dilihay
  William 161
Dillahay
  Mary 78
  William 211
Dillard
  John 125
Dillelay
  Charles 38, 210
Dilliha
  Charles 154
Dillihay
  John 166
Dinkins
  Ann 121
  Lydia 91, 121
  Rosannah 111
  Thomas 61
Dixon
  Mr. 184

Doake
  Samuel 86
Dobey
  Peter 34
  Robert 13, 34
  William 13, 34
Doby
  John 125, 145, 159, 160, 162, 201
  Joshua 162
  Nathaniel 204
  Peter 16, 60, 120, 126
  Rob 62
  Robert 16, 62, 92, 125, 162, 201
  William 62, 115, 125, 132
Dortch
  John 45
Dowdy
  Thomas 107, 163, 164
Drake
  Lazarus 94, 120, 151, 198
  Lazerus 168
  Samuel 85
Drew
  Mary 82, 110, 112
Duncan
  Elisabeth 48
  Elizabeth 51, 74
Dunkin
  Nathaniel 164, 192, 203
Dunn
  John 99, 119, 183, 206
  Lewis 206, 222, 231
  Morrice 234
  Morris 132, 163
  Nathaniel 204, 224, 226, 228, 229, 231, 233, 234, 236, 237, 239-241
  Thomas 13, 14, 43, 60, 76, 95, 119, 148, 175, 176
  William 71, 125, 162, 201, 214, 222, 229, 231, 239
Durgn
  Nathaniel 204
Eacols
  Edward 15, 37, 65
  John 221
Earwood
  Catharine 117
  Catron 180
  John 88, 104, 106, 108, 109
  Mrs. 161
  nfn 138
Eckels
  John 170
Eckles
  Edward 40, 88
  John 89, 128, 152
  William 152
Ecols
  Edward 157
  John 230, 238
  William 127
Edmund
  John 68
  William 83

Edmunds
  David 8, 18, 26
  J. 170
  John 18, 87, 94, 104, 119, 120, 126, 144, 146, 151, 168, 170, 185, 198, 210
  Joseph 155
  Thomas 201
  William 8, 18, 26, 55, 58, 94, 107, 120, 151, 168, 198
Edwards
  John 13, 126, 151, 199
  Nathaniel 17
  Sarah 173, 199
Elbeck
  Mountfort 16
Eldredge
  William 189
Eldridge
  Judith 16
  Mr 4
  Mr. 72
  Thomas 23, 35, 59
  W. 174
  William 40, 66, 71, 90, 93, 127, 174
Eldrige
  William 121
Ellbeck
  Munford 34
Ellet
  William 66, 91
Ellis
  Benjamin 16, 42
  Caleb 203, 224
  Edward 12, 13, 45
  Edwin 229, 237
  John 4, 9, 45, 72, 137, 195
  Joseph 67, 101, 114, 122, 123, 149, 162, 171, 181, 189, 220
  Joshua 38, 67, 90
  William 126, 155, 156, 203, 224
Ellit
  nfn 69
Epes
  Daniel 57
Eppes
  Edward 8, 16, 35, 59, 83, 92, 114, 127
  Francis 13, 34, 94, 130
Epps
  Daniel 201
  Edward 173, 199
  Frances 154, 174, 201
  James 199
Eskredge
  Thomas 193, 196
Eskridge
  Thomas 187, 200, 213
Evans
  Abram 17
  James 12
  Sarah 48, 74, 106
  William 7, 26
Even
  William 158

Evens
  Benjamin 176, 200
  Sarah 198
  William 171
Evins
  Sarah 50, 59
  William 54, 58
Evinton
  Edward 137
Exum
  Mical 137
  nfn 137
Ezel
  Joseph 72
  Thomas 119
  Timothy 119
Ezell
  George 167
  Infant 173
  Isham 124, 176, 200
  James 199, 220
  John 44, 45, 167
  Joseph 70, 97, 98, 118, 132
  Mary 142, 146, 160
  nfn 185
  Thomas 45, 70, 167, 198, 227
  Timothy 16, 17, 34, 35, 39, 59, 78, 92, 99, 111, 124, 127, 143, 145-147, 151, 160
  William 9, 43, 44, 64, 65, 84, 115, 123, 160, 176
Ezill
  Timothy 63
  William 55
Ezzel
  William 27
Facecy
  Edward 51
Facey
  Edward 58
Facie
  Edward 109
Facy
  Edward 107, 110, 134, 143
Farrington
  Amy 153
  Edward 17
  John 35
  Mary 130
  Robert 8, 17, 19, 20, 22, 24, 27, 29, 35, 38, 46, 91
Farrinton
  John 66, 91
  Mary 117
  Robert 51, 55, 57, 66, 67, 77, 80, 81, 84, 86, 90, 101, 105, 117, 134
Fason
  Henry 149
Fauson
  Benjamin 220
Fawn
  James 168
Fedder
  Benjamin 163

Surry and Sussex Counties, Virginia, 1742-1786   251

Feild
  Ann 149
  Anne 111
Feilds
  Anne 148
Felps
  Frances 61
  Francis 11, 41
  Thomas 14
  William 67
Felt
  William 122
Feltes
  Frances 70
Felts
  Alice 110
  Alse 109
  Burrell 201
  John 119, 167, 198
  Mary 159, 228, 232
  Nathaniel 44, 70, 95, 118, 119, 167, 182, 184, 187, 192, 198, 216, 223, 232
  Richard 43, 102, 119, 206
  Thomas 44, 70, 85, 116, 118, 119, 192, 201, 223
  William 101, 149, 171
Fennon
  Mr 218
Ferrington
  Amy 166, 172
  John 172
Field
  Ann 95
  Jane 105
Fields
  Green 180-182, 195
Fig
  Benj. 150
Figg
  Benjamin 121, 171
Figgure
  Bartholomew 16
Figgures
  Batholomew 7
Finia
  Alexandria 61
  John 61
Finney
  Alexander 38
Finnia
  Alexander 14
  John 175
Finnie
  Alexander 96, 121, 150
  Elisabeth 163
  John 202
  Mary 209, 213, 216
Finning
  Mr 211
Fire
  William 154
Fires
  William 236
FitchPatrick
  Joshua 29

Fitzpatrick
  Joshua 46, 72
  Richard 16, 46, 72, 100
Fleming
  Addam 217
Floide
  Thomas 124
Flood
  Ardrich 132
  Charles 87
  Fredrick 132
Flowers
  Simon 75
Floyd
  Thomas 124
Forbes
  Isabel 243
  James 243
Ford
  Fredrick 222
Fort
  Frederick 164, 206, 232
  Holloday 201
  John 131, 157
Four
  Parham 142
Foy
  Hugh 123
Freeman
  Agness 89, 90
  Arthur 38, 43, 68, 70
  Edward 44, 98
  Fed 170
  Hamlin 129, 131
  Henry 27, 38, 39, 68, 70, 100, 131, 154, 165, 205
  Jesse 65
  Joel 90
  John 15, 37, 51, 73, 88, 128, 149, 152, 166, 170, 171, 190
  Jones 90, 129, 152, 166
  Josiah 90, 129, 152, 166
  Nathan 89, 152
  William 15
Garland
  John 170
Garrison
  Benjamin 125
Gary
  John 158, 171, 198, 227, 229, 231
Gearton
  James 37
Gee
  Cap: 110
  Capt 177
  Charles 16, 66, 90, 121, 150, 173, 174, 199
  Henry 121, 127, 135, 137, 146, 158, 175, 179, 180, 182, 186-188, 197, 215, 223-226, 229, 233

Gee
  James 2-4, 7, 16, 19-24, 26, 28, 33, 46-48, 52-54, 57, 58, 66, 71, 77, 79, 81, 82, 86-88, 90, 101, 103-105, 107-111, 113, 118, 134, 140
  Jesse 174
  John 64
Genings
  John 70
George
  Lord 60
  Wilson 219
Gesswit
  Anne 159
Gesswitt
  Ann 193
  Anne 112
Gibb
  Matthew 9
Gibbens
  Lawrence 68
Gibbeons
  Lawrence 112
Gibbins
  John 155
Gibbons
  Capt 142
  John 126
  L. 217
  Laurance 233
  Laurence 212-217
  Lawrance 172, 180, 186-188, 235
  Lawrence 14, 42, 103, 113, 118, 129, 133, 134, 136, 139, 141, 143, 144, 147, 184, 206, 207, 209, 210, 229, 238, 240
  Major 142
  Mr 142, 211
  Mr. 138
  Thomas 203, 224
Gibbs
  Matthew 13, 20, 21, 34, 62, 92, 126
Gilbert
  Hannah 13
  James 205
  Martha 75
  William 119, 170
Giles
  Morris 228
Gillam
  Burrell 13
  Burwell 43
  Charles 13, 20, 22, 25, 29, 43, 46, 48, 51, 57, 78, 213, 223
  Elizabeth 213
  Fibby 223
  Hincha 46
  Hinchea 25, 29, 51, 56-58, 78
  Hinchia 13, 20, 22, 27
  Jesse 65
  John 13
  Sarah 17, 43
  Thomas 13
  William 27, 55

252   The Vestry Book of Albemarle Parish

Gillan
  Martha 216
Gilliam
  Anselin 119
  Anselm 43
  Anslum 226
  Burrell 116, 119
  C. 217
  Charles 80, 82, 86, 119, 145, 195, 208, 211, 216, 217, 226, 228, 233-236, 240
  Drewy 119
  Edmund 119, 220
  Gilliam 64
  Hansel 124
  Hichia 201
  Hinchea 80, 82, 85, 86, 116, 119, 121, 169
  Hinchey 205, 206
  Hinchie 162
  Isham 205, 242
  John 137, 162, 205, 220, 239
  Levi 41, 205
  Levie 70, 232
  Levy 100, 131
  Lucy 212
  Markus 202
  Martha 213, 232
  Patty 195, 211, 217
  Samuel 204
  Thomas 119
  William 8, 38, 58, 67, 68, 90, 94, 122, 129, 130, 201, 204, 224
Gillium
  Anselm 191
  Anslem 206
  Austin 222
  Charles 182, 183, 187, 193, 206
  Edmund 206
  Hinchia 170
  Isham 157
  John 191, 221, 222
  Levi 165
  Levy 154, 180, 181
  Patty 178, 180-182, 184, 187, 193, 206
  Sarah 206
  William 172, 174
  Willium 154
Gillum
  Hinchia 43
  James 39
  Jesse 43
  William 39
Glover
  Joseph 220
  Robert 62, 106
Glovier
  James 155, 157, 172
  Jones 163
  Joseph 197
Goff
  David 88, 109
  Davis 102
  Sarah 88, 102, 109
  Susanna 102

Goff
  William 88
Goging
  William 137
Goldey
  Dr. 72
Golightly
  John 11
Golikely
  Christopher 41, 44
Golithely
  Christopher 40
Goodwin
  John 16, 66, 71
  nfn 127
Goodwynn
  Thomas 90
Gordin
  John 68
Granthum
  James 174
Gravely
  Thomas 230
Graves
  Benjamin 204, 213
  David 200, 227
  Soloman 176
  Solomon 37, 63, 65, 123, 160, 178, 190, 200, 221
  William 137, 228, 230, 238
Greehill
  nfn 128
Green
  Anne 46
  Ben 228
  Burrel 13, 68, 152, 174
  Burrell 90, 94, 130
  Burrill 64
  Burwel 154
  Burwell 166
  Burwil 204
  Burwill 224
  Edward 86
  Fed 172
  Fred: 130
  Frederick 66, 153, 172
  Fredrick 91
  Lewis 13
  Mary 24, 29, 48
  Nathaniel 38, 46, 55, 67
  Peter 2, 4, 8, 19, 20, 22, 27, 91, 108, 114, 117, 130, 135, 136, 141, 145, 147, 153, 160, 172, 179, 181, 183, 184, 187, 190, 193, 208
  Robert 40
  Tad: 130
  William 38, 94, 137, 157, 158, 174, 204, 224
Greene
  Burrell 129
Gresswett
  Ann 79
Gresswit
  Anne 178
  Thomas 18

Gresswitt
  Amey 211
  Ann 74, 143, 144, 182, 195, 211
  Anne 110, 185, 187
  Mrs 211
  Thomas 101
Greswit
  Ann 50, 180
Greswitt
  Ann 184
Griffin
  Edward 125
  Richard 1, 18, 38
Griffis
  Edward 45, 69, 175
  Thomas 175
  Travis 61, 198
Grosswitt
  Anne 140
Groves
  John 16, 37
Gunn
  Benjamin 227
Gus
  John 64
Guthry
  Daniel 37
Haddon
  Frances 171
  Francis 199
Hadon
  Francis 232
Hail
  Benj. 132
Hairgrove
  John 206
Hale
  John 38
Hall
  James 221, 230, 238
  nfn 38
  William 18, 64, 94, 96, 121
Ham
  Frances 177
Hamelton
  Marmaduke 125
  William 62
Hamilton
  Marmaduke 11
Hamlin
  Stephen 18, 54, 58, 67, 83, 101, 103, 122, 149, 171, 185
Hancock
  Anthony 126
  Benj. 149
  Benjamin 95, 197, 203
  Clement 27, 34-36, 56, 59, 61, 62, 85, 92, 93, 127
  John 54, 58, 95, 197
  Mary 149, 197
  Nicholas 95, 197
  Nicolas 149
  Robert 34, 35, 59, 61, 85, 92, 93
  Thomas 197
  William 26, 37, 83, 113, 122, 149, 168, 199, 206

Surry and Sussex Counties, Virginia, 1742-1786 253

Handcock
  John 37
  Joseph 37
  William 7
Handcocke
  Clement 12, 16
  John 18
  Robert 16
  William 18
Hardy
  John 173, 202
Hargrave
  Augustine 18, 37
  Elizabeth 73
  Jesse 171, 235
  John 43, 67, 70, 95, 100, 119
  Joseph 18, 37, 122, 149
Hargrove
  John 60, 204, 220
Harison
  Thomas 62
Harper
  Edward 65, 128, 129, 152, 170
  William 15, 35, 37, 39, 65, 66, 68, 90
  Wyat 91, 172
  Wyatt 37
Harrington
  Robert 48
Harris
  Edward 97
  William 119, 167
Harrison
  Benja: 122, 123
  Benjamin 12-14, 16, 18, 35, 36, 42, 43, 61, 66, 71, 89-91, 94, 101, 103, 164
  Captain 144, 195
  Charles 149
  Coll: 112
  Colonel 44, 68
  Henry 60, 112, 113, 116, 119, 120, 133, 141, 142, 144-148, 156, 161, 169, 182, 187, 188, 191, 197, 206, 210
  Infant 128
  James 152
  John 18, 38, 39, 130, 153, 172
  Nathaniel 150, 164, 171, 197, 198, 203, 207, 210, 215
  Peter 203
  Richard 128, 150, 174
  Robert 129
  Thomas 12, 36, 93, 126, 199
  William 127, 158, 171, 198
Hartgrave
  Sarah 149
Harthorn
  John 55, 56, 199
  Joshua 92
  nfn 114, 191
  Peter 55, 92, 127
  Rachel 92
  Rebeckah 92
Harthorne
  Rebekah 84

Hartley
  Clemant 227
  Clint 229
  Joseph 227
Harwell
  Mark 129
  Mason 242
  Sterling 233, 234, 236, 237
Harwood
  Daniel 167, 206, 222, 227, 232
  Joseph 11, 41, 95
  Philip 11, 41, 206
  Phillip 95, 98, 109, 110, 118, 167, 192
  Samuel 72, 145, 159, 160, 175, 204, 220
Harword
  Joseph 61
  Phillip 61
  Samuel 61
Hatch
  Henry 89
Hatley
  John 12
Hatly
  John 12
Hatt
  James 219
Hawthon
  John 13
  Joshua 13
  Peter 13
Hawthorn
  Elizabeth 201
  John 26, 34, 173, 226
  Joshua 34, 62
  Peter 16, 25, 35, 60, 62, 173
  Rebecca 35
  Rebekah 60
Hawthorne
  Elizabeth 162
  Isham 162
  John 201, 228
Hay
  Gilbert 11, 69, 125
  John 47, 59, 92
  Peter 26
  Richard 11, 45, 69, 102, 106, 109, 110, 125, 138, 175, 177
Hays
  John 106, 127
  nfn 4
  Richard 163
Haywood
  George 175
Headley
  Nathan 229
Hearn
  James 108, 140, 143, 144, 226
Heath
  Adam 16, 66, 90, 121
  James 39, 63, 64, 99, 124, 151
  John 16, 64, 120, 174, 199, 219
  Josiah 66
  Mark 174
  Nathan 237

Heath
  Rebeccah 174
  Rebeckah 150
  Thomas 17, 39, 63, 64, 99, 118, 121, 124
  Urpley 199
  William 16, 66, 90, 121, 150, 174, 220
Henry
  I. 227
Hern
  Frederick 186, 234, 236
  James 44, 159, 160, 165, 180-183, 185-187, 193, 195, 208, 211, 213, 216, 227, 232, 234, 236, 240, 242
  Mary 219
  Sarah 232-234
Heron
  James 218
  Mary 218
  Sarah 218
  William 218
Hewet
  William 154
Hewett
  William 174
Hewit
  Mr 204
Hewitt
  Mrs 224
  William 130
Hicks
  Child 187
  Joseph 20
  Tubert 213
  William 67, 101, 187, 193, 195, 211, 216
Hige
  James 122
  William 122
Higgs
  Christian 110
  Izodoniah 50, 59, 79, 108
  Joseph 67
  Widow 74
Hill
  Benjamin 162, 163, 205
  Capt. 194
  Green 202
  John 12, 39, 45, 67, 72, 90, 97, 98, 129, 132, 163, 233
  Matthew 35
  Mial 68
  Mical 90
  Michal 129, 152
  Miles 39
  Peter 77
  Richard 38, 39, 55, 58, 67, 68, 84, 90, 114, 129, 152, 153, 166, 173, 177, 181, 190
  William 72, 73, 132, 152
Hinchia
  John 201
Hind
  John 168

Hind
  William 150
Hinds
  David 151, 168
  John 151, 168
  Joshua 151, 168
  Peter 149, 151, 168
  Richard 151, 168
  Thomas 151, 168
  William 151, 168
Hines
  David 68, 94, 120
  Hartwell 198, 204
  Harwell 236
  Jed 211
  John 120
  Joshua 64, 68, 120, 198
  Peter 68, 94, 120, 122
  Richard 68, 94, 120
  Thomas 18, 68, 94, 120, 136, 198
  William 18, 38, 39, 60, 64, 68, 90, 94, 120, 125, 170, 198, 202
Hinnibrough
  John 150
Hite
  Mrs 234
  William 96, 197, 210, 213, 216, 234-236
Hiter
  William 211
Hix
  Child 177, 184
  Cupel 180
  James 123, 149, 171
  Joseph 9, 22, 149
  Josh 9
  Josiah 8
  Mary 177
  Nancy 185
  Sarah 142
  Seloy 211
  Trubel 163
  Tubal 181
  William 97, 98, 123, 132, 143, 144, 149, 171, 180, 182, 184, 211
Hobbs
  Frederick 124
  John 94, 130, 174
  Sarah 145
  Thomas 199
Hogwood
  Andrew Wilburn vii
  George 167, 205, 239
Holliman
  John 18
Holloman
  John 37
Holloway
  Absalom 76
Holman
  William 9
Holmes
  William 4, 21

Holt
  Dred 149
  Ethelred 122
  Henry 61
  John 68, 90, 152, 166
  Nathaniel 124, 158, 176, 182, 187, 192-196, 200, 205, 222, 227, 228, 234
  Thomas 194
Holts
  John 129
Homes
  William 20
Hood
  Fanny 110
  Frances 57, 78, 80, 86, 102, 104, 105, 109, 117, 133-135
  John 2, 78, 109, 110, 117, 123, 135, 138, 160, 176, 200
  Mr. 72, 73
  Nathaneel 63
  Nathaniel 40, 57, 75, 95, 122, 173, 202
  nfn 235
  Thomas 137, 176, 233
Hoomes
  John 204
  Joseph 200
Horn
  James 122, 173, 202
House
  Capt. 242
  John 174
  Laurence 214-216
  Lawrance 226
Housman
  John 13
  Stephen 13
Howe
  James 118
Howel
  William 60, 94, 120
Howell
  Hannah 151, 168, 198
  John 13
Hubbard
  Matthew 177
Hubbud
  James 132
  Matthew 98, 132
Hubert
  Matthew 163
Hughlins
  William 100
Huit
  William 94
Huland
  Selah 108, 110, 112, 118, 140, 143
  Widow 142
Hulin
  John 160
Hulmne
  Ann 92
Hunicut
  Glaster 90

Hunicutt
  Mr 143
  Wyke 66, 90
Hunnicut
  Wike 16
Hunnicutt
  Gloster 150, 174
  Wyke 121
Hunt 61
  Benjamin 61, 93, 115, 122, 126, 168
  John 18, 36, 94, 151, 168
  Jurkins 170
  Sarah 235
  Thomas 35, 37, 65, 66, 89, 91, 172
  William 94, 120, 151, 168, 198, 199
Hunter
  David 27, 42, 56, 58, 76, 84, 139
  Mr. 25, 72-75
Huron
  T 238
Hurst
  Thomas 14
Huson
  Richard 15, 17, 35, 37, 57, 65, 78, 80, 86, 87, 89, 128
  Thomas 35, 37, 66, 89, 91, 130, 136, 143, 152, 153, 170, 172
Hutchens
  Francis 41
Hutching
  Epharaim 206
Hutchings
  Anne 206
  Francis 17
Ingram
  Joseph 90, 152, 153, 166
Ingrum
  Joseph 172
Irby
  John 13, 57, 84, 170, 201, 224, 237
  Mary 170
  William 201
Ivey
  Adam 12, 17, 163, 228
  Daniel 164, 227
  Henry 164
  Hugh 16, 26, 164, 192, 231
  John 16
  nfn 7
Ivie
  Hugh 218
Ivoy
  Daniel 203
  Hugh 203
  Jesse 203
  Richard 203
Ivy
  Adam 45, 72
  Hugh 54, 71, 214, 222
  John 48, 71
  Peter 202

Jackson
  Frances 170
  John 15, 37, 65, 89, 128, 152, 170
  Robert 89, 128
James 19
  Emanuel 42, 126, 155, 203, 224
  John 197
  Nathaniel 42
Jarend
  John 83
Jarrad
  Fadde 158, 171, 192
  Faddy 116, 127, 128
  Fady 198
  Henry 39, 60, 88, 90, 96, 114, 122, 125, 150, 165, 170, 192, 201, 222
  John 39, 54, 60, 82, 90, 114, 125, 150, 201
  Nicholas 150, 164, 167, 170, 198, 202, 206, 222
Jarrard
  Henry 165
  John 26
Jarrat
  Henry 231
  Nicholas 231
Jarratt
  Faddy 227, 229
  Nicholas 227
Jarrett
  Faddy 231
Jarrot
  Faddy 222
Jean
  Christopher 42
Jeen
  William 64
Jeffrey
  John 37
Jeffries
  John 16, 18, 20
Jelks
  Dread 97, 98
  Ethelbert 132
  William 132
Jenkins
  John 49, 58, 83, 87
Jennings
  John 70
Jennson
  John 118
Johnson
  Barnet 29
  Henry 18
  James 200
  Lewis 61, 91, 93, 122, 165, 181, 200, 205
  Mary 148, 159
  Mildred 242

Johnson
  Moses 3, 7, 12, 20-24, 26-29, 33, 36, 46, 48-54, 56-58, 61, 62, 77, 78, 80-82, 85-88, 91, 101-105, 107, 108, 110, 111, 113, 116-118, 121, 134-136, 139, 141-145, 148
  Mr. 74
  Nathaniel 60, 96
  Pettway 83, 162, 164, 181, 184, 195, 200, 209, 232
  Petway 96, 122, 216, 227
  Phillip 192
  Pittway 200
  Richard 94
  Roe 74
  Susannah 75
  Thomas 122, 163, 202
  Waddle 206
  William 7, 12, 13, 26, 36, 37, 54, 60, 64, 94, 96, 122, 150, 164, 165, 200
Johnston
  Elizabeth 220
  Petway 217, 222
Jones
  Allen 204, 243
  Capt. 181, 184
  Captain 143
  David 7, 13, 16, 26, 54, 58, 59, 66, 71, 83, 90, 94, 114, 120, 121, 127, 148, 150, 158, 160, 162, 169, 171, 174, 189, 190, 198, 204, 210, 213, 242
  Edmund 148, 165
  Edmunds 60
  Edward 68, 103, 129, 136
  Elizabeth 78
  Frederick 66
  Fredrick 91
  Hamilton 225
  Henry 93
  Holmes 162, 174, 205
  Howell 18, 26, 37, 188, 193-196
  Jacob 68, 158
  James 37, 60, 64, 78, 94, 96, 107, 117, 119-122, 130, 141, 143, 145-148, 150, 154, 158, 159, 161, 162, 165, 169, 171, 174, 175, 179-182, 186-189, 191, 195-198, 201, 204, 209, 212-214, 218-221, 229, 230, 234, 239, 240
  Jesse 164, 165, 201
  John 14, 22, 35, 60, 66, 90, 91, 93, 125, 150, 174, 205, 218, 221, 229, 237
  Lucretia 150
  Mary 130, 153, 200
  Molly 232
  Morledge 232
  Mr. 73
  Mrs 228
  Nat. 149
  Nathaniel 67, 101, 122, 171
  nfn 106

Jones
  Nicholas 18, 85
  Owen 25, 46, 47
  Owin 3, 20, 22, 23, 29
  Peggy 187, 193, 208, 211, 213, 216, 217
  Peter 122, 164, 165, 200, 201
  Prudence 240
  Richard 12, 44, 64, 93, 94, 126, 128, 130, 137, 154, 172, 174, 204
  Robert 4, 8, 9, 12, 18-25, 28, 29, 33, 36-39, 44, 46, 49, 51, 58, 60, 62, 64, 77, 79-82, 85, 91, 94, 96, 102, 104, 110, 115, 118, 120-122, 139, 165, 169, 174, 185-188, 190, 196, 201, 204, 206-209, 212-215, 217, 219, 221, 224, 225, 228-230, 233, 234, 236-238, 240, 241
  Roger 150
  Sally 232
  Samuel 220
  Sarah 18, 38, 39, 60
  Stephen 14
  Susannah 53, 125
  Thomas 14, 42, 68, 140
  Widow 61
  William 8, 9, 12, 20, 22, 23, 25, 29, 46, 47, 148, 155, 161, 168, 199
  Willie 243
Jons
  Robert 140
Jordan
  Benja. 126
  Benjamin 16, 42
  William 203, 224
Judkin
  Charles 14
Judkins 27
  Charles 27, 44, 55, 58, 70, 71, 85, 89, 95, 116, 118, 131, 157, 176, 204, 205, 211, 227, 229
  Gray 233, 234, 237
  John 18, 126, 155, 156, 201, 227, 228, 231
  Nicholas 42, 242
  Robert 16, 42, 56, 58, 84, 115, 126, 155, 156, 203, 224
  Ruana 75
  Samuel 219
  William 42, 73, 126, 155, 156, 203, 224, 242
Junkins
  Mary 151
Kainborough
  Duke 17
Kelley
  John 91, 153, 172, 220
Kellie
  John 66
Kelly
  John 35, 91, 130
Kennebren
  John 90, 202

Kennebrew
  John 60
Kennebrough
  John 125, 170
Kerr
  George 178, 195, 196
Kersey
  Elizabeth 82
  George 72
  Thomas 97
Killie
  John 66
Kinart
  William 227
King 105
  Andrew 37, 108, 109, 152
  Ann 142, 143, 169, 176
  Anne 156, 160
  Drusilla 117, 137, 142
  Elisabeth 147
  Elizabeth 3, 160, 176
  Ephraim 220
  Ephriam 219
  James 176
  John 23, 43, 49, 51, 57, 65, 77, 78, 80-82, 86, 87, 102, 105, 108, 110, 111, 117, 123, 134-136, 141, 144, 160, 228, 236
  Joseph 38
  Rebecca 117, 137, 142
  Richard 13, 43, 82, 86, 89, 111, 123, 133
  Sarah 142
  Widow 138, 160
  William 123
Knight
  Ephraim 89, 95
  Henry 242
  Joell 219
  John 13, 43, 44, 48, 49, 51, 65, 78, 89, 102, 107, 124, 133, 160, 169, 177, 184, 196, 206, 211
  John 158
  Jordan 33, 169
  Jorden 156
  Jordon 156
  Moses 173, 202
  nfn 218, 228, 236, 240
  Peter 176
  Richard 40, 41, 63, 95, 107, 122
  Sarah 209
  Susannah 158
  William 8, 11, 27, 41, 55, 61, 70, 84, 95, 98, 115, 118, 167, 206
Lamb
  John 60, 96, 100, 122, 123, 126, 149, 155, 156, 191, 201, 203, 221, 224, 230
  William 193, 211, 225, 238
Lambarc
  John 115
Lancaster
  Samuel 20, 24, 25, 29, 46, 48

Land
  Bird 165, 205
  Carter 233
  Curtis 17, 41, 70, 100, 131, 154, 165, 205
  Isham 242
  John 36, 61, 86, 91, 121, 165, 180, 184, 200
  Joseph 149
  Robert 70, 100, 131, 154, 165, 205, 234, 239, 242
  Susanah 242
  Webb 209
  William 13
Lane
  Joseph 67, 101, 122, 171, 193, 213, 216
Lanier
  Benjamin 228, 233, 234, 236, 237, 241
  Richard 137
  Samuel 18
  William 229
Lashley
  James 205
  John 59, 121
  nfn 138
  Patrick 162, 205, 236
  Thomas 59, 109, 121
  Walter 59, 121
  William 162, 205
Lashly
  nfn 137
  Walter 13
Lattance
  John 125
Leath
  Charles 17, 63, 96, 120, 157, 171
  John 63, 96, 157, 171, 199
  William 171, 199
Lee
  Daniel 219
  Edward 26, 35, 55, 59, 60, 82, 83, 92, 127
  Henry 8, 16, 34, 45, 56, 58, 72
  John 59
Leeth
  Charles 40
  John 40
Lells
  Peebles 202
Lester
  Andrew 13, 170
  Patty 119
Letcher
  John vii
Lightfoot
  Colonel 36
  Philip 12
  William 61, 93, 126, 168, 199, 200
Liles
  John 199
  Morrice 231
  Morris 199
  Moses 199

Liles
  Peter 232, 236
Lilley
  Anne 155, 160
Lilly
  Anne 193, 211
  Susan 216
Linn
  Robert 98, 132, 206, 236
Linsey
  Edward 98, 132
Lister
  Andrew 201
  William 137
Llewellin
  Thomas 198
Lofling
  Burrel 205
  William 205
Loften
  Cornelius 13, 17
  William 13, 17
Loftin
  Cornelius 43, 56, 70, 85, 89, 100, 116, 133, 154, 156, 165, 169
  Frederick 206
  William 41, 43, 70, 100, 119, 131, 154, 165, 177, 205, 206
  [illeg.] 238
Long
  C W 227
  Charles 192, 204, 222, 232
  Edward 167
  George 11, 61, 95, 175, 176, 182, 184, 192, 204, 222, 232
  John 60, 67, 101, 219, 229
  Robert 18, 41, 67
Longbottom
  William 70, 167, 206, 225, 235
Love
  Amos 67, 90, 108, 114, 117, 130, 135, 136, 141, 145, 147, 153
Lowry
  William 39
Loy'd
  Edward 180
Lucas
  John 107
Lundy
  Edward 163
Lynn
  Robert 163, 164
Maberry
  Charles 11, 13
  Frances 13
Mabry
  Abel 118, 157, 167, 192, 198, 201, 223, 227, 228
  Abell 227, 232
  Charles 41, 60, 78, 95, 175, 204
  Cornelius 98
  Francis 16, 34, 35
  Hinchia 17
  Hinchy 35
Macanish
  Donald 160, 188

Surry and Sussex Counties, Virginia, 1742-1786   257

Macklemore
  Burrel 184
  Burrell 97
  Burwell 163
  Joel 163
Maclamore
  Burrell 98, 132
  Burril 72
  Joel 132
  John 97, 132
Maclemore
  Burrel 45
Magee
  Anne 206
  Drewy 206
  Magee 235
  Ralph 43
  Robert 206, 226
  William 206
Maggee
  Ralph 13, 119
Magget
  Samuel 27, 56, 95, 100, 115
Maggett
  Samuel 84, 103
Maggot
  Samuel 123, 197
Magnum
  Child 177
Magot
  Samuel 16, 149, 162, 203
Magy
  Simon 230
Mahany
  Semore 137
Malone 238
  Ann 50, 53, 79, 88
  Anne 74
  George 24
  John 68, 128, 129, 152, 166, 170, 190, 230, 238
  Mical 166
  Michael 230, 238
  Nathaniel 39, 68, 90
  Thomas 15, 37
  William 20, 37, 38, 65, 67, 88-90, 128, 129, 152, 170
Manery
  Henry 41, 205
Mangam
  James 152, 153
Mangum
  Child 177
  James 67, 90, 130, 166
Manncey
  Henry 95
Mannery
  Henry 11, 146
Mannry
  Charles 43
Manry
  Henry 61, 167, 175, 204
  John 175, 204
Marable
  Hartwell 173

Marble
  Hartwell 44
Marks
  Richard 168
Marrable
  Hartwell 92, 155, 218, 230, 239
  Hartwill 199
  H[illeg.] 229
  Nathaniel 238
Marrablle
  Hartwell 226
Marrible
  Hartwell 84, 88, 128, 172
Marribles
  Henry 127
Marsengill
  Henry 67
  Thomas 67
  William 67
Marten
  Peter 11
  William 11
Martin
  James 132
  Peter 45, 49, 57
  William 11
Marvel
  Hartwell 16
  Henry 55, 58
Marvell
  Henry 15
Masinggill
  Thomas 149
Mason 161
  Capt. 9
  Christopher 72, 74, 139
  Daniel 72, 74, 139
  David 71, 72, 75, 92, 115, 125, 139, 140, 146-148, 158, 159, 161, 175, 176, 179-183, 185-189, 191, 193, 194, 196, 197, 200, 206-209, 211, 212, 214, 215, 219, 222, 223, 225, 226, 228, 229, 234, 236-242
  James 4, 16, 17, 20, 27, 39, 40, 55, 64, 99, 124
  John 2-4, 7, 14, 16, 18-26, 28, 29, 33, 37, 38, 46-49, 52-55, 58, 60, 61, 64, 71-75, 77, 79-82, 86-88, 96, 101, 103, 104, 106-108, 110, 111, 113, 116, 118, 121-123, 128, 134, 135, 139, 141, 144-148, 150, 151, 155, 157, 158, 161, 163-165, 169, 179, 180, 182, 196, 200-203, 206, 208-210, 214, 215, 217, 218, 220, 221, 223, 225-229, 233-237, 240, 241
  Joseph 7, 16, 34, 38, 46-49, 51
  Major 161
  Richard 227, 228
  Thomas 228
  William 150, 163, 188, 193, 194, 210, 221, 229, 233, 244
Massenburg
  Coll. 210, 211

Massenburg
  Colonel 160, 161, 178, 184, 196
  John 226, 227, 233, 234, 236, 240, 241
  Major 117
  Mr. 72
  Nicholas 88, 104, 107, 108, 110, 111, 113, 115-118, 128, 133-139, 143-147, 155, 156, 158, 172, 188, 189, 197
  Nichols 136, 137
  Nicolas 148, 155, 161, 180, 182, 190
  William 237, 240, 241
Massenburgh
  Nicholas 217
Massengill
  Thomas 195
Massinburgh
  Nicholas 215
Mathis
  Jane 51
Matthews
  Jane 33, 50, 51, 74
Mattis
  Jane 73, 78, 80, 86
Maven
  John 121
McGary
  John 23, 29, 46
Mcgee
  Robert 225
McKenish
  Donald 217
Mclemore
  Burrel 12
  John 12
McLimore
  Ann 242
  Burw[ell] 242
Meacham
  Ann 236
  Henry 16
Meachum
  Banks 174
  Edward 136
  Henry 34, 35, 59, 86, 92, 127
  Joshua 127, 174, 199
Meade
  William vi
Mecham
  Joshua 24
Mechum
  Banks 199
Meglemry
  John 204
Mias
  Thomas 95
Miers
  Thomas 149
Milone
  John 221
Minor
  John 13
Mitchel
  Daniel 172

258   The Vestry Book of Albemarle Parish

Mitchel
  Henry 34, 35, 39, 42, 56, 62
  John 42
  Nathaniel 125, 162
  Peter 42
  Robert 66
  Thomas 34, 42, 62, 125
  William 153
Mitchell
  Daniel 91
  Henry 8, 13, 14, 17, 34, 62, 64, 99, 124
  John 14, 68, 103, 129, 202
  Nathaniel 92
  Peter 14
  Randal 68
  Robert 42, 66, 68, 91, 220
  Samuel 129
  Sarah 68
  Thomas 25, 42, 62, 84, 92, 103, 115, 129, 151, 202
  William 4, 14, 42, 91, 103, 129, 130
Mongammie
  John 126
Montague
  John 125
Montgomary
  John 203
Montgomery
  John 156, 224
Moody
  Joseph 14
  Thomas 63, 121
Moore
  Barham 176, 200, 205, 228, 230, 238
  Eppes 39, 63, 124, 151
  Henry 151
  James 77
  John 200
  Sarah 176
  Thomas 13, 17, 41, 43, 65, 70, 100, 124, 131, 133, 154, 165, 183, 205, 211, 226, 235
  William 8, 17, 39, 41, 63, 87, 124, 151, 165, 169, 205
More
  Eppes 99
  Michael 219, 220
  William 99, 114
Moreing
  William 221
Mores
  Thomas 18
Morgan
  John 11, 12, 45, 69, 98, 125, 132, 175
  Robert 137
Morrice
  Edward 1
Morris
  Edward 79
  Joseph 236
  Lewis 219

Morriss
  Joseph 105
Morris'
  Thomas 156
Morton
  William 151
Mosley
  George 204, 211
Moss
  David 120
  Edmund 229, 238
  Gabrial 199
  Hannah 119
  Henry 34, 35, 59, 92, 127, 174, 190, 199, 221, 228, 230, 239
  James 17, 35, 66, 77, 91, 130, 172
  Jesse 92, 127
  Joanna 170, 193, 201, 208, 213, 218, 235
  John 13, 14, 41, 61, 95, 137, 175, 204
  Joshua 168, 199, 216
  Mary 204
  Widow 142
  William 16, 34, 35, 59, 60, 92, 175
Mumford
  Edward 65
  Thomas 121
Munford
  Edward 37
  Thomas 93
Munns
  Ephraim 88
  John 88
Muns
  Ephraim 104
  John 109, 137, 141
Murfee
  Arthur 101, 122
  Simon 67, 101
Murphey
  Simon 18
Musselwhite
  Thomas 214, 215, 218
Musslewhite
  Thomas 82
Mustlewhite
  Thomas 233
Myers
  John 29
Myrick
  John 167
  William 167, 206
Nance
  Benjamin 65
  Daniel 89
Nancy
  John 69
Nanney
  John 101
Nanny
  John 17, 36, 131
Negroe
  Leonora 243

Negroe
  Regulus 243
Newman
  Robert 59, 63, 77, 95, 122, 202
Newsom
  Benjamin 194
  Holliday 194
  Nathaniel 228, 232, 234, 237, 239
  nfn 211
  Thomas 11
Newson
  Nathaniel 233
  Thomas 41
Newsum
  Amos 132
  Benjamin 167, 195
  Child 194
  Jesse 167
  Nathaniel 159, 163
  nfn 217
  Robert 213
  Sampson 167
  Silvia 183, 213
  Thomas 61, 95, 167, 175
  William 128
Nicholson
  Flood 233
  Harris 197
  James 16
  John 117, 213, 217, 225, 235
  Mary 197
  Robert 28, 46, 48, 86, 113
  William 191, 222, 224, 226, 235
Nickels
  Edward 63
Nicolls
  James 42
Nicolson
  Flood 230
  Henry 184
  James 42
  John 108, 126, 135, 136, 141, 145, 147, 156, 179, 182, 187, 193, 208
  Mary 149
  Robert 7, 18, 22-24, 26, 37, 51, 54, 57, 58, 77, 80, 81, 83, 101, 105, 134
  William 155, 201, 231
Noble
  Mr. 74
Norcress
  Richard 70
Norcross
  James 70
  Richard 14
  Richrd 70
Northcross
  Richard 118, 167, 198, 227
Northington
  Nathan 123, 128, 164, 175, 192, 206, 223
  Samuel 118, 131, 157, 192, 201, 231

Northinton
  Samuel 70, 157
Nott
  Nathaniel 231
Nouse
  Lawrance 226
Numans
  Robert 173
Nun
  nfn 138
  Sucrese 138
Nunn
  Lucy 137
Nusum
  Benjamin 182, 212
  Jacob 198
  Lewis 206
  Nat 206
  Samson 212
  Silve 193
  Silvia 211
  Thomas 167, 198, 205
Obly
  Joseph 20
  Joshua 4
  Tosa 8
Odonally
  Hugh 102, 105, 134
  James 102, 105, 134, 135, 142, 145
  Mical 102
Odonnally
  D. 138
  Daniel 105
  James 105, 108, 109
  John 138
Odonnolly
  James 137
Ogborn
  Augustin 226
  John 61
Ogbourn
  John 14
Ogbun
  John 114, 121
Ogburn
  John 71, 83, 96
Oliver
  Isaac 118, 157, 198
  Isaeck 167
  James 35
  Thomas 15, 64, 94, 130, 154
  William 64, 130, 154, 174, 204, 223
Orvin
  David 204
Owen
  Benjamin 157, 197
  David 91, 157, 192
  Elizabeth 242
  John 43, 70, 157, 177, 184, 228, 236, 240, 242
  Robert 174
  Sarah 80, 140, 143, 180
  Widdow 228, 240
  Widow 236

Owens
  John 131
Owin
  Benjamin 224
  Frederick 224
  Robert 14
  Sarah 53
Owing
  Benjamin 160
  David 205, 212
  John 205
Pain
  John 93, 211
  William 93
Painter
  Ann 232
  John 112, 144
  Mary 145, 159, 160
  Susannah 145
Pair
  Jane 213, 216, 228
  John 168, 199
  Rebecca 142, 143, 146, 147, 195
  Rebeccah 160, 177, 180-182, 187, 193
  Rebeckah 210
  William 137, 200
Pandex
  Alexander 25
Pandix
  Alexander 29
Pare
  Bethel 61, 126
  Jane 218, 234, 236
  John 126
  William 36
Pareham
  Mathew 224
Parham
  Abraham 17, 40, 63, 96, 120
  Abram 157, 199
  Ephaim 2
  Ephraim 3, 7, 19, 21-25, 27, 28, 33, 46, 48-55, 57, 64, 75-79, 81, 82, 84, 86-88, 94, 103-106, 108, 110, 111, 113, 116, 118, 130, 133, 135, 136, 139, 141, 143, 145, 146, 153, 166, 230, 238
  Ephraim 15, 141, 221
  Ephriam 190
  Epraim 58
  George 88, 128, 152, 170
  James 17, 40, 63, 96, 120, 157, 171, 199
  John 17, 40, 63, 96, 120, 157, 191, 199, 222, 226, 231
  Kith 226
  Lewis 84, 90, 114, 129
  Lucresa 107
  Mathew 154, 204
  Matthew 15, 17, 27, 40, 55, 56, 63, 64, 84, 85, 94, 96, 115, 116, 120, 130, 157, 171, 174, 199

Parham
  Nathaniel 115, 130, 154, 174, 175, 190, 204, 221, 224, 230
  Robert 93, 127, 156, 172
  Stith 40, 93, 127, 156, 171, 172, 191, 202, 222, 231
  Susanah 224
  Thomas 56, 63, 85, 116, 120, 157, 171, 191, 199, 224
  William 8, 17, 27, 39, 40, 63, 64, 82, 94, 96, 130, 143, 154, 174, 221, 230
Parker
  Dury 11
  Federick 156
  John 56
  Richard 18, 38, 94, 120, 151, 168, 197, 198, 212-214, 219, 223, 225, 229, 235, 238, 240, 241
  William 8, 26, 29, 38, 55, 64, 83, 94, 114, 120, 150
Parkerson
  Capt 236
Parkes
  Mary 233
Parsons
  Henry 229, 237
Partin
  William 15, 44, 128, 155, 193, 210, 218
Partridge
  Mary 164
  Nicholas 26, 37, 54, 60, 83, 88, 114, 122, 164, 227, 232
  Nicolas 192, 200
  Wills 96, 122
Partrige
  Nicholas 222
Parvell
  Semore 204
Pasmore
  George 2
Passmore
  John 15
Pate
  Edmond 12
  Edward 97, 232
  John 132, 192, 222, 232
  Thomas 12, 45, 72, 97, 98, 116, 132, 140, 163
Patridge
  Nicholas 7
Pear
  William 12, 75
Pedington
  John 85
  Joseph 85
Pedinton
  Thomas 65
Peebles
  David 7
  John 14, 16, 18
  Nathaniel 71, 127
  Sarah 16
  Thomas 9

Peet
  Thomas 209
Peete
  Dr. 72
  Samuel 51, 94, 105, 111, 119, 120, 151
  Thomas 198, 236, 244
Peets
  Doctor 138
Pendix
  Alexander 20, 22
Pennenton
  John 61
Pennington
  David 154, 165
  John 12, 13, 36, 43, 88, 156, 165, 191, 231, 239
  Joseph 165, 169
  Joshua 165
  Marcus 156, 169
  Thomas 43
  William 200, 227, 229
Peoples
  Thomas 175
Pepper
  Archibald 35
  Richard 14, 17, 27, 42, 68, 75, 103
Pete
  Doctor 216
Peter
  John 106, 183, 215
  Mr. 73
  Walter 235
Peters
  James 190, 204
  John 184, 195, 209, 219, 220, 226, 229, 231, 233
  nfn 106
  Thomas 9, 18, 55, 58, 83, 94, 114, 120, 151, 168, 190, 198
Pettaway
  Edward 55
Pettway
  Edward 64, 83, 87, 114, 115, 124, 127, 172, 173, 190, 191, 231, 239
  John 124, 162, 230
  Joseph 95
  Micajah 89
  Mr. 72
  Robert 116, 127, 128, 172
  Sterling 197
  William 116, 127, 128, 172, 191
Petway
  Edward 8, 15, 27, 39, 40, 44, 45, 47, 93, 99, 151, 156, 222
  John 201, 221
  Joseph 7, 18, 149
  Michael 37
  Robert 40, 93, 156, 157
  William 8, 15, 27, 40, 45, 93, 155-157
Phelps
  Richard 13

Phips
  Benjamin 175, 204
Pidington
  David 131
  John 89, 91, 105, 110, 115, 133, 136
  Joseph 91, 115
Pinnenton
  John 61
Pinnington
  Howel 176
  John 177, 222
  Thomas 176
  William 176
Pinninton
  John 121
  Joseph 121
  Moses 122
  Thomas 124
Pleasant
  Beauford 197
  Buford 95, 149
  Peter 149
  William 149
Pooke
  Richard 151
Porch
  Bridges 173
  Henry 34, 35, 59, 92, 127, 173, 183, 197, 199, 211
  James 14, 34, 35, 69, 103, 127, 129
  Peter 199
  Porch 42
  Solomon 219
Pothress
  Peter 170
Potts
  John 123, 176
  John 177
Powel
  Edward 70, 91, 130, 157, 172
  John 157
Powell
  Edward 44, 70, 153
  Seymore 166
  Seymour 238
Poythress
  Elizabeth 37
  Joshua 40
  Mr. 15
  Peter 17, 39, 151, 152
Poytress
  Joshua 63, 96, 120
  Peter 64, 65, 89, 99, 124, 128
Preson
  John 197
Presson
  John 95, 149
  Thomas 149
Prichard
  Swan 147
Pride
  Halcott 173, 199
  Holt 203

Pridlow
  Thomas 204
Prince
  Edward 16, 71, 97, 98, 132, 159, 163, 177, 211, 215
  Gilbert 11, 45, 72
  Hannah 228, 234
  James 69
  John 242
  Joseph 16, 69, 72, 97, 132, 160
  Nicholas 82
  William 167, 206
Pritchard
  Henry 43
  Maurice 13
Pritloe
  Mr. 73
  Thomas 74
Pritlow
  Joshua 176
Procter
  Abner 126
  James 42
  Joshua 42
Proctor
  Abner 155
  Joseph 16
Pryer
  George 94
Pulley
  Spittle 43
Pully
  James 17
Purdie
  Mr. 184
Rachel
  John 43, 73, 89, 100, 124
Rachell
  John 70
  William 91, 103
Rae
  Mr. 73
  Susannah 188
Railey
  Peter 18
Raine
  Robert 128
  William 88
Raines
  John 162
  Robert 210, 217
  William 37
Rainey
  Nathaniel 66
  William 17, 55, 66, 67
Rains
  William 65
Ramsey
  William 216
Rand
  Peter 225
Randal
  Peter 235
Randall
  Geo: 130
  George 66, 187, 193

Randall
  Mary 14, 17, 66
  Peter 225
Randolph
  Colonel 43
  George 35, 91, 103, 153, 172, 179, 182
  Peter 103, 213
Ranes
  Wynne 188
Raney
  Nathaniel 91, 130, 153
  Robert 217
  William 35, 84, 90, 91, 131, 153, 166, 172
Ransom
  Richard 17, 36
Rawlings
  Gregory 8, 11, 20, 22, 24, 28, 41, 46, 48, 81, 86, 95, 101, 105, 108, 117, 134-136, 141, 145, 147, 167, 175, 179, 196, 205
  Howell 204
  Richard 95, 175, 204
  Sarah 204
  William 137
Rawlins
  Gregory 9, 51, 57, 61, 77, 80
Read
  John 17
Reddin
  John 151
Redding
  Francis 16
Reding
  John 123
Redwood
  John 219, 220
Reeves
  George 34
  John 34
  Richard 40
  Richard2 40
  Stith 40
  William 202
Reives
  Christopher 92, 125, 162
  Frances 62, 92, 125
  George 62, 92, 125, 162, 242
  John 62, 126, 127, 156, 162
  Peter 62, 63, 85, 95, 116, 122
  Richard 59, 63, 87, 93, 95, 102, 122, 127
  Timothy 126, 162
  William 95, 173
Renn
  David 238
  James 94, 103, 120, 151, 168, 195
  John 177, 180, 182, 195, 211, 236
  Joseph 61, 131, 154, 165, 177, 190, 205, 211, 221
  Thomas 36, 37, 61, 68, 94, 115, 126, 191, 222
  William 106

Richardson
  Benjamin 11, 41, 95, 175, 204, 236
  Henry 95
  John 11, 16, 41, 95, 175
  Jos. 129
  Joseph 152, 166
  Martha 38
  William 38, 90, 119, 130, 167, 175, 192, 198, 201, 223, 228, 232-234, 237, 239
Richarson
  Benjamin 61
  Henry 61
  John 60
  Joseph 67
  William 67, 70
Riddles
  William 123
Ridley
  Doctor 177, 180, 184, 185
  James 166
Rieves
  Christopher 191
  George 13, 182, 191, 195, 207, 212-215, 217-220, 222, 223, 225, 228, 229, 231, 233, 234, 236, 237, 239-241
  Richard 106
  Timothy 220
  William 219
Rigbey
  William 105
Rigbie
  William 134
Rivers
  John 152, 170
  Robert 14
Rives
  Christopher 202
  George 197, 202, 208, 226
  John 201
  Peter 56
  Richard 40
  Timothy 201, 202
  William 158, 177
Roane
  John 125
Robards
  Joseph 72
Robarts
  Willut 201
Roberson
  Drury 38
  George 153, 172
  Isaac 39, 153
  James 170
Roberts
  Benj 201
  Benjamin 162, 170
  Daniel 12, 45
  Joseph 97
  nfn 159
  Willard 56, 115
  Willert 205
  Willet 3, 84, 121

Roberts
  Willitt 170
  Willit 13, 159
  Willot 162
  Willute 119
Robertson
  George 66, 91, 94, 130, 153
  Isaac 50, 57, 68, 74, 90, 110, 112, 133, 140, 143, 166
  Nathaniel 129
Robinson
  George 35
  Robork
  Joseph 132
Rochel
  Hinchia 176
  John 156
  Mary 156, 169
Rochell
  Hinchae 200
  John 13, 133, 200, 205
Rodgers
  William 179, 181, 183, 184, 187, 193, 208
Roe
  Cannon 28
Roes
  Cannon 50
  William 232
Roger
  William 126
Rogers
  Benj. 149
  Benjamin 16, 162, 197, 203
  Celia 23
  Elizabeth 227, 234, 236, 240
  Frances 174
  Jesse 156
  Mary 227, 232-234, 236, 240, 242
  Nathan 137
  Reubin 81, 162
  Samuel 95
  William 13, 20, 22, 23, 25, 29, 42, 43, 46, 81, 89, 95, 100, 102, 123, 126, 133, 144, 147, 149, 155, 156, 160, 169, 208, 210, 212, 213, 216, 217, 225, 235
Roland
  Burwell 212
  Elizabeth 212, 218, 234, 240
  Jesse 70
  John 89, 90, 109, 129, 131, 137, 138, 175
  Joseph 44, 57, 70, 77, 131
  Joshua 14
  Phebe 233
  Susanna 232, 234
  Tabitha 140, 143, 144, 160, 177, 212, 242
  Webb 174, 192, 231
  William 14, 44, 70, 89, 131, 200, 204
Rolans
  Elizabeth 236

Rolin
  Joseph 57
Rollings
  John 125
  Susanna 232
Rolun
  Joseph 52
Rooking
  James 16
  Rookings
  James 13
Roper
  James 137
  Thomas 125
Rose
  Hannah 160, 177
  Richard 14, 70, 176
  William 4, 9, 16, 19-21, 25, 44,
    89, 118, 131, 157, 192, 194,
    201, 223
Roser
  Francis 203
Rosers
  Francis 164
Ross
  Arthur 238
  William 22, 29, 42
Rossenbery
  Susannah 157
Rosser
  John 16
Rotenberry
  Widow 63
Rottenberry
  John 40
  John1 40
  Susanna 93
  Susannah 95, 127
Rouse
  James 62
Rowland
  Elizabeth 216, 228
  John 167, 198
  Joseph 157
  Joshua 228
  Samuel 157
  Tabitha 180, 182
  Timothy 184
  Webb 158
  William 77, 157
Rowlings
  John 11
Ruffin
  Capt. 73
  Edmund 13, 27, 56, 79, 81, 146
  Mr. 161
Samman
  James 215
Sammons
  James 11, 45, 69, 81, 125, 175,
    228, 232, 235, 236
  John 125, 175
  Lucrecia 158
  Lucrecy 176, 180, 181
  Thomas 163
  Widow 178

Sammons
  William 98, 132, 163, 195, 234
Sandafer
  John 98
  Robert 132
Sandaford
  John 98
Sandefour
  Robert 44
Sanders
  John 158
  Thomas 230
  William 158, 233, 240
Sandress
  John 198
Sandrus
  John 71, 171
  William 71, 127
Sands
  John 206
Sante
  Timothy 197
Santee
  Samuel 137, 233
  Timothy 95, 149, 233
Saunder
  William 16
Saunders
  Thomas 166, 221
  William 228
Sawrey
  Henry 67
Scarbrough
  Thomas 87
Scoggin
  Jane 210, 218
  Richard 228
Scoging
  William 137
Scot
  Robert 14
Scott
  John 13
Seaburn
  Benjamin 206
Sears
  Frances 70
Seat
  Robert 44, 70, 85, 116, 118, 201
Seats
  Robert 70
Seborn
  William 163
Sebrel
  Samuel 76
Seburn
  Benjamin 132
  Isaac 116
Seebom
  Benjamin 164
Senal
  Brian 95
Serewsbury
  Benj. 206
Sermont
  Mr. 74

Servard
  Samuel 126
Seward
  James 149
  Samuel 199, 200
Sewell
  Joseph 35
Shackelford
  Banister 155
Shairmon
  Ebenezar 176
Shands
  Augustine 171, 174, 227
  Austin 164
  John 8, 11, 12, 45, 69, 150, 164,
    171
  John 40
  Phebe 228, 232, 234, 236, 239
  Thomas 71
  W. B. vii, 229
  William vii, 16, 66, 71, 90, 121,
    123, 128, 158, 164, 174, 203
  Willison 198
Shane
  Thomas 158
Shanns
  John 43
Sharp
  Frances 95
Shearman
  Ebenezer 200
  Mary 242
Shele
  Lemmon 173
Shell
  Mary 233, 234, 236
Shelton
  Edward 8, 9, 11, 20, 22, 24, 28,
    29, 46, 48, 51, 52, 57, 61, 80,
    81, 86, 95, 102, 105, 108,
    117, 118, 134, 135
Sikes
  Thomas 91
Sillis
  Aron 213
Sills
  Isom 65
  Peter 234, 240, 242
  Widow 65
Simon
  John 206
Singleton
  Michal 64
Slate
  Edward 89, 107, 131, 157
Sledge
  Amos 121, 150, 163
  Charles 61, 96, 132, 163, 181
  Daniel 38
  John 14, 38, 61, 96, 120, 121,
    150, 163, 169, 202, 204, 220
  Rebekah 61
Smith
  Amy 133, 137, 138
  Ann 68, 69

Smith
  Arthur 67, 83, 114, 131, 149, 162, 189
  Bell 110
  Benja: 137
  Berry 103
  Dane 227
  Ed: 229
  Edward 63, 152, 213, 218, 233-235, 238
  Isham 69, 94, 103, 114, 129, 130, 154, 174, 190, 221, 230
  Jesse 224
  John 7, 17, 21, 22, 25, 26, 39, 54, 58, 63, 67, 99, 124, 149
  Joshua 201
  Josiah 103, 114, 129
  Laurence 222
  Lawrance 164, 170
  Lawrence 200, 201, 231, 242
  Law[rence] 242
  nfn 151
  Peter 16, 106, 133, 138, 211
  Sarah 239
  Thomas 151, 219
  William 14, 42, 89
  [illeg.] 238
Snensick
  James 12
Solomon
  Lewis 9, 11, 45, 69, 125, 160
  William 11, 45, 69, 125, 175, 177
Sorrons
  Henry 101
Sorrow
  Henry 18
Southald
  Mary 213, 216
Southard
  John 154
  Mary 208
Southward
  Mary 179, 204
Southwort
  John 175
Southworth
  John 165
  Mary 177, 181, 182, 184, 187, 193, 211, 217, 218
  Widow 178
Sowersberry
  Benjamin 43
Sowsberry
  Benjamin 119
Spain
  Drewry 95, 122
  Elizabeth 79, 196
  James 200, 224, 227
  John 63, 95, 122
  Miles 224
  Thomas 89, 131, 157, 205
  William 122, 173
Spane
  Elisabeth 140, 143
  Thomas 205

Speirs
  William 202
Stacey
  Simon 238
Stacy
  John 126, 155
  Simon 42, 126, 155, 163, 191, 203, 221, 224, 229, 235
Staffod
  Cudworth 221
Stafford
  Cudburth 190, 200
  Cuthbud 121, 123
  Cuthburt 76
Stark
  nfn 157
Stevens
  John 27, 43, 44, 55, 64, 65, 84, 115, 123
Stewart
  Charles 198, 206
  John 101, 190, 221
  Richard 198, 206, 227
  William 15, 44, 227, 228, 232
Stoakes
  Jones 232, 233
  Samuel 182
Stoaks
  Christopher 201
  Cisla 205
  John 176
  Jones 154, 160
  Marcus 154, 165, 176
  Nathaniel 200
  Samuel 180, 181, 184
  Sarah 176
  Silvanius 200
  Silvanus 157, 176
  Thomas 176
  Young 176
Stokes
  David 51, 65
  Drury 44
  James 11
  John 43, 65, 124
  Jonas 14
  Jones 17, 65, 70, 100, 131, 218
  Marcus 70, 131
  Samuel 43, 65, 118, 140, 181
  Sil: 85
  Silvanus 41, 43, 44, 55, 58, 71, 89, 116, 131
  Silvester 14
Strange
  William 158
Stuart
  Charles 164
  James 45, 85, 97, 118, 132, 164, 167, 175, 194
  John 131, 166
  Rd 229
  Richard 167
  William 44, 56, 62, 63, 65, 85, 95, 116, 122, 173, 200, 202

Studivant
  Henry 41
  William 231
Sturdavant
  Henry 8, 85, 93, 127
  Hollumn 127
  Holm 93
  James 142
  John 95, 122, 228
  Matthew 95, 123, 200
  William 228
Sturdivant
  Anderson 204, 224
  Charles 172
  Henry 27, 40, 56, 58, 63, 157, 172
  Holemn 172
  Hollemn 75
  Hollman 40
  Hollom 157
  Holman 40, 63
  Jesse 173
  John 40, 63, 157, 172-175, 202, 204, 219, 224, 226
  Matthew 63, 65
  Thomas 172
  Willam 222
  William 157, 173, 192, 202, 226
Suder
  Mary 233
Swonsby
  Benjamin 13
Sykes
  Thomas 103, 129
Tacon
  Henry 177
Tatum
  Bridget 53, 76
  Christopher 2-4, 7-9, 13, 19-26, 28, 29, 33, 34, 46-53, 62, 92, 125
  Drury 62
  Henry 62, 125, 162, 201
  Howell 220
  John 16, 53, 56, 62, 77, 80, 81, 84, 86, 88, 92, 101, 115, 125
  Joseph 72, 75
  Joshua 53, 56, 62, 76, 77
  Josiah 73
  Mary 162, 201
  Nathaniel 121, 150, 162
  nfn 139, 239
  Peter 16, 66, 90
  Robert 62
  Samuel 13, 27, 59, 162
  Thomas 174
Taylor
  Thomas 16
Teete
  Thomas 235
Tenning
  Rachel 172
Tharp
  Joseph 69
  Lewis 221

Thompson
  John 174, 198
  William 45, 72
Thorn
  William 227
Thorp
  Denis 230
  Joseph 8, 17, 27, 36, 55, 58, 84,
    101, 103, 115, 125, 131, 166,
    175
  Lewis 175, 238
  Peterson 166
  Timothy 17, 36, 101
Thos
  Hubbard 11
Threewit
  Edward 63
  John 172
  Peter 63
Threewits
  Frances 160
  nfn 157
Threewitt
  Peter 224
Threewitts
  Frances 127
  John 93
  Peter 154, 174, 175, 204
Threwitt
  John 40
Thrower
  Thomas 16
Thweat
  David 220
Tillar
  Major 36
Tiller
  Major 11, 17, 69, 101, 131, 166
Tius
  Thomas 176
Toby
  John 115, 119, 126
  Mary 155
Tomkins
  John 22
Tomlinson
  Benjamin 66, 89, 121
  James 61, 96, 127, 128, 150
  John 13, 71, 121, 127, 128, 171
  Nathaniel 35, 60, 92
  Richard 13, 35
  Thomas 16, 126, 155, 191, 194,
    201, 222, 224, 231
  William 38, 92, 120, 127, 174,
    199
Tompson
  William 56
Tomson
  Captain 150
  John 127, 158, 171
  William 12, 58
Toy
  Adam 96, 132
  George 132
  Henry 127
  Hugh 83, 116

Trippet
  Morris 11
Troughton
  Andrew 122
Tucker
  Daniel 68
  David 128, 130, 152, 153, 170,
    172
  Joel 84, 88, 114, 128, 152, 170,
    171, 190
  Joseph 15
  Robert 13, 152, 170, 226, 231
Tuder
  Henry 106, 110, 163
  John 220
  Robert 219
Tudor
  Henry 105, 109, 117, 140, 143
Turner
  Daniel 164, 204
  Edmunds 170
  James 18, 67, 101, 122, 123, 148,
    149, 170, 171, 187, 189, 195,
    202, 220, 233, 237
  William 170
Turville
  Francis 73
Ty
  Henry 97
Tyas
  John 84, 90, 114, 128, 129
  Lewis 95
  Thomas 124
Tyler
  Henry 11, 41, 85, 88, 95, 96, 98,
    116, 132, 163, 167, 206
  Mr. 74
  nfn 61
  William 98
Tyus
  Absalom 152
  Benjamin 204, 224
  John 39, 200
  Rebeccah 166
Underhill
  John 4, 14, 16, 38, 61, 96, 110,
    112, 220
Underwood
  Absolum 201
  Bedels 45
  Isham 220
  John 137
  Lewis 242
  Mark 177, 239
  Thomas 11, 45, 69, 125
Vaughan
  Harry 18
  Thomas 42, 68, 73, 103, 129,
    148, 186
Vent
  Peter 85
  Thomas 222
Verel
  John 196
Veril
  John 179

Verrel
  John 137
Verret
  John 62
Vines
  Thomas 14, 27, 42, 55, 68, 69,
    84, 103, 128, 129, 152, 170
Vinson
  Thomas 132
Wade
  Mary 242
  Thomas 68, 103, 129
Wadkins
  J. Thomas vii
  John 154, 174
  Thomas i
Waide
  Thomas 39
Walker
  Edward 102, 105, 108, 117,
    134-136, 141, 145, 147, 162,
    179
  John 165, 199
Wall
  John 2, 3, 19
Wallace
  James 67
  John 100, 107
  Sarah 21
  Selah 21
  Thomas 107
  William 21, 25
Waller
  Jamimah 136
  Thomas 118, 138, 140, 143, 159,
    177, 180-182, 184, 187, 193,
    195, 208, 210, 211, 213, 215,
    218, 226, 228, 232, 234-236,
    240, 242
  Unity 215
Wallis
  Jesse 202
  Thomas 39, 60, 77, 90, 125, 150,
    170
Warbintons
  John 126
Warbirton
  John 42
Warbitons
  John 16
Warburton
  John 156
Ward
  Thomas 35
Warren
  Thomas 73
Warrick
  Jacob 3, 9
  John 29
  Sarah 242
Warwick
  Job 104
Wasdon
  John 18
Washer
  John 220

Surry and Sussex Counties, Virginia, 1742-1786

Washington
  John 76
Watkins
  James 203
  John 94, 130
  Sarah 132
Watkinson
  Benjmain 220
Weather
  Michael 227
Weathers
  Benja: 128
  Benjamin 44, 155, 222, 231
  John 155, 172
  Lidia 172
  Lydia 127
  Mical 167, 192
  Michael 198, 223, 232
  Thomas 14, 44, 70, 71, 118, 201
  William 40, 93, 127, 156, 172
Weaver
  Edward 7, 14, 26, 38, 61, 83, 96, 114, 121, 150, 163, 190, 202, 221
  Gilbert 16
  Henry 121, 123, 150
  John 46, 53, 77, 229
Webb
  Harmon 205
  Robert 11, 17, 27, 39, 41, 55, 68, 70, 78, 84, 90, 103, 115, 129, 131, 152, 154, 165
Weldon
  Benjamin 79
  Daniel 28, 34, 46
Wever
  Edward 55
  John 57
Wheeless
  Joseph 40
White
  Benjamin 144
  Charles 18
  James 123, 203
  John 58, 220
Whitehead
  Elisabeth 140, 143, 147
  Elizabeth 79
  Isham 202
  Matthew 40, 63, 95, 122
  nfn 217
  Robert 63, 137, 176, 177, 179, 181, 182, 184, 187, 189, 193, 195, 200, 208, 210, 212, 216, 217, 226, 232, 235
  Thomas 122
Whitehorn
  John 125, 175, 191, 231
  Thomas 239
Whitehorne
  John 222
Whiteledon
  John 229
Whitfeild
  Matthew 57, 78, 80, 111, 112, 118, 134, 138

Whitfield
  Elijah 220
  Mathew 81, 160
  Matthew 82, 86, 102, 105, 107
  Thomas 199
Whitington
  John 123
Whittington
  Edward 137
  John 46, 75
  William 137
Whuett
  William 66
Wickes
  Benjamin 120
Wiggens
  Richard 45
Wiggins
  James 225, 235
  Richard 12, 108, 109, 117, 135-137, 141, 142, 145
Wilborn
  Benjamin 211
  John 94, 130, 131
  William 73, 129, 152
Wilborne
  Benjamin 204, 224
  Burrel 175
  Burwel 224
  John 130, 154, 174
  Mary 195
  William 152
Wilbourn
  John 15
Wilbourne
  Benjamin 220
Wilburn
  Benjamin 193
  John 70, 76, 89
  William 39, 67, 90, 166
Wilburne
  William 166
Wilie
  William 226
Wilkason
  John 16
  Matthew 12, 14, 45
Wilkenson
  Thomas 35
Wilkerson
  Child 176, 180-182, 187, 193
  Elizabeth 153
  John 42, 66, 69, 71, 86, 103, 123, 129, 141, 153, 172
  Matthew 70
  nfn 210
  Thomas 42, 66, 91, 103, 129, 130, 153
  William 90, 123, 157, 171, 199
Wilkinson
  nfn 212
  Thomas 35
Willborne
  Burwil 204
Willburn
  John 64

Willcocks
  William 169, 202
Willcox
  William 204
William
  Willie 146
Williams
  Agnes 36
  Benjamin 220
  Charles 176, 200, 216
  Gary vii
  George 72
  Isaac 17
  James 13, 44, 49, 51, 57, 65, 78, 82, 111, 124, 176, 200
  Mr. 193
Williamson
  Arther 222
  Arthur 156, 169, 178, 183, 191
  Auther 231
  Grace 12
  Jesse 156, 160, 169, 183, 191, 222, 228, 231, 233, 234, 236, 237, 239-241
  John 15, 37, 65
  Joseph 65
  Lewelling 152
  Major 196
  Mr 217
  Person 242
  Thomas 164, 206
  Valentine 164
  Vol 45
  Vol: 97, 132
  William 169
Willie
  Elizabeth 243, 244
  Jacobina 243
  Mrs 223
  William vi, 1-4, 7-9, 12, 19-26, 28-30, 33, 34, 46-49, 51, 53, 54, 56, 58, 59, 72, 73, 75, 77, 79-82, 85-88, 91, 101, 103, 104, 106-113, 116, 118, 121, 127, 133, 134, 136-148, 158-161, 173, 177-180, 182, 183, 185-189, 193-197, 199, 208-220, 223, 225, 235, 243, 244
Willis
  Colonel 13
  Frances 119
  John 157
  Thomas 170
Williss
  John 89
Wills
  William 127
Wilson
  George 214, 219
  Nicholas 221, 230, 238
  William 220
Winfeild
  Jarvis 68
  John 129
  Peter 128

265

Winfeild
  Robert 129
  William 68, 129
Winfield
  John 152
  Peter 65, 89, 129, 152
  Robert 152
  William 152
Wingfield
  Peter 166
  William 166
Winkfield
  Jarvis 39
  William 39
Winkles
  Esther 39, 60
  James 90
Winne
  Mathew 221
Winther
  Micajah 118
Womack
  William 131
Wommock
  Thomas 166
Wood
  Charles 234
Woodard
  John 17, 42, 69, 103, 129, 208, 210
Woodham
  Mary 33, 50, 74
  Thomas 50, 193
Woodland
  William 14, 44, 70, 118, 201
Woodroff
  Richard 15
Woodroof
  Richard 44
Woodruff
  David 200
Woodward
  John 172, 176, 180, 182, 184, 187, 193, 195, 212, 214, 216, 218, 226, 239, 241
Wooten
  William 220
Wooton
  Edward 177, 180, 181, 189
Wootten
  Edward 149

Worrick
  Mr 228
Worsdon
  John 68
Wowdon
  John 94
Wren
  Ann 199
  Joseph 93, 230
  Thomas 12, 93, 155, 168, 199, 231
Wrenn
  Thomas 18, 128, 137
Wright
  Edward 100, 123
  John 104
Wyatt
  Edward 14
Wyche
  Benj. 150
  Benjamin 18, 64, 94
  Elizabeth 204
  George 18, 26, 38, 55, 64, 94
  J 240
  James 8, 17, 27, 36, 55, 58, 69, 84, 103, 115, 125, 131, 166, 175, 230
  Nathaniel 36, 69, 101, 131, 166, 175, 190, 209
Wynfield
  Jarvis 90
  William 90
Wynn
  John 222
  Robert 47, 48
  Sloman 123
Wynne
  John 40, 93, 127, 145, 152, 157, 172, 192, 202, 231
  Major 1, 75
  Mathew 55, 88, 172
  Matthew 40, 58, 84, 93, 115, 128, 155, 157, 190, 230, 235
  Robert 1, 2, 8, 15, 21, 27-29, 33, 37, 40, 49, 51, 52, 54, 58, 65, 72, 77, 79, 82, 110, 139, 157, 173, 202
  Sloman 8, 27, 40, 41, 56, 58, 85, 93, 122, 127, 138
  Stith 156, 157, 172
  Thomas 8, 15, 27, 37, 55, 64, 65, 89, 94, 128, 142, 152, 154, 166, 170, 174
  William 68, 80, 130

Wynns
  William 38
Yarbrough
  William 42, 68, 103, 129, 190, 221, 230
Yearwood
  Catharine 138
  Catherine 110
  John 110
  Kathrin 177, 183
  Widow 177
Yell
  John 222
Young
  Dorrell 92
  John 13, 16
  nfn 35
  Thomas 16, 66, 90, 121, 162, 201
  William 35, 60, 127
Zeels
  John 36
  Lambert 36
  Morris 36
Zell
  Drewry 177
  John 12
  Lambert 12
  Maurice 12
  Peter 177, 228
  Thomas 76
  William 77
Zells
  David 168
  John 168, 191
  Lambert 168
  Morris 168
Zilk
  David 126
  John 126
  Lambert 126
  Morris 126
Zill
  Isham 93
  John 61, 93
  Lambert 93, 95
  Morris 61
  Merriss 93
Zills
  Isom 65
  Morris 239

www.ingramcontent.com/pod-product-compliance
Lightning Source LLC
Chambersburg PA
CBHW061436300426
44114CB00014B/1715